Delivering Aid

Squatters in an area between 10th and 11th Streets and between the south side of Canyon Boulevard and the north side of Boulder Creek (present-day site of city hall), Boulder (Boulder County), Colorado, 1920. Photograph by Edwin Tangen. Courtesy of Boulder Historical Society Collection of the Carnegie Branch Library for Local History, Boulder, Colorado.

DELIVERING AID

IMPLEMENTING PROGRESSIVE
ERA WELFARE IN THE AMERICAN WEST

THOMAS A. KRAINZ

UNIVERSITY OF NEW MEXICO PRESS | ALBUQUERQUE

PRINTED IN THE UNITED STATES OF AMERICA

11 10 09 08 07 06 05   1 2 3 4 5 6 7

LIBRARY OF CONGRESS CATALOGING-IN-PUBLICATION DATA

Krainz, Thomas A., 1965–
    Delivering aid : implementing progressive era
welfare in the American West / Thomas A. Krainz.
        p. cm.
    Includes bibliographical references and index.
    ISBN 0-8263-3025-8 (CLOTH : ALK. PAPER)
    1. Public welfare—Colorado—History—20th century. I. Title.
    HV98.C6K73 2005
    361.9788'.09'04—dc22

                    2005016500

Portions of *Delivering Aid* originally appeared in the following:

"Transforming the Progressive Era Welfare State: Activists for
    the Blind and Blind Benefits" in *Journal of Policy History*.
    Used by permission.

"Culture and Poverty: Progressive Era Relief in the Rural West,"
    Copyright © 2005 by the Pacific Coast Branch of the American
    Historical Association, reprinted from *Pacific Historical Review*.
    Used by permission of the University of California Press.

Author's note: I have not altered the spelling or punctuation of
residents' letters asking for assistance from county commissioners.

Book design and type composition: Kathleen Sparkes

Body type is Utopia 9.5/14; 26P6
    Display Type is Century Gothic,
    Frutiger, and Copperplate

For Laura Knotts

Contents

List of Illustrations

Tables

Preface and Acknowledgments

For several years before entering graduate school, I was employed as a social worker for various nonprofit organizations in the West. In the most challenging yet rewarding of these jobs, I monitored six adults with developmental disabilities who lived independently in the community. Together, these six adults and I grappled with a wide range of issues—money management, grocery and clothes shopping, meal preparation, loneliness, depression, violence, medical concerns, and employment—to name just a few. I received a great deal of satisfaction when someone either mastered a new skill, especially one that had been a long-term goal such as using the bank, or took a bold new step toward greater independence such as successfully riding a bus route which required a transfer. Of course, not all aspects of the job were always so positive. Even though many of these adults were amazingly resilient, determined, and hardworking, many also exhibited self-destructive behaviors, suffered from neglectful families, or struggled with crime-ridden neighborhoods. Often it seemed as if each day brought a new set of problems, problems that required a quick response and, with luck, a solution. I had to maneuver through the often maddening welfare bureaucracy of food stamps, Supplemental Security Income, Medicaid, and subsidized or public housing. Yet, I found it deeply satisfying when, despite all the obstacles, I succeeded in gaining the goods and services that one of these six adults rightly needed and were entitled to receive. Obtaining a new hearing aid, for example, required such persistence in negotiating a series of "Catch-22" rules that my colleagues warmly congratulated me on my accomplishment after weeks of efforts.

My co-workers and I often eagerly looked forward to attending training sessions or daylong seminars addressing new ideas in social work. At these meetings, we not only got a much needed break from our regular schedules but we also had a chance to share ideas with others in the field and to hear some of the leading thinkers on the legal and social issues facing adults with developmental disabilities. The concepts gleaned from these meetings often inspired us, but usually for only a few days. For the reality of implementing new ideas was a very different matter than discussing social work theories. Many times, the ideas were simply not appropriate to a given circumstance or required too much time and effort to carry out. Often, we had already been enacting a so-called new idea under a different name or under no name at all. Likewise, new regulations did not necessarily change our practices; we may have mentioned a new policy's terminology in our daily log books without actually altering our routines.

Because of these experiences as a social worker, I was a bit surprised to read the historical literature on poverty and social work when I entered graduate school. Most scholars have focused on social work theories while ignoring or skirting the daily practices of social workers. In addition, poor people are, ironically, largely absent from discussions of poverty and welfare policies. The daily implementation of welfare measures and how these practices affected poor people form the foundation of this book. To investigate Progressive Era relief practices, I have chosen a diverse sample of Colorado communities—Native Americans on an Indian reservation, Protestant cash-crop homesteaders, Catholic Hispanic subsistence farmers, miners in a dying mining center, residents in a dominant regional city, and farmers and workers in a stable mixed economy.

Research and writing can be lonely experiences. Locating material and piecing together sentences, paragraphs, chapters, and arguments can often be a frustrating and time-consuming endeavor that one must usually bear alone. Luckily, I received support and encouragement from a community of organizations and individuals.

I received financial support from numerous organizations. The Center on Philanthropy at Indiana University, Indianapolis provided support during the last year of writing this study when it was at the dissertation stage, and the Thomas Edwin Devaney Dissertation Fellowship from the Center for Humanities and the Arts at the University of Colorado offered generous monetary funds. The John Reinthaler Memorial Fund, the Beverly Sears Award, and the Douglas A. Bean Memorial Fellowship, all from the University of Colorado, enabled me to travel to county offices throughout the state and to photocopy essential material. The University of Colorado History Advisory Board provided funds for obtaining photographs for the final manuscript. To all these organizations, I express my gratitude for their assistance.

In the course of doing research and writing, a number of people skillfully directed me toward needed material. County clerks and recorders throughout Colorado took time away from their busy schedules to show me their collections of documents. The staffs at the Colorado Historical Society, the University of Colorado Archives, the Western History Collection at the Denver Public Library, the National Archives—Rocky Mountain Region, and the Interlibrary Loan Service at the University of Colorado all diligently located my most obscure requests. Archivists at the Colorado State Archives deserve special mention for providing top-notch professional service with an ever-shrinking budget. Terry Blevins shared with me both his extensive collection of photographs of Lincoln County and his enthusiasm for the region's history. I am also grateful to Ray McGeorge for locating the minutes of the Society of the United Workers for the Blind of Colorado.

Numerous scholars read all or parts of the manuscript and offered valuable suggestions for improving the final version. Mark Pittenger thoroughly read and provided detailed comments on an early draft. Lee Chambers pushed me toward incorporating more gender analysis. Carol Byerly offered numerous suggestions to streamline the narrative flow. Vine Deloria Jr. and Christopher Riggs answered my questions about U.S. Indian policy and commented on drafts about the Ute Mountain Ute Indian Reservation. Catherine Kudlick read and commented on an early draft of the blind benefits material. Julie Greene continually encouraged me to tighten my argument while at the same time placing it in a larger context. At the University of New Mexico Press, Durwood Ball and then David Holtby showed confidence in my work from the very beginning. Joanne Goodwin commented on a conference paper, which was a small portion of this project, and read several complete drafts of the manuscript. Her remarks have influenced how I approached my study of welfare and have made this book much stronger. Susan Sterett enthusiastically supported my work from the first day we met, read many drafts, and offered critical insights about the welfare state as well as encouraged me to celebrate each professional accomplishment. Finally, Ralph Mann has directed my graduate and professional career from the very beginning. He has allowed me to grow as a scholar while gently demanding more from each set of revisions. Ralph's comments have proved insightful, often highlighting core issues that I missed.

Over the course of researching and writing, friends and family members offered support and encouragement. My fellow graduate students at the University of Colorado, Ellen Aiken, John Enyeart, and Todd Laugen, all sympathetically listened to my latest problems with poor relief and offered valuable suggestions on the manuscript. Maria Timmons, Victor Flores, Chris Barr, Trish Shanley, and Scott Miller always assured me that I was making rapid progress despite feeling overwhelmed and discouraged at times. Jim Denton offered invaluable advice about the historical profession. Sawad Brooks graciously agreed to apply his artistic skills to the dust jacket, a process which was a joy for me to follow.

Closer to home, Ruth Kinney, my former landlady and neighbor, charted my daily progress while trying to pry me away from the computer to perform "just one more chore" for her. Paulette Foss has assisted with this study from the beginning. She has answered literally hundreds of questions concerning this project, and I feel fortunate to have benefited so much from her help. Bettina Nicely Johnson generously used her impressive editing skills to sharpen my prose, smooth out the rough spots, and push me to clarify my thoughts. Most of all, I thank Bettina for sharing her excitement about this project with me. To my parents, Ron and Millie Krainz, I thank them for offering their ongoing support. Over the years, they have watched this study develop from the earliest stage of vague ideas to a published book. They have, no doubt, eagerly awaited the finished product.

Finally, I thank Laura Knotts for sharing her life with me. She provided unwavering encouragement throughout this project. Through successes and disappointments, Laura always kept her faith in me, and her love for me. One could not ask for more.

Introduction

ON OCTOBER 23, 1912, MARY YODER BEGAN RECEIVING PUBLIC POOR RELIEF from the county commissioners of Lincoln County, Colorado. Born in Shell Rock, Iowa, Yoder and her family settled in the town of Limon on Colorado's High Plains just three months prior to starting relief. The family's hopes for the future took a sudden turn for the worse when Yoder became a widow. With three children to raise, she asked the county commissioners for help. For the next two years and eight months, commissioners provided Yoder and her children with assistance in the form of supplies, coal, and medicine. On May 1, 1915, Lincoln County's poor records list Yoder's name for the last time, after she had received a total of almost $390 in public relief.[1]

The limited information about Yoder provides only a glimpse into her circumstances, yet her brief story challenges some deeply held assumptions about the delivery of Progressive Era welfare from the mid-1890s to 1920. Absent from Yoder's entries are several key characteristics that scholars have identified as representative of turn-of-the-century assistance. County poor records do not mention trained social workers assisting Yoder. Instead, elected county commissioners determined the level and type of support for her family. Nor is there any sign of a shift from private to public relief in Lincoln County. Publicly funded welfare was, in fact, the only form of long-term aid available in this rural county. In addition, there is no indication that Yoder received a mothers' pension, a new form of aid for single mothers, during her nearly three years on assistance even though Colorado's voters approved pensions just a few weeks after Yoder began receiving help from the county. Being a widow with three children, she surely would have qualified for such a pension.

By no means were the abnormalities in Yoder's case isolated to Lincoln County. Other communities also showed little evidence of change due to Progressive Era welfare reforms. Indeed, by examining county-level poor records like Yoder's, the lack of change in relief policies becomes a prominent feature of the period. At the same time, however, significant variations in aid practices among communities surface when comparing Yoder's experiences with welfare recipients from other counties. Yoder, for instance, received relatively high levels of monthly assistance compared to most other aid recipients in Colorado. In the end, Yoder's incomplete, yet simple, short tale, and thousands of other individual stories found in various county poor records throughout Colorado, disrupts long-held assumptions about the development of America's Progressive Era welfare state, forcing a rethinking about turn-of-the-century relief practices.

Historians and the Welfare State

The substantial body of literature on poverty and the welfare state has, over the past decade, both explored new issues and followed some old patterns. For years the study of the poor and the aid that they have received had occupied a peripheral position in the historical profession. Few historians devoted their full attention to the subject matter, and the teaching of welfare history was often left to schools of social work. Surprisingly, the emergence of "new" social history in the 1960s and 1970s largely ignored the stories of people dependent on charity and public assistance. Thus, the field of welfare history stagnated, remaining isolated from new developments in studying the past.[2] In recent years, however, welfare history has undergone a dramatic transformation, maturing into a vibrant and growing area of inquiry. Scholars, especially those interested in gender issues, notions of citizenship, and the formation of state policies, have begun a close examination of poverty and the development of welfare programs, producing a flood of new works. Yet, despite this vitality, many of the same broad underlying themes or concerns that had guided an earlier generation of scholars continue to mold much of the present-day literature. A focus on several closely intertwined topics—influential individuals, policymaking, and the ideology or motivation behind welfare programs and the accompanying rhetoric—binds this new expanding field of welfare history to earlier studies.

Scholars of welfare history, both then and now, have directed their attention to individuals who influenced the policies, practices, and public opinions about relief and the poor. In 1956, Robert H. Bremner's *From the Depths* established not only much of the foundation for welfare history but also the trend of concentrating on "movers and shakers." Bremner examines both prominent leaders who advocated for reforms and for the professionalization of social work as well as intellectuals who chose to write, photograph, paint, and draw about the conditions that poor people encountered.[3] Following Bremner, authors have tended to move away from intensely studying intellectuals' views of poverty while still maintaining an emphasis on a much smaller circle of "movers and shakers," those directly involved in policymaking or institutional formation and maintenance. Nathan Irvin Huggins, Allen Davis, Clarke Chambers, and others researched the men and women who led various groups, such as voluntary reform associations, settlement houses, and social service agencies.[4]

This focus on leading reformers has continued with recent scholarship but with a modification. Because feminist and gender theories have strongly influenced the focus of contemporary authors who examine poverty and the development of the welfare state, influential women, especially those from the Progressive Era, have come to occupy center stage in the literature. Josephine Shaw Lowell, Edith and Grace Abbott, Jane Addams, Sophonisba Breckinridge, Florence Kelley, Julia Lathrop, Mary Richmond, and Lillian Wald for instance, dominate the pages of inquiry. Scholars have diligently charted the careers and thoughts of these nationally known reformers. Accompanying these individuals into the historiography are the organizations that they controlled. These elite and middle-class groups or societies—New York City's Charity Organization Society, the Children's Bureau, the National Federation of Women's Clubs, the Hull House "network," and the Parent Teacher Association—all supported leading policymakers, formulated reform efforts, and possessed access to political power.[5] In the end, historians of poverty and welfare have been able to tell us a lot about influential reformers and their organizations.

Essentially inseparable from this focus on "movers and shakers," has been the examination of policymaking. Scholars have not only discussed the reformers who shaped welfare policies, but also the social movements behind broad changes in relief. Walter Trattner, for instance, chronicles the transformation from colonial era aid to scientific charity to professional social work to the War on Poverty.[6] Other authors have written extensively about the development and practices of various institutions, associations, and organizations like orphanages, homes for the mentally disabled, and Charity Organization Societies. Likewise, the evolution and changing directions of various policy debates among activists, politicians, social workers, and academics concerning workmen's compensation, mothers' pensions, aid to dependent children, old age pensions, and Medicare have received substantial attention from scholars. Charting the process of developing and enacting new welfare policies from germination to legislative victory to societal acceptance or rejection has been a constant trend in the field of welfare history.[7]

Over the last few years, authors have often framed their discussions of welfare policy formation in either a state-centered or a society-centered analysis. Those supporting a state-centered approach argue that the state acts independently of broader socioeconomic forces in setting relief policies. Theda Skocpol, for instance, explores how the "fit" among political institutions, existing policies, and a social group's capacities for political action determined the success or failure of Progressive Era reform legislation.[8] Edwin Amenta, likewise, places the structure of political institutions central to understanding the successes and shortcomings found in establishing modern welfare policies during the New Deal.[9] Other scholars, however, favor a society-centered framework which contends that social and economic elements shape how the state creates and enforces policies. With this model, the state does not act independently, but rather it embodies the beliefs and customs of society as a whole. Gender, class, and racial values, argues Linda Gordon, determined the form of government welfare policies during the first half of the twentieth century. This division between state- and society-centered researchers has frequently been very heated, with opposing sides vigorously defending their positions.[10] These strong passions have heavily influenced historians' study of welfare policies and practices during the last decade.

The ideological motivations of prominent reform leaders as well as the philosophical framework and rhetoric of different welfare measures have likewise received a great deal of attention from researchers. Protestantism, for example, helped to shape Josephine Shaw Lowell's and Mary Richmond's involvement with the Charity Organization Society movement and later Jane Addams' participation with settlement houses.[11] In the early 1970s, scholars increasingly turned to social-control theories to explain motivations for

welfare policies. David Rothman, for instance, argues that American societal disorder in the early nineteenth century spurred the use of asylums as a
means to create healing, controlled environments that supposedly "cured"
or "reformed" criminals, the poor, or the insane.[12] Social-control theories
also heavily influenced Frances Fox Piven and Richard Cloward's explanation of welfare policies since the 1920s in their influential *Regulating the
Poor*.[13] To support their analyses of ideological motivations, historians have
tapped into a voluminous supply of rhetorical evidence found in the form
of articles, speeches, essays, correspondences, and autobiographies of
reform leaders. The minutes and records of reform organizations, government documents, and legislative bills provide additional sources of evidence
to support an ideological focus.

Recently, scholars have tended to highlight the influence of gender on
welfare policies, especially during the Progressive Era, and on how welfare
programs affected ideas of citizenship. According to historian Molly Ladd-
Taylor, female reformers used notions of maternalism to mold the welfare
state. Their biggest and earliest success came with the establishment of
mothers' pensions, a form of public welfare aimed at keeping the children
of poor mothers in their homes.[14] Paula Baker, however, takes a slightly
different approach as she argues for a "domestication of politics" as "women
passed on to the state the work of social policy that they found increasingly
unmanageable," forcing the state to assume new authority and responsibilities during the early twentieth century.[15] For some writers, the influence of
gender created essentially two different welfare tracks, with men generally
qualifying for more generous social insurance programs with set qualifications while women received less generous welfare benefits with means-
and morality-tested criteria.[16] The type of welfare benefits a person received
or was eligible for, argues a growing group of scholars, clearly influenced
one's claims to citizenship.[17]

Even though the literature on the welfare state has generally focused on
these three closely linked themes—influential individuals, policymaking,
and ideological motivations and rhetoric—still, as we have seen, important
differences in interpretations remain. For our purposes, the most crucial
issue is the degree to which scholars' view the Progressive Era as a period of
meaningful change in this nation's welfare practices and policies. Almost all
scholars acknowledge that the period did indeed witness many new theories and ideas about welfare. But how significant these theories and ideas

were in actually changing practices is open to debate. Robert Bremner sees the Progressive Era as an important start in reform, while Walter Trattner notes the long list of reform measures enacted at this time. James Patterson, however, is less impressed with Progressive Era changes. For him, these reforms retained the same essential goal of trying to instill middle-class values or behaviors in the poor just as previous relief practices had tried to do.[18]

Central to this debate over Progressive Era change is the role of mothers' pensions. Recently, many historians view these pensions, as well as the Progressive Era, as a major turning point in America's welfare development. Mothers' pensions, according to Linda Gordon, represent the "first modern public welfare in the United States."[19] And Gwendolyn Mink goes so far as to state that "'Welfare' began eighty years ago in state-level mothers' pension programs designed to mitigate the poverty of worthy mothers without husbands to depend on."[20] For Gordon, Mink, and others, Progressive Era mothers' pensions began the bifurcation of America's welfare state by largely channeling men and women into two very different types of welfare.[21] Most older scholars have been far more hesitant to give mothers' pensions so much credit. Bremner calls them a type of superficial reform, while both Patterson and Chambers claim that the pensions were hardly more than mere modifications of existing relief practices and beliefs.[22] Roy Lubove contends that mothers' pensions "failed . . . to modernize the public welfare system."[23] Thus, scholars have not been able to agree on the Progressive Era's importance in shaping relief measures nor on which changes were the most significant.

Shifting the Focus

This study will both build on the vitality and strength of the existing welfare-history literature as well as diverge from it. As noted above, Progressive Era relief practices have received intense scrutiny from scholars inspired by gender analyses, by recent debates over the state and the polity, and by social-control theories. This project continues that examination. At its core, *Delivering Aid* will address two questions: Does the Progressive Era mark a period of significant change in the nation's welfare practices? What forces were affecting relief policies? Although contemporary historians have concentrated heavily on early-twentieth-century developments, they have oddly failed to explain adequately the transformations that occurred and what elements shaped policies during this period. Instead, their focus has mainly been linking Progressive Era programs with the New Deal in the 1930s.[24] This project will analyze Progressive Era policies on their own terms to determine the degree of meaningful change and what influenced practices. But to answer these questions I will take a different approach than most of my colleagues. The focal point of this study will be the experiences of those individuals and families who actually received assistance. As a result, the implementation of relief efforts at the local level will take center stage. In addition, this book will examine assistance from a community-wide perspective so that the analysis mirrors how poor people may have encountered or at least viewed their relief options. Finally, this investigation of Progressive Era relief practices will take place in the American West, allowing for both an exploration of diverse communities largely overlooked in the literature and an analysis of welfare practices in the one region that most strongly embodied Progressivism.

A focus on the implementation of welfare practices shifts the emphasis away from prominent reform leaders and their ideology and rhetoric to the daily experiences of poor people. Thus, in lieu of measuring the importance of poor relief programs by how and why reformers advocated for particular policies, this study measures the importance of poor relief programs in light of the tangible actions that did or did not alter a poor person's circumstances. The danger of relying on rhetoric and ideology only to validate the success or failure of a program is that the rhetoric and ideology rarely matches the implementation. What reformers hoped to enact and what they actually accomplished did not always correspond. Even achieving legislative approval did not, of course, guarantee the full enactment of a relief measure. Only through an investigation of implementation can we accurately determine the significance of aid efforts.

Some historians have realized the need to address implementation. For years Michael Katz has been arguing that the study of poverty has been "insufficiently concerned with the actual experience of people."[25] Clarke Chambers echoes Katz's concerns and chides the field for paying too little attention to the "recipients of public assistance."[26] And Molly Ladd-Taylor states that "any understanding of a welfare system must come from examining the administration of services, rather than the political campaign or ideology behind them."[27] Joanne Goodwin, more recently, has completed one of the first monographs to examine the problems of implementing

welfare programs. Selecting Chicago, Goodwin explores the political con-
flicts over administering mothers' pensions. She investigates battles over
controlling mothers' pensions, disagreements over funding levels, and
debates about eligibility. Goodwin concludes that "virtually from the beginning of implementation, the initial promise of mothers' pensions disappeared."[28] Goodwin's conclusion thus differs dramatically from the rhetoric
and ideology used to promote mothers' pensions.

With implementation occupying center stage, a shift in analysis to the
local delivery of assistance becomes a necessity. During the Progressive Era,
welfare policies remained largely a local issue as neither federal nor even
state governments, for the most part, dictated or controlled relief. Instead,
county officials were responsible for the needy as individual counties appropriated funds and administered local poor relief programs. And most private charities also depended almost solely on local fund-raising efforts and
personnel to aid the poor. The "profoundly local nature" of this nation's welfare system, states Katz, is one of the dominant features of the American
state.[29] Due to this local responsibility, it becomes problematic to speak of
welfare reform or policies in a national manner. Theda Skocpol acknowl-
edges this dilemma when discussing mothers' pension programs. "Any
detailed analysis of the implementation of mothers' pensions in this period," concludes Skocpol, "would have to deal with many different local patterns" because the funding and administering for the pensions were "left
almost entirely to thousands of local communities."[30] If we want to understand turn-of-the-century relief policies, we need to examine how communities carried out the implementation of assistance at the local level where
policies were funded and administered.

Directing our attention to the local distribution of aid greatly expands
the possible topics for inquiry. Most studies of welfare history have claimed
a national perspective while focusing almost exclusively on prominent
reformers. These leaders, no doubt, were nationally known, and they truly
acted as national speakers rallying support for various issues. Yet, these
reformers worked in only a few eastern or midwestern cities. Reformers from
the American West remain largely absent from the literature. In addition,
when authors do cite instances of welfare rhetoric or policies, the overwhelming majority of these examples come from a select few places. The debates
and policies of Boston, Chicago, New York City, and Philadelphia dominate
the historiography. Examples from locations west of the Mississippi River or

from rural communities are indeed scarce.[31] Even Progressive Era social workers were keenly aware of how location could influence relief practices. "I have been told always since I have been in social work, that New York and Chicago are in a class by themselves," stated Baltimore's J. W. Magruder, a participant in the 1912 National Conference of Charities and Corrections, "and the rest of us are not necessarily concerned in what New York and Chicago may do in a given case."[32] The inclusion of the American West into the field of welfare history will not only enrich an already vibrant body of literature but will also add complexity to conclusions about aid policies.

Equally as important as diversifying the field of knowledge, an examination of welfare practices in the West allows a focus on the region that most enthusiastically embraced Progressive Era reforms. Westerners generally had much weaker alliances to political parties, resulting in a willingness to engage in split-ticket voting, to defect to the opposition, or to support third-party candidates. With such weak local political parties, efforts to abolish political machines and their patronage systems, one of the key aims of Progressivism, succeeded, not only more easily but also to a much wider extent in the West than in the South, Midwest, or Northeast. Indeed Westerners were willing to embrace "candidate-centered" or "issue-oriented" electoral politics and to approve efforts to facilitate direct democracy, which only further bypassed political parties.[33] Measures like the recall, the initiative, the referendum, and the direct primary as well as a host of other reforms—women's suffrage, eight-hour workday laws, protective labor legislation for female employees, and workmen's compensation—often originated or quickly took hold in the West.[34] Given this broad reform climate, the West would be the one region where Progressive Era welfare ideas would seem to have the best chance of succeeding at the local level.

Prioritizing the local implementation of relief forces a rethinking of the use of broad theories to explain welfare developments. The application, in particular, of state- or society-centered approaches to analyze relief programs becomes problematic when examining policies at the local level. For an either/or debate proves unsatisfactory since such a wide range of elements has contributed in shaping the implementation of assistance. At certain times or with certain programs, for example, societal forces such as religious beliefs, economic trends, attitudes about women, or professionalization impulses profoundly directed how communities responded to the poor. Yet, at other times or in other programs, the state (in this case county governments) acted as an independent entity, ignoring trends or pressures from society at large. No clear pattern emerges that would completely exclude either state- or society-centered influences. Instead, an ever changing mixture of the two approaches best explains the many elements that helped to determine how communities implemented aid.[35]

Finally, a community-wide overview of relief practices is required in order to highlight the daily experiences of poor people receiving assistance. Usually scholars have isolated artificially specific welfare programs in their discussions, addressing only a single type of relief as if other forms of aid were unavailable. Yet, officials and, to a lesser degree, the poor often had a choice as to how they wanted to address an impoverished situation. Many counties dispensed a range of assistance including outdoor relief (assistance outside of formal institutions and within one's home), indoor relief (assistance inside of institutions in the form of county poor farms, poorhouses, or hospitals) and blind benefits (assistance to blind people). Plus, most communities also maintained several private charities as well as informal methods of aid. Oftentimes, the poor easily and quickly moved among various forms of assistance as their circumstances changed and evolved. Daniel Hopkins from Teller County exemplified the shifting needs of an aid recipient. In his seventies and having suffered an injury, "blown up while at work in one of the mines," Hopkins began receiving outdoor assistance, and for a while supplemented his relief payments "by tilling a small farm." He eventually became "practically helpless" as his condition worsened, forcing county officials to bring Hopkins to the county hospital where he would "spend his declining years."[36] Taking into account all types of public relief, private charities, and informal help allows for the possibility of following a person through different types of assistance and to inspect relief from a community-wide perspective in a manner that reflects how the poor themselves experienced turn-of-the-century aid practices.

Arguments and Sources

In order to examine the local implementation of aid, this study employs a comparative case-study approach. I have selected a diverse set of counties that vary in terms of local economies, cultures, geographies, settlement patterns, population densities, ethnic/racial compositions, philanthropic

Colorado State Map Showing County Divisions, 1913

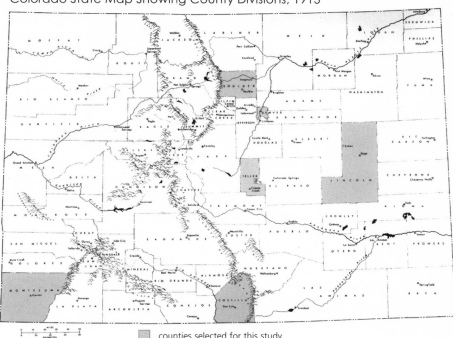

counties selected for this study

Source: Adapted from Kenneth A. Erickson and Albert W. Smith, Atlas of Colorado *(Boulder, Colo.: Colorado Associated University Press, 1985), opposite of title page.*

traditions, and religious backgrounds. Yet, I have also confined my research to a single state, Colorado, so that all communities share a common state government, encounter similar laws at similar times, and allow for an investigation of welfare practices in the American West. Using Boulder County, Costilla County, Denver County, Lincoln County, Montezuma County, and Teller County (see map), this project spans the years from roughly 1890 to the late 1920s, with the majority of the data covering the years 1900 to 1920. In order to achieve a community-wide perspective of assistance practices, I will examine the four types of public poor relief that counties distributed during the Progressive Era—outdoor assistance, indoor relief, mothers' pensions, and blind benefits—and address each community's private charities and informal methods of assistance. This set up offers a chance to measure the degree of change in welfare policies during this period in a diverse sample of communities. Can we see a difference in the implementation of welfare policies because of Progressivism? If the answer to this question is yes, then how did reformers make a difference? If Progressive Era policies did not alter relief practices, then what did determine or structure assistance? If welfare policies were not altered during this period, then a rethinking is in order as to how effective the Progressive Era was in state building, especially in terms of modern welfare practices.

The use of a comparative case-study approach that examines the implementation of welfare at the local level has profoundly shaped my arguments and conclusions. Using local implementation as my lens, I have found that in terms of altering the welfare state the Progressive Era was a period of disappointment. By the mid-1920s, Colorado's delivery of poor relief looked strikingly similar to nineteenth-century relief practices. In a sense, this lack of change really should not be surprising—one of the enduring characteristics of America's welfare state is that it remains "so impervious to real reform."[37] But recently historians have been unwilling to apply this observation to the Progressive Era, a time of seemingly great transformation in the welfare state. The changes that scholars have cited exist, for the most part, only in terms of rhetoric and ideology and not in terms of implementation. Many of the ideas that reformers advocated simply never made it into the daily relief practices of local communities. The professionalization of charity work and the adoption of individual casework methods, for example, rarely appeared at the county level. And even in places where officials made a diligent effort to professionalize relief, still these attempts were often so compromised as to result in little meaningful change. In addition, the often-cited shift of welfare from private to public control is misleading and exaggerated. In most counties, public funds and elected officials dominated local welfare practices well before Progressivism.

If Progressive Era welfare reform ideas were not filtering down from prominent leaders, then what was directing or dictating the implementation of local poor relief efforts? Local circumstances largely determined the type and method of relief practices. Local economies, geographies, settlement patterns, ethnic/racial compositions, population densities, philanthropic traditions, religious beliefs, decisions by local officials, and existing policies or institutions all altered how communities distributed assistance. Even in places like Denver, where officials such as Gertrude Vaile, a professionally trained social worker, tried hard to enact many of the key elements of Progressive Era welfare reform, local conditions still shaped these attempts. This wide-ranging list of local circumstances embodies a combination of society- and state-centered influences on various poor relief practices. This combination of influences is fluid, changing not only over time but also according to the type of assistance. Because local circumstances strongly affected how communities implemented their aid programs, significant variations appear among county practices. As a consequence, diversity in welfare policies best characterizes the Progressive Era welfare state.

These various local circumstances also shaped mothers' pensions. Even though one of the key aims of the pension movement was to instill uniform policies and practices across an entire state, important local differences continued to surface in the implementation of mothers' pensions. In the end, mothers' pensions did not operate in a vacuum; instead, they interacted with many other local factors which influenced the delivery of aid. In fact, mothers' pension programs mirrored a county's existing poor relief practices as opposed to establishing new trends. In some counties, outdoor assistance programs had already incorporated similar policies as found in mothers' pensions but had done so long before, and independent of, the pension movement. Thus, any connection between Progressive Era reform and the emergence of maternalism in the modern welfare state needs to be highly qualified. The notion that mothers' pension programs represent a "new beginning" or a transformation in poor relief is difficult to support when looking at implementation.

Despite its failure to live up to claims of change, the Progressive Era did alter Colorado's welfare state in one unexpected area: blind benefits. Unlike mothers' pensions, the successful implementation of blind benefits dramatically improved the living conditions of its recipients. Blind benefits imposed a uniform relief policy, regardless of location, which mothers' pensions never could accomplish and established statewide guidelines that determined who should receive assistance and at what levels while removing some authority away from county officials. Benefits also altered the funding of relief, with the state government taking a portion of the responsibility for the first time. Equally significant, blind and non-blind activists, and not welfare professionals, played a crucial role in designing and obtaining benefits. Once voters approved benefits, activists then managed to gain complete administrative authority over the benefits, even blocking attempts by professional social workers to wrest away control. Blind benefits represent an early form of interest-group politics that will come to dominate the political landscape, especially the welfare state, during the 1930s. The success of blind benefits, however, proved only temporary. By the mid-1920s, an odd assortment of groups and individuals—the Ku Klux Klan, local professional social workers, the American Foundation for the Blind, and Helen Keller—all attacked blind benefits and together succeeded in largely rolling back the one significant social welfare reform of the Progressive Era. On the eve of the Great Depression, Colorado's relief practices still looked much as they did in the nineteenth century.

My arguments and conclusions rest on being able to examine the implementation of poor relief in Colorado through the use of some unique sources. As a consequence, a brief explanation concerning these main sources is needed. The existence of county poor records or county pauper records, as they were sometimes called, allows for just such a thorough inspection of implementation from 1891 to 1925. Under pressure from Denver reformers, the Colorado legislature created the State Board of Charities and Corrections in 1891 to investigate the "whole system of public charities and correctional institutions."[38] Reformers wanted to remove any political involvement from the operation of the state's institutions and to instill an efficient centralized board to oversee charitable activities. The board's authority always remained purely advisory, but it did manage, despite the lack of universal compliance, to collect some statistical information on the operation of public charities, including county assistance programs.[39] Many counties did indeed begin keeping record books listing recipients of public assistance and many counties also began filing yearly reports with the State Board of Charities and Corrections. These record books and reports form the foundation of my evidence for this research project.

Although some counties kept track of their poor, the records were not necessarily easy to find. The majority of present-day county officials had no idea that such records existed, especially not prior to the mid-1930s, since most assumed that welfare began with the New Deal. I visited over one-third of the county courthouses throughout the state, and I literally crawled through some vaults on my hands and knees, climbed up shelving to reach the last box way up on top, and pushed file cabinets out of the way to peer behind them. Many counties never kept poor relief records, a few maintained only sporadic accounts, others discarded them long ago, and some lost them to fires and floods. Yet, I was able to locate a half-dozen counties with usable records. By combining county poor records with annual reports to the State Board of Charities and Corrections, or by relying solely on superb annual reports, I was able to add two more counties to the pool. From these eight counties, I chose six representing a diverse sampling of Colorado.

These county pauper records possess a wealth of information about individual recipients of public relief. While the quality of information varies from county to county, nevertheless, all the records generally consist of the recipient's name, sex, age, cause of distress, months receiving aid, and type and amount of aid received. I took the information in the county poor records and annual reports and entered it into a simple statistical computer program.[40] The statistical program allowed me to condense multiple entries about a particular relief recipient to a single entry containing all the information on that person. As a result, I was able to track an individual's entire welfare history, taking into account starts and stops in assistance and changes in the type of aid received. For all the selected counties except Denver, I entered the complete poor records into the computer program. In the case of Denver, I used a sample consisting of every third entry. Also, because Denver's records did not give the recipient's name, I was only able to track an individual's welfare history for a year's duration at a time. In total, this work charts the experiences of over five thousand individuals and families receiving public aid, often tracing these recipients over several years. My arguments and conclusions rest on these recipients' daily encounters with the welfare state.

Other records from the State Board of Charities and Corrections are also essential for this study. The board consisted of six members, almost always from Denver and Colorado Springs, appointed by the governor to serve six-year terms without compensation. The board's secretary, the only paid member, would make unannounced visits to investigate county relief practices, county poor farms, county poorhouses, and county hospitals. *The Minutes of Meetings of the State Board of Charities and Corrections* and the board's published biennial reports contain the descriptions of many of these visits as well as the board's recommendations for changing local policies. These reports about local charity operations provide some of the best information about how communities delivered assistance, even though the reports often originate from an urban, outsider's view. In addition, these sources from the board provide a link to national trends and debates about social welfare theories and practices. Board members, for instance, regularly attended and participated in annual national meetings, like the Charities and Corrections Conferences. As a result, many of the board's recommendations represent the latest and most "progressive" relief ideas.

Finally, I have added an element of comparison into this work in order to avoid some of the problems inherent in social historians' use of local studies. By selecting six counties with different socioeconomic structures and environments within Colorado, this work hopes to address some of the criticism of community-based research. Critics have argued that social history has fragmented the profession into increasingly smaller and smaller segments. And, as a result, an understanding of broader historical processes is often lost. In addition, scholars have often dismissed community-based studies as history simply pertaining to an isolated area. Studying six communities at once makes it difficult to regard this work's arguments and conclusions about the development of the welfare state as relevant only to a few counties or to a single state. Instead, the comparisons reveal patterns of behavior and trends that clearly show the powerful influence that local conditions had on Progressive Era poor relief practices.

The Settings

Using Colorado as the basis for a study of Progressive Era welfare development may seem a bit exotic or unusual. Indeed, Colorado's relatively small population raises questions about how important or representative the state was in comparison to larger states. Plus, the state may seem isolated or at least removed from the many changes that happened during the late nineteenth and early twentieth centuries. And in some ways, Colorado's political system was far less entrenched than many other eastern or southern states, thus allowing for greater changes through electoral politics.

But the state's many advantages far outweigh its few potential disadvantages. From 1890 to the mid-1920s, Colorado enthusiastically embraced or encountered almost all political trends and social developments that historians usually associate with the period. Voters from the Centennial state, for instance, battled Denver's political machine, fervently used the initiative to bypass political parties, and approved prohibition. The state experienced some of the nation's most violent battles between labor and capital with the 1894 and 1903–4 Cripple Creek strikes and the 1914 Ludlow Massacre. The populations of the state's three largest urban communities, Denver, Pueblo, and Colorado Springs, more than doubled between 1890 and 1920.[41] And like other non-southern states, Colorado experienced an influx of immigrants from eastern and southern Europe. In 1910, just over 16 percent of the state's population was foreign born while the nation averaged 14.7 percent.[42] For some of the period's developments, Colorado was, in fact, at the forefront. Colorado, for example, became the second state to grant women suffrage in 1893 and became one of the few states to elect both a Populist, in the 1890s, and then a Klan governor, in the 1920s. Clearly Colorado was not isolated or removed from turn-of-the-century events.

More important, Colorado provides a diverse setting for inspecting the welfare state, letting us see the delivery of relief in a variety of rural and urban communities. The three rural counties each show Colorado's residents in different social and economic settings, including Native Americans on the Ute Mountain Ute Indian Reservation in Montezuma County, newly arrived Protestant cash-crop homesteaders in both Montezuma and Lincoln Counties, and Catholic Hispanic subsistence farmers in Costilla County. The three remaining communities further diversify the study. Denver provides the opportunity to inspect aid in a medium-sized western city that actively embraced Progressive Era welfare reform. Teller County allows for an examination of relief practices in a declining industrial mining center. Finally, Boulder County represents a stable, mixed economy. Together, these communities are fairly representative of the American West, and even of large sections of the nation outside of the South.

Because the six counties differ so much from one another, a quick historical survey of each community will give the reader a firm understanding of each location's background. Costilla County sits in the San Luis Valley along the New Mexico state line. Surrounded by the Sangre de Cristo Mountains on the east, the San Juan Mountains to the west and southwest, and the La Garita Mountains in the northwest, the San Luis Valley is about fifty miles wide from east to west and runs 120 miles from Villa Grove, Colorado, in the north to near Taos, New Mexico, in the south. The valley, with its lowest point seven thousand feet above sea level, averages only four to nine inches of precipitation per year.[43] Sagebrush, yucca, and prickly pear cactus fill the valley, while juniper and piñon grow in the foothills and aspen,

Douglas fir, and blue spruce scale the surrounding mountains.[44] The Rio Grande begins its eighteen-hundred-mile journey to the Gulf of Mexico in Colorado's San Juan Mountains, and its many tributaries drain the central and southern portions of the valley.

Non-Indian settlement of the San Luis Valley came from the south, from New Mexico. The Mexican governor of New Mexico, Manuel Armijo, granted two residents of Taos the Sangre de Cristo land grant in 1844. Consisting of slightly less than one million acres, the Sangre de Cristo grant followed the Spanish, and then Mexican, policy of awarding individuals or groups huge tracts of land in return "for establishing settlements, bringing the lands into production, and defending themselves" and Mexican sovereignty from aggressors.[45] This policy of using land grants to expand colonization provided an inexpensive way to control territory since the government bore virtually no cost in giving the land grant. Meanwhile, the land grantee or grantees funded the initial settlements in hopes of recouping expenses through future land sales. In 1845, Utes and Apaches drove back the first attempt to settle the Sangre de Cristo grant. Four years later, a small group successfully settled along the Rio Costilla, establishing La Plaza de los Manzanera (now Garcia, Colorado). In 1851, twelve colonists ventured farther north and formed La Plaza de San Luis de Culebra (San Luis, Colorado) along the Rio Culebra.[46] The 1,771 square miles that make up Costilla County encompass most of the original Sangre de Cristo grant.

Isolation would dramatically shape these early settlements and Costilla County for decades to come. From the beginning, the mountain ranges isolated communities in the San Luis Valley from market outlets. As a consequence of the valley's inaccessibility, towns fostered a subsistence and barter economy revolving around agriculture. Settling along rivers and digging irrigation ditches, communities assured themselves of water for their crops. Families tilled small farms and grazed a few head of cattle or sheep.[47] San Luis Valley's isolation also influenced Costilla County's culture and social structure. In southern Colorado and northern New Mexico, the Roman Catholic lay organization, La Fraternidad Piadosa de Nuestro Padre Jesús Nazareno (the Pious Fraternity of Our Father Jesus Nazarite), commonly referred to simply as the Penitentes, was active in almost every Hispanic community.[48] Strong kinship ties and small communities likewise characterized the settlements scattered throughout Costilla County. Generation after generation of family members continued living in the region, passing

Street scene in San Luis (Costilla County), Colorado, 1899. Courtesy of Colorado Historical Society, CHS X4730.

down land obtained from the Sangre de Cristo grant. Finally, Spanish persisted as the dominant language of Costilla County well into the twentieth century, further separating Hispanic residents from the Anglo world beyond the mountains.

Located west of Costilla, in the Four Corners region, Montezuma County is the second southern Colorado county in this study. The Dolores and Mancos Rivers, along with numerous seasonal washes and creeks, drain this rugged county of deep canyons, dry mesas, expanses of barren land, and the timbered La Plata Mountains. Formed in 1889, Montezuma County covers slightly over two thousand square miles and ranges from a high point of just over thirteen thousand feet to a low of four thousand feet in elevation.[49]

Like many sections of Colorado and the West, Montezuma County tempted settlers with promises of vast amounts of mineral wealth. During the 1870s, a series of gold and silver rushes percolated throughout the San Juan Mountains of southern Colorado. One group of California prospectors journeyed across northern Arizona into the Four Corners region and camped in the Mancos Valley. Impressed with the tall grass, clear water, and nearby timber, six members of the California party decided, after a summer of prospecting in the La Plata Mountains in 1874, to settle permanently in the valley. Soon others began arriving, searching not for mineral deposits but rather for range land. During the late nineteenth and early twentieth centuries, the cattle industry dominated the local economy as more and more settlers took advantage of the abundant grasses. Herds ranged in size from a few head to as many as five thousand. Yet the success of the cattle industry also spelled the region's environmental downfall. With so many cattle grazing on the open range, the tall bluestem grass or western wheat grass gave way to sage brush by about 1910.[50]

At the same time that sage brush spread through the area, a wave of homesteaders were also putting down roots in Montezuma County. A number of outside investors funded two irrigation projects during the 1880s to bring water from the Dolores River to the Montezuma Valley.[51] With the availability of water from these projects beginning in 1889, homesteaders began to arrive in Montezuma. These new settlers turned to farming rather than ranching, raising alfalfa, fruit, and pinto beans. Other homesteaders experimented with dry-farming techniques in sections of the county that lacked irrigation.

As in Costilla County, the land being settled in Montezuma County was not empty. Rather, the land had been part of the Ute domain. The Utes consisted of seven different bands that shared a common language and culture. The Utes' hunting grounds spread from Utah to Kansas and covered almost the entire state of Colorado, but the Weeminuche band of the Utes primarily occupied the Four Corners region. Before the United States gained control of the area with the Treaty of Guadalupe Hidalgo in 1848, the Weeminuche band had largely been isolated from Spanish and Mexican contact. However, with settlers pouring into Colorado, especially into the San Juan Mountains beginning in 1859, various Ute leaders and bands signed a series of treaties. The end result of these treaties was a persistent reduction in land controlled by the Utes. By 1895, the Weeminuche band had settled on a reservation at the foot of Sleeping Ute Mountain in the southern portion of Montezuma County. Consisting of slightly over four hundred thousand acres, the Ute

Main Street in Cortez (Montezuma County), Colorado, ca. 1913. Photograph by George L. Beam. Courtesy of Colorado Historical Society, CHS X4411.

Mountain Ute Indian Reservation made up about 30 percent of the county.[52] In a sense, there were two separate communities within Montezuma County: the Weeminuches on the reservation and residents in the remaining part of the county.

Far away from the canyons and mesas of Montezuma County and across the state sits Lincoln County, the third and largest county in this study. Created in 1889 and located in eastern Colorado on the Great Plains, Lincoln County is shaped like a backwards "L" covering almost twenty-six hundred square miles.[53] Level ground, gently rolling swells, and hilly sections characterize this area of the High Plains stretching from a low elevation of forty-five hundred feet in the southeast to fifty-four hundred feet in the northwest portion of the county. No major rivers cut through Lincoln County; instead, a number of creeks drain the county into the watersheds of the Platte and Arkansas rivers.[54]

Ute horsemen at Towaoc (Montezuma County) on the western end of the Ute Mountain Ute Indian Reservation, 1908. Photograph by H. S. Poley. Courtesy of Denver Public Library, Western History Collection, P-47.

The grasses of the Great Plains attracted people to the area. The Arapahoe and Cheyenne roamed the western portions of the Great Plains hunting bison and other large game that came to feed on the grama, or buffalo, grass. This short, tough grass that grew on the High Plains could tolerate drought, cold weather, close grazing, and trampling.[55] With the discovery of gold in 1859, miners and settlers poured through the hunting grounds reserved for the Arapahoe and Cheyenne by the federal government just eight years earlier. After a series of atrocities by both Indians and whites that led to warfare that engulfed much of the central and northern plains, the Arapahoe and Cheyenne agreed, in the Medicine Lodge Creek Treaty of 1867, to leave Colorado for the Indian Territory (Oklahoma).[56] With the removal of Native Americans and the elimination of bison, stockmen, first from Texas, and their cattle flocked to the empty grasslands of Colorado's eastern plains. Bovina, a town in Lincoln County, got its name as a waterhole stop along the Texas-Montana cattle trail.[57] During the 1870s and 1880s, the area became a huge open range as cattlemen settled to take advantage of the same short, tough grass that had drawn buffalo. One of

County Fair, Hugo (Lincoln County), Colorado, 1908.
Courtesy of Terry W. Blevins.

the main purposes for the local weekly paper, the *Range Ledger*, published in Hugo, the Lincoln County seat, was to advertise local cattle brands so that stray cattle could be reunited with their proper owners.

With the coming of cattle, railroads soon followed and at times even led the settlement of the eastern plains. The Kansas Pacific Railroad (later purchased by the Union Pacific) first passed through Lincoln County in 1870, connecting Denver with Kansas City. The Chicago and Rock Island Railroad cut across the northern portion of the county in 1888 on its way to Colorado Springs. The need to service the tracks and trains and to care for workers and passengers spurred the development of several towns in Lincoln County. Hugo became a division point for the Union Pacific with a roundhouse, a water tank, a hotel, and an eating house. The Union Land Company created Limon as another service center for the Union Pacific Railroad. And the towns of Arriba and Genoa grew up along the tracks of the Chicago and Rock Island Railroad.[58]

While overgrazing spelled the demise of the cattle industry in Montezuma County, dry farming halted the dominance of stockmen in Lincoln County. The peak for the open-range cattle industry came in 1877 when just over three hundred railcars filled with cattle departed from Hugo.[59] Beginning in the 1880s, Lincoln County experienced its first wave of homesteaders. These early farmers fenced their crops and limited access to the range. Yet, the drought of the mid-1890s halted any further settlement and drove many of these early homesteaders off the land. By the turn of the new century, a second homestead boom was under way. Fueled by the popularity of dry-farming methods, the number of farms in Lincoln County grew from only ninety-eight in 1890 to 1,334 twenty years later.[60] With essentially no irrigation and an average of only slightly more than fourteen inches of precipitation per year, dry farming seemed to be the answer to growing crops on the arid Great Plains.[61] Wheat, corn, and hay became the three most important crops in Lincoln County, and by 1906 farms and houses occupied every section of the county.[62]

Due west from Lincoln County, across the last of the Great Plains, through the foothills, up several thousand feet in altitude, and over Pikes Peak, sits Teller County, the next community included in this study. Teller County did not exist until the state legislature carved out 547 square miles from neighboring counties in 1899 to create a separate county encompassing the Cripple Creek Mining District, one of the world's richest sources of gold. Much of Teller County is situated in high-altitude country that until 1890 had only been used by a few ranchers to graze their cattle in pastures along the western side of Pikes Peak.

Quickly the quiet, wind-swept pastures would be transformed into a bustling mining camp. Robert Womack, a heavy-drinking local cowhand, had been searching the area, on and off, for valuable ore since 1878. In 1890, his persistence paid off as he discovered a gold-bearing vein near Poverty Gulch.[63] By the following spring the rush was on as investors from around Colorado began to purchase mining claims. What had been pastures a few months earlier suddenly housed several growing urban settlements. By May 1891, the city of Cripple Creek had electricity as well as the services of three hotels and two banks.[64] Within a few years, the towns of Gollitt, Mound City, Anaconda, Elkton, Altman, Independence, Goldfield, and Victor sprung up as mining developed around the region. By 1895, two railroads reached the district, and a third railroad would arrive in 1901. During this time of rapid development, setbacks only temporarily slowed growth. In 1896, fire essentially destroyed all of Cripple Creek, and neighboring Victor met a similar fate three years later. Yet, in both cases, reconstruction began instantly with the requirement that only brick be used for central business district buildings. Ten years after Womack's discovery, the Cripple Creek gold rush peaked. In 1900, the district produced slightly over eighteen million dollars in gold, and Teller County's population reached just over twenty-nine thousand inhabitants.[65]

Cripple Creek's gold rush created a distinctive community. Because of the late date of discovery and the difficulty of deep hard-rock mining, the Cripple Creek Mining District almost immediately resembled an industrial mining center. The romantic image of the lone miner panning in a stream had long since passed by the time Cripple Creek boomed. Large amounts of capital and labor were needed to remove several layers of hard rock while sinking shafts, often one hundred feet or more, to profitable veins.[66] Frequently this capital came from outside the district. By 1900, investors from Colorado Springs, Denver, the East Coast, or foreign nations owned about 90 percent of the district's mines.[67] And turn-of-the-century industrial mining was not a pretty sight. "The whole region looked as though thirteen-inch guns had been playing upon it from every quarter," wrote Walter Wyckoff during his visit to Cripple Creek. "At points along the gulches and crowning the neighboring hills were high wooden structures built over the shafts with power-houses belching black smoke from tall iron chimneys."[68] In many respects, the Cripple Creek Mining District mirrored stable industrial mining towns like Butte, Montana, which had large shifts of laborers working underground and a more stable community core than most boom towns. Teller County's workforce consisted of older and more experienced miners, with over 58 percent of all adults in the community married.[69] In addition, workers excluded essentially all Asians and southern and eastern Europeans from the mining district.[70]

"Labor," according to historian Elizabeth Jameson, "built one of the most impressive working-class communities in the history of the United States" in the Cripple Creek Mining District.[71] In 1894, miners organized under the Western Federation of Miners and won the right to unionize, an eight-hour workday, and a three-dollar minimum daily wage. A labor victory in the middle of the nation's worst nineteenth-century depression (1893–98) was surprising. A strong alliance between workers and local merchants, in part, explains the 1894 victory. Also contributing to the miners' victory was Governor Davis Waite, a pro-labor Populist, who intervened on the side of strikers, preventing mine owners from using local deputies to break the strike. Unlike other gold rushes, laborers in Cripple Creek received some of the district's immense wealth.

Two counties north of Teller sits Boulder County, the fifth county in this study. In many ways, Boulder County geographically and economically mirrors Colorado. Located some twenty miles northwest of Denver and roughly

The central portion of Cripple Creek (Teller County), Colorado, 1896.
Photograph by Andrew James Harlan. Courtesy of Denver Public Library,
Western History Collection, X-819.

sixty miles south of the Wyoming border, it contains both the High Plains and mountains. Approximately 40 percent plains and 60 percent mountains, the county covers 764 square miles. Its elevation ranges from approximately five thousand feet along the eastern border to Longs Peak, at 14,256 feet, in the extreme northwest corner. The St. Vrain, Boulder, Coal, and Left-Hand creeks, along with their tributaries, drain Boulder County into the South Platte River. The diverse geography attracted farmers, ranchers, and miners, producing a mixed economy.

Precious metals found in the mountains first brought newcomers to Boulder County. In 1859, a party of Missourians on their way to Denver discovered gold near present day Gold Hill.[72] Within a year of the yellow metal's discovery, Gold Hill supported over a thousand people. Despite initial success, within two years both the placer and quartz mining began to play out.[73] Caribou, south and west of Gold Hill, followed a similar boom/bust pattern. In 1869 a group of prospectors brought back mineral samples from a location near the Continental Divide that proved to be one of the "richest silver mines in Colorado."[74] By 1873, Caribou's population peaked as approximately one thousand people, mainly Cornish residents, lived and worked at an altitude of 10,500 feet above sea level.[75] While miners continued to extract gold, silver, lead, and copper from western Boulder County, precious-metal mining's importance and magnitude substantially decreased during the early twentieth century.[76]

The growth of mining communities like Gold Hill and Caribou spurred the development of the city of Boulder. Located at the eastern edge of Boulder Canyon, next to the mountains, Boulder acted as a supply town for the mountain mining communities. Later the city of Boulder grew and even briefly attempted to challenge Denver for control over the region. With the 1877 opening of the state's premier higher education institution, the University of Colorado, in Boulder, the city solidified its paramount position in the county and guaranteed its importance in the state. In 1910, Boulder, dominated by Protestants, was the fifth largest city in Colorado, with 9,539 residents, and continued to serve as a market center linking the county's mining and agricultural sectors.[77]

The plains of eastern Boulder County followed a different settlement pattern than the mountain communities and the city of Boulder. In the eastern part of Boulder County, settlers produced a variety of agricultural products including barley, potatoes, alfalfa, sugar beets, wheat, cattle, and sheep.[78] In the southeastern corner of Boulder County, coal mining became the most important industry. During the 1880s and 1890s, Catholic Italians started to come to the area, eventually dominating the mining communities of Louisville and Lafayette.[79] By 1908, twenty-five coal mines seasonally employed approximately fourteen hundred miners in the county.[80]

Denver, Colorado's smallest but most populated county, is the final county for this study. Consisting of slightly more than fifty-eight square miles, the city and county of Denver, the city and county shared boundaries beginning in 1902 after separating from Arapahoe County, housed the state capital and contained 213,381 residents in 1910, making up slightly over 26 percent of the state's total population.[81] Ten years later, these figures would increase to 256,491 citizens, accounting for about 27 percent of Coloradans (see Table 1).[82]

Boulder (Boulder County), Colorado, 1900. Photograph by William Henry Jackson. Courtesy of Colorado Historical Society, CHS J3288.

While Denver's dominance of the state, and indeed of the Rocky Mountain West, seems assured now, the city's humble beginnings hardly foreshadowed its future claim as the Queen City of the Rockies. Denver's beginning rested more on rumors of riches than on any actual unearthing of precious metals. William Russell and his two brothers set out from Georgia in 1858 to prospect in the Rocky Mountains. By the time Russell reached the Rockies in the spring, his party numbered over one hundred, and they set up camp where Cherry Creek flows into the South Platte River. During that summer, the Russell party panned out several hundred dollars of gold from a nearby creek before they exhausted the find. Word of the discovery, long since depleted, along with other claims of gold in the Pikes Peak region, spurred those eager for quick riches to head to the small settlement in 1859. Fortunately for the soon to be arriving miners, prospectors, braving winter conditions, had unearthed three substantial gold fields in the surrounding mountains. With the rush now in full swing,

View of 17th Street in Denver, Colorado, ca. 1917. Photograph by Ford Optical Company. Courtesy of Colorado Historical Society, CHS X5356.

it was clear that the future of Denver would be as a supply town for nearby mountain mining communities and farming settlements.[83]

By the turn of the century, Denver had begun to diversify its economy, although the city still relied heavily on agriculture and mining. Denver added manufacturing, banks, stockyards, and meat-packing plants, while smelters processed precious metals from nearby mountains. Denver's boosters advertised the city's climate and location to draw tourists and health seekers.[84] With Denver gaining a sense of permanence, the city experienced an influx of immigrants from eastern and southern Europe. Italians, Poles, Russians, and Slovenians, to name a few, all congregated in the Queen City, largely accounting for the city's rapid expansion during the late nineteenth and early twentieth centuries.[85]

In order to use these very different communities as a lens to inspect the implementation of Progressive Era relief policies, I have organized this study more topically than chronologically. Chapter 1 examines and explains the differences among the five smaller counties—Boulder, Costilla, Lincoln, Montezuma, and Teller—in their use of outdoor assistance as well as the debates and struggles on the Ute Mountain Ute Indian Reservation over what constituted relief. This focus on outdoor aid continues in chapter 2 with an inspection of Denver's relief program and the local conditions that molded it. Chapter 3 investigates how local circumstances shaped the role (or absence) of charitable institutions and private relief organizations in all six counties. The disappointing implementation of mothers' pensions is the subject of chapter 4. Chapter 5 explores blind benefits and how they transformed relief practices. Chapter 6 briefly follows events through the 1920s and early 1930s before finally concluding with a short summary of arguments concerning the development of America's Progressive Era welfare state.

CHAPTER ONE

The Diversity of Relief

OUTDOOR AID IN SMALLER COMMUNITIES

ON APRIL 8, 1916, MONTEZUMA COUNTY COMMISSIONERS MET TO CONDUCT regular business. Near the end of their meeting, Mrs. Winifred Nero appeared before the commissioners asking for help. Mrs. Nero requested "that she be provided with funds in the sum of $20.00 with which to pay for transportation for herself and family from Cortez to Durango." The commissioners agreed to Mrs. Nero's request but with one condition. In exchange for the money, Mrs. Nero had to reimburse the commissioners by turning "over to the County, for sale, all her House Hold goods." The commissioners then directed the county sheriff to dispose of Mrs. Nero's belongings "for the best price" and "to deliver the proceeds of such sale to the County Treasurer."[1] These commissioners, untrained in charity or social work, were making decisions that would seem to lessen Mrs. Nero's chance for success at her new location. In a sense, the behavior of Montezuma County commissioners seems almost alien to our present characterization of the Progressive Era, a period when professional social workers supposedly directed assistance.

Almost a year later and several counties to the east, Costilla County commissioners gathered in San Luis's adobe courthouse to alter their poor relief system. The commissioners unanimously decided to abandon the practice of dispensing aid through local merchants. In the past, storeowners kept individual accounts for each relief recipient as the poor received all assistance in the form of goods purchased from various retailers. In place of this system, the county would now give all relief directly to the poor in the form of cash or check.[2] This change would be one of the greatest modifications of Costilla's poor relief program during the early twentieth century. Yet, as with Montezuma's practices, the change in Costilla's distribution of aid would hardly pass as representative of our current understanding of Progressive Era assistance. Indeed, the idea of giving the poor money without supervision or guidance from trained social workers would seem to run counter to the goals of individual casework. The actions taken by commissioners in both Costilla and Montezuma hardly conjure up images of the beginnings of a "modern" welfare state that historians have so often labeled the Progressive Era.

While the examples from Costilla and Montezuma challenge our view of turn-of-the-century assistance, they also reveal dramatic differences in the direction and tone of each county's relief efforts. In Costilla, the commissioners seemed to be operating a relaxed system with little oversight and control. By giving cash directly to the needy, the commissioners were confident that the poor would properly manage their own affairs. At the same time, Montezuma's public assistance appeared highly regimented and punitive, the exact opposite of Costilla's. Montezuma's commissioners were actively involved in the most trivial decisions concerning their relief efforts. In addition, Montezuma seemed determined to make relief a humiliating and painful experience. What accounts for these profound differences in approach?[3]

This chapter will explore both the discrepancies in the implementation of public outdoor relief (assistance outside of formal institutions and within one's home usually in the form of goods—food, clothes, fuel, or medicine—and rarely in cash) found among the smaller communities of this study—Boulder, Costilla, Lincoln, Montezuma, and Teller Counties—as well as the efforts on the Ute Mountain Ute Indian Reservation to transform annuities and rations from legal obligations into a type of poor relief. Denver's outdoor relief policies will be analyzed in the following chapter. Public outdoor aid was the dominant form of Progressive Era assistance in all five counties and in some locations it was the only type of aid offered. Yet, historians have written very little about publicly funded outdoor relief practices. The few authors who have addressed the topic mainly limit their analyses to turn-of-the-century debates over whether relief should be privately or publicly funded and administered, and stress attempts made by certain communities to restrict or abolish outdoor assistance.[4] The recent wave of research on the development of America's Progressive Era welfare state has produced almost no new analysis of outdoor relief.[5] By examining the implementation of outdoor relief in these five diverse counties, our understanding of the forces acting on outdoor assistance becomes much clearer. Dramatic differences, for instance, among county relief practices were not confined to just Costilla and Montezuma. In fact, variances appeared among all five counties. Local circumstances—economies, settlement patterns, environmental conditions, religious beliefs, kinship ties, philanthropic practices, and decisions by commissioners—largely accounted for these differences and shaped the type and form of assistance that each county adopted. On the Ute Mountain Reservation, previous relief decisions, the economy, the environment, protests, laws, and a treaty shaped how and if annuities and rations would be implemented as a type of poor relief or as legal agreements.

Even though their local practices varied considerably, all five of these counties were well aware of Progressive Era trends in social welfare reform.[6] Cripple Creek, the county seat of Teller County, hosted two sessions of Colorado's seventh annual conference of Charities and Corrections in 1902. Reformers, politicians, academics, and administrators from throughout the state converged on the mining district. The first session at Cripple Creek discussed "Truancy and Parental Neglect," while the evening meeting dealt with local systematic charity organizations. Inspired by the talks, Teller's citizens immediately formed a committee to create a local charity organization society.[7] Boulder County residents became informed about poor relief policies through university events and guest speakers at social clubs. In 1914, Gertrude Vaile, supervisor of Denver's outdoor assistance program, spoke about "Some Social Problems of Public Outdoor Relief" at a sociological conference held at the University of Colorado. This same conference also brought Fr. William O'Ryan, president of the State Board of Charities and Corrections, to the county.[8] Mary McDowell, Jane Addams' assistant, delivered the university's 1907 commencement speech, and the Woman's Club of Boulder held a talk about visiting Hull House.[9] Throughout the period, the secretary of the State Board of Charities and Corrections repeatedly visited all five counties. During these unannounced inspections, the secretary conferred with local county officials and advocated changes in relief practices. A formal letter from the board almost always followed these visits, stating the exact recommendations and changes that the board desired. Thus, while these five counties were largely rural, they were neither isolated nor shut-off from social welfare developments or discussions.

Although all five counties shared a common preference for outdoor assistance, there were still profound differences in how they dispensed that relief. The average amount of aid that a person received, for example, varied considerably among the counties. In Montezuma, recipients averaged almost thirty-one dollars per month in assistance, an amazingly high figure. Lincoln and Teller gave out more modest monthly amounts in the high teens, while Boulder averaged just over nine dollars per month. At the low end of the scale stood Costilla, doling out about five dollars each month (see Table 2). When looking at the two extremes, Montezuma and Costilla, it appears, at first glance, that Montezuma ran a generous welfare system, with high monthly averages, while Costilla operated a stingy, if not harsh, public assistance program. In fact, this data seems to go against the two brief examples that introduced this chapter. In those descriptions, the roles of each county appeared reversed, with Montezuma being rather punitive and with Costilla giving the poor some degree of freedom and compassion. When considering additional data that indicates how long a needy person received assistance, our picture becomes even cloudier. In Montezuma, Lincoln, and Teller Counties, recipients remained on welfare roles for an average of only six to eight months. Poor folk in Boulder faired considerably better by averaging over sixteen months of aid. However, Costilla more than doubled Boulder's average by allowing its residents to stay on assistance for over thirty-four months (see Table 3). Once again, Costilla and Montezuma seem to be reversing places on our spectrum. Local circumstances account for this seemingly contradictory data.

Subsistence, Extended Families, and Penitentes

Costilla County's use of outdoor aid stands out among the five communities as being exceptional. Several characteristics account for the county's distinctiveness. On the one hand, the poor remained on welfare rolls for very long durations; most averaged close to three years of assistance. In the most extreme case, Silverio Madrid, a sixty-five-year-old blind resident, received aid for at least twelve years, from 1894 to 1906.[10] On the other hand, Costilla's poor folk received the smallest amounts of monthly support. The surviving records, 1891 to 1906 and 1913 to 1919, indicate that levels of assistance remained remarkably consistent. The county commissioners generally allotted each individual between $3.50 and $8.00 per month, regardless of a person's reason for distress. Finally, the high number of elderly individuals receiving aid in Costilla sets it apart from the other counties. In Costilla, 30 percent of relief recipients cited "old age" as their reason for needing assistance (see Table 4). In sum, long durations, low levels of monthly support, and a sizable number of elderly people characterized Costilla County's outdoor relief. Of course, the important question is, why did Costilla's public assistance program take on these distinctive elements? As with all the counties, there are several interlocking reasons that explain a community's outdoor relief program. In Costilla's case, a series of economic determinants, settlement patterns, kinship behaviors, and religious practices account for the county's distinctive poor relief practices.

Costilla was one of Colorado's poorest counties during the late nineteenth and early twentieth centuries. At the time, Costilla, one of the state's sixty-three counties, had the twelfth lowest tax value in the state and the lowest among the six communities in this study.[11] Causing much of Costilla's financial problems were hostilities between the largely Anglo residents of the northern end of the county and the majority Hispanic residents in the southern portion.[12] Anglos disliked being governed by Hispanics and were especially upset at the use of Spanish and at what they perceived to be unfair taxation rates. Unable to end Hispanic control and physically separated from one another, Anglos advocated a splitting of the county. "As far as the residents of this district are concerned," stated an English-language newspaper, "the county of Costilla can be divided at any time. If the south-enders do not like our attitude, their recourse is division."[13] To this end, north-enders met in November 1912 to "discuss the feasibility of carving a new county out of Conejos and Costilla counties." By the following year, Anglos realized their goal when the state legislature created a new county, Alamosa, out of the northern portions of Costilla and Conejos.[14] Costilla County shrunk from 1,771 square miles to 1,185 square miles. The division sent the county's already shaky financial situation into further crisis as it struggled with mounting debt.[15] "The county was in a bad way financially," reported William Thomas, secretary of the State Board of Charities and Corrections, "as the creation of the county of Alamosa had taken away 40 percent of its taxable property."[16]

Despite Costilla's financial problems, the county never discontinued nor reduced its payments to recipients of outdoor relief. Likewise, there is no evidence that the commissioners began a "get tough" policy with new applicants because of a shortage of funds. Yet, the county's limited resources, no doubt, contributed to keeping monthly payments low throughout the period. As the county attempted to repay its debt, commissioners were in no position to raise relief payments, thus, partially accounting for the very consistent, but low, levels of support found in Costilla.

Besides lacking money, Costilla possessed a unique settlement pattern. Charles Beaubien, who had gained control of the Sangre de Cristo land grant in 1847 by inheritance and by purchasing the remaining interests, decided to set aside three different types of lands and land uses for the community. He gave or sold, for small sums, strips of land or *varas* (a vara is a Spanish unit of linear measurement that varied from 32 to 43 inches in different countries) for cultivation by original settlers. Since Beaubien intended this land for agriculture, each strip fronted a water source, the Rio Culebra or a stream, so that each settler had access to irrigation. Family size determined how many varas a settler could obtain. A "single man received a strip of land 100 varas wide, a married man a strip 200 varas wide, with additional frontage up to 500 varas according to the number of male children in the family."[17] While the strips of land were relatively narrow in width, each strip did extend for quite a distance, in some cases, for several miles.[18] In addition to the vara strips, as the narrow strips of land are now called, Beaubien also set aside two tracts of common land. Settlers had access to common land in the mountains, called La Sierra, which provided timber, firewood, berries, nuts, and game. Closer to the vara strips, settlers also had access to 633 acres of common grazing land, named La Vega, located adjacent to San Luis, the county seat.[19] The three-way division of the Sangre de Cristo grant was not a new scheme. Beaubien had simply duplicated a land disposal system that had been used previously in New Mexico. Under this scheme, each settler received a prime plot of irrigable land (the vara strips), access to grazing land (La Vega), and access to forested mountain tracts (La Sierra).[20]

This system of land ownership and use had a profound influence on Costilla's poor relief. The combination of the vara strips and communal lands provided "all the natural resources needed to survive in an isolated rural village."[21] Most residents raised their own meat, vegetables, and grain and could gather or hunt additional foods—piñon nuts, choke cherries, and venison—

from La Sierra. Each household produced almost all its own clothing and local store owners "accepted produce in exchange for merchandise."[22] Even with the development of some income-producing opportunities, wool production and increasingly available cash-paying jobs outside of the county, Costilla's land system and subsistence economy continued to support, either wholly or partially, large segments of the population. So while Costilla was removed from both markets and accessible market outlets, it was still able to provide for its poorer residents through Beaubien's land distribution. Thus, low levels of monthly support reflected the fact that residents, even impoverished ones, needed little cash to survive in Costilla County's cash-poor economy. Commissioners had little reason to provide high levels of assistance when the subsistence and barter economy provided a safety net for needy people.

The centrality of the communal lands to the communities of Costilla can clearly be seen in the battles over their control. The 1848 Treaty of Guadalupe Hidalgo theoretically protected Beaubien's division of the Sangre de Cristo. American courts, however, have been less willing to recognize some of these land uses and ownership arrangements despite the treaty. In 1916, Judge J. D. Wiley ruled that the communal lands mentioned in Beaubien's deed referred to only La Vega and not to La Sierra. Although the government tried to undo Beaubien's intentions, local citizens simply ignored Judge Wiley's legal ruling and continued accessing the communal mountain tract. The willingness of residents to defy the courts showed the vital role that the subsistence economy, especially the communal lands, played in the lives of local citizens well into the twentieth century.[23]

Working in harmony with the subsistence and barter economy were kinship networks. The kinship patterns that developed in Costilla County were similar to those in portions of northern New Mexico that also had land grants. Original settlers passed down to the next generation vara strips that they had obtained from Beaubien. Families divided the vara strips "into equal strips for all heirs, as long as there was sufficient land for the subsistence of all." These land divisions produced a residential pattern that tightly clustered siblings and cousins. The end result was a "fraternal network that unified the community."[24] While this system of land division and residential living helped sustain the subsistence and barter economy, it also assisted the needy. Costilla County's poor almost always had at least one relative within the immediate area. However, the presence of relatives did not disqualify one from help. In fact, the commissioners relied on relatives, in a sense, to subsidize the county's meager payments. "Most all the [Costilla] paupers have some relatives," stated the State Board of Charities and Corrections, "who assist them in a small way."[25] Thus, extended family members who might house, feed, or care for their relatives provided another safety net for poor residents in Costilla County.

The tightness of Costilla's communities produced an informal application process for relief. In fact, it was a process that relied on face-to-face interaction, skirting formal bureaucratic procedures. While in other Colorado counties family members, neighbors, or actual applicants occasionally appeared before commissioners to plead their cases, in Costilla an unusually high number of applicants made personal appearances. "On this day," to cite one such example, "Virginia Montoya, a cripple, 40 years of age, appeared and requested and petitioned the Board for aid and assistance."[26] The informality and personal nature of Costilla's application process continued with the manner in which the commissioners decided each case. There is no indication that a formal investigation ever took place. Instead, with the poor person often before them, the commissioners approved or disapproved each request for aid. The basis for each decision rested on what was generally before their eyes: blindness, old age, illness, broken-down bodies, and widows and their children. And of course, given Costilla's tight community structure, "personal acquaintance" among the poor and the county commissioners further assisted in determining relief efforts.[27] The net effect of this informal system was that commissioners did not refuse aid to any applicant. And given this close community interaction, the use of cash assistance comes as no surprise since people clearly knew one another.

Finally, Catholicism, especially the Catholic lay organization the Penitentes, contributed in shaping Costilla's public assistance program. In southern Colorado and northern New Mexico, the Penitentes were active in almost every Hispanic community in the region, including Costilla County. Until World War I, "a sizable majority of Hispanic males" belonged to local Penitente chapters.[28] In brief, the Penitentes were a mainly male brotherhood that attempted to lead "Christ-like" lives. "The pious observances of these Brothers are centered around the Passion of Jesus and the spirit of penance."[29] During Lent, and especially during Holy Week, the Penitentes engaged in a complex series of rituals. Some of these practices centered around local retreats restricted to the Penitentes, while other Lenten practices were public rituals in which devout members participated. Penitentes used self-flagellation and other forms of self-inflicted bodily punishment as a means of expressing penance during many of the Holy Week public processions.

The unique practices of the Penitentes generated a lot of attention, most of it negative. Protestant missionaries were especially shocked at the use of self-flagellation and used these practices as a launching pad for anti-Catholic rhetoric.[30] However, the Catholic hierarchy was none too pleased with the Penitentes' rituals either. In 1833, when Bishop José Antonio Laureano de Zubiría y Escalante toured northern New Mexico, the Penitentes' "excessive zeal disturbed and concerned him," prompting the Church to begin a campaign to rein in the brotherhood.[31] Yet, the Church's efforts to control and moderate the Penitentes largely failed. To avoid negative publicity and to protect the spiritual meanings of their practices, the Penitentes became a secretive organization that nonetheless served the community. Due to a lack of priests in the region, the Penitentes filled a spiritual void by performing some of the religious services normally administered by priests. In the absence of clergy, the Penitentes would "perform their own rituals for weddings or christenings or funerals," and they also celebrated other religious occasions such as holy days and feast days for patron saints.[32] The Catholic hierarchy was unable to manage the brotherhood because of the Church's institutional weakness, and because the Penitentes enjoyed widespread community support for the services they provided.

The literature on the Penitentes has concentrated on two main concerns. Writers have debated to great lengths the origins of the brotherhood. Some authors link the Penitentes to the Third Order of Saint Francis (a lay organization); others argue that they descended from medieval flagellants in Seville, Spain; some contend that *confradias* or "religious brotherhoods" also from Spain are the most direct link; still others cite the influence of Pueblo Indians. Obviously no one knows the definitive answer and some mixing of the above traditions probably best explains the brotherhood's beginnings. Besides debating the origins of the Penitentes, authors have also devoted a great deal of attention to chronicling the public displays of penance that occurred during Holy Week. The descriptions of these processions range from those fixated on the more "spectacular" forms of penance—being tied to crosses, kneeling on sharp stones, or whipping one's back—to those authors more interested in providing a religious and cultural context for understanding these practices. In either case, the focus on the Holy Week processions and the origins of the brotherhood has slighted the year-round work of the Penitentes.

In an attempt to lead "Christ-like" lives, the Penitentes went beyond acts of penance and the reenactment of the Passion of Jesus, engaging in good deeds or pious works of charity throughout the year. For, in addition to fulfilling the spiritual needs of isolated communities, the group also organized and directed charitable efforts. As almost all authors have acknowledged, the Penitentes were "essentially a charitable organization" or a "mutual aid" society.[33] Like the brotherhood's acts of penance, their acts of charity were to be carried out with humility and, if possible, anonymity. The most visible form of these good deeds centered around the supervision of funerals. Penitentes provided assistance in the form of cooking meals during the wake, building the casket, digging the grave, preparing and burying the corpse, and leading prayers and hymns.[34] The female auxiliaries of Penitente chapters, know as the Auxiliadoras de la Morada, played a key role in these acts of charity. The Auxiliadoras went to the homes of the deceased and "cook[ed] meals, clean[ed] house, [and] comfort[ed] members of the family." These women, in addition, were responsible for nursing and caring for the sick. As they did at funerals, the Auxiliadoras did not just nurse the ill; they also washed the family's clothes, prepared meals, and cleaned the house and yard.[35]

Each local Penitente chapter had one member in charge of charity-related activities. The *Enfermero* (Nurse) or *Hermano Caritativo* (Charitable Brother) was responsible for arranging for the care of the sick and for organizing other charitable acts. The Enfermero would often assign women from the Auxiliadoras to attend the sick, or would assign fellow members to "take a night and donate food and aid."[36] Penitentes also assisted the needy by harvesting their crops or by providing firewood.[37] Widows, likewise, received fuel and goods from Penitentes.[38] The brotherhood often paid doctor bills and provided money to those in need.[39] The Penitentes assisted members and nonmembers alike in almost any area of relief throughout the year.

In order to provide for these good deeds, many local Penitente chapters maintained a *fondo* (fund) to help the poor. From the fondo, Penitente members supplied the needy with goods or cash. In Petaca, New Mexico, local Penitentes kept a storehouse of "several hundred pounds of grain, flour, potatoes, numerous articles of clothing, shoes, etc. ready for issue to the poor."[40] Other Penitente chapters maintained their "own flock of sheep or goats" as a means to generate money for their fondo.[41] Through the use of the fondo and the guidance of the Enfermero, the brotherhood maintained a durable and responsive charitable structure that relied on community resources, through material goods and individual services, to support needy residents.

The well-organized and extensive means of assistance that the Penitentes provided to the isolated communities in southern Colorado shaped county relief practices. Obviously, the Penitentes, drawing on the subsistence economy and kinship networks, supplemented the efforts of county commissioners in helping the poor. Thus, Costilla's low levels of monthly support reflected, in part, the efforts of Penitente chapters to aid the needy. But the brotherhood may have also molded the county's relief practices by assuming responsibility for many, if not most, of the short-term relief cases. The Penitentes' distribution of goods, cash, and services seemed directed mainly to those experiencing brief periods of distress. As a result, those encountering temporary difficulties had no reason or need to apply to the county commissioners for assistance. Due to the brotherhood's practices, Costilla County poor rolls largely supported residents dealing with long-term, irreversible causes of poverty, mainly elderly and disabled folks. "Old age" accounted for almost a third of the reasons given for obtaining assistance in Costilla. In fact, the county had the highest average age per recipient—57.76 years for females and 64.91 years for males—compared to the other counties in this study (see Tables 4 and 5). The combination of "old age" and "cripple" made up just under half of all the causes of distress for Costilla.[42] Because the condition of these elderly and disabled residents only deteriorated with time, and because these residents could no longer physically participate fully in the subsistence economy, they remained on Costilla's poor rolls for long periods, usually until death. The dominance of irreversible causes of poverty listed in Costilla's relief records partially explains recipients' extremely long durations on county welfare.

But in addition, and probably most important, the Penitentes offered the county a view of charity and poor relief that rested on notions of Catholicism. Pious good deeds that aided the poor, the sick, the disabled, and the aged, took on a spiritual significance. These charitable acts reflected a "life of grace." For it was "Christ-like" to assist the needy. Due to the influence of Penitente members, residents of Costilla County viewed poor relief, whether from the county commissioners or from the Penitentes, as more than just a community responsibility or duty that should be minimized. Poor relief was, indeed, a worthy and key component in maintaining Costilla County's social fabric and values. As a result, these religious-based beliefs and acts of charity along with the subsistence economy, family members' assistance, and county relief practices all contributed to build a safety net for needy residents.

Dry Farming and Homesteading

While religion, kinship networks, and settlement patterns molded Costilla's poor relief system, these same factors also determined, in part, how Lincoln and Montezuma (the portion of the county north of the Ute Mountain Ute Indian Reservation) Counties operated their public assistance programs. The poor relief systems in Lincoln and Montezuma appear, however, the opposite of Costilla's in every way. Aid recipients in Lincoln and Montezuma Counties, as already mentioned, averaged the shortest time on relief, in Montezuma 7.57 months and in Lincoln just 6.38 months (see Table 3). Yet at the same time, these two communities averaged some of the highest monthly payments, with Lincoln at $18.51 per month and Montezuma topping the five counties with $30.90 per month (see Table 2). Besides these two traits, the two counties also shared a third characteristic, the dumping of the poor on neighboring communities. In both Montezuma and Lincoln, county commissioners used public funds to pay for transportation costs, mainly railroad tickets, to remove the needy from their jurisdiction. Lincoln sent the highest percentage away, almost 33 percent, while Montezuma was a distant second at a little over 6 percent (see Table 6). The question arises as to why Lincoln and Montezuma Counties' poor relief systems took on the characteristics of high monthly aid, short durations of assistance, and the removal of the poor? Dry farming, homesteading, rapid settlement, and Protestantism all help to answer the question.

The lack of water had a profound influence on the societies of Lincoln and Montezuma. Early-nineteenth-century expeditions by Zebulon Pike and Stephen Long into the Great Plains labeled the area as the Great American Desert. And even as late as 1878, John Wesley Powell's *Report on the Lands of the Arid Regions of the United States* warned that "the climate is so arid that agriculture is not successful" west of the 100th meridian.[43] East of the 100th meridian, farmers could count on at least twenty to twenty-eight inches of precipitation each year. But once one headed west of the 100th meridian, annual precipitation fell to less than twenty inches per year. Lincoln County,

in fact, averaged only a little more than fourteen inches of annual precipitation.[44] Montezuma County's agricultural districts varied from thirteen to seventeen inches of precipitation per year.[45] The low amounts of precipitation
meant, according to Powell, that traditional forms of agriculture used in the
more humid eastern portions of the United States would eventually lead to
failure in the nation's arid western portions.

Despite Powell's warning, settlers streamed into the Great American
Desert during the 1880s. At the same time that newcomers poured into arid
regions west of the 100th meridian, precipitation increased to levels well
above normal. This dramatic rise in precipitation seemed to offer proof of
the widely popular, but untrue, notion that rain would follow the plow, transforming deserts into fertile farmland. What the settlers were actually experiencing was not a changing of the environment due to farming, but rather,
one of the Great Plains' wet cycles. Eastern Colorado boomed between 1886
and 1889 as thousands of optimistic farmers broke sod in hopes of a new
beginning and prosperity. But the rains did not last. Beginning in 1889 and
continuing into the mid-1890s, drought struck the Great Plains, forcing at
least two hundred thousand settlers from the region. Conditions required
those residents of eastern Colorado that chose to stay to seek help.[46] "One
family," reported the *Rocky Mountain News*, "has lived six weeks on nothing
but squashes."[47] The citizens of Denver and Colorado Springs responded by
collecting food, clothing, shoes, and coal for drought-stricken farmers.[48]

The disastrous experiences of the late nineteenth century only temporarily discouraged settlement of the Great Plains. Beginning in the early
twentieth century, a new wave of farmers descended on the region. But these
settlers were no longer hoping to alter the climate; instead, they believed
that they had found a farming method that corresponded to the climate of
the Great American Desert. The answer seemed to be dry farming. While the
exact methods of dry farming varied from farmer to farmer and from promoter to promoter, the most widely publicized dry-farming system was that
of Hardy Webster Campbell. Campbell homesteaded in the Dakota Territory,
and from this experience he devised his dry-farming practices. Campbell
advocated packing the subsoil, making the topsoil into a dust mulch, plow-
ing deep furrows, and allowing the land to lay fallow in the summer. All these
techniques aimed at preserving moisture in arid western regions.[49]
Campbell was so convinced of his methods that he believed that drought-
resistant crops were unnecessary and that "eastern Colorado . . . can grow

better average crops than they are growing in Illinois to-day." Railroad companies, the Northern Pacific and the Burlington, latched on to dry farming and began promoting Campbell and his dry-farming system to encourage settlement along their rail lines. By 1906, Campbell was receiving national attention, and, a year later, the first Dry Farming Congress gathered in Denver to promote farming on the arid Great Plains.[50]

All the publicity about dry farming drew settlers to Lincoln and Montezuma Counties during the turn of the century. Land that had once been characterized as a desert now seemed to hold great potential. "Hardly a day passes nowadays," observed Lincoln County's *Range Ledger*, "that there are not land buyers and homesteaders in town."[51] In just ten years, Lincoln County went from 138 farms in 1900 to 1,334 farms.[52] In 1907, Lincoln residents gathered to celebrate their recent good fortune by holding a dry-farming festival with races, games, music, and food and drink for all.[53] Montezuma County also boomed during this period. Settlers homesteaded lands lacking irrigation using dry-farming methods. Montezuma's dry farmers turned to pinto beans and potatoes as cash crops and, as late as 1913, dry farmers were still pouring into the county.[54] Like Lincoln, Montezuma County thrived in these years. "From all parts of the county," reported the *Montezuma Journal*, "comes the most cheering reports of the prospect for bountiful crops of all kinds."[55] It was not just Lincoln and Montezuma that experienced prosperity. The whole region had once again entered another wet cycle as precipitation throughout the Great Plains, "despite some droughts, was above average" between 1900 and 1920.[56]

Yet, despite the relative good times, homesteading and dry farming were extremely risky and uncertain. Conditions in Lincoln were harsh, unrelenting, and unpredictable, even in good years. Drought was only one of several natural forces that could wreak havoc on homesteaders. "Severe hail-storms in different parts of this county, in the last two or three weeks," reported the *Range Ledger*, "have caused destruction to crops and much other damage."[57] Martha Kollath, who came to Lincoln in 1918, recalled that it seemed as if "we always got hailed out."[58] Heavy snowstorms and blizzards could also cause considerable damage, especially to livestock. The winter of 1911–12 was particularly difficult. J. Carl Harrison remembered how his father lost over half of his six hundred head of cattle during that winter despite heroic efforts to remove snow and purchase feed.[59] And if the snow and cold did not kill off the cattle, then the cattle could become a potential threat to

*Sanford "Sant" Daniel with his wife, Levia, and their three daughters,
from left to right, Bernice, Ova, and Lela, on their homestead located
three miles south and a half mile west of Hugo (Lincoln County),
Colorado, ca. 1910. Sanford earned an income through a variety of
occupations including farming, raising cattle, driving a school bus,
delivering mail, and digging wells. Courtesy of Terry W. Blevins.*

homesteaders. Carrie Wheeler, a widow with small twins, was completely
dependent on what she raised on her homestead. When a neighbor's livestock broke through her fence and ate and trampled her crop, Wheeler knew
that she was in a dire situation.[60] Finally, if drought, hail, snow, and cattle
were not enough, prairie fires were always a possibility during hot, dry spells.
"Prairie fires," stated the *Range Ledger*, "have been doing much damage to
the range in this part of the state."[61] Homesteading on the arid Great Plains
was, no doubt, an uncertain undertaking at best.

Homesteaders in Montezuma County encountered less extreme weather conditions than Lincoln County farmers, but they still faced trying circumstances. Unlike Lincoln where settlers had taken almost all the available land
by 1909, Montezuma experienced a dry-farming boom late enough to allow
farmers to take advantage of the 1909 Enlarged Homestead Act which permitted settlers to claim 320-acre dry-farming tracts as opposed to 160 acres.[62]
Nevertheless, Montezuma's dry farmers faced the difficult task of clearing
their land. While Lincoln's treeless plains allowed farmers to begin breaking
sod immediately, in Montezuma, the land was extremely rocky and covered
with sagebrush. The process of removing sagebrush was backbreaking work.

Settlers without horses "tackled the sage brush with ax and grubbing hoe. Father, mother and all the 'kids' large enough to work frequently engaged in the task." Those homesteaders with teams of horses hooked up some type of heavy apparatus to "drag back and forth over the brittle sage dragging it down and breaking it off."[63] The exhausting process of clearing the sagebrush consumed the time and resources of would-be farmers.

Due to the difficulties in homesteading and dry farming, settlers had a very small margin of error. The difference between success and failure was a mighty thin line as dry farming often pushed homesteaders to the very edge of disaster. In Montezuma County, the importance of clearing the sagebrush was literally "a race between getting some production from the soil or starving out."[64] Nora Marie Dreier recalled how once her family moved to Lincoln, times were hard. Her father had only eight dollars left after arriving, which was "not much to start with, with five kids . . . and two grown people . . . no crop the following year."[65] Faced with the need to obtain food and goods, families devised strategies to cope. In both Montezuma and Lincoln, homesteaders sought out paid work to cover expenses. "It was next to impossible to make a living on a dry farm," stated Montezuma's Henry McCabe, "so they worked where ever they could find anything to do."[66] In eastern Colorado, it was common for women and children to operate the farm, planting and harvesting crops, while men sought out wage work in Colorado Springs and other nearby communities.[67] Even paid work was frequently not enough to help homesteaders. In Montezuma, "some of the early settlers were so poverty-stricken that they had very little to eat. Quite often they would [steal and] kill a calf or a yearling and trade half of the meat for flour or whatever they could get."[68] Out along the eastern plains, women and children collected coal along the railroad tracks. If a train came by while they were scavenging, the engineer "would shovel some more off to them instead of into the engine because he felt sorry for them."[69]

Yet, despite these attempts to compensate for the lack of money and resources, many homesteaders were unable to avoid failure. Numerous dry farmers simply moved away, finding conditions too unfavorable to remain. "Some of the older settlers had to give up after several years of hardship and want. It was a pitiful sight," remembered Montezuma's McCabe, "to see them load up the few things that they had and then watch them drive away."[70] Lincoln's John Stelter decided to sell his land and goods after homesteading for almost eleven years.[71] Some residents chose not to move away, at least not initially. These individuals turned, instead, to county commissioners for assistance.

The difficulties and uncertainties of raising a crop under such harsh conditions molded the relief systems of both Lincoln and Montezuma Counties. Only Lincoln's poor relief recipients cited "crop failure" and "bad weather" as reasons for distress. Clara Robbins listed her cause of poverty as "no way of living since crop failed," and Owen Schenk stated that his reason for destitution was due to "crop failure and inability to get work."[72] Although only a little over 8 percent of Lincoln's poor cases listed "bad weather" or "crop failure," nevertheless, the inability to grow enough seems to explain, at least partially, the causes of poverty for others. In letters to Lincoln County commissioners, those requesting help often mentioned that they were unable to grow more. "As you know," wrote Maud Armack, "I have only 160 acres of land and only 48 acres broke so I don't get much for my part."[73] The harsh and unpredictable environmental conditions of the Great Plains simply prevented many dry farmers from growing enough cash crops to earn an adequate living.

But more than environmental circumstances pushed residents onto poor rolls. The unforgiving surroundings would simply not allow settlers the ability to recover from setbacks. Any type of physical ailment, for example, could quickly push homesteaders into despair. John Stelter, mentioned above, sold his land, in part, because of "being in poor health."[74] Despite achieving some measure of success after farming for over a decade, Stelter's success could not protect him from the demands of the region. In the case of Pluma Scott, her child's illness caused her to receive public relief. Her child had "been out of bed once in 3 months and she no means making a living."[75] Montezuma's Mr. Adams suffered from old age and was unable to scratch out a living growing vegetables on five acres.[76] A spouse's illness, injury, or death could likewise suddenly spell hard times. "My husbun been sick a year," pleaded Mrs. Gust Velander, "and could not work and we have no money come in."[77] Single homesteaders, widowed or deserted women, and single men, shouldered workloads that would have strained couples. Being a bachelor compounded Stelter's problems, as he lacked a spouse to bear some of the farm's burdens while he was ill. And when Albert Vanardsdale deserted his family in Montezuma County, they quickly entered "a destitute condition."[78] For homesteaders, crises had immediate consequences, often quickly forcing a family to ask for county aid.

Few alternatives to county assistance existed for the needy of Lincoln and Montezuma Counties. Unlike in Costilla County, Lincoln and Montezuma lacked the extensive kinship networks that could help cushion poor relatives. The dry farming and homesteading boom of the early twentieth century brought in a flood of newcomers to both counties. Yet, for the most part, these settlers arrived as individual families and not in large kin groups. Thus, in times of need, the poor could not easily turn to nearby relatives for assistance as people in Costilla did.

Other traditional sources of aid were also unreliable or scarce in Lincoln and Montezuma Counties. Homesteaders, at least those dry farming during the early twentieth century, could offer little help to one another. Almost all homesteaders were pushed to the limits and had little spare money, time, or goods to give to those in need. As a consequence, many neighbors chose to help the poor by alerting county commissioners of those in need. "We the undersigned," began a letter signed by eight Montezuma residents to their county commissioners, "do hereby petition that you at once investigate the condition of the family of Albert Vanardsdale."[79] Even though the neighbors were aware of the family's need for assistance, they decided to pass that responsibility on to county officials. In Lincoln, a committee of farmers appeared before the commissioners petitioning "for an appropriation from the County funds for the purpose of procuring seed grain for the destitute farmers of the County."[80] The idea of using public funds to purchase seed was not new. During the 1890s drought, the Colorado legislature spent over three thousand dollars buying seed for farmers along the eastern Plains, and neighboring Kit Carson County provided seed for its needy farmers.[81] Despite these precedents, Lincoln's officials voted down their farmers' request for seed. Still, Lincoln's citizens were turning to publicly funded solutions to aid the destitute. The lack of relatives and the inability of neighbors to help meant that the poor were almost totally dependent on the county for assistance. Unlike in Costilla, where relatives and the Penitentes subsidized the county's poor relief, in Lincoln and Montezuma, county commissioners were essentially responsible for complete support of the poor. As a result, monthly relief payments were high in both Lincoln and Montezuma as compared to Costilla.

Furthermore, the poor in Lincoln and Montezuma seemed to be in more desperate circumstances than those from other counties, and the degree of destitution contributed to the high monthly payments. Often, by the time residents applied for aid, they seemed to have already reached bottom. "We are bad in need of some clothing for the children," wrote Montezuma's Henry Wolf, father of seven.[82] In Lincoln, there were numerous reports of people fearing starvation. "I got to have somthing to Eat" pleaded James Gariss of Lincoln County.[83] Deserted and with two small children, Martha Stetson wrote that she had "no money, no way of getting anything to eat no resorses . . . to keep from starving."[84] Part of the problem was that Lincoln's poor were trying to hold on to their homesteads. Time and time again, poor folk mentioned the need to hang on for only a little while longer so that they would not lose their land. "This is the year that I got to finish Braking the 80 acres or loose my farm," wrote James Gariss. "I havent a cent to my name," continued Gariss, "and I have Bin here two years Without raising anything to live on and I come here with $650.00."[85] After livestock ate Carrie Wheeler's crops, she asked the commissioners for groceries "so I can remain in my homestead and thus save an expense of paying rent for some other place in which to live."[86] In a desperate attempt to succeed, homesteaders poured all available resources into their land, and when that land failed to produce, for whatever reason, farmers were left with essentially nothing to fall back on. By the time county commissioners intervened, aid recipients required high levels of immediate support.

Definitions of success contributed to the desperate circumstances of Lincoln and Montezuma's poor. Unlike in Costilla where subsistence farming was acceptable, the dry farmers of Montezuma and Lincoln defined success in terms of achieving a place in the market economy. These homesteaders came to make money by means of cash crops, whether wheat in Lincoln or pinto beans in Montezuma, or by increased land values. Subsistence was not the main goal in either community, although some subsistence practices—hunting deer and rabbits and growing gardens—did exist in Lincoln and Montezuma.[87] Yet, despite these customs, the point of homesteading was not "simply to make a living," according to historian Donald Worster, "but to make money."[88] The culture of capitalism, argues Worster, "drove Americans into the grassland and determined the way they would use it."[89] As a consequence, settlers channeled their limited resources into trying to generate money by means of cash crops and improvements to their homestead.

This underlying assumption of participation in the market economy dictated not only the definition of success but also how long a poor relief recipient would receive aid. If it appeared that a person was unable, for whatever reason, to make a successful attempt at engaging the market, then aid would be cut. County officials did not have the patience for those who would take a long time to recover from crises or begin to operate their homesteads. As a result, county commissioners quickly cut off aid or shipped the poor out, giving Lincoln and Montezuma Counties the lowest average duration and the highest percentage of dumping the poor (Tables 3 and 6). Lee Newport typified those dumped by the county governments. Newport, age twenty-eight, arrived in Lincoln "in bad condition" suffering from tuberculosis. He was given a meal and quickly put on an eastbound train to Cheyenne Wells in the neighboring county.[90] This habit of removing the needy to other locales and passing the responsibility for caring for them onto other communities was a well-established practice, begun first in England and then in British North America. The New England colonies enforced strict settlement laws, clearly spelling out the requirements for becoming an "inhabitant" and thus qualifying for assistance.[91] Commissioners in Lincoln and Montezuma Counties were partially following this tradition of limiting relief only to people who they considered their long-term residents or to individuals who could quickly sustain themselves once again.

High rates of mobility and rapid population growth in both Montezuma and Lincoln made it easy for commissioners to halt aid or to move the poor out of the county, but it also created a need for formal procedures. From 1900 to 1920, Montezuma's population more than doubled from 3,058 to 6,260. During the same twenty-year span, Lincoln County experienced even greater growth, increasing from 926 residents to 8,273, almost an 800 percent increase (see Table 1). Unlike Costilla where families had lived in the county for decades and where the lack of available land as well as the strong local traditions that kept outsiders at a distance would have discouraged new arrivals, newcomers dominated Montezuma and Lincoln Counties. Mobility became a defining element of each community, especially Lincoln, with many new settlers coming to stay and many choosing to leave.[92] Thus, when county commissioners forced the poor to leave the county, either by suspending aid or transporting them out of the county, these actions simply reinforced the acceptance of mobility as a community characteristic. Since extended families were rare in Lincoln and Montezuma, commissioners did not have to account for their actions to other relatives. In addition, the high mobility rates of both counties required that commissioners formally investigate most aid applicants. In Lincoln, for example, commissioners delayed action on Rosa Fisher's case "until more information could be obtained," and Mr. V. Jenkins seemed to act as a type of field agent for the commissioners by granting temporary emergency aid while reporting back to the commissioners about applicants.[93] In Montezuma, residents requesting aid often had to file a formal application or an affidavit with the commissioners, who would then investigate each case.[94] The poor relief systems in both Montezuma and Lincoln Counties were more structured and bureaucratic than the informal system in Costilla.

Religious beliefs may have also shaped the relief efforts in Montezuma and Lincoln Counties. While Costilla was almost completely Catholic, Montezuma and Lincoln were almost completely Protestant.[95] At the time, many Protestants attributed poverty to an individual's moral shortcomings, poor character, and lack of effort. Thus they believed that relief should be highly supervised and given in limited amounts. For if charity became excessive, it had the potential of ruining a person's character, perhaps even causing pauperism.[96] Although a direct link between these views of poverty with relief practices in Montezuma and Lincoln could not be established, the brief, but polite, letters from residents requesting aid do hint at this mentality. "I am very sorry," wrote Montezuma's Georgia Denby, "but I will have to ask a little help of the county."[97] "I do hate to bother you," penned Lincoln's Mr. H. W. Edwards, "but I cant help my self at present but I am in need badly if you can help me with a small a mount Pleas do so."[98] In a sense, the poor seemed to view their own dire circumstances as a personal failing. And the manner in which commissioners from Lincoln and Montezuma County enacted assistance also seems to support the notion that they viewed poor relief as a burdensome chore that must be closely monitored and controlled.

Very Different Concerns

So far, the discussion of Montezuma has included only the northern portion of the county. The Ute Mountain Ute Indian Reservation, accounting for approximately 30 percent of Montezuma County, did not share in the dry farming and homesteading boom of the early twentieth century that so profoundly shaped Montezuma's public assistance. Instead, the Ute Mountain Reservation had a different history, economy, and a very different set of circumstances shaping relief issues even though the reservation fell almost completely within Montezuma County's borders. Because the federal government, under the direction of the Office of Indian Affairs, operated the reservation, a treaty, federal laws, and a federal bureaucracy molded debates over which practices did or did not constitute poor relief on the reservation. The Weeminuche band of the Utes considered annuities and rations as legal obligations while federal officials wanted to use these same practices as a form of poor aid. Although the Utes encountered one of the most developed areas of the American state, the Office of Indian Affairs, local conditions, as in the five counties, still largely resolved if annuities and rations would be implemented as a type of poor relief or as legal obligations. In the end, the environment, the economy, local customs, previous aid policies, and protests by Utes, along with a treaty and laws, all influenced how annuities and rations were distributed on the reservation.

In 1895, the Weeminuches had agreed to settle on a reservation in southern Colorado. At the time, the federal government offered the Weeminuches a choice as to whether or not they wanted to divide their reservation into individually owned allotments of land.[99] The Weeminuches had long maintained few outside contacts as the harsh geography of the Four Corners region had isolated them from Spanish, Mexican, and then American settlers. They had also grown increasingly frustrated with the ever changing plans of the federal government and had chosen to limit contact by avoiding governmental officials and remaining far away from agency outposts. Thus, when it came time to decide on allotments, the Weeminuches selected the course that would minimize interaction with outsiders. They voted against allotments, maintaining a common land holding. The Ute Mountain Reservation, as the Weeminuche reservation became known, consists of 412,067 tribally held acres in Colorado's southwest corner.[100]

Life on the Ute Mountain Reservation was very different from the rest of Colorado. The land that the Weeminuches settled on was harsh. One late-nineteenth-century visitor described the reservation as "an arid desert" while another visitor characterized the area as "land that is about as low in utility as one can find in Colorado."[101] Yet, with water the land is actually quite productive. The federal government had promised to irrigate the reservation but failed to carry through with its commitment.[102] Lacking water and not especially eager to farm anyway, the Weeminuches turned to raising livestock, mainly goats, sheep, and horses, on their tribal lands. The approximately

Bob Beecher and his wife (Emma South?) at their home near Mancos River Farm, Ute Mountain Ute Indian Reservation (Montezuma County), Colorado, 1923. In 1920, the Office of Indian Affairs listed no permanent homes on the Ute Mountain Reservation. Consolidated Ute Narrative Report, 1923, Microfilm Publications, Roll 26, Record Group 75. Courtesy of National Archives and Records Administration.

510 Weeminuches who resided on the reservation in 1912 lived a seminomadic life following their herds across the desert landscape. At the time, they lived in tepees or brush shelters, before turning to tents.[103] The Office of Indian Affairs listed no permanent houses on the Ute Mountain Reservation in 1920 as the entire Weeminuche population lived in tents.[104] This seminomadic life, confined within reservation boundaries, resulted in little contact with outsiders. As a result, only a handful of Utes learned English, and Indian dress and customs remained largely unchanged well into the twentieth century.[105]

The ability of the Weeminuche band to maintain essentially their old way of life while on the reservation upset some Indian Affairs workers. By refusing allotments, the Utes had thwarted any attempts to force them to

farm and countered efforts to break up tribal lands into individual hold-
ings.[106] The continuance of a seminomadic lifestyle, Indian dress, native customs, and their native language sparked hostility from government workers.
The Weeminuches, reported Francis E. Leupp after his 1895 visit, cared "simply to ride their horses, hunt, and indulge in savage pastimes."[107] Four years
later, Indian Agent Louis A. Knackstedt stated that the Weeminuches "live in
tepees, wear the blanket, and are in the same condition they were before,
with no signs of improvement in the future."[108]

Even though the Ute Mountain Utes maintained many of their former
ways, they were unable to support themselves fully or adequately. Indeed,
poverty permeated almost every aspect of reservation life. The livestock
operations failed to provide the Utes with much income since horses made
up the vast majority of these roving herds. At the time, horses had little market value and thus provided little money. The arid landscape compounded
the difficulty of raising livestock. The reservation contained good winter pastures but lacked sufficient summer grazing land due to the lack of water.[109]
Diseases, especially highly contagious trachoma, an eye infection that often
leads to blindness, ravaged the reservation during the late nineteenth and
early twentieth centuries.[110] The Office of Indian Affairs estimated that slightly more than 40 percent of the Weeminuche band had trachoma in 1912.[111]
Tuberculosis and the 1918 influenza epidemic also took their toll on the
Utes.[112] In just seven years, from 1913 to 1920, the Weeminuche lost over 9 percent of their population, dropping from 510 to just 462 residents.[113] With
little economic activity and with diseases and death rampant, the Ute Mountain Reservation was, in many ways, a grim place during this time.

Due to these harsh conditions, survival for the Weeminuches rested
largely with their reliance on rations and annuity payments from the Office
of Indian Affairs. "They (Ute Mountain Utes) didn't have much," recalled
Paula Maria Allen, "they just lived on rations."[114] On the first day of each
month and during the middle of the month, the reservation superintendent
oversaw the distribution of rations. With sacks in hand to carry their rations,
"Indians lined up," remembered former superintendent S. F. Stacher, as "the
doors opened and they were given in order named: flour, baking powder,
sugar, salt, soap, and fresh beef." During the middle of the month, the superintendent followed a similar routine, only substituting pork and beans for
the fresh beef.[115] In addition to bimonthly rations, the Weeminuches also
received yearly per capita annuity payments. Treaty stipulations, interest on

Ration day on the Ute Mountain Ute Indian Reservation (Montezuma County), Colorado, 1908. Rations were distributed twice a month in accordance with a treaty and federal agreements. Photograph by S. F. Stacher. Courtesy of Colorado Historical Society, F-39597.

trust funds held by the Department of Treasury, and income from grazing fees constituted these annuity payments. The Office of Indian Affairs usually paid these yearly annuities in cash to each reservation member. Through a combination of receiving rations and annuities, raising livestock, and hunting and gathering, the Weeminuches pieced together a livelihood, albeit an inadequate one.

Utes and federal officials held dramatically different interpretations concerning the value and legitimacy of rations and annuities. To Indians, including the Ute Mountain Utes, the bimonthly rations and yearly cash payments were compensation for land vacated. Utes agreed to allow settlement on land once used by them in exchange for food and cash. This bargain seemed appropriate considering that with settlement wild game disappeared, thus ending any opportunity for Indians to continue hunting and thereby support themselves. The 1868 treaty with the Utes, the first agreement between the

Utes and the federal government, stipulated that Congress must furnish not only "beef, mutton, wheat, flour, beans, and potatoes" but also "clothing, blankets, and such other articles of utility." Congress must provide these goods "until such time as said Indians shall be found to be capable of sustaining themselves."[116] The 1874 Brunot Agreement and the 1895 Hunter Act guaranteed the continuation of these practices while also establishing annuities for the Utes. "The United States agrees to set apart and hold," stated the Brunot Agreement, "as a perpetual trust for the Ute Indians, a sum of money, or its equivalent in bonds, which shall be sufficient to produce the sum of twenty-five thousand dollars per annum."[117] So when Standing Wolf, a Ute Indian, went to Washington in 1900 "to solicit an improvement in rations" he was simply trying to convince the federal government to honor its half of the exchange for Ute lands.[118]

Federal officials understood rations and annuities in a completely different manner. Instead of viewing rations and annuities as legal obligations under treaties and laws, federal officials essentially skirted the legal questions involved and focused on what they perceived to be the negative consequences of these practices. During the turn of the century, federal representatives began to attack the use of rations and annuities as customs that prevented Indians from progressing from "savagery to citizenship." These practices, according to the Board of Indian Commissioners, were "working grave injury to the character and prospects of Indians."[119] Criticism of rations and annuities revolved around two main issues. Federal officials believed that these policies curtailed Indian desires to work and thus caused poverty. Rationing "encourages idleness and destroys labor; it promotes beggary and suppresses independence; it perpetuates pauperism and stifles industry."[120] According to this view, the poor economic opportunities on many Indian reservations did not cause widespread poverty. Instead, the use of rations and annuities fostered laziness that resulted in poverty. "The pauperizing effect of the steady issuance of rations which supported able-bodied Indians in direct idleness has become manifest to all."[121] Second, government workers thought that the use of tribal funds and rations unduly perpetuated tribal identity, stifling individual initiative. Tribal funds were "paralyzing individual effort" and preventing attempts at recognizing "the individual and not the tribe."[122]

Government reformers advocated controlling rations and annuities, regardless of previous treaties or federal laws, as the best way to address these criticisms. Federal officials proposed the breakup of tribal funds into Individual Indian Accounts (I.I.A.). "We should now break up the tribal funds," stated President Theodore Roosevelt, "doing for them what allotment does for the tribal land; that is, they should be divided into individual hold-ings."[123] The creation of I.I.A., according to reformers, would instill a strong work ethic, acknowledge individuals, and end tribal identity. Congressional enactment of Individual Indian Accounts in 1913 perpetuated federal attempts, along with the Dawes General Allotment Act of 1887, to detribal-ize Indians during the late nineteenth and early twentieth centuries. Individual Indian Accounts took money that Indians would have received from annuities and placed the funds into bank accounts for each person. These accounts were supposed to create a "system of individual accounta-bility. . . which is essential to our ideal of American citizenship."[124] Reformers also placed greater controls on the delivery of rations. Reformers hoped, in spite of past agreements, that the Individual Indian Accounts and the limit-ing of rations were simply the first steps toward their ultimate goal of com-pletely abolishing all tribal funds and rations.

Despite all the rhetoric about increasing "individual responsibility" and removing "obstacles to self-support," the formation of Individual Indian Accounts and the limiting of rations essentially tried to transform annuities and rations from legal obligations into a form of poor relief. Government reformers, from the beginning, clearly stated their desire to eliminate tribal funds except "as a 'poor fund' for the infirm and helpless" Indians.[125] Even though Congress placed tribal funds into individual ac-counts, Indians still could not access their own funds, as they needed approval from an Office of Indian Affairs representative before using their own money. The Office of Indian Affairs advised its agency superintendents to limit approving use of I.I.A. funds to old, indigent, and disabled Indians. And agency superintendents should allow able-bodied Indians use of their accounts only "in cases of an emergency."[126] In addition, able-bodied people were to work for their rations or not receive any at all. These new restrictions not only superseded past treaties and acts, but they also clear-ly made rations and Individual Indian Accounts into a type of poor relief for Indians. In many respects, Progressive Era Indian policy mimicked the gen-eral practices of county-level poor relief despite the unique legal status of Indian nations. All counties in this study, regardless of differences, restrict-ed poor relief to those people deemed dependent or unable to provide for themselves. While the definitions of dependence and the treatment of dependents varied dramatically from county to county, nevertheless, dependency formed a common baseline for all communities. These changes in Indian policy aimed to establish dependency as the sole criterion for receiving rations and funds from Individual Indian Accounts instead of the legal obligations originally stated in the treaties and laws.

The actual implementation of these policy changes on the Ute Mountain Reservation proved difficult. Agency superintendents used Individual Indian Accounts not only as a poor fund, as federal reformers had desired, but also as a way to obtain needed goods that fell outside traditional notions of relief. "This girl," stated Lurene Whyte's I.I.A. request form, "is an orphan and needs a little money (fifteen dollars) from her account each month for living expenses."[127] Whyte's reason for using I.I.A. funds almost perfectly mirrored how other Colorado counties justified poor relief in their own communities, as a way to care for dependents such as orphans. Yet, at other times, the use of I.I.A. funds on the reservation looked dramatically different from county poor relief practices. Weeminuches often used their children's accounts to provide their families with basic necessities. Jesse and Enterpa Bancroft, eleven and twelve years old, received permission to purchase lumber, a stove, a stove pipe, and a tent for housing their family during the winter as their father lacked "sufficient means to buy" the needed items.[128] Ute Mountain Utes also used their Individual Indian Accounts to acquire livestock as a way to support themselves. Ida Fields, for example, requested five hundred dollars from her account to purchase a herd of sheep, which she then combined with the flocks of her husband, father, and brother.[129]

The use of Individual Indian Accounts and rations for reasons other than traditional poor relief on the Ute Mountain Reservation upset officials in Washington. "It is understood that you are issuing a large number of monthly checks against the individual bank accounts of your Indians in their favor," began a stern letter to Ute Mountain superintendent Alfred H. Symons, "with which they may purchase food, supplies, and defray other expenses of a temporary nature. The Office is not certain," continued the rebuking letter, "whether you are confining the issuance of such checks to the old and indigent and disabled."[130] This was not the first time that Washington had questioned Symons' practices. A few months earlier, the Office of Indian Affairs demanded to know why able-bodied Weeminuches continued receiving rations.[131]

In both cases, Symons's response reveals how local conditions on the Ute Mountain Ute Reservation thwarted attempts to transform previously agreed to practices into a type of poor relief. With the federal government unwilling to fulfill its commitment of bringing water to the reservation, the Weeminuche band had "no opportunities of bettering their condition."[132] Given these economic circumstances, superintendents were unwilling to curtail access to Individual Indian Accounts and rations. The problems of poverty on the reservation were so great that traditional poor relief practices simply would not work. Unlike other communities where poverty afflicted only a small number of people, on the Ute Mountain Reservation, poverty was essentially universal. Thus, the notion of restricting relief—either rations or money from Individual Indian Accounts—to the able bodied seemed inappropriate, if not inhuman. In addition, the practices of previous super-intendents established a precedent that Symons found difficult to break. "It has been the custom here," wrote Symons, "through the reign of my prede-cessor to pay considerable money to Indians even though some of them are able bodied."[133] Concerning the issuing of rations to the able-bodied, Symons remarked that it "has always been the custom here as far back as I am able to learn."[134] These previous practices, along with the lack of gainful employment, created a situation that made it difficult to alter suddenly the use of rations or tribal funds.

The actions of the Weeminuches also contributed to the difficulty of using rations and Individual Indian Accounts as poor relief. Each time that Symons tried to limit rations and I.I.A. funds, Ute Mountain Utes immedi-ately protested. When Symons attempted to remove Utes from federal assis-tance it "always caus[ed] a scene and considerable friction."[135] Weeminuches fought these reductions in several ways. Often, Utes would turn to their friends off the reservation for help in writing a letter of complaint to Washington. "When the white man's parents are old and hungry," questioned one such letter, "does Washington let them starve?"[136] At other times, a group of Indians directly confronted the superintendent and voiced their displeas-ure over policy changes. And at still other times, individual Utes expressed disapproval. In some of these protests, the threat of violence loomed.[137] Symons warned of a possible "uprising" if access to rations and Individual Indian Accounts were limited. "The friction of dealing with this tribe," wrote Symons, "is something unequaled elsewhere."[138] He also cautioned that the Weeminuches were "dangerous when they can not have their own way."[139]

The Utes' view of rations and tribal funds as legal obligations established by a treaty and laws no doubt emboldened them to voice their disapproval of policy changes. Clearly, Utes believed they were entitled to these supplies and money. Thus, these protests, along with the reservation's poor economic possibilities and previous aid practices, prevented officials from treating rations and Individual Indian Accounts as simple poor relief measures.

The debates about relief on the Ute Mountain Ute Indian Reservation were completely alien to the rest of Colorado. Treaties, federal laws, and the huge bureaucracy of the Office of Indian Affairs all contributed in molding the delivery of annuities and rations on Indian reservations. And yet, despite the developed nature of this segment of the American government, local conditions still altered, at least partially, reform policies. The Weeminuches were unable to stop the official change in status of rations and annuities from legal obligations to a form of poor relief. But, protests and dire economic circumstances at the local level halted the implementation of these changes. Ute Mountain Ute superintendents essentially continued to distribute rations and money from Individual Indian Accounts in a manner that reflected previous practices. Still, the attempt to limit the responsibilities of the Office of Indian Affairs runs counter to most historians' depiction of the policies of the period. Most scholars have presented the Progressive Era as a period of massive state expansion into a variety of new concerns; at the same time, however, one of the most developed parts of the American state, the Office of Indian Affairs, was actively trying to shed responsibilities.

Widows and Women's Employment

In Boulder and Teller, the two remaining counties, stark differences appear in terms of who qualified for assistance. When a person received assistance, the county clerk and recorder generally noted, with only a word or two, the reason for receiving aid or the cause of distress. Even though a person's cause of distress may have changed over time, nevertheless, this information provides a basis for examining how local conditions determined who qualified for public poor relief.[140] When comparing data from Boulder and Teller Counties, the number of widows listed in each community's poor records is strikingly different. Boulder County cited thirty-two widows, making up just over 21 percent of its known female causes of distress between 1912 and 1920.

Meanwhile, Teller County listed only a single widow for the same span of years, the fewest number among all the six counties. Why such a great disparity between counties in the number of widows? This difference is especially puzzling considering general attitudes toward widows and each community's local economic structure. Yet, upon close inspection, the availability of employment for women explains why so many widows in Boulder received aid while so few did in Teller.

During the late nineteenth and early twentieth centuries, society agreed about the need for widows to receive some type of assistance. Charity and social workers alike viewed widows as permanent and high-ranking members of the deserving poor for several reasons. A woman became a widow through no fault of her own. In fact, a widow was "the victim of circumstances and conditions for which society and the state and not she are responsible."[141] In a 1910 survey of widows living in various cities and receiving private relief, 50 percent of their husbands had died from tuberculosis, pneumonia, and industrial accidents.[142] Thus, for Frederic Almy, a leading charity worker from Buffalo, New York, "widowhood [was] a most innocent cause of poverty."[143] A husband's death during the Progressive Era plunged all but the wealthiest of women into dire economic circumstances. Life and funeral insurances often covered only the most immediate short-term needs, and many husbands left their wives with no resources.[144] Needing money, widows sought out wage-paying jobs. Yet, women had few employment opportunities during the period. Most women earned money in domestic, service sector jobs, and for the most part, these jobs paid insufficient wages to support a family. In addition, widows had to juggle child-care obligations, which often further restricted employment opportunities. As Almy observed, the "poverty of widowhood is not usually due to a lack of thrift." Unable to earn adequate wages, widows often received poor relief or moved into a son or daughter's household. A widow's children also elicited society's sympathy because they shared their mother's hardships. The consequences of a father's early death could reverberate for future generations according to Almy "because the poverty is apt to increase in geometrical progression, twofold, fourfold, or even more in each generation, as the neglected children mature."[145] Given these general attitudes toward widows, one would expect to find relatively similar percentages of widows among the counties and not the great discrepancy found between Boulder and Teller Counties.

Differences between the local economies of Boulder and Teller further complicate an explanation as to why the two communities differed so dramatically in their percentages of widows. Boulder's and Teller's economies were in many ways opposites. In Boulder's mountains, precious-metal mining continued into the twentieth century, although at a magnitude greatly reduced from the county's early settlement years. Out along the High Plains, coal mining dominated the southeastern corner of the county. Ranching and farming operations filled the remaining portions of the county's plains region. The city of Boulder acted as a service center for the mining and agricultural communities, as well as housing the state's flagship university. With an economy combining mining, ranching, farming, and a large state institution, Boulder County possessed a healthy, stable, mixed economy.

Teller County's economy was far less diverse and stable than Boulder's. Teller's economy rested almost completely on gold mining. By the turn of the century, the mining boom peaked as 475 mines removed over eighteen million dollars worth of gold in 1900 alone. However, at the same time that the boom peaked, it also became increasingly clear that the good times would not last. Engineering difficulties and increasing costs in mining at deeper and deeper levels, as well as a shortage of capital, slowed mining activity. Despite the beginnings of a gradual downturn in gold production, mining activity did not completely halt. By 1910, miners still extracted just over eleven million dollars worth of gold from 145 operating mines in the county.[146] Thus, gold mining continued to dominate Teller's economy during the early twentieth century.

Teller County's almost complete dependence on mining placed its women at a far greater risk of becoming widows than the women in Boulder County. Throughout the nation, turn-of-the-century workplaces could often be dangerous and deadly. For the year 1913, according to conservative estimates, twenty-five thousand American workers suffered fatal industrial accidents, and another seven hundred thousand missed work for more than four weeks due to injuries.[147] During the seven-year period from 1914 to 1920, 147 people died due to accidents in Boulder County alone.[148] A variety of mishaps inflicted injury and death. In Boulder, for example, a threshing machine killed William Bevans, and Rhodes Ackers severed his right leg just above the knee while switching rail cars.[149] Mining, however, inflicted a far greater toll on its workforce than any other job. The Bureau of Labor Statistics ranked metal mining as the nation's most hazardous occupation.[150] Hard-rock roofs lessened the possibility of cave-ins throughout Teller County's mines; still, mining remained dangerous. Teller newspapers constantly reported, often in vivid detail, the killing and maiming of miners due to various accidents. Ed Black, reported the *Cripple Creek Times*, was "horribly mutilated" as his "head was severed and both arms and both legs were torn from the body" as he fell one thousand feet down a mine shaft.[151] The same local newspaper announced the death of two more miners with the headline, "Explosion of 40 Sticks of Giant [Dynamite] Blow 2 To Atoms."[152] In addition to fatal accidents, the steady development of occupational diseases posed another threat to a miner's health. The use of machine drills increased the dust hazards that often led to silicosis, a respiratory disease that set the stage for fibrosis, tuberculosis, and pneumonia. At first, these respiratory ailments disabled workers, forcing men to quit mining; later, they frequently caused them to cease working altogether. As these diseases progressed, death often resulted.[153] Given this dangerous work environment and the fact that over thirty-seven hundred men worked in Teller's mine industry in 1910, one would expect a higher percentage of widows on the poor rolls in Teller than in Boulder.[154] And yet, as already mentioned, the number of widows on public relief in Boulder far exceeded that in mining-dominated Teller County.

Several circumstances help to explain why so few widows appeared in Teller's poor records. Due to Teller's economic decline, many women, and men, left the county for better job possibilities. Teller County's female population dropped almost 50 percent from 11,915 in 1900 to 6,478 ten years later, while the number of males decreased even more dramatically from 17,087 to 7,873. And widows, no doubt, joined in this exodus. In fact, the percentages of widows living in Boulder and Teller Counties were essentially equal in 1910, just above 9 percent, despite the dangers of mining.[155] This similarity between the counties indicates that widows were probably leaving Teller for better opportunities. While women had few employment options, regardless of location, urban centers did provide women with a slightly greater range of job possibilities. Both Denver and Colorado Springs had substantially higher percentages of widows, 12.7 percent and 13.4 percent, than either Boulder's or Teller's roughly 9 percent.[156] Widows moved to these two cities in hopes of better providing for themselves and their families.[157] Widows in Teller may have also quickly remarried. Although the disparity between males and females was no longer as great as during Teller's early days, males still outnumbered females by slightly over 21 percent in 1910, while in Boulder the difference was only a little over 6 percent. Teller widows may have been able to find a new husband from this readily available pool of men. The possibilities of remarriage or relocation may have contributed to the low number of widows on Teller's public assistance.

Local economic opportunities for women, however, best explain this clear difference between Boulder and Teller Counties' poor relief. Even though a male occupation, mining, dominated Teller County, the concentration of men created job opportunities for women as boarding house managers, cooks, laundresses, prostitutes, retail clerks, waitresses, and school teachers. During the peak years, women, according to one newspaper, "flock[ed] in by droves" to Teller "with the idea that fortunes await them—if not through employment, that a rich husband can be easily caught."[158] By the 1910s, women were obviously no longer flocking to Teller due to the county's economic downturn; however, Teller still offered women more options for employment than Boulder. After Anne Ellis's husband died in a mining accident, for instance, she tried supporting her family by operating a bakery and then a boarding house.[159] In November 1914, to cite one more example, a local prostitute complained that Cripple Creek had become a dull town with little excitement. Yet, this same prostitute remarked that she was able "to make two to three dollars a day."[160] Although two to three dollars a day was by no means extravagant, it was still a decent daily wage.

Data from the 1910 census confirms this anecdotal evidence. Teller County's widows were more likely engaged in paid employment than widows from Boulder. Almost 59 percent of Teller's widows earned wages while just under 46 percent of Boulder's widows did so in 1910 (see Table 7). Despite Boulder County's stable and diverse economy, it lacked any type of substantial or reliable female employment. Boulder did not have any manufacturing that might depend on female workers. Nor did its economy encourage large concentrations of men who would have created a demand for traditional female occupations. Precious-metal mining operations in Boulder County had become small and widely scattered throughout the mountains. Family-run farms and ranches dotted the eastern sections of Boulder. Thus, even though Boulder County had a healthier overall economy than Teller County, Teller's depressed mining economy offered women more employment opportunities. At a time when women had few job possibilities, the greater employment options in Teller County, no matter how slight, enabled widows to remain off the poor rolls at a far greater rate than in Boulder.

The favorable job opportunities for women in Teller altered relief practices not only for widows but for other women as well. The greater availability of jobs for Teller's women meant that women from Teller County were not as dependent on men as Boulder's women.[161] In Boulder County, over 53 percent of women who received aid did so because of circumstances "beyond their control": a husband's death or injury, desertion, nonsupport, or even a woman's lack of employment. For thirteen women in Boulder, "no work" appeared as their cause of distress, adding weight to the notion that the county lacked employment opportunities for women. At the same time, just 5 percent of Teller women on relief received aid for reasons "beyond their control," with no women receiving assistance due to a lack of work (see Table 8). Once again, census data support these trends. In 1910, slightly over 64 percent of Teller's unmarried women—single, divorced, and widowed—listed a paying occupation, while just under 46 percent of Boulder's unmarried women did (see Table 7). Nationally, 46.5 percent of single, divorced, or widowed women held jobs, almost identical to Boulder County.[162] The vast majority of Teller women received assistance because of their own physical inability to work as a result of old age, illness, or injury. Thus, in Teller County it was not enough to be a widow or to be deserted to qualify for aid. Instead, because of the availability of jobs, women received public relief only when they could no longer physically work. In Boulder County, meanwhile, being widowed or deserted qualified women for public assistance. Local economies in both Teller and Boulder Counties profoundly affected the delivery of public relief in ways that, at first, do not seem apparent or reasonable. For impoverished women, the degree of economic opportunities determined their chances of receiving public assistance in Boulder and Teller Counties.

■

The public outdoor relief systems among these five smaller counties appear radically different when implementation becomes the lens. Each community's poor relief programs clearly exhibited distinctive characteristics that would have made them appear very different to residents from a different county. The levels of support, the length of time one received assistance, how commissioners treated aid recipients, and who qualified for help all varied from community to community. At times, these variations could be quite stark. Local circumstances molded very different relief practices. Thus, settlement patterns, religious beliefs, kinship relations, local economies, philanthropic practices, environmental conditions, and decisions by public officials all affected how county commissioners cared for poor folk. On the Ute Mountain Ute Reservation, previous practices, the environment, the economy, protests, laws, and a treaty influenced how Weeminuches and federal agents viewed and implemented annuities and rations. The ability of local conditions to shape the method and manner of relief remained a constant throughout the Progressive Era.

This pattern of local circumstances shaping how communities distributed aid was not isolated to only these smaller counties. In Denver, the region's urban hub, social reformers not only knew about new Progressive Era social welfare practices, but they also enthusiastically embraced these changes. Reformers tried hard to remake Denver's poor relief practices during the early twentieth century. Yet, local conditions either diminished these attempted changes or continued to exert such a strong influence on the implementation of relief that many of these changes failed to alter aid practices.

CHAPTER TWO

Relief, Reform, and "Lungers"

OUTDOOR POOR RELIEF IN THE
CITY AND COUNTY OF DENVER

"DENVER IS DOING PIONEER WORK IN ATTEMPTING TO HANDLE ITS DEPENDENT families in the modern and humane way," observed Frank Bruno, superintendent of New York City's Charity Organization Society, in 1914. "The success which has come in its first year should bespeak for it the heartiest backing by the public. A good part of the country will watch the experiment Denver is making with keen interest," continued Bruno. "If it is found that it fails here—either through political interference or apathy of public support—it will give a setback to honest and efficient outdoor relief throughout the country."[1]

As Bruno's remarks indicate, Denver, beginning in 1912, initiated some of the most innovative Progressive Era social welfare practices and policies, transforming its public outdoor relief program into one of the nation's most respected welfare operations. Largely under the direction of Gertrude Vaile, Denver's leading social welfare reformer, the city attempted to demonstrate "that municipal government could maintain an efficient and humane administration of charity."[2] Vaile believed, in brief, that public relief could

successfully appropriate the methods and practices of private charity societies. Through this appropriation, Vaile contended, public relief efforts could
responsibly answer to poor people's needs without wasting funds or bowing
to political pressure. In many ways, Vaile's reforms embodied Progressive Era
social welfare thoughts, trends, and practices.

Denver differs dramatically from the five smaller counties that we
explored in the previous chapter. Unlike the five smaller communities,
Denver possessed a more sophisticated welfare state with a wide range of
different policies and institutions caring for the city's needy in addition to a
more developed county government to carry out its agenda. And while the
other five counties knew of Progressive Era welfare developments, Denver's
position as the state's capital and largest urban center made the city a hub
of reform activity. Denver, for instance, hosted the National Conference of
Charities and Corrections in 1892 and 1925, and the State Board of Charities
and Corrections met regularly in the city to report on charity practices and
institutions. Denver, unlike the other counties, also possessed an emerging
professional class of social workers and reformers who actively embraced
and formulated many leading turn-of-the-century welfare policies.

In another sense, however, Denver provides a familiar story of Progressive Era changes. The city's efforts at municipal political reform mirrored
those of urban centers in other states that struggled to break the grip of fraud
and corruption. Denver's citizens successfully overthrew Mayor Robert
Speer's political machine and challenged law enforcement's close ties with
prostitution and gambling interests. Reformers abolished the city's "all powerful" mayor system and established a commission form of government.
Some of these changes, however, proved only temporary as voters quickly
repealed the commission form of government and reelected Speer. And like
many other major cities, Denver housed a political establishment that
fiercely resisted these reform efforts. All these elements played a role in shaping how the city structured its relief department and policies.

Denver offers a unique opportunity to inspect Progressive Era welfare
reform using a "before and after" analysis. The year that Vaile overhauled the
city's relief efforts, 1912, provides a clear division between pre- and post-
social welfare reform. By comparing relief practices before and after Vaile's
reforms, we can assess to what degree policies were or were not transformed.
On one level, the changes that Vaile initiated profoundly altered the direction and tone of the city's welfare programs. Vaile strove hard to eliminate

political meddling in the city's relief efforts while establishing professional standards. She introduced individual casework techniques and required that staff members be trained social workers. In many ways, Vaile's reforms pointed to a new beginning for the welfare department. But when implementation becomes the gauge of change, these new policies suddenly appear far less successful. Vaile's reforms occurred more at the administrative level than at the ground floor where poor people received assistance. As a result, poor residents noticed little change in their interactions with the city's outdoor relief program in spite of Vaile's efforts.

As in the five smaller counties, a range of local circumstances molded Denver's responses to the poor. Gertrude Vaile brought a unique vision to social welfare reform, one that profoundly shaped the city's relief strategies. But in the process of trying to change policies, she encountered an entrenched political structure that challenged her efforts. The difficulty of dislodging existing relief practices, the constant budgetary restraints, and the outright resistance to change, all limited Vaile's ability to transform Denver's welfare programs. The national tuberculosis problem also deeply affected how the city responded to those in need. A constant stream of indigent tubercular sufferers came to Denver in hopes that the city's climate and altitude would cure their illness. Efforts to grapple with this needy migrant population drained resources from the city's underfunded poor relief programs. The influx of poor tubercular patients to Denver and other western locations forced officials, like Vaile, to call for a radical expansion of the welfare state by requesting assistance from the federal government. Debates over the proposal for federal involvement in the care of migrant tubercular sufferers reveal how Denver's local situation biased Vaile's stance toward federal assistance.

The City, Its Poor, and Its Relief

Boris D. Bogen, manager of the United Jewish Charities, visited Denver in 1907. After touring the city, he concluded that Denver did not suffer from the same extreme congestion and overcrowding that plagued many eastern cities. In fact, the city did not seem to have "very much destitution" at all according to Bogen.[3] Bogen was only partially correct in his observations. Denver did indeed lack the high-rise tenements that occupied block after block of most eastern cities. The images of clotheslines strung high above a narrow city street and poorly lit stairways by photographers Lewis Hine and Jacob Riis would be almost alien to Denver's landscape. As Denver experienced rapid growth during the turn of the century, more than doubling its population from 106,713 in 1890 to 213,381 in 1910, the city spread out instead of up.[4] Unlike many cities, Denver had plenty of room to expand on the High Plains.

Nevertheless, one should not confuse, as Bogen did, the lack of crowded tenements with adequate housing or an absence of poverty. Like other cities, Denver had its wretched housing and slums filled largely with immigrants and African-Americans. "Take in the Russian or Italian Settlement on both banks of the [South] Platte river," warned Martha Coates, assistant secretary of the State Board of Charities and Corrections, "and you will see sights that are sickening, and have smells wafted to your nostrils that stifle and choke you and remain with you through the night hours and chase away sleep. An intangible, contaminating influence pervades the atmosphere of these neighborhoods," wrote Coates, "and you feel a desire to flee from the appalling squalor and to turn your head so as not to see the disagreeable things that the odors warn you exist." Down along the banks of the South Platte River, eastern and southern European immigrants constructed single-story homes, fences, stables, and outhouses out of "old corrugated iron, tar paper, tin cans, bed springs, iron beds and old lumber."[5] These river-bottom residents paid a small sum to wealthy individuals or corporations that owned the land. Sanitation was poor, as flooding constantly inundated these communities, and stagnant water often remained for weeks and months. The city dumped its garbage nearby, while the Burlington Railroad had unloaded "a long string of cars" filled with manure to reclaim land along the river.[6] "Almost all these houses," concluded Coates, "are absolutely unfit for human habitation."[7]

Along with recent arrivals from eastern and southern Europe, African-Americans occupied many of the city's poorly constructed homes. In 1910, foreign-born whites accounted for 18.2 percent of Denver's population. Germans, Russians, and Swedes made up the three largest foreign-born groups. African-Americans, meanwhile, totaled 5,426, or 2.5 percent of the city's residents.[8] These different ethnic and racial groups congregated in separate neighborhoods. Blacks settled in the Five Points area, while Poles, Slovenians, German-Russians, and other eastern European groups resided in the Globeville section near smelter and meat-packing jobs. Italians lived

*Woman and child at the corner of Lipan Street and W. 33rd Street,
near the South Platte River, Denver, Colorado, 1914.* Minutes of the
State Board of Charities and Corrections, 1914, *366, Box 18626.
Courtesy of Colorado State Archives, Denver, Colorado.*

along the river bottoms in "Jumbletown" and in "Little Italy" located in north
Denver. The city also housed a floating, fluctuating army of single men seeking employment or moving through town to mountain mining camps or to
the High Plains for agricultural jobs.[9]

The city's rapid growth exposed the corruption and inadequacy of its
government. State officials regularly meddled in municipal affairs, while
political machines made a mockery of democracy with stuffed ballot boxes
and graft. Public service corporations—tramway, water, gas, and electric
companies—exploited customers, provided shoddy service, and were
"unwilling to compensate the city adequately for franchise privileges."[10]
Denver, observed historian Robert Perkin, "entered the twentieth century
stewing in a vat of malodorous municipal and corporate corruption."[11] In
hopes of cleaning up the city's political mess, state voters passed a 1902 constitutional amendment, the Rush Amendment, that guaranteed home rule

for Denver. The Rush Amendment not only prevented state involvement in municipal affairs but it also created the new county of Denver. Until 1902, Denver was part of Arapahoe County, a largely agricultural county that extended eastward all the way to Kansas. Not surprisingly, the interests of Denver often conflicted with the rest of Arapahoe County. Plus, Denver's citizens wanted to join together city and county offices for greater efficiency and accountability. With the approval of the Rush Amendment, the city of Denver became the city and county of Denver with the same city and county boundaries encompassing just over fifty-eight square miles. Although in 1905 the state supreme court ruled against the merging of city and county offices, the courts did allow the creation of the new county to remain intact. As a result, Denver's combination of city and county boundaries offers a unique opportunity to examine how a municipal government dealt with poverty. In most of the nation, the county government was responsible for caring for the needy, thus making it more difficult for scholars to separate out city and county practices and policies. In Denver, however, the two were essentially the same, beginning in 1902, despite the court's ruling.

During the turn of the century, Denver appropriated two sets of funds to support its poor. The city government annually gave nine to twelve thousand dollars to the privately operated Charity Organization Society of Denver to supplement various local institutions and to distribute outdoor aid for nonresidents who did not qualify for publicly administered relief. Meanwhile, the county government funded and operated its own outdoor relief program for its residents. In 1903 the county commissioners set aside fifteen thousand dollars for support of poor residents; two years later that amount had risen to twenty thousand dollars.[12] The following chapter will more closely examine the relationship between the publicly funded relief provided by the city and county of Denver and the private charity work of the Charity Organization Society of Denver. At the moment, we will focus solely on publicly funded and administered outdoor relief. During the five-year span from 1906 through 1910, Denver's public outdoor welfare assisted 4,937 individuals or families.[13]

The poor had very little contact with the county's relief program. The needy applied for aid at a small room across from city hall through a small aperture that opened onto the hallway where "the applicants stood, their backs to a noisy, crowded hall, their faces to an equally crowded office." Here at the window, the county agent recorded the applicant's name, address, sex and ages of family members, place of birth, date of arrival in Colorado and in Denver, and cause of poverty. The Denver county agent, similar to his counterpart in the five smaller counties, usually used only a word or two, such as "widow" or "sickness," to describe a person's cause of distress. At this point, the county generally gave out some relief before initiating any formal investigation of the applicant.[14]

Denver distributed the same basic relief to almost all its needy citizens. Outdoor relief recipients received a grocery lot and a coal order per month. The grocery lots, or family lots as they were sometimes called, consisted of "twenty-five pounds of flour, twelve pounds of potatoes, two pounds of rice, one bar of soap, quarter pound of tea, two pounds of sugar, one pound of coffee, two pounds of navy beans, two pounds of salt pork, quarter pound of baking powder, two pounds of lard, two pounds of crackers and ten pounds of cornmeal." Families, however, could substitute various items from the standard grocery lots. Recipients could request beef or butter, for example, instead of pork and could exchange other goods for items of equal value.[15] Each morning, aid recipients formed a line outside the county agent's office with baskets in hand to receive their lots.[16] The city's Board of Charities and Corrections believed that the groceries were "about as good as that of the average laboring man's family with an income of $10 a week." The city contracted with a local grocer to supply the goods, and each lot supposedly fed two people for two weeks at a cost of $2.90 per lot in 1911. Even though the city calculated that each lot would last for only two weeks, it nevertheless distributed the goods only at monthly intervals. For families larger than two people or, in rare cases, for families with greater needs, the city gave them more than one lot each month. "There is an old couple, living out near Englewood, to whom we allow two of the 'lots' each month," reported John Parsons, chief clerk of the city's Board of Charities and Corrections. "We also allow them a half ton of coal monthly . . . but all they get in the way of food is the $5.80 worth of groceries which the city gives them." Coal orders seemed to have been either in ton or half ton amounts.[17] In addition to the food and coal orders, the city also provided nightly meal and bed tickets for single men. The "application window was beset every afternoon by throngs of single men, one hundred per day, asking for meal and bed tickets." These meal and bed tickets paid for a single meal and a place to sleep in a lodging house.[18]

Denver devoted few resources to following up on applicants' claims of distress. In the case of single men, for example, the city's Board of Charities and Corrections made little effort to track them. According to reformers, the city gave meal and bed tickets out "sometimes as regularly as five times a week to the same man."[19] The city employed only one investigator who researched recipients' circumstances; however, he could not promptly visit each applicant, nor visit very often. "Frequently," claimed reformers, the investigator "did not visit the home at all if the applicant's story or recommendation satisfied him."[20] In order to assist the lone investigator, the county commissioners occasionally requested help from the privately operated Charity Organization Society of Denver.[21] After "passing" an investigation and regardless of a family's situation, the city's Board of Charities and Corrections continued offering only grocery lots or coal orders to its needy citizens. About the only difference "passing" an investigation made was an increase or decrease in the number of lots or in the amount of coal that one received.

Statistics on Denver's outdoor public relief confirm this image of a bare-bones operation. Compared to other Colorado counties, Denver ranked near the bottom in both the amount of aid received per month and the duration for receiving assistance. Denver's relief recipients averaged just $5.52 per month in the form of grocery and coal lots. Only Costilla County offered lower average monthly allowances, $5.03 per month, than Denver, while Lincoln, Teller, and Montezuma Counties provided substantially higher average monthly aid (see Table 9). Even though Costilla and Denver were in many ways extremely different from one another, both communities shared a common assumption that others would supplement their meager welfare benefits. In Costilla, as the previous chapter argued, kinship networks, a subsistence economy, and the Penitentes all helped to support the community's poor. Denver relied on the numerous resources found in an urban environment to supplement its low levels of public assistance. Not only could Denver's needy turn to various local private institutions for aid (which we will explore in the following chapter), but they could also depend on neighbors for help. In fact, the city's Board of Charities and Corrections anticipated assistance in caring for the needy. Denver expected poor residents to "supplement the [grocery] allowance[s] a trifle" by adding additional foods and covering the remaining two weeks of each month. "Friends supply them with fruit or vegetables," reported the *Denver Post*, "so they are not confined exclusively to the diet provided by the city." The elderly couple near Englewood, for instance, received clothes from friends.[22] Denver relied on these acts of kindness to support its poor as it openly acknowledged that its food lots were inadequate in both quantity and variety of goods.

Although Denver operated a very strict welfare program, variances within that system still arose depending on an applicant's ethnicity. As in Montezuma and Lincoln Counties, Denver's poor citizens received aid for extremely short durations. Denver's outdoor relief recipients averaged only 3.57 months per year on the city's welfare roll, while Lincoln and Montezuma's poor averaged 3.52 and 4.48 months per year (see Table 10). Denver had no intention of permanently supporting the poor or of providing long-term assistance. The city spread its limited relief resources thinly among a large number of needy people. Denver's county agents, however, did not distribute this aid evenly among the poor. The city's Board of Charities and Corrections claimed that, in most cases, family size solely determined the amount of aid, especially the number of grocery lots received by each applicant. Yet, the city actually gave more aid to Americans than to immigrants regardless of household size. Americans received an average of $5.72 per month, while Italians averaged only $4.39 per month, and Russians fared even worse by averaging $4.33 per month (see Table 11). Russians and Italians, nevertheless, had substantially larger household sizes than Americans. The average household among Russians held 3.89 members, 4.49 for Italians, but only 2.77 for Americans (see Table 12). This discrimination did not, however, cut across all aspects of outdoor poor relief. Italians and Russians did manage, for example, to remain on Denver's relief rolls longer than Americans. Italians averaged 6.36 months per year on assistance, Russians averaged 4.03 months, but Americans averaged just 3.23 months (see Table 13). Poor employment opportunities for eastern and southern European immigrants best explain their long durations on county poor rolls.

Gertrude Vaile and Reforms

Beginning in 1912, Denver's municipal government underwent massive changes. First, Colorado's Supreme Court reversed its 1905 decision barring the official merging of city and county offices. Thus, the city and county of Denver truly became a consolidated government. Second, reformers finally were able to defeat Mayor Robert Speer's political machine. With the failure of a reform city charter in 1902, political corruption, machine politics, graft, and exploitation by public service corporations continued infesting every aspect of Denver's municipal government. But reformers also persisted in their attacks on the city's administration. Muckraking journalist George Creel used the *Rocky Mountain News* to expose Mayor Speer's corruption and close ties to the city's red-light district. Juvenile Judge Ben Lindsey penned a series of articles for *Everybody's Magazine* that revealed the strength of Speer's political machine in controlling Denver's public offices and political processes. Creel, Lindsey, Edward Costigan, Josephine Roche, and other reformers formed a Non-Partisan Charter League in 1911 in an attempt to clean up Denver's administration through the creation of a commission form of government. While Speer and his aides at first succeeded in blocking the Non-Partisan Charter League, their heavy-handed tactics angered citizens and eventually resulted in the defeat of Speer's political machine with the election of a reform ticket to every city office.[23]

With Speer and his supporters completely removed from power in 1912, reformers had accomplished only the first of their two major objectives. Next, they wanted to abolish the powerful mayoral form of government, replacing it with a commission government. The commission government gained widespread acceptance during the Progressive Era after Galveston, Texas, turned to it following the 1900 hurricane that devastated the island community. Crippled by corruption, inefficiency, and a huge debt, Galveston teetered on the brink of a complete collapse as it tried to rebuild. In order to restore Galveston, business leaders successfully obtained state authorization to replace the mayor, aldermen, and boards with a commission of five citizens.[24] The commission government rested on the notion of combining legislative and administrative duties in a few officials whom voters could hold directly accountable.[25] In 1913, reformers savored a victory when Denver's electorate adopted a new city charter that created a five-member commission government. Yet Denver just as quickly abandoned these changes. The city's commission government failed to deliver on promises of improved efficiency as political infighting and weak leadership resulted in the collapse of Denver's reform movement. Tired of inadequate city services and political squabbling, voters, in 1916, repealed the commission charter and reinstated the mayoral form of government as Speer once again captured the mayor's seat. Speer would remain Denver's mayor for only two more years before dying of pneumonia in 1918.[26]

The many changes in Denver's governmental structure repeatedly altered the city's outdoor public relief department. With the approval of a 1904 city charter, a three-member, nonsalary, advisory board oversaw a City Department of Charity and Correction. Appointed by the mayor, the advisory board made few, if any, attempts to alter the delivery of assistance prior to 1912.[27] Mayor Speer's 1912 defeat instilled new life into the advisory board, and, in November, the new reform mayor selected Gertrude Vaile to fill a vacancy on the newly formed Board of Charities and Corrections. At the time, each board member assumed direct administrative control over a segment of the city's relief operations, with Vaile supervising the outdoor relief program. After the 1913 approval of a new city charter forming a commission government, the city's relief structure changed once again. The Commission of Charity and Correction, under the direction of an elected commissioner of the Social Welfare Department, now managed all of Denver's charitable functions, as well as several other public services. Under this new system, Vaile became the paid supervisor of outdoor relief beginning in June 1913. Two years later, the commissioner promoted Vaile to executive secretary in charge of Denver's entire publicly funded charitable efforts. The return in 1916 to a strong mayoral municipal government once again restructured the city's charity operations. The Department of Health and Charity replaced the Commission of Charity and Correction, and Vaile became the assistant director and then the director of the Bureau of Charities. Vaile remained with the new bureau until August 1917 when she accepted a position with the Red Cross assisting in the nation's war effort.[28]

Through all these confusing changes—various city charters, several administrations, and numerous reorganizations—Gertrude Vaile remained not only a constant but the most important player in shaping Denver's Progressive Era welfare reforms. Born in 1878, Vaile came from one of the city's most prominent families; she was, according to one journalist, "one of the Denver girls of wealth."[29] Her father, Joel F. Vaile, became a leading attorney representing railroads and large mining interests. Her mother, Charlotte M. Vaile, exhibited "estimable character, superior culture and refinement" and authored several books for young readers. Vaile graduated from Vassar College in 1900 with a sociology degree and came back to Denver briefly before departing on a nine-month European tour with her family.[30] Shortly after her return, Vaile assumed housekeeping duties after her mother died, and she became involved in several local organizations including the social science department of the Woman's Club of Denver.[31] By 1905, Vaile sat on the executive board of the social science department and had become active on the Club's public baths committee.[32] Vaile left Denver in 1909 to study at the Chicago School of Civics and Philanthropy. After graduation, she worked for two years with the Chicago United Charities, first as a district visitor and later as a district superintendent near Hull House.[33] In 1912, Vaile briefly returned to Denver before accepting a month-long Russell Sage Foundation assignment investigating "the workings and results of the Illinois Mothers' Compensation act."[34] While in Chicago, Vaile received notice that she would be able to "give her services to her own city" when Denver's mayor selected her for the city's Board of Charities and Corrections.[35] The mayor's appointment began Vaile's long association with Denver's public outdoor relief.

Gertrude Vaile's views on publicly funded and administered assistance would not only profoundly shape Denver's welfare system but also differed dramatically from those of her fellow charity and social workers. During the mid-teens, debates over the merits of private versus public welfare reached new levels of intensity with the widespread passage of mothers' compensation or pension laws (we will explore the implementation of Colorado's · mothers' compensation in chapter 4). At this time, Vaile offered a practical approach that seemed to bridge the differences between the supporters of private aid and the defenders of public welfare. She argued "that all public outdoor relief is dangerous," particularly new forms of assistance "which deliberately aim to remove the stigma of dependency from the recipients." Yet, Vaile understood that spreading across the nation was a trend "demanding larger and larger public relief for more and more people. . . . [W]e find group after group being added with startling rapidity to those already dependent upon public funds." Despite her misgivings about public welfare, Vaile also realized that "public outdoor relief is necessary and a matter of social justice." Given that public welfare was not disappearing but, in fact, increasing, Vaile sought to reform outdoor assistance instead of joining "the ranks of the reactionaries" who opposed all public aid. Her solution rested on applying the methods and standards of private charity organizations to public outdoor relief practices. Thus, individual casework stood at the center of Vaile's reform agenda. She wanted to eliminate the practice of simply giving material relief without seeking "the cause of the trouble" and without trying to change the individual's circumstances. The use of individual casework methods, according to Vaile, would prevent unnecessary dependence on public welfare and would allow individuals to lift themselves out of poverty. "Only in constructive, individual, case-by-case treatment," wrote Vaile, "lie the hope and safety of public outdoor relief."[36]

Vaile's plans for rehabilitating public welfare drew widespread praise. After presenting her ideas, "Principles and Methods of Outdoor Relief," during the 1915 National Conference of Charities and Corrections held in Baltimore, Vaile received broad backing.[37] Public officials from Kansas City and New York City supported her reform plan, and even executive officers from private relief organizations applauded her ideas. Buffalo's Frederic Almy, one of the most vocal opponents of public outdoor relief testified, according to the *Survey*, "that Miss Vaile had given him a new star to hitch his wagon to and that he for one was going home to get more and better public service."[38]

Attempting to apply private charity methods and practices to Denver's outdoor relief programs, Vaile initiated a series of changes that aimed to transform almost every aspect of the city's previous welfare policies. First, and in many ways foremost, she introduced new record-keeping procedures. For some time, state law had required counties to collect basic information on each relief recipient. Counties, including Denver, used large, heavy volumes to record this information, and officials often entered a recipient's name and data two or three times throughout these enormous books. Vaile initiated a new system that would be "more convenient and which makes it possible to deal more intelligently with the situations of the needy."[39] Denver adopted the Russell Sage Foundation record forms used by many private charities. These new forms could be arranged alphabetically and allowed for more detailed case histories, including information about "members of the family, their physical and industrial conditions, their relatives and associations, and the place where they live."[40] Even the process of collecting personal data changed. No longer would recipients stand at the noisy window giving information; instead, in a separate, quiet office a staff member interviewed all aid applicants while filling out the detailed case-history forms.[41]

Vaile also altered the method and purpose of investigating each applicant. After the interviewer completed the case history, but before giving any aid, an investigator visited each applicant's home. Three, then four, full-time investigators spent most of their time in the field "following up the various sources of information indicated in the preliminary applications in order that the precise degree of responsibility on the part of the applicants may be fixed."[42] This investigation was "not merely to see if the applicant is telling the truth, but to understand him, his character, his resources, his handicaps." Vaile wanted to put an end to the old practice of providing a standard dole for each needy person without making an "effort to change the applicant's situation."[43] Individual casework tried to lift the relief recipient out of poverty while "bringing to him all the most natural and beneficent help" available.[44] The search for "natural" and "beneficial" aid meant involving relatives, religious organizations, neighbors, employers, and other community members in assisting the applicant. Not only did the investigators contact these individuals and agencies but two recently hired stenographers also communicated with out-of-town relatives and charity organizations.[45]

Vaile pushed hard to train her staff members and professionalize Denver's outdoor relief program. The changes in record keeping and the use of individual casework all introduced the latest developments in the field. Since none of the staff members had received training in social work, Vaile arranged to instruct her workers. At night, she taught her staff the methods of casework by studying early case records, by reading social work bulletins published by the Russell Sage Foundation, and by discussing record keeping and interviewing procedures. Persistent political meddling, in the form of political appointees, presented an obstacle to professional development. Vaile managed each political appointee by either developing a loyal and trusting relationship or by diplomatically transferring the appointee to another municipal office. In an attempt to reduce political involvement and raise standards, Vaile, in 1917, formally required that all social work staff hold college diplomas and informally demanded that they be former volunteers in the Bureau of Charities. During these early years, staff members brought a type of missionary zeal to their work. Vaile and her assistants worked long hours, often working during holidays and Sundays. Vaile's enthusiasm spread to her staff and the "constant fear of political interference" bonded the workers. Each member felt as if she were "supporting a cause" and loyalty to both the "cause" and to fellow staff members ran high.[46]

Vaile also strengthened ties between Denver's Bureau of Charities and the community. Private relief organizations had been very successful in recruiting volunteers and depending on widespread community support. But public relief agencies had not tried these same methods. Vaile saw no reason why these private practices could not be transferred to Denver's public welfare programs. Vaile encouraged volunteers to assist in running the city's outdoor relief. She used volunteers as "friendly visitors" to help in monitoring relief recipients and to assist regularly in the office. Further, Vaile allowed Mrs. Charles Denison, a wealthy benefactor, to pay the salary for an additional visitor and stenographer for five months.[47] Vaile established a weekly "case conference" open to "interested public-spirited citizens, representatives of churches," and other organizations. These weekly conferences educated the public about the bureau's work and in turn generated funds and recruited additional volunteers. A "clothing committee" organized and distributed clothes from the bureau's storeroom.[48] Most important, Vaile maintained strong community ties through an unpaid advisory board that consisted of representatives from various religious groups and the business community. While Vaile kept the board informed of policy developments, the board in turn kept the public abreast of the city's charity work, offered suggestions to Vaile, and at times acted as a buffer between Vaile and partisan pressure.[49]

Did the Reforms Make a Difference in Poor People's Lives?

Gertrude Vaile and her staff, no doubt, ambitiously initiated many changes in the delivery of Denver's public poor relief. But how successful were these changes in actually altering the practices of the city's welfare programs? From the point of view of the needy, her efforts do not seem to have dramatically transformed the bureau's daily interactions with the poor. In fact, it is shocking how in many areas so little changed despite all of Vaile's commitment and energy. This is not to argue that her efforts were in vain or that absolutely no change occurred. Instead, the reforms that Vaile implemented had a far greater influence on staff members and the bureau's relationship with politicians than on how the poor encountered relief. Multiple reasons—political resistance, tight budgets, overly optimistic expectations, and difficulty in dislodging previous practices—accounted for the mixed record.

Professionalizing the city's relief work and distancing the bureau from partisan influences were the two interrelated areas where Vaile's reforms largely succeeded. The introduction of individual casework management and new record-keeping methods raised the standards of the bureau's work. Vaile successfully recruited new female staff members who were indeed college graduates and were committed to social work as a profession. Due to her efforts, Denver's Bureau of Charities became a "female dominion" composed entirely of female staff members with Vaile as their mentor. As historian Robyn Muncy has so clearly demonstrated, a "female dominion" came to rule American welfare reform during the early twentieth century. The situation in Denver mirrored, on a much smaller scale, the trends that Muncy found in both Chicago and in the nation.[50] Vaile's hand-picked successor, Florence W. Hutsinpillar, continued the fight against partisan intervention as she successfully fought to keep all case files confidential and out of the political arena.[51] By 1920, Denver's poor relief administration and the relationship between public outdoor aid and partisan politics had fundamentally changed as professionalization dominated the city's charity efforts.

While Vaile succeeded in altering the bureaucratic end of relief, she and her associates were far less successful in changing how poor folk experienced Denver's outdoor assistance. One of their biggest disappointments must have been the inability to investigate relief applicants properly. Prompt investigation and the ability to maintain regular contact with aid recipients were two of the key components in carrying out effective individual casework. Before Vaile took control of the city's outdoor relief program, Denver employed one visitor or investigator and relied on help from the local charity organization society. Vaile increased the number of paid investigators from one to four; however, she no longer received assistance from the Charity Organization Society of Denver. Instead, she used her own volunteer visitors to supplement the work of the paid ones. Still, from the very beginning of Vaile's reforms, the need for additional investigators became a pressing concern. Frank Bruno observed that "more visitors" were needed in order for Denver's welfare reform to succeed. "Denver is placing about three times as much on each worker [visitor]," wrote Bruno, "as the private societies in New York and Chicago are requiring."[52] "The urgent need is for more visitors," stated the bureau's second annual report, as the "386 cases per visitor are fully twice as many as such workers should be held responsible for."[53] In reality, Vaile's reforms had hardly transformed the ability of investigators to maintain contact with recipients. Most poor people on aid "received scant attention once they were given an allowance." Only when a crisis or an "acute situation came to light" did relief recipients receive casework services.[54] The only difference between the pre- and post-reform practices was the prompt investigation of new applicants. In the past, the city often gave aid prior to investigation. Under Vaile, the bureau did manage at least to investigate quickly all new applicants. Thus, after the initial investigation, poor residents experienced no great difference in the adoption of casework methodology since the bureau could not successfully implement the new procedures.

Of course, budgetary restraints limited Vaile's ability to carry out her reform plan. Vaile and her associates painted an extremely bleak picture of Denver's relief efforts prior to reform. They presented an image of chaos, fraud, corruption, and general waste. Relief offices were "crowded," hallways were "noisy," and assistance was given "on the mere word of the applicant."[55] With so little supervision of applicants, reformers believed that fraud must have run rampant through the outdoor relief program. Vaile and her supporters promised to deliver not only a more humane and responsive relief, but also, and just as important, they guaranteed a more efficient and cost-effective welfare operation. And indeed when the city's Board of Charities and Corrections disclosed in 1913 that over the previous year there had been "one hundred cases of obvious fraud and the expenditure of many hundreds of dollars for charity to the unworthy," it seemed to confirm the worst fears of municipal waste.[56] The board claimed that the use of thorough investigations would rapidly weed out "old cases of fraud."[57] In addition, the city's various public and private charity organizations established a confidential exchange to prevent applicants from simultaneously receiving assistance from both the city and private charities.[58] Yet, despite halting so many supposedly fraudulent claims and using the confidential exchange, Denver's relief spending did not decrease, but actually went over budget.[59] Reformers had clearly overstated the degree of waste and fraud in the outdoor relief program. Given that each applicant only averaged 3.57 months of aid per year at an average of only $5.52 per month prior to reforms, there was not a great deal of waste that reformers could actually trim. Thus, Vaile's promises of massive savings due to the adoption of casework methods simply never materialized, resulting in an inability to hire more social workers to investigate aid recipients.

Other areas of reform also fell short of anticipated goals. In March 1913, Denver's Board of Charities and Corrections established a municipal store to supply groceries to all the city's institutions as well as outdoor relief recipients. The poor quality and high price of goods distributed under the previous administration provided the rationale behind the city-operated store. In the past, grocers who had provided supplies for the poor often "'adulterated and rendered unfit for consumption much of the food sent out,'" claimed the charity board.[60] The possibility of saving money through wholesale purchasing strongly motivated the establishment of a municipal store. Yet, the store remained open for less than a year, closing in January 1914. The city's other institutional operations never used the store, and the savings from wholesale purchases were never great enough to offset the operating costs. The store could only provide a limited number of staples and could not stock fresh vegetables and fruit. After closing the store, the city once again contracted with grocers to provide food orders. The only difference was that unlike in the past, when a single large wholesaler distributed food lots, now small neighborhood grocers near the applicants' homes filled out the orders and provided the goods.[61]

The city's attempts to cure alcoholism also quickly proved unsuccessful. Beginning in April 1913, Denver began giving liquor cures to those individuals whose intemperance seemed to contribute to their poverty.[62] Each patient took a formula that made him or her nauseated during the three-to-five-day treatment. In 1913, the city paid $853.06 for liquor cures at a rate of approximately $20.00 per treatment. While no one questioned the "desirability of attempting to provide a cure for the liquor habit," some raised concerns about the effectiveness and methods of the cures. For instance, the city could not determine the exact medicine or remedy used to produce the nauseating feeling since it was a "secret" formula. The use of an unknown formula on the poor without a physician's supervision seemed unwise and unethical. And since the city kept no follow-up records on these liquor cures, there was no clear evidence that the cures actually worked, if even for a short time. As a result of these concerns, Denver "almost wholly discontinued, except in rare cases," the use of city poor funds for liquor cures. "Only when men and women show considerable strength of character," stated the Social Welfare Department's annual report, "do we consider the matter of the cure." In 1914, only eight people received liquor cures with only two benefiting from the treatment. Thus, like the municipal store, the generous use of liquor cures, another element of Denver's Progressive Era reform efforts, experienced an extremely short life.[63]

One of the practices that Vaile and her associates particularly wanted to abolish was Denver's reliance on a dole consisting of a standard food lot and coal order. Vaile had hoped to eliminate the use of a dole by relying, in part, on casework methodology that would provide a "definite intelligent plan to improve permanently the conditions of the recipient."[64] A thorough investigation would reveal the core reasons for an individual's poverty as well as the solutions. For many supporters of casework methodology, including Vaile, the possible solutions for a poor person's circumstances seemed to entail more then just handing out food and coal to each recipient. For if a dole could alleviate the problems of the poor, then there would be no need for trained visitors, casework methods, or even Vaile and her reforms. Yet as we have seen, due to the limited number of paid investigators, Vaile failed to implement effective casework practices. One consequence of this failure was a continued reliance on the dole. With a limited number of visitors, "very little could be accomplished except to grant regular relief."[65]

Yet, the lack of investigators only partially explains the persistence of this practice. The city, even after Vaile's reforms, offered little else to its relief recipients besides the dole. Most poor folks on aid still received a lot of groceries and coal. In fact, the food lots remained essentially the same except for a two-pound reduction in flour as the only difference between the pre- and post-welfare reform grocery orders. In some cases, the social welfare department did begin giving recipients cash. This was done, however, only for emergency situations and only in amounts of three dollars or less.[66] So despite Vaile's efforts, Denver basically continued to provide the same type of aid that had previously been offered to the city's poor.

The situation for homeless men also did not improve enough to satisfy those in need of shelter. Beginning in 1912, the city and county of Denver halted its annual supplement to the privately operated Charity Organization Society of Denver (COSD). Prior to 1912, the COSD had agreed to aid all non-residents while public outdoor relief cared for the city's residents. Once officials stopped supplementing the COSD, the city eventually assumed responsibility for all resident families as well as for nonresident and transient homeless men, while the COSD still cared for nonresident families and single women.[67] Although Denver had increased its commitment to the needy by assuming direct responsibility for nonresident and homeless men, nevertheless, the city's ability to care for them remained unsatisfactory, at least according to the men themselves. In February 1915, a delegation of destitute and unemployed men appeared before the State Board of Charities and Corrections protesting Denver's inadequate facilities for them. The city provided heat, electricity, and clothes-washing facilities on two floors of an empty building. The city also furnished two meals a day and, on occasion, towels and laundry soap. Yet, the delegation complained of overcrowding as four to six hundred men slept on the two dirty floors. The "men are so crowded together that it is impossible to walk around" and most had "little or no bedding." The delegation considered the meals insufficient and the washing facilities inadequate thus "rendering it impossible to keep clean." These men, largely floating common laborers, wanted an improvement in how Denver treated them; more important, they demanded work, not charity, from the city.[68] Despite Progressive Era welfare reforms, the one instance in which we have direct feedback from the poor clearly shows unhappiness with the city's relief efforts.

One contributing reason for the general lack of change was that Vaile often had to devote a great deal of effort to fight off attacks on the city's charities services. On at least two occasions, the business community or politicians attempted to shut down Denver's relief programs. The most serious challenge happened in 1914 and 1915 when a committee of taxpayers and businessmen recommended that the city completely abolish its charity department and simply give an equal amount of funds, minus any salaries, to private charities. The committee believed that salaries were too high, and that the city's relief programs largely duplicated existing services already provided by private organizations. Vaile and her supporters successfully fought back by explaining that the adoption of individual casework practices had actually saved the city money by preventing fraud and encouraging independence among poor residents.[69] Several years later, when Speer won reelection in 1916, rumors quickly surfaced that he planned to abolish the public welfare department and halt all casework investigation. No one clearly knew Speer's intentions; nevertheless, word rapidly and quietly spread, especially among members of the unpaid advisory board. Soon letters poured into the mayor's office demanding the continuance of the department's work. This strong community support most likely helped to save the department.[70] But fighting these battles obviously drew energy and attention away from the core changes that Vaile wanted to accomplish.

A few years after Vaile and her associates had initiated their welfare reforms, it would have been difficult for a relief recipient to have noticed much of a difference. By 1917, when Vaile left for the Red Cross, little had changed in the city's delivery of aid. The municipal store had quickly opened and closed, and liquor cures had mostly been discontinued. Attempts to use individual casework largely failed due to budget constraints and too few investigators. The large savings promised from ending the fraud and inefficiency of the previous administration never materialized. Aid recipients still had little contact with the city's relief staff, and they still received the same basic dole of grocery lots and coal orders. The few successful changes mainly affected office personnel. The office staff learned new record-keeping procedures, received casework training, and were expected to meet higher educational requirements. Likewise, the increased professionalization minimized political meddling in poor relief affairs. Only when they picked up food orders at neighborhood grocers, received prompt first-time investigation, were allotted small amounts of cash for emergency cases, or took advantage of some of the new, albeit inadequate, services for homeless men would Denver's poor have experienced any changes in the city's outdoor relief practices.

There was, however, one unintended consequence of Vaile's reforms. By depicting previous welfare practices as corrupt and fraudulent, Vaile and her supporters implied that many—perhaps even most—relief recipients were undeserving of the city's assistance. After Vaile's staff had investigated recipients, they discovered that in fact most deserved aid. Of the 1,931 families who applied for assistance in 1914, for example, 735 were found not to need material relief. Yet, the remaining 1,196 did require the city's assistance. By passing the investigation, these 1,196 families now had a degree of legitimacy to their claims for public relief. No longer could reformers dismiss them as undeserving or reject their petitions as fraudulent claims. Likewise, by passing the investigation, these applicants had clearly demonstrated that they had either few or no other resources with which to solve their poverty. Until their circumstances changed—and for many the circumstances were intractable—they could continue to demand assistance. In the past, the city could, and probably did, discontinue recipients after a few months, only to have them reapply and start the cycle all over again. "The 1,196 families given relief constitute Denver's real problem of dependency," stated the Social Welfare Department's 1914 report. "They call for large relief on the average, because there seems no other way to meet their need."[71]

Although Denver did not increase the amount of monthly aid in the form of grocery lots and coal orders it allotted to assist this dependent group, this new sense of legitimacy did seem to result in slightly longer durations on relief rolls after Vaile's reforms. While the existing data do not allow a

direct comparison of durations, the data do indirectly indicate that durations did increase after 1912. From 1906 through 1910 recipients of Denver's
outdoor public relief averaged from a low of $12.80 per year to a high of
$17.87. During the five-year span from 1915 through 1919 the average yearly
amount of aid sharply increased. Recipients in 1915 averaged $21.49 but by
1919, they averaged $36.49 (see Table 14). Wartime inflation accounted for a
large portion of these increases; still, inflation does not completely explain
all the increases in aid. Given that the amount and the type of aid did not
dramatically change between the two five-year periods, only an increase in
duration adequately accounts for the remaining portion of increases in
relief.[72] Even though the delivery of assistance changed little due to welfare
reforms, the poor, at least those who passed the investigation, did experience an unintended change in Denver's relief practices as they remained on
public assistance for slightly longer periods.

Tuberculosis

In addition to all the political, budgetary, and policy issues impeding reform,
caring for tubercular sufferers became one of the largest obstacles to change
as the number of people needing help simply overwhelmed the city's
resources. Tuberculosis, according to Vaile, was "the heaviest and most
difficult among all the problems" facing Denver's poor relief.[73] Tuberculosis
had ravaged the nation for years, earning the name the "white plague." Yet,
tuberculosis did not quickly kill its victims as did most plagues. Instead,
tuberculosis was a chronic illness that slowly weakened a person. The disease
could last for years, often decades, as it alternated between attacks and remis-
sions. For most of the nineteenth century, society viewed tuberculosis, or consumption as it was then known, as a hereditary and noncontagious illness
that infected all social classes and all regions of the nation. In 1882, Robert
Koch discovered the specific bacteria, tubercle bacilli, that caused consumption. During the early twentieth century, tuberculosis still extracted a heavy
toll on the nation's population, accounting for 10 percent of all deaths.[74]

By the twentieth century, tuberculosis had become a disease of poverty-
stricken urban immigrants. Although the overall tuberculosis rates began to
decline during the late nineteenth century, in poorer neighborhoods, consumption still claimed extremely high numbers of people. In New York City, for

example, the citywide tuberculosis mortality rate stood at 256 per 100,000 in 1900, but in crowded and impoverished tenement districts the rate was about 500 per 100,000.[75] The tenements' crowded living conditions, lack of ventilation, and limited access to fresh air made for easy and rapid spread of the contagious disease. Inadequate nutrition and overwork weakened immune systems, contributing to the high rate of tuberculosis among the poor.

Koch's 1882 discovery altered the method for treating tubercular patients. During the mid-nineteenth century, patients sought vigorous exercise through a variety of outdoor activities including hunting, horseback riding, hiking, and camping. By the late nineteenth century, however, doctors would recommend plenty of rest, fresh air, lots of healthy food, and isolation in a sanatorium under the direction of a trained medical staff of doctors and nurses. The sanatorium provided nutritious meals and encouraged eating large quantities, including dozens of eggs and several quarts of milk each day to build up the body's strength. Patients spent as much time as possible outside in fresh air. During warm weather only bathing was done inside and during cold weather meals were also taken indoors. Bundling up in warm clothes and using hot bottles, patients "slept outdoors and sat outdoors all day happily and successfully . . . in Denver when it was twenty below."[76] Tubercular patients could not neglect the importance of rest in their recovery. In fact, for some patients, resting became a full-time job as they put "every atom of . . . will power into recovery."[77] Throughout every part of the day, patients followed "the doctor's orders for that hour: taking temperature, swallowing raw eggs, walking five minutes, resting two hours—whatever it may be."[78]

While many aspects of treating tuberculosis changed with Koch's discovery of the infectious bacteria, the importance of climate and altitude in combating the disease remained a vital, albeit controversial, component for most recovery plans. For years physicians had prescribed climatic treatment for those with consumption. In the early nineteenth century, for instance, some doctors recommended sea voyages to temperate climates. Beginning in the 1840s, those with consumption often headed west to take advantage of the climate and active outdoor lifestyle. Many physicians, according to historian Katherine Ott, believed that "elevation increased heart and lung action so that 'aseptic' oxygen got deeper into the lungs and aided healing."[79] Yet, there was by no means any clear consensus on just which type of climate or how high an altitude would be most beneficial for tubercular patients. Physicians and local boosters recommended and promoted a number of locations with a

variety of climates and elevations. Pasadena and San Diego, California; El
Paso, Texas; Phoenix and Tucson, Arizona; Asheville, North Carolina; New
Mexico; NewYork's Adirondack Mountains; Colorado Springs; and Denver, to
name just a few, all drew tuberculosis sufferers in hopes of a cure. The widely publicized testimonies from infected physicians who had moved west in
search of better health encouraged many others to seek out this particular
region.[80] By 1900, one-third of Colorado's newcomers had come in hopes of
obtaining better health.[81] In fact, those "chasing the cure," people seeking a
cure from tuberculosis, had quite literally overwhelmed the state. "Colorado,"
observed Elizabeth Dobell in 1914, "is overrun with [tubercular] invalids."[82]

The influx of "lungers," those suffering from tuberculosis, made the
nation's tuberculosis epidemic into Denver's local charity problem. As a result,
several local organizations turned to their national affiliates for assistance in
dealing with the seemingly unending stream of "lungers." In 1892, Denver's
German Jews began constructing a hospital to care for the influx of indigent
Jewish tubercular sufferers. The Depression of 1893 halted all work, and the
project remained stalled until the national Independent Order of B'nai B'rith
stepped in to provide funds. The National Jewish Hospital finally opened its
doors in 1899, serving all religious faiths, although Jews largely dominated its
clientele. The National Jewish Hospital only admitted those who could not
afford proper treatment. The hospital's motto, "None May Enter Who Can
Pay—None Can Pay Who Enter," concisely summed up its mission. The
National Jewish Hospital admitted only those with incipient cases of tuberculosis and did not provide meals that followed Jewish dietary laws. In response,
the Jewish Consumptives' Relief Society opened its doors in 1904, providing
free tuberculosis care to the poor, welcoming all patients regardless of their
stage of infection, maintaining a kosher kitchen, and speaking Yiddish. Other
ethnic and religious groups quickly followed the Jewish pattern of establishing hospitals in the Denver area for their own consumptive patients. German
Lutherans opened the Evangelical Lutheran Sanitarium in 1905, and Swedes
operated the Swedish National Sanatorium beginning in 1909. Other smaller
institutions also sprang up. The Craig Colony of Brotherly Relief opened in 1910
helping homeless, tubercular men, while the Sands House began operations
in 1914 caring for destitute, tubercular women.[83]

Despite all these different private facilities, the influx of those "chasing
the cure," especially impoverished patients, still overwhelmed Denver's institutions. Even the Jewish community could not care for the influx of indigent

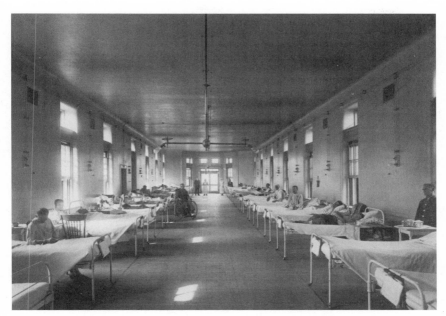

*Men's Tuberculosis Ward of Denver General Hospital (also known as
Denver County Hospital), Denver, Colorado, ca. 1905. Photograph by
Ford Optical Company. Courtesy of Denver Public Library, Western
History Collection, X-28573.*

tubercular sufferers despite establishing two large facilities for the very purpose of providing for impoverished patients. In the end, few beds were available to those unable to pay; the National Jewish Hospital had 149 beds in
1900, the Jewish Consumptives' Relief Society had 140 beds in 1915, the Craig
Colony offered 50 beds in 1915, the Sands House sheltered 18 impoverished
patients in 1915, and both the Evangelical Lutheran Sanitarium and the
Swedish National Sanatorium set aside a varying number of beds for non-
paying consumptive patients. Few public accommodations existed for
Denver's indigent tuberculosis sufferers. The Denver County Poor Farm
housed 25 consumptive patients in a separate building, and the Denver City
and County Hospital set aside 36 beds for tuberculous patients.[84] Thus, the
few hundred beds available to the consumptive poor could not possibly care
for the thousands of "lungers" who flocked to the Queen City each year.

The lack of facilities for both resident and especially nonresident indigent tubercular sufferers meant that consumptive men and women tried to patch together their medical care while somehow sustaining themselves. The nutritious meals, plenty of rest, and close medical supervision offered at local hospitals and sanatoriums were basically off-limits to the vast majority of tubercular sufferers who migrated to Denver with little, if any, savings. As a consequence, poor consumptive sufferers sought out local boarding houses. These inexpensive accommodations were often crowded, poorly ventilated, absent proper sanitation, and likely located in congested neighborhoods suffering the ill effects of industrial pollution. One impoverished tubercular woman, for example, arrived in Denver only able to afford a room in a facility that lacked outdoor sleeping accommodations, a key component, at the time, in fighting tuberculosis. As a result, "she went to the park and stayed in the open all day" and when she was weak, she laid "down on the seats of the street car."[85] Destitute "lungers," in addition, could ill afford the luxury of not working and resting for hours each day for months or even years at a time. Indeed, the consumptive poor had to seek out paid employment in spite of their weakened condition. With "lungers" flocking to Denver, however, the number of jobs suitable for tubercular sufferers, occupations requiring little physical exertion and yet lots of exposure to the outdoors, were scarce. "Denver is no place for tuberculosis patients," observed New York's Edward T. Devine, "who have to earn their living, or who have to live on an income which will not pay for a liberal diet and bright, sunshiny rooms."[86]

These indigent tubercular sufferers who were unable to gain admission to one of the charitable hospitals or sanatoriums overwhelmed Denver's public poor relief. "The tuberculosis problem is always appalling," stated Denver's 1913 Social Welfare Department report. "The expense of caring for tubercular families is heavy out of all proportion to the care of other families, and fraught with serious consequence to the community."[87] In 1920, Denver averaged 1 indigent tubercular person to every 156 city residents. In comparison, Los Angeles averaged 1 indigent tubercular person to every 186 residents, San Antonio averaged 1 to 264, and Cleveland averaged 1 to 231.[88] With such a large number of indigent tubercular persons, it is not surprising that Progressive Era social workers listed tuberculosis as one of Denver's leading causes of poverty. During the years from 1906 through 1910 and from 1915 through 1919, tuberculosis accounted for just over 11 percent of Denver's outdoor poor relief cases and represented the city's fourth leading cause of distress behind only sickness, old age, and unemployment (see Table 15). The percentage of tubercular poor may have been even higher depending on whether officials included tuberculosis cases in the sickness category. In fact, Vaile claimed in 1916 that consumption involved 16 percent of Denver's relief cases.[89] Tuberculosis accounted for so many of Denver's relief recipients that during the late teens or early twenties a single full-time investigator handled only consumptive cases.[90]

Tuberculosis and Expanding the Welfare State

As consumption strained local poor relief resources in Denver and in other western communities, reformers began searching for a solution. At first, local communities and charities tried to discourage migrant indigent tubercular sufferers from coming. Realizing that these local efforts were largely unsuccessful, politicians and reformers from the Southwest turned to the federal government for assistance. In the process of asking the federal government for help, these western Progressives considered proposals that would have radically altered America's welfare state. Denver's Gertrude Vaile exerted an extremely strong influence on the debates concerning nonresident tuberculous patients. Vaile's daily experiences with the city's indigent tubercular sufferers largely shaped her views and ideas about the nation's consumptive problem.

The crux of Denver's tubercular problem lay in the migration of indigent "lungers" to the city chasing a cure. Physicians and charity organizations located in the eastern United States encouraged and often paid for transporting impoverished tubercular patients to Denver. By 1899, the city's charity organization society had become "greatly annoyed by the shipping of people from other cities to our own. . . . We regard this treatment as uncharitable and weak in every way."[91] The Leahy family, for instance, arrived from Buffalo, New York, in 1902 with the husband suffering from "consumption," the wife an "invalid," and the child suffering from "tuberculosis of the brain." Despite their destitute circumstances and ill health, the Leahy family did not want to return to Buffalo.[92] A congregation in Tampa, Florida, to cite another example, sent a dying consumptive, his wife, and his three children to Denver "armed with a letter of introduction recommending them to all charitably inclined people." Upon their arrival, the family went directly from the train depot to Denver's charity office. All agencies refused to provide assistance except for offering to pay for transportation back to Tampa. Like the Leahy family, the family from Florida also refused to return to their place of legal residence.[93] With no power to deport or to hold a community responsible for sending their poor, eventually Denver or one of its local private charities would have to assume some responsibility for the migrant indigent tubercular sufferers that arrived daily.[94]

Realizing the strain that impoverished tubercular arrivals placed on the city's relief programs, Denver's charity leaders used speakers and sent out letters to discourage consumptives from coming. These efforts emphasized that both patients and physicians had placed too much importance on the role of climate and elevation in curing tuberculosis. "Pure air is of no value," stated one such letter, "unless other essentials for proper care . . . food, shelter, and wholesome environment among friends and relatives, freedom from anxiety for the necessities of life" were also present. These campaigns also highlighted the saturated job market, the overwhelmed local charities, the long wait lists at hospitals and sanatoriums that served the needy, and the irresponsibility of groups and physicians who sent advanced tubercular sufferers west when death was all but certain. Finally, speakers and letters urged officials in a patient's hometown to "guarantee" that their indigent consumptive residents would "not become a public charge" for another community.[95] In 1912, Colorado's Board of Charities and Corrections sent out a letter containing these ideas to other states in hopes of preventing indigent tubercular migrants from coming to Colorado. A few years later, Denver's Anti-Tuberculosis Society distributed over ten thousand leaflets, "Why Tuberculosis Persons Without Funds Should Not Leave Home," in Illinois, Georgia, Iowa, Kansas, Minnesota, Oklahoma, and North Carolina.[96]

Despite these efforts, reformers soon called for sweeping changes as the enormous size of the interstate migration of indigent tubercular sufferers to Denver and to the Southwest overwhelmed these local attempts to stem the flow. The National Association for the Study and Prevention of Tuberculosis estimated that between ten to fifteen thousand consumptives annually migrated to the Southwest and West.[97] In hopes of finding ways of "aiding the tuberculous stranger in the Southwest and to discourage further migration of indigent consumptives to southwestern states," Texas Governor O. B. Colquitt invited politicians and reformers to Waco, Texas, in 1912 for the second Southwestern Conference on Tuberculosis. Three of the four resolutions that emerged from the Waco meeting called for an expansion of state power to fight the "white plague." The first resolution simply advocated publicizing the deplorable conditions that impoverished tubercular sufferers found upon their arrival in the Southwest. Next, the conference proposed a number of legislative measures to improve living and working conditions so as to prevent the contraction of tuberculosis. Third, the Waco gathering called upon the legislatures of southwestern states to construct and fund sanatoriums and hospitals for impoverished consumptives. Finally, the conference stated that the migration of indigent tubercular patients was an interstate problem that the federal government should address by maintaining sanatoriums and hospitals in the region.[98]

The notion of federal involvement in caring for the indigent tubercular patient was not a completely new proposal. During the 1899 National Conference of Charities and Corrections, for example, delegates discussed the pros and cons of establishing a government-operated national sanatorium.[99] And in 1908, Frank Bruno, then with the Associated Charities of Colorado Springs, advocated a partnership among states and the federal government in building and maintaining a national sanatorium.[100] The Waco conference, however, succeeded in actually getting a bill sponsored in Congress, the 1914 Shafroth-Callaway Bill. The proposed legislation planned to turn "abandoned military reservations and other government property in the Southwest [into] tuberculosis hospitals for indigent consumptives."[101] The Shafroth-Callaway Bill never passed Congress; but, the act did begin attempts to get the federal government to take some responsibility for the nation's impoverished migrant tubercular sufferers.

Efforts to force the federal government to deal with the problem of indigent migrant consumptives continued in the next few years with what became known as the Kent Bill. Introduced by California Congressman William Kent and by Nebraska Senator George Norris in 1916, the Kent Bill aimed, in short, to reduce the burden that nonresident indigent tubercular sufferers placed on states by having the federal government assume a portion of the cost for their care. The proposed legislation authorized the secretary of the treasury to inspect and to designate certain hospitals and sanatoriums for the care of consumptives while also prescribing standards and methods of treatment. Most important, under the Kent Bill the federal government would pay seventy-five cents a day for the care of each nonresident patient provided that the designated facility also expend an equal amount for the patient's care.

If tubercular sufferers, however, left their legal place of residence for the purpose of taking advantage of the bill, then the seventy-five cent subsidy would be withheld. The federal government also offered to pay for a nonresident patient's return to his or her place of legal residence if they had secured medical treatment back in their home community. Once returning home, the patient would no longer be eligible for the federal subsidies.

The Kent Bill aimed to revolutionize the delivery of aid for tubercular sufferers. The proposed legislation would have addressed one of the main problems in poor relief—the dumping of the poor on other communities. Since the subsidies from the Kent Bill were only for indigent nonresidents, then those states, mainly western ones like Colorado that had become meccas for people chasing a cure for consumption, would have benefited the most from the federal payments. No longer would Denver have to provide for the nation's indigent consumptive on its own. Instead, the federal government, under the Kent Bill, would cover half the costs of a patient's treatment. In addition, the stipulation that the subsidies would not be paid to those purposely leaving their place of legal residence would supposedly aid in curtailing the migration of tubercular sufferers to places like Denver.

The proposed involvement of the federal government in caring for the indigent, albeit only indigent tubercular patients, represented a potentially huge transformation in poor relief. In the past, only with the Freedmen's Bureau following the Civil War had the federal government become involved in supporting the poor absent any service requirement. During the late nineteenth and early twentieth centuries, the federal government did provide military pensions. And while Theda Skocpol has shown that these Civil War pensions became a type of old age and disability relief, supporting one-third of all elderly men living in the North, these pensions nevertheless remained tied, although loosely, to some form of military service by family members.[102] The Kent Bill, however, did not require any type of prior service to receive federal funds. Instead, being poor, a nonresident, and suffering from tuberculosis qualified one for federal aid under the proposed legislation. The Kent Bill would have made the federal government a permanent player in poor relief, and, for the first time since Reconstruction, county and state governments would no longer have to assume the complete burden of supporting the needy.

Yet, despite all the changes and benefits that the Kent Bill would have initiated, the proposed legislation sparked a heated debate among health care providers and social workers. Leading the charge to defeat the bill was none other than Denver's Gertrude Vaile. Through her daily experiences with Denver's relief recipients, Vaile formulated her opposition to the proposed legislation. Physicians who supported the Kent Bill aligned themselves against Vaile. While the two camps were often sharply divided, both sides agreed on the need for the federal government to play a role in helping indigent tubercular sufferers. The actual form of that role, however, separated the two groups.

Those who supported the Kent Bill tended to rest their arguments on an idealistic vision of how society, especially poor relief, operated. Dr. Philip King Brown, medical director of San Francisco's Arequipa Sanatorium, for example, stated that fears of an increase in tubercular migration to health-resort locations due to the Kent Bill were simply unfounded as the "provision was so worded to meet the passing-on method." Any attempts to dump indigent consumptives, according to Brown, "would be too easily detected" and a "few prompt deportations" would quickly discourage any additional dumpings.[103] The issue of a nonresident indigent tubercular sufferer's place of "legal residence" was also a simple issue. For supporters, like Brown and Robert J. Newton, secretary of the Southwestern Conference on Tuberculosis, a person's legal residence boiled down to a clear legal matter. "Consumptives may return to their homes after an absence of years," reassured Newton, "and, if indigent, still receive assistance."[104] Advocates of the Kent Bill based their support on an exaggerated view of the power of laws, especially federal ones, to shape how local communities treated their needy.

Vaile challenged supporters of the Kent Bill by constantly referring to her rich daily experiences in dealing with Denver's indigent tubercular sufferers. Thus, Vaile rested her opposition to the proposed legislation not on theories or ideals but rather on the realities of implementing poor relief policies. Vaile argued, in short, that the Kent Bill would actually increase, not decrease, the burden that indigent consumptives placed on communities in the western United States. Citing how Denver's two national Jewish hospitals had acted like magnets, enticing destitute Jewish consumptives to come to Denver without securing prior admittance to hospitals, Vaile worried that the promise of federal payments would simply reproduce "the Denver Jewish problem on the universal scale of the whole American public" with thousands upon thousands flocking to the West searching for a cure. Vaile also argued that the Kent Bill's provision to protect against migration by denying benefits to those who purposely left their place of legal residence was completely "worthless."

It would be impossible, stated Vaile, to prove or to disprove the reasons for a person's migration. Likewise, the notion of returning consumptives to their place of legal residence after months or even years of treatment seemed equally unrealistic to her. Vaile in fact agreed with the general principle of returning tubercular patients to their legal residence, but her experiences had shown that communities simply would not extend assistance to those who had left for treatment. "I can find no way," wrote Vaile, "by which a patient who goes away from home for his health can secure the right to return home after a year and receive relief, no matter how desperately he may desire to do so."[105] And why, asked Vaile, should Colorado pay for half of the care for a patient from another state. Instead, that person's place of legal residence should pay for treatment.[106]

But Vaile's strongest objection to the Kent Bill rested with the limited nature of the subsidies. Under the proposed legislation, federal subsidies paid seventy-five cents per day for the care of only the patient. Vaile, coming from a social work background, pointed out that "the family dependent upon the patient" actually became the heaviest financial burden for charities. The Kent Bill, however, made no provisions to provide for these dependents, usually wives and children. These dependent family members represented a huge responsibility that could last for years. By not acknowledging these dependents, argued Vaile, the Kent Bill actually miscalculated the true cost that nonresident tubercular sufferers placed on health-resort communities like Denver.[107]

While Vaile criticized the Kent Bill, she also offered solutions to the problem. Vaile would not accept the argument that she should support the measure simply because it was the best "we can get" or that it represented "the beginning of federal activity in the national fight against tuberculosis."[108] At first, she advocated that states should adopt uniform settlement laws that would "determine the conditions under which a person is legally eligible for public aid."[109] Quickly, Vaile abandoned this solution, and instead she proposed an even greater increase in the federal government's responsibility than what the Kent Bill offered. Vaile suggested reversing the Kent Bill, giving aid "not in the care of non-residents, but of residents." This simple change, Vaile believed, would be "a strong incentive for tuberculous persons to stay at home" and thus reduce the migration of indigent consumptives to places like Denver. Vaile even succeeded in having Colorado Congressman Benjamin Hilliard introduce a bill that contained her ideas.[110]

Proponents of the Kent Bill rallied support for the measure by pointing to the medical benefits of the proposed legislation. The standardization in treating tubercular patients through inspections and certifications of hospitals by the U. S. Public Health Service drew praise among many doctors. In a sense, the Kent Bill would professionalize the treatment of tuberculosis. Most important to Dr. Wilbur A. Sawyer, secretary of California's State Board of Health and testifying before the Senate's Committee on Public Health and National Quarantine, was "that the institutions which will receive this subsidy shall attain certain standards in regard to equipment and diet and care and conduct and cleanliness and cheerfulness, and so on."[111]

Supporters of the Kent Bill used their status as physicians to attack Vaile and her views. Brown, for example, seemed irritated, if not insulted, that Vaile had defined the problem of indigent tubercular sufferers as a poor relief issue. Consumption, according to Brown, was a "fundamental public health problem" as tuberculosis was a communicable disease. "The problem is not," wrote Brown, "as indicated by Miss Vaile's objections, primarily one of social relief, care of ex-patients and dependent families, but one which must be seen first in its relation to public health." According to Brown, "it certainly is not the [federal] government's job to provide charitable relief" as Vaile had suggested. Brown instead argued for a narrow, medical definition of the tubercular issue. "Any problem concerned primarily with a disease," wrote Brown, "is concerned on its remedial side first and most urgently with measures for the eradication of that disease in the swiftest and most effective way."[112]

Brown's efforts to define the debate as a strictly medical issue highlighted a gender division between the two groups. Brown, and other male doctors, clearly preferred a narrow "scientific" approach that focused solely on the patient. By concentrating on the patient, the medical establishment devoted their skills and attention to, in most cases, the family's male head of household. The seventy-five cent payments would go to care for indigent consumptives who were mainly male. Meanwhile, Vaile's focus on the dependents reflected the outlook of female social workers who examined problems from a broader social perspective. Vaile understood that the Kent Bill would only partially address the suffering caused by tuberculosis since dependents received no assistance. Brown clearly thought little of the largely female-dominated social work profession. He dismissed Vaile's objections to the Kent Bill in a condescending manner as "solely from the social worker's viewpoint." In addition, Brown went on to belittle Vaile by portraying her as intellectually incompetent. Vaile's positions were, according to Brown, "beclouded with alarmist hysteria" and filled with "misconceptions and delusions."[113]

In the end, the Kent Bill failed to win approval. While the proposed legislation did receive the support of the National Tuberculosis Association, Treasury Secretary William McAdoo, Surgeon General Dr. Rupert Blue, and numerous charity boards, it never obtained widespread support among western states, except for California. Vaile's efforts seemed to have played an important part, if not the most important part, in the bill's defeat. "Miss Vaile has made a gallant fight against the bill," observed Newton, "and to her must go the credit if it fails."[114] In addition to publishing in the pages of the *Survey*, Vaile also expressed her views of the bill's deficiencies by writing to senators and congressmen and by engaging in debates at the National Tuberculosis Association Conference and the Southwestern Tuberculosis Conference. Even though the Kent Bill would have greatly expanded the role of the state in caring for the poor, that expansion was too small and misdirected to appease Vaile and most western states. Hilliard's bill, the proposal containing Vaile's idea of federal payments for the care of resident indigent consumptive patients, also met defeat.

Progressive Era attempts to alter the treatment of needy tubercular patients failed as indigent consumptive sufferers experienced no significant change in their care. Impoverished tubercular men and women continued to migrate to Denver and the Southwest even after the defeat of the Kent Bill. And health-resort communities continued to struggle with the influx of "lungers." "The disease is widely prevalent in our homes and our industries," reported Denver's Anti-Tuberculosis Society in 1919 and "there is practically no supervision or control of this infectious disease." The city still had few beds for indigent tubercular sufferers. Attempts to establish a three-hundred bed municipal tuberculosis sanatorium in 1919 failed when Denver's voters narrowly defeated the bond issue. A small conciliatory victory, however, was achieved when the city council appropriated fifty thousand dollars for a one-hundred bed tubercular addition to Denver's County Hospital.[115] By 1920, Denver's indigent consumptives, both residents and nonresidents, had witnessed only minor changes in their circumstances.

Local conditions in Denver, as in the other counties, shaped how the city distributed its aid. Gertrude Vaile's reform ideas, especially her notion that public welfare needed to adopt private charity practices, heavily affected the city's attempts to reshape its relief program. Vaile wanted to take a system of aid based on what she perceived to be outdated and ineffective methods of assistance and transform it into one the nation's most modern welfare operations. Vaile aimed to end the practice of simply giving poor residents a set amount of food and coal without trying to address the cause of their poverty. She wanted to use individual casework methods and a professionalized staff to create an efficient and humane relief system that would seek solutions to people's poverty as well as end any waste and corruption. Yet budget restraints, political resistance, and the inability to offer the city's poor anything other than the existing dole, all contributed in restricting the success of Vaile's changes to the administrative level only. Of course the influx of indigent tubercular migrants to Denver overwhelmed the community's resources. This seemingly unending stream of ill, needy people molded Vaile's proposals, especially her call for federal assistance to help pay for the care of resident tuberculous patients. But Vaile's idea, as well as the Kent Bill, went down in defeat, leaving "lungers" with no new options for aid. In the end, despite numerous and ambitious attempts at welfare reform, Denver's poor citizens experienced few permanent alterations in how they encountered the city's delivery of outdoor relief during the Progressive Era.

Local circumstances also affected the use and existence of charitable institutions and private charities. Some counties simply had no institutions or strong private charities, while other communities had an extensive array of publicly and privately operated facilities and organizations. How officials and residents of each locale utilized these different options varied considerably. Some groups avoided using institutions, while others embraced them. Each county's institutions developed differently. County poor farms, for instance, took on very unique characteristics that tended to reflect a community's resources, values, and attitudes toward relief. At times, the division between public relief and private aid appeared almost seamless, with an endless blurring of funding and responsibilities. Just as dramatic differences appear with how each county operated its outdoor aid, equally as stark differences also surface when examining the use of charitable institutions and private charities.

Poor Farms, County Hospitals, and Private Aid

ON JULY 12, 1913, WILLIAM THOMAS, SECRETARY OF THE STATE BOARD OF Charities and Corrections, visited Boulder County's poor farm. Thomas routinely made unannounced inspections of various benevolent institutions and organizations. On this particular day, he did not like what he saw: "Cannot say that this visit was satisfactory." Boulder County commissioners had failed to act upon Thomas' recommendations from his previous inspection. The dining room still lacked any windows, the kitchen still needed ventilation as it was "warm to suffocation," and the laundry appliances were still "insufficient." Despite these shortcomings in the poor farm's structural features, the relaxed management of the facility seemed to most disturb Thomas. Poor farm occupants, for example, were responsible for keeping "the dormitories in order." Thomas believed that "the class of men who drift into these institutions [were] mighty poor housekeepers" with the result that some aspects of the poor farm fell below acceptable standards. Still, the housekeeping skills of one resident did impress him. "Strange to say," reported Thomas, "the one who keeps his place cleanest is blind."[1]

Alice Fulton, the new secretary, spent the day, March 8, 1918, once again inspecting Boulder County's charitable facilities. This time, she visited the privately operated Associated Charities of Boulder (AC). The efficient organization of the AC deeply impressed her. "I found the Charities Rooms most interesting to observe," stated Fulton, as each room appeared "wonderfully systematized." The first room contained hats, shoes, undergarments, other clothing, and supplies. The next room consisted of "two generous closets and rows of shelves filled with all kinds of home made jellies, jams, preserves, vegetables, and every sort of delicacy required by the sick."[2] The Associated Charities seemed to represent the exact opposite of the county farm. Precise organization and order characterized the AC while informality typified the county poor farm. The president of the AC summed up the society's approach toward relief: "Let charity abound," stated Dr. Frank Burdick, "nevertheless, let it be scientific."[3]

The Boulder County Poor Farm and the Associated Charities of Boulder seemingly represent the differences between public and private aid. Public money from the county commissioners funded the poor farm, and public officials oversaw its operation. The poor farm cared for some of the county's most needy residents in an institutional environment, albeit a loosely structured one. Private citizens, on the other hand, organized, managed, and raised funds for the AC. Unlike the poor farm, the AC gave assistance within poor people's homes by giving them food or clothing.

The differences between public and private welfare organizations, and whether they provide institutional, indoor aid, or outdoor, in-home aid, have divided the field of social welfare history. Scholars, for the most part, have tended to focus on only one type of relief, a particular institution or program, while disregarding other forms of assistance.[4] The need to keep research projects manageable largely dictates this choice to limit the field of investigation. Yet, this tight focus makes little sense when trying to examine how an entire community grappled with caring for its needy citizens. Each type of assistance contributed to a community's overall relief strategy. The exclusion of any one form of welfare creates a glaring gap in the analysis of options available to the needy. Plus, from a poor person's point of view, these divisions would seem too rigid and too artificial. As an individual's circumstances changed, the type of relief, be it public, private, institutional, or in-home, may have also changed depending on a person's needs. As historian Michael Katz has pointed out, the division between private and public relief remains unsatisfactory as the "relations with each other have remained tangled" and "difficult if not impossible to dissect."[5] Thus, in order to understand fully how poor folk experienced relief, an examination of all forms of welfare available to them is required.

This chapter will explore how local conditions shaped a community's private relief societies, both outdoor and indoor, and charitable institutions, both private and public, in all six counties and on the Ute Mountain Ute Indian Reservation. Settlement patterns, time of settlement, population densities, and cultural preferences, to cite just a few influences, all played an important role in determining both the presence or absence of private charities or institutions and the use of these facilities. Likewise, decisions made by officials, such as whether or not to build a poor farm or a county hospital, how to manage the facility, and how much to fund the institution, all contributed toward giving each community a distinctive relief strategy. As a result, poor farms and county hospitals became either valued or marginal facilities depending on local policies. At some established institutions, existing problems such as overcrowding heavily dictated decisions. The type of relationship, an informal or a more formal one, that existed between private and public assistance also structured a community's aid. The close cooperation between private and public welfare providers in some locales challenges arguments of an expansion of state responsibility during the Progressive Era. Instead of indicating an expansion of welfare services, the Progressive Era, at best, signifies a consolidation of state responsibilities in urban areas. In rural communities, however, public assistance essentially maintained its role as the dominant form of relief. By the end of the Progressive Era, poor residents, for a number of reasons, would have noticed few changes in their encounters with private charities or institutions supported by private or public funds.

Philanthropic Societies and Institutional Use in Rural Communities

Even though Costilla, Lincoln, and Montezuma Counties were all largely rural, how these communities created and used private charities and institutions varied considerably. Lincoln and Montezuma failed to sustain any private charities, but Costilla's residents managed to support one. All three counties did share an absence of any private institutions located within their boundaries. Yet, how officials and citizens from each locale viewed and utilized facilities outside their own county once again differed substantially. And on the Ute Mountain Reservation the use of a hospital created a cultural battle. In the end, several differences characterize how these sparsely populated communities used private charities and institutions.

For two of the counties, Lincoln and Montezuma, private aid generally did not exist as citizens failed to maintain any type of philanthropic society geared toward helping the poor. This absence of private assistance helps to explain, in part, why public relief payments were so high in Lincoln and Montezuma Counties (see Table 2). Public aid, as previously mentioned, essentially supported the poor in both places. For Lincoln and Montezuma, the recent arrival of most homesteaders, the difficulty in establishing a home, the dispersed settlement patterns, and the small number of residents all hindered the establishment of private charity organizations.

Settlers had only just begun to establish themselves in Lincoln and Montezuma Counties during the turn of the century. Most of these recent arrivals poured almost all of their time, energy, and resources into setting up their dry farms in the region's harsh conditions. Lincoln's Glen R. Durrell remembered how his family lived in a tent for their first summer and fall because getting a crop planted and a fence constructed "were more immediate considerations than housing." Only after the family completed fencing and planting did they build a dugout to spend the winter in.[6] Settlers like the Durrell family struggled immensely just to carve out a secure foothold on the land. They obviously had little time to spare for establishing and maintaining philanthropic societies.

Even building and sustaining places of worship, usually the foundation for most private charities at the time, had generally only just started by the late nineteenth and early twentieth centuries. During the early 1900s, most of Lincoln's congregations consisted of only a few families meeting in a home or a schoolhouse and were often part of a circuit or mission. By the mid-teens, many of these groups had raised enough money to build a small church. The Methodist Church in Hugo, for instance, consisted of only forty-three members by 1908, yet six years later they had constructed their first church.[7] Since settlers arrived earlier in Montezuma than in Lincoln, churches developed at an earlier date. Mormons opened their first house of worship in 1886, and three years later citizens built a Congregational Church in Cortez.[8] But like Lincoln, Montezuma's churches had small congregations.

Besides the late settlement and the embryonic nature of churches, the widely dispersed population in each county also hindered philanthropic activity. Farming and ranching operations, as already mentioned, dominated both Lincoln and Montezuma Counties. The need for large amounts of land for survival meant residents were often spread out with rather long distances separating neighbors. "This country was once open, bare range," remembered Lincoln's Joe Cooper, "with only a few cabins of the few homesteaders to mar its loneliness." Poor road conditions or a lack of roads made travel among neighbors difficult and time consuming. Cooper recalled having trouble even locating his 1909 homestead claim since there were "no roads or any trails."[9] Thus while neighbors did congregate for cherished social occasions—dances, debate clubs, religious revivals, holiday picnics, and dinners—the distance and difficulty required to gather placed a burden on even starting, much less maintaining, philanthropic societies.[10]

The relatively low number of residents in Lincoln and Montezuma Counties further compounded the problem of establishing private charities. Not only were settlers widely scattered, but each county also lacked any sizable towns. Montezuma's county seat and largest community, Cortez, numbered only 565 residents in 1910. Ten years later, Cortez had actually decreased to 541 inhabitants. At the same time, Lincoln's county seat, Hugo, had only 343 residents in 1910 and 838 by 1920 (see Table 1). Limon, Lincoln's largest town, meanwhile, totaled 534 inhabitants in 1910 and a decade later had 1,047 residents.[11] Both Lincoln and Montezuma simply lacked the critical population mass needed to sustain philanthropic societies. Communities, in fact, struggled to operate the bare institutional necessities, and even these few establishments often limped along. The Liberty Baptist Church just south of Hugo, for instance, folded less than ten years after opening its doors. When Hugo finally received its first full-time Roman Catholic priest in 1923, Fr. Michael Hogan largely supported himself by farming and by operating a filling station.[12]

Not all rural counties, however, failed to sustain philanthropic societies. In Costilla County, as previously discussed, the Penitentes played an important, and crucial, role in supporting the needy. Costilla's ability to maintain the Penitentes rested on many of the same factors that were absent from both Lincoln and Montezuma Counties. Non-Indian settlers began to arrive in Costilla in the late 1840s and early 1850s, several decades prior to widespread settlement of Lincoln and Montezuma. By the turn of the century, Costilla's residents had already securely established their homes, their farms, as well as their community resources such as irrigation ditches, schools, churches, and *moradas*, the windowless meeting halls of the Penitentes. As a result, citizens of Costilla could devote their time, energy, and resources to concerns beyond their immediate survival, unlike the homesteaders in Lincoln and Montezuma Counties who struggled to hold on to their land claims.

Costilla's settlement pattern also helps to explain its ability to maintain a philanthropic organization like the Penitentes. Early arrivals to what became Costilla County generally clustered buildings tightly together as a means of protection from Ute and Apache raids. These first settlements, situated along the Rio Culebra for irrigation purposes, were relatively close to one another.[13] In addition, as families subdivided vara strips for their heirs, closely clustered family groups developed over time.[14] So while Costilla's towns remained small and the county kept low population levels like Lincoln and Montezuma, the clustering of settlements within a few miles of one another made it easier for residents to gather to sustain private charity work.

More important, Costilla was a far more unified community than either Lincoln or Montezuma Counties. Although Lincoln and Montezuma were overwhelmingly Protestant and different denominations did often share resources, disagreements over religious beliefs still divided both communities. One attempt in Lincoln County to hold a nondenominational Sunday school, for example, lasted for several years until discord over the use of interdenominational literature closed the school.[15] Lincoln and Montezuma residents divided resources to build and maintain separate places of worship. And the very act of homesteading prioritized individual success and advancement. In Costilla County, however, residents primarily practiced the same religion, Catholicism, allowing community resources to be directed toward a single unified purpose. The existence of communal lands (La Vega and La Sierra), a subsistence and barter economy, and an extensive community-built and operated irrigation system in Costilla required greater cooperation and unity than did homesteading. Costilla's unity, both religious and economic, made it easier for residents to support the Penitentes' good deeds.

Different local circumstances, no doubt, contributed to the presence or absence of philanthropic societies in Costilla, Lincoln, and Montezuma Counties; nevertheless, the three communities did share an absence of any privately funded or maintained charitable facilities. There were no orphanages, homes for wayward children, benevolent institutions caring for elderly or disabled adults, or hospitals operated by religious or ethnic groups. Nor did there exist any publicly funded county hospitals in any of the three communities. Two of the counties, Costilla and Lincoln, did not open a poor farm, and Montezuma's attempt to operate one was intermittent, at best, and largely unsuccessful (we will examine Montezuma's poor farm later in this chapter). For the most part then, Costilla, Lincoln, and Montezuma neither housed nor maintained any benevolent institutions, whether supported by private or public funds.

Small populations in each locale largely accounted for this absence of charitable institutions. Costilla, Lincoln, and Montezuma simply had too few residents to construct, maintain, or even occupy orphanages or hospitals. But the absence of charitable facilities does not mean that residents did not access these types of services outside of their counties. In fact, county commissioners often paid to support residents in institutions located in nearby communities. Not all groups or counties, however, utilized these neighboring charitable institutions in the same manner.

In Costilla, a clear split emerged between how Hispanic and non-Hispanic residents used benevolent institutions. From 1891 to 1906 and from 1913 to 1919, county commissioners did not pay for a single Hispanic resident to use an institution, including hospitals. Discrimination seems an unlikely explanation for this trend as Hispanics were almost always represented on the County Commissioner Board, and, more importantly, there is no evidence of commissioners turning down a request to support an impoverished Hispanic resident in an institution. Instead, cultural preferences appear to best account for this avoidance of benevolent facilities. Family members in Costilla, as observed earlier, played a key role in caring for the community's needy, with relatives assisting most of the county's paupers in some "small way."[16] This tight kinship network kept the poor, including those that might have used institutions, in the community. Instead of sending the ill, the aged, and the disabled to institutions outside of the county, they remained in Costilla under the watchful eye of local relatives. This cultural preference to care for the poor and sick at home parallels practices found in New Mexico, where most of Costilla's Hispanic families originated. In 1910, New Mexico remained the only state that did not maintain a single almshouse or poor farm.[17] Thus, the absence of an almshouse or poor farm in Costilla and the avoidance of institutions reflect a cultural practice of depending on families to care for and maintain their own needy, disabled, and ill relatives.

In contrast, Costilla's non-Hispanic population did use benevolent facilities; county commissioners supported C. L. Cowgill, Elizabeth Holmes, and Annie Mapes in institutions. Cowgill appears to have stayed in an unidentified hospital for almost five years during the 1890s, at a cost to the county of $1,765. Years later, Costilla County paid for both Holmes and Mapes to receive care at the Woodcroft Hospital for the insane located in Pueblo.[18] But commissioners were no longer willing to support residents for long durations in an institution, as they had done with Cowgill. When Dr. Hubert Work of Woodcroft Hospital reported in February 1917 that Holmes's mental condition was "getting worse," commissioners informed Holmes's father that the county would "no longer bear the expense of keeping" his daughter at the facility.[19] Costilla County seemed willing to fund those who wanted institutional help but only for short periods.

County commissioners from Lincoln and Montezuma sent residents to institutions far more frequently than did officials from Costilla. Of the three counties, Lincoln most aggressively used institutions outside its boundaries. From 1909 to 1922 Lincoln officials sent just over 17 percent of its total relief cases to hospitals, while 7.5 percent of Montezuma's poor relief recipients from 1901 to 1919 used institutions.[20] Lincoln mainly sent its aged, ill, and injured to Denver's City and County Hospital or to St. Anthony's Hospital run by the Sisters of Saint Francis in Denver. Michael Ewright, for example, went to St. Anthony's due to old age, while typhoid caused Alfred Kuruse to go to Denver's City and County Hospital.[21] Montezuma commissioners paid for care at Mercy Hospital, operated by the Sisters of Mercy, located in nearby Durango. Mrs. Cunningham, for instance, went to Mercy Hospital for her cancer, and Thomas Hesherington also went there after a horse kicked him.[22] Montezuma's commissioners even made use of more distant institutions by paying the transportation costs for Stout Atherton to go to the Soldiers' Home in Leavenworth, Kansas and for Helen Rosana Broan to go to the State Home and Training School for Mental Defectives in Wheatridge.[23] Lincoln and Montezuma commissioners, and the poor themselves, unlike in Costilla, regularly sought out the professional expertise that institutions offered as a legitimate means to solve problems.

The Utes had a very different experience with institutional help than did other Colorado residents. Institutional use on the Ute Mountain Reservation, specifically hospital use, became a cultural battleground between Native Americans and federal officials. As historian Robert A. Trennert has shown with the Navajo peoples, western medicine became another tool to assimilate native populations. While the desire to improve the health of Indians partially motivated the use of western medicine, medical care became "involved with the government's determination to destroy native culture and replace it with values of white America." The medical policies of the Office of Indian Affairs, argues Trennert, aimed "to demonstrate the superiority of Anglo-European culture," as well as "to minister to the sick."[24]

Events on the Ute Mountain Reservation offered no exception to this pattern. The presence of medicine men on the reservation remained a sensitive issue throughout the period. "The greatest difficulty as to health and matters pertaining to sickness," reported one Ute Mountain superintendent, "is the Indian Medicine Man. He must and will be eradicated."[25] Superintendents expected the contracted physician to lead the charge against medicine men. "The most important proposition for the Medical Man on this reservation," wrote superintendent U. L. Clardy, "is to oppose in some substantial way the Indian Medicine Man."[26] Yet, despite such bold statements medicine men remained extremely influential among the Weeminuches. In 1917, superintendent Alfred H. Symons observed that the "medicine men here have a wonderful hold on this tribe of Indians."[27]

Even the opening of a hospital in 1921 had little effect on the situation. Getting the Weeminuches to utilize the newly built hospital proved difficult, as the use of the institution quickly became a cultural tug-of-war. "There are many of their superstitions and customs which tend to prevent the maximum use-fulness of the hospital," wrote the 1922 superintendent. Not only did medicine men disapprove of the hospital, but Utes themselves would only use the facility if there was "no chance to get well."[28] In the 1930s, male Utes often fled the hospital if a woman was giving birth, and, according to Weeminuches, "deaths occurring in the hospital made the institution unfit for habitation."[29] Most Weeminuches continued to rely, at least partially, on medicine men for assistance regardless of the hospital's presence.

Besides this cultural conflict, the hesitation to use western medicine seems to have also rested on the inadequacy of services provided. Often, doctors employed by the Office of Indian Affairs were corrupt, lazy, and incompetent.[30] During the early twentieth century, for example, a Cortez druggist cared for the medical needs of the Weeminuches. "He staked his reputation as a medical man," reported superintendent Stacher, "mainly to the use of 45-caliber compound cathartic pills. It was not long until the

Indians dubbed him 'the pill doctor,' or something worse."[31] Superintendent Clardy described the efforts of the 1911 physician as "the most perfunctory kind."[32] The reliability of medical care also created obstacles. For Ute Mountain Utes, medical services, beginning in 1909, consisted mainly of weekly visits from a contracted doctor from Cortez.[33] The frequency of visitations varied considerably over the next decade. In 1910, for example, the lack of a saddle horse limited the physician's mobility; at other times, roads were impassable, and in the summer of 1920, no physician served the reservation.[34] Due to the long time between visits, follow-up treatment became problematic.[35] Thus, Weeminuches continued using medicine men well into the twentieth century, long after physicians began serving the reservation.[36]

Utes did seek out western medical care, however, if they believed that it was reliable, or at least somewhat creditable. Superintendent Stacher recalled Tom Root coming to him for help with an illness and thanking him later for his successful recovery.[37] Superintendents realized a relationship existed between competent medical personnel and the Utes' willingness to access medical services. "The Indians have great confidence in the physician," stated superintendent Symons, and two years later, superintendent Axel Johnson noticed that the field matron, a type of social worker or nurse on many reservations, had gained the confidence of Ute women.[38] During the mid-1920s, superintendent Edward E. McKean observed that if "competent physicians are available . . . Indians are very willing and anxious to patronize them."[39] The Weeminuches' willingness, or unwillingness, to utilize the reservation's hospital or other western medical services clearly rested, in part, on a physician's competency. Indeed, how communities, including the Utes, used charitable institutions depended on a range of local variables.

County Poor Farms and County Hospitals

While commissioners in Lincoln and Costilla did not maintain any publicly funded facilities for the poor, such as a county hospital or a county poor farm, the four remaining communities did. Montezuma opened a poor farm in 1913, Boulder operated a poor farm and later constructed a poorhouse/hospital, and Teller maintained a hospital. Denver, which we will examine later in this chapter, funded a range of institutions, including a sizable poor farm and a large hospital. Of Colorado's sixty counties in 1910, only eighteen maintained either a poor farm, or a hospital, or both.[40] Local circumstances influenced not only how these different publicly funded institutions served their communities but also each facility's characteristics. For some counties, Boulder and Teller for example, these facilities played an important part in local strategies to care for the poor, usually in a respectful manner, while in Montezuma the publicly maintained poor farm served few needy residents and did so in a generally unsatisfactory way.

Examining county hospitals and county poor farms can become a messy endeavor since these institutions were constantly changing. What may be a poorly maintained facility one year may in the next few years become a model operation. Five years after William Thomas' disappointing visit to the Boulder County poor farm, for instance, the State Board of Charities and Corrections was now "glad to commend the management" of the same poor farm.[41] Changes in personnel and policies could transform an institution from a highly controlling one to a loosely operating place or vice versa almost overnight. What may be a perfectly suitable living environment for one resident may seem unacceptable and oppressive for another occupant. Over time, commissioners devoted varying amounts of attention and resources to these facilities, which could quickly alter the nature of these institutions. Because of this constant state of flux, it is extremely difficult to generalize about conditions found in county poor farms or hospitals. To characterize these facilities as historian Alan Derickson does as places where "inmates surrendered all independence" or where "institutionalization meant disgrace" simply misses the complexity and fluidity of county poor farms and county hospitals.[42] In Boulder, Montezuma, and Teller Counties, these facilities received both praise and criticism.

Poor farms or almshouses originated in the early nineteenth century as an inexpensive means to both serve the poor and to discourage dependency or pauperism. In many ways, these supposedly self-supporting poor farms served contradictory purposes. These institutions aimed to care humanely for those "deserving" poor folk who could not maintain an independent existence. Yet, poor farms also hoped to discourage their own use by creating such harsh living conditions that applicants would not want to reside there. Poor farms, for example, required occupants to work and provided only the basic necessities.[43] The problem, of course, became balancing humane treatment while maintaining less than desirable living conditions.

This balancing act persisted, in a slightly modified form, well into the twentieth century, posing a dilemma for officials. During unannounced inspections of county farms, members of the State Board of Charities and Corrections constantly stressed the need for better bedding, housing, food preparation, and more attention to residents' care. In short, the board aimed to improve the general living conditions and treatment of poor farm occupants. At the same time, however, board members, and other Progressive Era reformers, were concerned about increasing the efficiency of public institutions like poor farms. Although Progressives no longer viewed work by poor farm residents as a way to "punish" inhabitants as during the nineteenth century, they still viewed work as one way to improve efficiency. As a result, authorities consistently commented on the amount of work, or more accurately the lack of work, that poor farm occupants performed. "Inmates are employed when able, but these are few," reported Thomas on a visit to Boulder's poor farm.[44] "Every inmate [at the Denver County poor farm] who can be kept busy should be kept busy" as there are "plenty of odd jobs to do."[45] One proposal even suggested that Denver's poor farm residents be given "small tracts of land to care for and to cultivate, according to their strength and ability."[46] Overall, the state's Board of Charities and Corrections concluded that "little is done with inmate labor at these institutions."[47] Trying to increase the amount of work that poor farm residents performed without eroding the living standards or the humane treatment of occupants became a challenge that the board never seemed able to resolve.

Montezuma County provides an excellent example of the difficulties in balancing a poor farm's competing purposes. In December 1913, Montezuma County commissioners appropriated four thousand dollars to purchase 160 acres and several buildings to serve as the county's poor farm. Prior to purchasing the land, Montezuma had, like Costilla and Lincoln, only provided outdoor aid and occasionally sent impoverished residents to institutions beyond its boundaries. The exact reasons for establishing Montezuma's poor farm remain a bit unclear. Officials initially stated that "in the opinion of the Board of County Commissioners an emergency exists," but no evidence indicates any type of crisis.[48] Instead, an attempt to save money seems to have motivated the commissioners.[49] These cost-saving calculations, however, proved terribly wrong as the poor farm rapidly drained funds from the treasury. Just four months after the purchase, commissioners had to transfer one thousand dollars to cover poor farm expenses.[50] Soon the phrase "there are not sufficient funds in the Poor Farm Fund," began appearing regularly in county records as commissioners continually struggled to cover the farm's bills.[51]

The purchase of the poor farm and its expenses quickly became a political issue. "Poor investment was the poor farm, surely," stated the *Montezuma Journal*.[52] The farm's mounting costs as well as allegations of using the poor farm to funnel county business to a commissioner's store persisted for the next two years.[53] The poor farm scandal and other accusations of financial shenanigans finally led citizens to elect an entire new slate of county officials in 1916. Much to the satisfaction of the *Montezuma Journal* "housecleaning in Montezuma county was most complete."[54] Yet, despite the electoral sweep, the poor farm remained in operation.

While Montezuma's political leaders fought, the poor farm, located five miles southwest of Cortez, already housed some of the county's needy. Although the "land appear[ed] to be productive and fairly well tilled," living conditions at the farm were clearly inadequate. "Stoves, oil lamps, bedding and everything about the premises," according to Thomas, "presented an uninviting appearance, to say the least." Thomas went on to write that the "housekeeping is manifestly indifferent,—there being a total absence of a homelike and comfortable atmosphere in any part of the premises."[55] Recommendations to improve the poor farm started with the very basics. "The house now occupied should be stripped of all rubbish and thoroughly cleaned," the "kitchen should be . . . remodled," the first-story floor "should be relaid," and "the entire premises should be scrupulously neat and clean."[56]

The inadequate conditions found on Montezuma's poor farm were not surprising. Given that a desire to save money seemed to be the sole justification for the farm's existence, it was not unexpected that commissioners would be hesitant to invest in the farm. And accusations of political wrongdoing only intensified public scrutiny of poor farm expenditures. The *Montezuma Journal* reported that the "poor farm cost the tax payers $280.92 in July," and a week later the paper estimated that the farm "will cost the tax payers $3,500 a year the way thing[s] are now going."[57] This type of public attention only further dampened any attempts to spend money to improve conditions at the farm. When Thomas visited the poor farm once again, two years later, commissioners had acted upon few, if any, of his suggestions. He described the place as "dirty" with "a neglected frame dwelling house and some squalid looking out-buildings." Thomas concisely summed up the Montezuma County poor farm as "an unlovely place."[58]

Montezuma's poor farm, for the most part, did not even provide proper care for its occupants. The poor farm's superintendent, observed Thomas, remained "indifferent" as he did not closely look after inhabitants.[59] Poor farm residents, in fact, seemed responsible for their own basic upkeep and maintenance. Thus, the farm could not serve those unable to care for themselves. County physician Dr. E. E. Johnson appeared before the Montezuma County commissioners in December 1914, for instance, to argue that Mr. W. M. McCormick could not "receive proper care" at the poor farm. He recommended that officials move McCormick to Durango's Mercy Hospital "where he can have the proper care."[60] Yet, not everyone disapproved of the poor farm's living conditions. In fact, one 1916 resident, William Pratt, was quite happy with what the farm had to offer. Pratt, age seventy-seven, lived "by himself in a dirty little cabin, happy and contented" on the poor farm, and he "would tolerate no interference with his dirty comfort," according to Thomas.[61]

Regardless of William Pratt's happiness, few poor folk ever lived on Montezuma's poor farm. Although the farm had beds for five county charges, usually only two or three residents inhabited the poor farm at any one time.[62] In 1915, though, the State Board of Charities and Corrections reported that for a while no one resided on the farm.[63] Payments to the superintendent of the poor farm, between twelve to fifteen dollars per month for each person boarded, restricted the farm's use.[64] Commissioners agreed in January 1915, for example, to remove Georgia Denby, her children, and two other children from the poor farm. Deserted by her husband, Denby struggled to support her "large family" so commissioners decided to pay Denby thirty dollars per month "to provide board and care" for herself, her children, and the other children instead of residing at the poor farm.[65] This arrangement not only gave Denby a way to maintain a portion of her independence, but, and possibly more important from the commissioners' view, the arrangement also saved the county money as it was cheaper to pay Denby than to pay the superintendent for boarding each person. Montezuma's poor farm never seemed to succeed in any area. The farm served few people, proved costly to the public treasury, contributed to political divisions, and failed to provide adequately for its occupants. And yet, the county government insisted on its continuation.

Boulder County's use of its poor farm and hospital facilities offers a very different story than Montezuma County. Boulder's poor farm was both larger and more stable than Montezuma's, playing a key role in the county's relief strategies, and even becoming an important element in the community's social fabric. In addition to its poor farm, Boulder had a unique arrangement with the University of Colorado to use campus medical facilities to care for the county's impoverished injured and ill.

Over many years, Boulder County operated various types and combinations of poor farms, poorhouses, and county hospitals. During the 1870s, the county rented several different houses to serve as county hospitals, or poorhouses, or both. By the early 1880s, officials had constructed a wood-framed hospital, which fire eventually destroyed in 1888, almost killing four occupants. Two years later, the county erected a brick building to serve the medical requirements of the community's needy. In 1902, county commissioners sold the brick building and purchased a 120-acre plot near the town of Valmont to house a new county poor farm. The poor farm near Valmont would serve the county's needy until 1918 when commissioners sold the farm and constructed a combined county hospital and poorhouse on the outskirts of the city of Boulder.[66] This long experience with building and operating various public institutions allowed Boulder County to avoid some of the mistaken expectations that plagued Montezuma's efforts. Turn-of-the-century Boulder understood that these institutions could be both costly and successful when serving those in need. And Boulder's population in 1910, more than six times larger than Montezuma's, provided sufficient clientele to sustain the various institutions (see Table 1).

During most of the Progressive Era, the 120-acre poor farm near Valmont cared for Boulder County's needy residents. Located about five miles northeast of the city of Boulder, the farm cultivated one hundred acres while the remaining twenty acres housed buildings, roads, and "eight cows" that supplied "milk and butter for the institution."[67] The poor farm's agricultural production received praise when it won over a dozen awards at the 1915 Boulder County Fair.[68] In 1902 when the county purchased the land, a two-story farmhouse and several farm buildings sat on the property.[69] Two years later, the county added a two-story dormitory to board residents. With the dormitory, Boulder's poor farm provided between eighteen and thirty-four beds for the poor.[70] Between 1907 and 1919 an average of thirty-eight people per year stayed at the farm for various lengths of time.[71]

The Boulder County poor farm housed a variety of people. As in the rest of the nation, the elderly dominated the poor farm, resulting in an average age of 62.8 years. Yet, both the very young and the very old lived there. In 1912, for example, a one-month-old boy with his deserted mother and year-old brother resided at the county farm and, at the other extreme, a 102-year-old man from New York lived at the farm in 1919. Some poor folk remained at the farm for long periods. Berry Faust, an elderly blind man, entered the farm in June 1905 and stayed until his death, almost five years later on April 28, 1910. Others, like sixty-four-year-old David Brash, stayed for short periods: in Brash's case, for just five days as he recovered from an illness. While Boulder County's farm housed both males and females, males accounted for slightly more than 88 percent of poor farm residents. A range of circumstances and ailments afflicted occupants, including death of parents, drunkenness, illness, desertion, old age, injury, blindness, insanity, and homelessness. Old age, blindness, sickness, and disabilities, however, affected over 76 percent of Boulder's poor farm residents.[72]

In order to care for such a diverse population and maintain the farm, the county relied on both paid employees and volunteer assistance from poor farm residents. Four employees, two men and two women, managed the farm. The two men devoted most of their attention to farm production, while the two women cared for the residents and performed housekeeping duties.[73] State authorities believed that the workload for the two women was too great, and that the county should hire more help to assist in caring for the residents.[74] Although old age and disabilities slowed most poor farm residents, making the vast majority of occupants unable to work, the few who were able to work did help in running the farm. In 1912, for instance, twelve of the twenty-seven residents performed "some light employment."[75] In addition, a small number of occupants were responsible for keeping the dormitories clean and orderly.[76] Even though state officials sometimes disapproved of the lack of cleanliness and the lack of required work for occupants, both residents and paid employees seemed comfortable with the informal organization of work on Boulder's farm. The county's paid farm employees accepted the reality of poor farm residents' health, allowing occupants to judge for themselves how and if they could reasonably assist. This informal arrangement permitted residents to maintain a degree of control and dignity in their own lives while living on the farm.

Boulder's poor farm, unlike Montezuma's, became an important part of the county's relief strategies. The farm mainly provided care for those poor residents who could not independently maintain themselves. "We find most of these people far advanced in years," reported the State Board of Charities and Corrections during a visit to Boulder's poor farm, "others are helpless cripples, and some blind."[77] Most farm residents did not need the specialized medical treatment that hospitals offered, but they also could not perform all the daily tasks required to live on their own. Lacking relatives or friends willing or able to assist them and lacking the funds to employ assistance, impoverished aging and disabled county residents turned to the poor farm as the only way to sustain themselves. The farm provided free room and board and assumed the major daily chores—cooking, cleaning, and laundry—while still expecting residents to be at least partially self-sufficient.

Not only did Boulder County's poor farm become a vital form of relief but it also became a valued community institution. Historians have depicted poor farms or poorhouses as places with "wretched conditions" and places to be avoided by all but the most desperate.[78] While this characterization may hold true for Montezuma's poor farm, Boulder's poor farm presents an entirely different picture. Boulder's citizens did not fear their poor farm. "When people got older and didn't have anybody or anything," remembered one Boulder County resident, "they would go to" the poor farm. County citizens simply did not view residency at the poor farm as a disgrace; rather, they understood that those who went to the farm were "people [who] couldn't take care of themselves."[79] Ruth Kinney recalled that her father, Charles Wahlstrom, regularly visited old mining friends on Sunday afternoons at Boulder's combined county hospital and poorhouse during the 1920s. Wahlstrom deeply enjoyed these visits. He praised the comfortable living conditions, the quantity and quality of meals served, and the care provided. Wahlstrom even eagerly anticipated spending his last years at the institution.[80] Boulder's poor farm and later its county hospital and poorhouse became integral community institutions that local citizens counted on to serve them if the need arose.

The combined county hospital and poorhouse was, surprisingly, Boulder County's first attempt to sustain a county hospital since 1902. The absence of a county hospital was unusual given the county's relatively large population. Instead of maintaining their own hospital, officials took advantage of the community's proximity to the University of Colorado, joining forces with them to construct the University Hospital. The county of Boulder contributed five thousand dollars and the city of Boulder contributed three thousand dollars toward the construction of a hospital adjacent to the campus. In exchange for the funds, the city received one free bed for indigent patients and the county received two free beds for the next ten years.[81] The University Hospital opened in 1898, serving as a general hospital and training school for medical students and nurses. By 1910, the hospital could house a maximum of twenty-five patients at a time, and a year earlier forty impoverished residents, twenty-nine men and eleven women, had received care at the hospital.[82] In 1917, county commissioners and university regents reached a new five-year agreement that ended the use of free beds and instead charged the county eight dollars per week for each patient.[83]

Boulder's use of the University Hospital was not a completely satisfactory arrangement. The location of the hospital meant it could only serve a portion of the county's ill and injured. Those living in the northern portion of Boulder County could not reasonably access medical services on or near the University of Colorado campus. In an attempt to address this problem, commissioners both appointed a deputy county physician to serve the northern regions of the county and paid for care at the privately operated Longmont Hospital.[84] More pressing, the use of the University Hospital was clearly not a long-term solution to the county's need for a hospital. Since the 1890s, the University of Colorado had tried to relocate its medical school from Boulder to Denver. In 1911 it finally succeeded.[85] With the move, Boulder County could no longer rely on the hospital for future care. In response to this situation, the county commissioners decided, in 1918, to sell the poor farm near Valmont and construct a county hospital and poorhouse on a twenty-acre plot just north of the city of Boulder that already contained a spacious house, large barns, poultry houses, and an eight-hundred-tree fruit orchard.[86] By 1921, the new poorhouse had twenty-seven residents, while the new county hospital had eleven beds.[87]

Teller County's need and use of philanthropic organizations differed from the other counties. Unlike the other communities, Teller experienced a dramatic shift from a dominance of private aid to a dominance of public assistance. Yet, this shift occurred not because of Progressive Era theories but rather due to social, economic, and political changes that damaged the county's private relief structure. But much like Boulder, and unlike Montezuma, Teller developed a county hospital that would become an important community resource.

Unions, lodges, and fraternal associations inundated Teller County. Following the mine workers' 1894 strike victory in the Cripple Creek Mining District, all types of workers unionized. Bakers, barbers, butchers, cooks, musicians, plumbers, retail clerks, and waiters, to name just a few laborers, all organized unions by the early twentieth century, making the Cripple Creek Mining District one of the most unionized areas in the nation. During the peak of labor's power in 1902, "at least fifty-four union locals operated" in Teller County, and, according to historian Elizabeth Jameson, at least one-third of all residents belonged to unions.[88] In addition, more than a hundred local chapters of some forty lodges and fraternal associations existed in the county.[89]

Because unions, lodges, and fraternal organizations constructed a welfare safety net for their members, who often worked in highly dangerous occupations, these groups became the backbone of Teller's poor relief during the turn of the century. Unions offered sick benefits and paid for burial expenses, while lodges and fraternal associations provided life insurance policies and also assisted with burial costs. In 1902, the Victor Miners No. 32, for instance, spent four thousand dollars on funeral expenses and sick benefits.[90] Unions often also provided informal support. Kathleen Welch Chapman recalled the importance that union benefits and union members played in people's lives. "Now if there was a family that was very hard up or very tight for money, why [the unions would] help them out. . . . I can remember people . . . coming . . . when Papa'd maybe have a cold or be sick or couldn't go to work or something. There'd be maybe a half a dozen men come at night to see if he was getting along and if he needed anything."[91] Many laborers also maintained membership in a lodge or fraternal group. When Anne Ellis's husband died after mistakenly drilling into a stick of dynamite, the next day his lodge brothers, the Knights of Pythias, visited Anne and made all the funeral arrangements.[92] Lodges and fraternal associations regularly held benefit dances and used subscription lists to help the ill, injured, and widowed. The ability of workers to support their families adequately through union wages and their own benefit system became a source of masculine pride for laborers.[93] The role of unions, lodges, and fraternal societies did not go unnoticed by Teller officials. County Commissioner E. W. Pfeiffer told an audience of social and charity workers that because there "were so many unions, lodges, benefit balls and subscription lists in circulation . . . there was little call for county help."[94]

The legendary generosity of Winfield Scott Stratton also lessened the need for public assistance. A carpenter by training, Stratton moved to Colorado Springs where he began prospecting and studying mineralogy while still working as a part-time carpenter. In 1891, Stratton staked two claims in the Cripple Creek Mining District, the Independence and the Washington. The following year, Stratton became Cripple Creek's first millionaire as he dug into a gold vein on the Independence claim. In 1898, after removing just under four million dollars in ore, Stratton sold the Independence mine for eleven million dollars to a London investment company.[95] Unlike most millionaires, Stratton did not spend his money on luxury items or extended tours of Europe. Instead, he poured his immense fortune back into Cripple Creek and Colorado Springs. Not only did Stratton reinvest in business ventures, but he also gave away thousands, if not millions, of dollars to people in need and to various charitable organizations. After a fire destroyed Cripple Creek in 1896, Stratton, within hours, collected, paid for, and transported relief supplies—tents, blankets, diapers, and food—for two thousand people.[96] Each Christmas, he provided coal for every impoverished family in the town of Victor. He contributed money to building Catholic, Presbyterian, Baptist, and Methodist churches throughout the mining district. He gave the Salvation Army thousands of dollars each month to transport, house, and feed homeless men from Cripple Creek. He even purchased supplies and goods for destitute miners and laborers.[97] Stratton's generosity not only helped needy individuals but also lessened dependency on public aid.

Teller County's informal relief system—the combination of unions, lodges, fraternal organizations, and Stratton's good deeds—seemed to go unnoticed by state officials who were looking for more common, middle-class forms of relief. When Mr. C. L. Stonaker, secretary of Colorado's State Board of Charities and Corrections, visited Cripple Creek in 1901, the apparent lack of visible relief societies disturbed him. "There are many calls for relief," wrote Stonaker, "and there is no other organization in the [Cripple Creek Mining] district, consequently the county commissioners have a great problem in the proper disposition of all appeals coming to them. The different municipalities in the district do nothing and there is no form of private relief." Stonaker seemed unaware of local efforts or was possibly unwilling to credit the efforts made by Teller's unions, lodges, fraternal associations, and Stratton toward assisting the mining district's needy. In order to solve this apparent problem, Stonaker proposed a middle-class solution, the creation of a privately operated charity relief society. "What is needed," wrote Stonaker, "is a first class, experienced investigator, who will make proper inquires regarding each case and act accordingly, and I would suggest that at some early date an effort be made by this board to secure the organization of a central relief bureau in that district, supported by private contributions."[98] Stonaker advanced his plan by holding a session of the state's seventh Conference of Charities and Corrections in Cripple Creek, addressing the very topic of organized charities. Out of this session an exploratory committee was formed to investigate the creation of a charity organization for the mining district, but the idea never developed beyond this early stage.[99]

While state officials failed to alter fundamentally Teller's relief practices, other forces succeeded in ending the county's informal reliance on unions, lodges, fraternal associations, and Stratton to assist its needy. County commissioners moved to address the need to care for aged and infirm residents who were not adequately helped by the informal relief system by opening a county hospital in April 1902.[100] The county hospital provided a place for those needing long-term care and also offered medical treatment. At the time, only St. Nicholas Hospital, an eighteen-bed facility operated by the Sisters of Mercy, served Cripple Creek. Since almost all of Teller County sat above nine thousand feet in altitude, resulting in an extremely short growing season, the county could not operate a working farm as Boulder and Montezuma Counties did. Constructed in 1901 and 1902, during the height of the mining boom, Teller's hospital reflected the community's wealth. While Boulder and Montezuma Counties' poor farms consisted of basically modified farmhouses often lacking electricity and sewer lines, Teller built a two-story state-of-the-art hospital with the most modern conveniences. Made of brick at a cost of almost twenty thousand dollars, the Teller County Hospital had the latest comforts including steam heat, electric light, sewer lines, and fire protection.[101] Community members could rightfully have a sense of pride in their modern hospital.

Not long after the opening of the hospital, Teller County began an economic decline. Millionaire Winfield Stratton's death on September 14, 1902 at the age of fifty-four contributed to the district's slowdown. Stratton's death ended a seemingly limitless supply of money flowing into the Cripple Creek Mining District. During the previous years, Stratton had poured more than

Teller County Hospital, Cripple Creek, Colorado, no date. The former Teller County Hospital is presently used as a hotel. Courtesy of Colorado Historical Society.

eight million dollars back into Teller County through his attempts to develop new mines, especially the Plymouth Rock. While his mining efforts failed, his money had kept many laborers employed, and his generosity had helped hundreds of impoverished citizens.[102] In addition, as early as 1902, subterranean water and poisonous gases increasingly interrupted mining operations. The completion of several drainage tunnels only temporarily solved the problem of underground flooding.[103] In 1904, when the town of Anaconda burned, residents made no attempt to rebuild, even though both Victor and Cripple Creek had been rebuilt just a few years earlier.[104] From 1900 to 1910, gold production decreased from just over eighteen million to eleven million dollars per year, and the county's population dropped from 29,002 to 14,351.[105]

Finally, labor's defeat in the 1903–04 strike destroyed unions and weakened lodges and fraternal organizations. Just ten years after securing a victory, workers now found themselves on the losing end as the political and economic situation had changed. Mine owners and their supporters drove out union leaders, blacklisted union members, attacked union supporters, destroyed union halls, and wrecked union cooperative stores. The complete defeat of labor during the 1903–04 strike halted the union benefits that so many residents had relied on in times of need. In addition, the conflict shattered the cross-class brotherhood that had sustained lodges and fraternal associations.[106] While lodges and fraternal societies persisted after the strike, their importance greatly decreased. Labor's 1903–04 defeat damaged Teller's informal relief structure by greatly diminishing the prominent role that unions, lodges, and fraternal organizations played in sustaining the county's needy.

With the destruction of Teller's informal relief system, the county government became increasingly responsible for caring for its needy citizens, and its hospital played an important role in that care. Five employees, all women, ran the hospital, which could hold between thirty-four and forty patients at a time.[107] Like other hospitals, Teller's hospital cared for patients with various ailments and injuries. But, like poor farms, Teller's hospital also housed a group of old and disabled patients for long periods. In 1909, the county hospital listed eleven patients as "permanent patients," and these patients lived up to their classification as they each spent years in the hospital. Sixty-year-old Elizabeth Yerrick checked into the Teller County hospital in 1904 and remained there for the next fifteen years until her death in 1919.[108]

Regardless of the hospital's modern facilities, the management of the hospital did not always obtain such high marks. In 1914, a grand jury convened to investigate allegations of corruption and criminal misconduct by Teller County officials. The grand jury found no evidence of criminal behavior; however, it did cite several officials for incompetence and failure to perform their duties properly. The matron of the county hospital probably received the harshest and most pointed criticism of any county employee. The report found the matron to be "careless and incompetent" and demanded that officials "immediately" remove her from her position. The report went on to state "that at times the patients are not provided with either proper or sufficient food; that patients have been at times treated in a cruel and inhuman manner, and that they have been deprived of certain comforts furnished them by charitable people or charitable societies." Five months after the report became public, commissioners finally removed Mrs. A. R. Salt as matron of the county hospital.[109]

Despite the shortcomings of Mrs. Salt's tenure, Teller's county hospital, for the most part, seemed to be a respected and important community institution. Much like Boulder's poor farm, Teller's hospital and its "permanent patients" became an integral part of the community. During the Spanish Influenza epidemic, for example, health authorities decided to use the county hospital exclusively for treating epidemic victims. As a result, all other patients were evacuated. The county removed eight patients who needed medical care to St. Nicholas Hospital. Five patients stayed in a house near the county hospital, and "six old men," probably a portion of the "permanent" group, took up residency in the county jail. According to the local newspaper, these men were "well satisfied with their new abode," and they were "free to go anywhere they chose and to walk as far during the day as their health and years" would permit.[110] George C. McKnight, who had been at the county hospital for about a year trying to "cure" his epilepsy, insisted that officials allow him to remain at the hospital to help care for flu patients. County authorities granted McKnight's request. For several days he repaid the community for the assistance that he had received by tending to the ill. Soon, however, McKnight, "about 36 years of age," died of influenza.[111]

Although Teller, Boulder, and Montezuma Counties each operated a publicly funded poor farm or hospital, generalizing about these facilities is difficult. Local conditions, including policy decisions, funding levels, and personnel, all shaped these institutions into distinctive establishments. In addition, the roles that these poor farms or hospitals played in each community's welfare efforts varied considerably.

Denver's Publicly Funded Charitable Institutions

Although five of the six counties in this study had only one or no publicly supported charitable institutions, the city and county of Denver maintained six to serve its needy population. Two hospitals, Sand Creek and Steele, cared for those with contagious diseases. Sand Creek Hospital, "a small frame building" located approximately six miles from the city "in the middle of the open prairie," housed nine or ten smallpox patients. Steele Hospital cared for diphtheria and scarlet fever sufferers, accommodating about one hundred people. While both Sand Creek and Steele provided services free of charge for those unable to pay, neither hospital's main purpose was to provide for the poor.[112] Denver's four other publicly funded facilities—the County Poor Farm, the City and County Hospital, the Municipal Lodging House, and the Municipal Coal and Wood Yard—did, however, cater almost exclusively to Denver's needy.

Denver's charitable facilities, like its outdoor assistance program, experienced little change during the Progressive Era. Yet, the city's institutions did not follow exactly the same path as outdoor aid. Reformers like Gertrude Vaile had generated a great deal of publicity and excitement about transforming outdoor aid from a supposedly corrupt and inefficient program to a professional and efficient operation. Those interested in overhauling Denver's publicly funded institutions never succeeded in grabbing the spotlight. But like Vaile, institutional reformers inherited problems in some of the city's facilities that had taken on their own inertia. Overcrowding and a large number of infirm residents became the two issues that blocked any changes at the poor farm. Likewise, solving the severe overcrowding problem at the county hospital became the most pressing concern at the time. Denver did add two institutions, the coal and wood yard and the lodging house, during this period. Both these new facilities were simply modifications of existing or previous relief strategies, and both remained open for only a brief period. In the end, neither the coal and wood yard nor the lodging house radically changed Denver's relief practices. By the end of the Progressive Era, Denver's institutions remained, for the most part, much as they had been in the beginning of the period, although overcrowding had been greatly reduced.

With the defeat of Mayor Speer and the election of reform candidates in 1912, officials began altering relief practices by establishing the Municipal Lodging House. The city rented two upper floors of a three-story brick building to provide "a home for the man without a dime."[113] The lodging house consisted of twenty-four sleeping rooms with seventy-one beds, two bathrooms, a kitchen, an office, a fumigating room, a dining room, and a reading room.[114] "A night's lodging consist[ed] of supper, bath, fumigation of clothes, a good clean bed, [and] breakfast."[115] The superintendent of the lodging house also operated a free employment bureau that secured jobs for the unemployed. Each occupant's name went on the employment bureau's rolls with the expectation that lodgers would take any work that was found for them.[116] In 1914, the lodging house's second year of operation, the superintendent secured 1,208 jobs and furnished just over seven thousand beds for the homeless.[117]

The Municipal Lodging House aimed to reform relief practices. In the past, the city had dispensed meal and lodging tickets to those needing a place for the night. Reformers claimed that "the application window was beset every afternoon by throngs of single men, one hundred per day, asking for meal and bed tickets." Some men supposedly received tickets five times a week.[118] The lodging house eliminated extended stays by screening repeat applicants. Lodgers could stay up to three days; however, the superintendent allowed "exceptional cases" to remain longer.[119] The superintendent estimated "that $100 a month is saved over the former system of giving out meal and lodging tickets."[120] In 1914, the city spent just over thirty-three hundred dollars to operate the establishment.

In many respects, however, the Municipal Lodging House hardly altered previous relief practices. Women and African Americans, for example, noticed few changes. During the first year of operation, the lodging house generally did not accept homeless women as the city preferred instead to continue giving women meal and lodging tickets. Although a year later the superintendent did reserve one room for women and children, some still went off-site for care and services.[121] The city, likewise, placed fifty-one African American men in other facilities besides the lodging house.[122] The impoverished white men who did stay at the lodging house most likely viewed it as simply another rooming establishment, much like others in the city that they had frequented in the past with their meal and lodging tickets.[123] Finally, and most importantly, the Municipal Lodging House had a limited effect on relief practices because it only operated for a brief time. By 1919, it appears to have existed in name only, and two years later even its name disappears from records.[124]

The Municipal Coal and Wood Yard, Denver's other new public institution, opened just a few weeks before the new lodging house. In October 1912, officials leased a lot in the railroad district where the city's park and street departments could bring downed trees and wastepaper and where railcars could bring in coal. Unemployed men, and some women, sawed and chopped the wood, unloaded and shoveled the coal, and sorted and baled the paper in exchange for aid. The labor performed by the unemployed at the coal and wood yard partially, or completely, repaid the city for relief

Coal and Wood Yard at Nineteenth and Kalamath Streets, Denver, Colorado, 1912. Often those receiving poor relief or staying at the Municipal Lodging House were required to work at the Coal and Wood Yard. City of Denver, *21 December 1912, 1. Courtesy of Denver Public Library, Western History Collection.*

received. Once the Municipal Lodging House opened its doors, the superintendent required all lodgers to work three hours per day at the coal and wood yard if other employment could not be found.[125] Denver saved money by disposing of wood and paper at little or no cost and by buying coal at wholesale prices. The city gave the chopped wood to poor families receiving outdoor aid. While the paper-baling operation did not bring in much money, it did manage to "employ" two men who received public assistance. The two men did not receive cash for their labor; instead, the division of outdoor relief was credited one dollar per day in exchange for their work.[126] The wholesale purchase of coal saved the cost of a dealer's profits while quickly providing fuel to families receiving outdoor relief.[127] In its second year of existence in 1914, the operation cost the city just over two thousand dollars while supplying 1,333 tons of coal, ninety wagonloads of wood for 2,458 fuel orders, and fourteen railcars of wastepaper.[128]

First appearances would seem to credit the Municipal Coal and Wood Yard with radically overhauling Denver's relief practices. That occupants of the lodging house and some outdoor relief recipients were required to work at the yard to reimburse the city for assistance is clearly a change from previous practices. In the past, the city had indeed given lodging and meal tickets and outdoor aid without requiring work.

But upon closer inspection, the new work requirement was not as new or as strictly enforced as appearances might suggest. The notion of using a wood yard as a means to test the "worthiness" of charity applicants while supposedly protecting their "self respect" had been tried before. As early as 1887, Denver had operated a wood yard under the direction of the Ladies Relief Society. That wood yard, much like the Municipal Coal and Wood Yard, provided "comparatively light work of cutting wood" in exchange "for food and lodging for hungry and tired men." During the 1893 depression, Denver once again briefly opened a wood yard for unemployed men.[129] Through their experience in operating the wood yard, the Ladies Relief Society learned "that a majority of the poor are worthy."[130] Years later, the Municipal Coal and Wood Yard would once again teach similar lessons about poor folk. The ability of many relief applicants to perform physical labor for several hours quickly challenged the spirit, if not the intention, of the work requirement. During the coal and wood yard's second week of operation, the physical shortcomings of laborers became clearly evident. "Each man does according to his ability. Some of the applicants are in such poor health they can do almost nothing, but they stay at the yard, to do as much as possible." Whether the city continued to make sickly and disabled men work at the yard remains unknown, but the feasibility of the whole operation seemed seriously questioned by the workers' limited abilities. Echoing the statement of the Ladies Relief Society, the Municipal Coal and Wood Yard superintendent observed that "we don't have to watch these men. They are not loafers. They are fellows who have tried hard to get work but can't."[131] But much like the lodging house, the Municipal Coal and Wood Yard's brief existence largely limited the degree to which it reshaped Denver's relief practices. By 1918, the yard had closed its gates.[132]

While the Municipal Lodging House and the Municipal Coal and Wood Yard quickly opened and closed, Denver's poor farm and county hospital were far more permanent. The poor farm and hospital constituted the two largest and oldest publicly funded institutions in the city. Unlike institutions in Boulder, Montezuma, and Teller Counties, Denver's poor farm and county hospital became chronically overcrowded. This problem of overcrowding so overwhelmed these two established facilities that it became the dominant concern during the early twentieth century.

The poor farm sat outside Denver's boundaries for most of the Progressive Era. In 1899, the Arapahoe County commissioners closed the county's poorhouse, located in the immigrant neighborhood of Globeville, and opened a new poor farm near the farming community of Henderson, approximately seventeen miles northeast of Denver. At the time, the poorhouse had cared for only impoverished men, housing seventy-eight men. Indigent women, meanwhile, resided at the county hospital. With the opening of the new poor farm, the county brought together impoverished men and women.[133] When Denver formed its own county in 1902, it retained control of the poor farm despite the farm's location outside of the city's limits.

All accounts of Denver's poor farm agree on its excellent location and fertile land. Originally consisting of 160 acres, the poor farm by 1906 occupied 340 acres along the banks of the South Platte River. According to some observers, "a more beautiful or appropriate spot could not be selected" for a poor farm.[134] "The productivity of the land is unquestioned," stated a 1918 report, as the farm had "splendid water rights" which made it "susceptible to the highest kind of irrigated farming."[135] In 1913, the poor farm annually produced 230 tons of hay, 630 bushels of wheat, 1,200 bushels of oats, 300 bushels of barley, 250 gallons of canned tomatoes, 10 barrels of kraut, 10 barrels of pickles, and 450 pounds of honey, as well as 65 pounds of butter weekly and 50 gallons of milk daily.[136] The farm also had 69 head of cattle, 14 horses, 340 pigs, and 1,000 chickens by 1916.[137] "There is absolutely nothing in the way of farm or dairy products," reported Alice Fulton and Sarah Walling, members of the State Board of Charities and Corrections, during a 1917 inspection, "which has not been produced in great abundance." According to the two women, the poor farm's storerooms held "hundreds of glass jars filled with berries, apple butter or jam, pears, peaches, tomatoes, corn, beans, peas, succotash, asparagus, in rows and rows." All of this farm production resulted in excellent meals for poor farm residents. "The quality and quantity of food served to the inmates," wrote Fulton and Walling, "would do credit to any hotel."[138]

While the agricultural side of the farm obviously proved a success, other aspects of the poor farm did not always receive such high praise. In 1899

Denver County Poor Farm, Henderson, Colorado, 1913. Denver's poor farm was located approximately seventeen miles northeast of the city along the South Platte River. First Annual Report of the Social Welfare Department of the City and County of Denver, Colorado, 1913, 74. *Courtesy of Denver Public Library, Government Publications.*

when residents moved into the new poor farm, the county constructed a two-story brick building consisting of a kitchen, dining room, and two wards for residents, along with two connecting dormitories. "The buildings," reported the *Denver Times*, "are finished throughout with natural pine and are light and airy." Each dormitory had a sitting room or sun parlor, and all the buildings had steam heat and electricity.[139] Despite such promising, almost inviting, accommodations, the poor farm quickly encountered overcrowding problems. By 1906, the farm had 108 residents in seven wards, six for men and one for women.[140] Three years later, and just ten years after the farm's opening, city officials described it as "badly crowded" and in need of an additional building.[141] Yet in 1912, there were 175 residents crowding the poor farm's same seven wards "to its utmost capacity."[142] By 1914, the overcrowding slightly eased as the number of inhabitants dropped to 162 people, but beds still stood only "about two feet apart."[143]

Other problems, some caused by overcrowding, also plagued the poor farm. Bedbugs, for example, seemed a rather persistent problem, occasionally forcing officials to place bedposts in cans of water to prevent the bugs from crawling into the beds. The use of straw mattresses and "cheap shoddy blanket[s]" made it difficult for older residents to stay warm and comfortable.[144] At times, some occupants, especially men, received little attention and care from the staff. In 1914, one female attendant, for example, oversaw the needs of the seventeen female residents. At the same time, however, only a single male attendant looked after the 129 male occupants. Many of the poor farm residents required "considerable care" and the one male attendant could not properly address all their needs. Thus, the male attendant "found it necessary to detail an inmate as an aide in charge of each ward."[145] With so many shortcomings, the poor farm seemed a prime target for reform.

When reformers took control of Denver in 1912, John W. Ford, president of the Board of Aldermen, proposed sweeping changes for the poor farm. Ford envisioned constructing several new buildings to care for indigent tubercular patients, the mildly insane, those convicted of misdemeanors, and elderly couples who wished to continue living together. In addition, Ford aimed to reshape the daily routines of poor farm residents. During the summer, physically competent male occupants would perform general farm labor or care for the city's vacant lots and streets or perform other types of "light employment." Come winter, male residents would "engage in the manufacture of cement articles, culverts, sewer pipes and other accessories." Female residents would, according to Ford, make overalls, gloves, and other articles of commercial value as well as do laundry and housework for the farm plus take classes in domestic economy. Ford had "given considerable thought and attention" to his comprehensive reform plan, and he believed that these proposed changes were "eminently worthy of trial."[146]

Regardless of Ford's ambitious plan, Denver's poor farm changed little. The notion of using occupants to supply labor completely mistook the reality of these inhabitants. As with Boulder's poor farm, elderly and disabled residents dominated Denver's farm. "The popular notion," wrote Mr. G. E. Richardson, Denver's poor farm superintendent, "that those at the County Farm can each do a full day's work is totally wrong. More than seventy-five per cent of the wards are grey haired, too old to do more than simple tasks. Of the others they are affected with nervous disorders, epilepsy, palsy, heart trouble and the like. Not a single inmate is able in mind and body."[147] In 1915, Denver's poor farm residents averaged sixty-four years of age, and 53 percent were over the age of fifty while only five occupants were under the age of thirty.[148] Ford also overestimated the city's willingness or ability to construct new buildings on the poor farm. During the Progressive Era, the city only managed to construct one additional dormitory, for forty people, and a new hospital ward. Additional housing for couples never materialized. The city, however, did manage to find the funds to improve the agricultural operations by building a new barn, silo, and ice house.[149] In fact, an increase in

Dinner at the Denver County Poor Farm, 1925. Municipal Facts,
*November–December 1925, 17. Courtesy of Denver Public Library,
Western History Collection.*

agricultural production accounted for the only substantial change to the
poor farm during the early twentieth century, perhaps indicating the prior-
ities of officials.

Despite the large size of Denver's poor farm and its inability to change,
the overall operation seemed relaxed, allowing for individual residents to
maintain their sense of dignity. Denver's poor farm had "few rules."[150] In the
1920s, for instance, no strict guidelines existed except for the basic request
that everyone be courteous toward one another. Residents could move about
the farm as they pleased, they could smoke in bed, and they were not
required to work.[151] Yet, many residents did volunteer their labor. Some
washed dishes, several helped in the wards, and others assisted with farm
operations. Otto Prein, known as "Sheriff" Prein, had resided on the poor

farm for over a quarter century, becoming a proud permanent resident of the farm. Prein had "missed hardly a day's work" in over twenty-five years as he was always "busy about the farm buildings." Another resident, "Grandma" Brown, took "upon herself the guardianship of a troop of chickens. Day in and out she is seen from 4 A.M. until late in the afternoon caring for her little flock of White Leghorns which are the pride of her life."[152] Denver's poor farm clearly did not disgrace its residents nor did it completely take away their individuality. In fact, the examples of Brown and Prein seem to indicate that the poor farm encouraged, or at least allowed, residents to carve out their own niches.

Unlike the farm, Denver's county hospital never compelled local Progressive Era reformers to generate bold plans for the institution's transformation. The clearly defined medical mission of the hospital along with the strong professional presence of doctors and nurses may have discouraged outsiders like Ford from proposing grandiose reforms. But Denver's county hospital, even more than the poor farm, faced a severe overcrowding problem and had to manage insane patients. The City and County Hospital of Denver held the position as the city's largest publicly funded charitable institution. Originally founded in 1873, the hospital by 1910 had three hundred beds, making it the state's largest hospital. The medical staff of physicians and surgeons, composed of some of the city's best, gave their services free of charge. The hospital trained interns and operated a comprehensive nurses training program. "The County Hospital," wrote superintendent Dr. William H. Sharpley in 1914, "is solely for the purpose of caring for the poor and unfortunate, sick and helpless, who . . . are not in a position to pay their expenses in a private institution."[153] Put more concisely by a later superintendent, the "County Hospital is the Poor Man's Hospital."[154] Denver's county hospital cared for all ailments and injuries except for contagious diseases, which went to either Steele or Sand Creek Hospitals. In addition, almost all the city's emergency cases came to the county hospital, which did bring in some clients who were able to pay for their medical treatment.

The hospital had numerous shortcomings. "The County Hospital," wrote Sharpley, "is far from being an up-to-date institution." The buildings were old and, for the most part, badly in need of repairs. Floors needed replacing, x-ray equipment was antiquated, kitchen and laundry facilities were inadequate, and the accommodations for nurses were overcrowded and dilapidated. Too few interns worked at the hospital, and an understaffed nursing force struggled to provide proper care. In 1914, approximately sixty nurses cared for roughly four hundred patients.[155]

Despite all these deficiencies, overcrowding became the most serious problem facing the county hospital. By 1909, excessive crowding at the institution required the construction of an annex.[156] Yet, the new addition only briefly solved the problem. By 1914, if not sooner, overcrowding once again strained existing facilities. Chronically ill and insane patients were the main source of excessive crowding. The needs of these two groups, especially the insane, demanded resources that the hospital could ill afford to provide. "When this hospital was built," wrote William Thomas, secretary of the State Board of Charities and Corrections, "it was intended that it should minister to the sick and injured of the city, but since its inception, it has involuntarily assumed the care of others who should not be admitted to this class of institution."[157] In a sense, the hospital served as a place of last resort for needy residents.

Through the years, the county hospital had become a type of convalescent or old folks home for many residents. Due to overcrowding at the poor farm, thirty to fifty elderly or disabled patients stayed at the county hospital instead of being transferred to the farm. These patients did not require the medical or surgical care that the hospital offered, but they were also "not in condition to be discharged from all supervision" as they still needed nutritional meals and custodial care.[158] The practice of housing impoverished elderly or disabled citizens at a hospital was not unique to Denver. Teller County, as we have seen, housed a small band of ten to fifteen "permanent patients" at its hospital. Yet, the large number of chronic patients and the lack of room at Denver's county hospital did distinguish the Queen City's situation from other counties. In 1912, officials moved many of the hospital's chronic patients to the poor farm, resulting in the highest number of poor farm occupants, 175.[159] But this transfer, much like the annex, did not solve the problem. The following year, "the usual chronic invalid contingent was [still] in evidence."[160]

Denver's insane residents faced far harsher and more desperate circumstances than did its elderly and disabled citizens. In January 1914, a total of 140 insane patients, seventy-nine males and sixty-one females, lived at the county hospital. Their living conditions and treatment were, to say the least, deplorable. One building divided into small rooms housed most of the insane patients, although officials had also set up extra quarters in the basement. Originally, each small room slept only one person, but due to overcrowding, four to six people occupied each room. "These rooms are cell-like and cheer-less, with barred windows and heavy doors. There is a small opening or peep hole in each door about three inches in diameter." Insane patients had little opportunity to exercise, and the hospital made no attempt to segregate according to different types of mental disorders. For the insane, the county hospital was to "all effects and purposes a jail without the comforts and conveniences which even prisoners are allowed in the county jail."[161]

Conditions at the state's insane asylum in Pueblo aggravated the overcrowding at Denver's county hospital. Under Colorado law, once a court declared a person insane, he or she became the responsibility of the state. Yet, because the state asylum refused to take additional patients due to its own shortage of space, counties had to care for many of their own insane citizens. Thus, Denver was not the only community to face the problem of how to provide for its insane residents. In 1909, for instance, Boulder, Lincoln, and Teller Counties all used public funds to maintain insane people either at privately operated facilities like Dr. Hubert Work's Woodcroft Hospital in Pueblo or at their own poor farms or county hospitals.[162] But Denver faced a much larger burden than did the other counties. In 1914, Colorado counties supported 307 insane patients not provided for by the state. Denver's share of this total accounted for almost half.[163] State officials finally addressed this crisis in 1916 by completing a major expansion of the asylum.[164] During an inspection the following year, members of the State Board of Charities and Corrections found that the county hospital had "been wonderfully improved during the past year." There were now only 246 total patients, down from 415 in 1914, only ten of whom were insane. While some chronic patients still remained, overcrowding no longer burdened the hospital.[165]

At the end of the Progressive Era, Denver's poor residents probably noticed few changes in the public charitable institutions that served them. In fact, the city's institutions looked much as they had at the beginning of the period. By 1920, the only publicly funded facilities that cared for the city's needy were still the poor farm and the county hospital. The Municipal Lodging House and the Municipal Coal and Wood Yard had opened and closed their doors. Although overcrowding at the county hospital had largely been solved by the end of the Progressive Era, the poor farm still continued to struggle with the problem. Consequently, except for changes at the county hospital, poor folks probably saw few changes in Denver's institutional relief efforts.

Mixing Private and Public Relief

While public assistance dominated relief strategies in Boulder, Costilla, Lincoln, Montezuma, and Teller Counties, private philanthropy played a far more prominent and formal role in Denver. As we have seen, substantial private aid did exist in two of the smaller counties; in Costilla with the Penitentes and in Teller with labor unions, lodges, fraternal societies, and Stratton. The relationship between private and public relief in both Costilla and Teller, however, always remained informal, as a kind of unspoken assumption about how each community would care for its needy. In general, privately operated charitable institutions were either minimal or nonexistent in the less populated communities. In Denver, and to a much lesser degree in Boulder, many philanthropic societies had formal arrangements with the city to assist in providing aid. As a result, the boundary between public and private relief often blurred, as it did for many urban centers. Nonetheless the prominent role played by the Catholic and Jewish communities in structuring relief efforts set Denver apart from many other cities, especially midwestern and eastern ones.

Denver had an abundant collection of charitable institutions. As already mentioned, numerous tubercular hospitals and sanatoriums dotted the city's streets. In addition to their involvement with caring for indigent tubercular sufferers, the local Jewish community also maintained the Denver Sheltering Home for Jewish Children and the Jewish Relief Society, which gave outdoor aid. Protestant groups operated a number of different facilities. The Episcopal Church ran St. Luke's Hospital, the Salvation Army had a home for unemployed men, the Colorado Christian Home cared for orphans, the Florence Crittenten Home housed unwed pregnant girls and their babies, and the Colored Orphanage and Old Folks Home struggled to keep its doors open while serving the African American community. Numerous Protestant organizations operated outreach programs that served, but did not house, the poor. The Woman's Christian Temperance Union ran the Frances Willard Settlement, Presbyterians operated the Olivet Mission, and others maintained the Neighborhood House, the Deaconess Settlement, Epworth Mission, and the Sunshine Rescue Mission, to name just a few. These various settlement houses and missions usually provided meals, clothing, activities for children, and classes for adults while trying to proselytize. Catholics, like Jews and Protestants, established and maintained their own charitable institutions. The Sisters of Charity opened St. Joseph's Hospital and Mount St. Vincent's Home for boys. The Sisters of St. Francis founded St. Anthony's Hospital while the Sisters of Mercy established Mercy Hospital. Franciscan Sisters maintained St. Clara's Orphanage for boys and girls and the Sisters of Sacred Heart cared for only girls at the Queen of Heaven Orphanage. The Sisters of the Good Shepherd housed wayward girls and dependent children at their House of the Good Shepherd. In addition to these religiously motivated benevolent efforts, the city also had dozens of lodges, fraternal associations, and unions that provided some support for needy members. This brief listing of charitable facilities and organizations only partially encompasses the city's many philanthropic institutions and outreach programs.

Although many of these philanthropic establishments tried to control the poor, the ability to obtain free meals, coal, clothing, medical care, a place to sleep, or a place to put their children or a relative's children helped the poor in their daily struggles to make ends meet. The wide range of charitable options available to Denver's impoverished residents not only lessened the burden on public relief but also provided a choice for the city's needy in grappling with their situation. Poor people could pick and choose, to a degree, how, when, and where they wanted to address their problems. And because different establishments offered different services, poor folk could at least tap into the appropriate agency that provided the specific assistance required. Residents in the five smaller counties simply did not have the wide range of charitable options that Denver's citizens had access to.

While Denver's numerous philanthropic institutions differentiated it from the smaller counties, the city's private charitable facilities often mirrored national trends. Large institutions across the nation tended to locate in urban centers so as to have a ready supply of available clients. And, to a lesser degree, Denver's Protestants, Catholics, and Jews used their philanthropic organizations to battle one another for the souls of the poor as in other locales. During the Progressive Era, Protestants established, often for the first time, charitable institutions in the nation's slums that were filled with eastern and southern European immigrants. Most of these facilities offered material comfort to the poor but also attempted to transform the lives of recent immigrants. Many Protestant institutions tried to alter how and what immigrants ate, how they dressed, how they performed household chores, how they cared for their children, and how they used their leisure time. Most of all, however, Protestants tried to convert Catholic, Jewish, and Christian Orthodox immigrants.

Thus, the formation of Catholic and Jewish institutions and outreach programs were at least partially prompted by a desire to check Protestants' proselytizing. Catholics and Jews were also suspicious of many public institutions because Protestants largely controlled these facilities.[166] Since children were most vulnerable to conversion, Catholics focused their benevolent efforts on child-care activities, such as schools and orphanages. Having a large workforce in the form of religious orders, but also having little money, urban Catholics favored constructing large institutions. "Religious sisters and brothers," states historian Mary J. Oates, "could care for large numbers in a single facility, minimizing costs of land, building, and maintenance."[167] For Jews, the desire to maintain dietary laws and Yiddish motivated, in part, the opening of the Jewish Consumptives' Relief Society. The maintenance of charitable institutions by Catholics and Jews also served as a means to curtail nativism. These large institutions gave physical witness to efforts by Jews and Catholics to help their needy members so that they would not become society's burdens. The Jewish Consumptive Society and the National Jewish Hospital were both inspired, in part, by these concerns. In a sense, these facilities provided proof of the civic responsibility of Catholics and Jews.[168]

Although the development of Denver's Jewish, Catholic, and Protestant benevolent associations paralleled those of other cities, the relationship among these three local religious communities differed in some substantive ways from other urban centers, especially eastern and midwestern cities. In the 1880s, a diverse collection of Denver's leading citizens came together to address the city's need for more efficient and organized charity. Mrs. Frances Jacobs, who helped establish both the Hebrew Ladies' Benevolent Society in 1872 and, two years later, the secular Ladies' Relief Society, led efforts to assist Denver's poor residents. During this same time, Rev. Myron Reed, a Congregational minister, and Dean H. Martyn Hart, an Episcopalian, arrived. When Reed came to Denver in 1884, he brought his experience in running the Indianapolis Charity Organization Society with him. Hart, likewise, came to Denver with philanthropic experience through his work in London. Two Catholic priests, Fr. William O'Ryan and Fr. Patrick F. Carr also contributed to the city's early charity efforts. Fr. O'Ryan, like Dean Hart, had worked in England where he encountered attempts to coordinate fundraising, and Fr. Carr had teamed up with Hart in directing a local relief agency. These five citizens—Jewish, Protestant, and Catholic—joined together in the late 1880s to establish the Charity Organization Society of Denver (COSD).[169]

Denver's cooperation among its three major religious bodies distinguished the city from many other urban centers. The role that Catholics (especially Fr. O'Ryan) and Jews (especially Rabbi William S. Friedman, who soon joined the new organization) played in the formation and maintenance of the COSD was unusual. "Jew and Gentile, Catholic and Protestant, and those connected with no church," observed Richard E. Sykes, president of the COSD, "have worked together in harmony, actuated by a common purpose."[170] In many midwestern and eastern cities, Protestants largely controlled local charity societies. In Detroit, according to historian Olivier Zunz, Catholics and Jews avoided the local privately operated charity organization because of a deep mistrust toward Protestants. They turned instead to public officials for assistance.[171] But in Denver, no similar pattern developed, at least not for Catholics. In 1906 and 1909, Italian and Irish residents accessed both COSD and Denver County aid at similar rates. In fact, of all the ethnic groups, only Russians showed a significant preference for public aid over COSD assistance (see Table 16). Russians, overwhelmingly Orthodox Jews, may have avoided the COSD because of the strong influence of reform Jews in the relief organization.

The cooperation among Denver's Jews, Catholics, and Protestants in trying to grapple with the needs of the poor may illustrate a general Western characteristic rather than a unique characteristic of Denver. According to historian Mary J. Oates, religious animosity appeared to have been less in the West than in the Midwest or eastern sections of the nation. Since Catholics and Jews were often among the first settlers in the West, they could play a role in developing a community's philanthropic institutions and poor relief policies. San Francisco's Board of Supervisors, for example, invited the Sisters of Mercy to administer the county hospital. In Colorado prior to the construction of the Industrial Home and School for Girls in 1895, the state contracted with the House of the Good Shepherd to care for "all incorrigible girls and petty offenders."[172] Meanwhile, back East, Catholics hesitated to join in cooperative efforts with other religious groups. Catholics in New York City, Chicago, Boston, St. Louis, and Baltimore, for instance, strongly resisted joint fundraising efforts. In Denver, however, St. Joseph's Hospital and Mount St. Vincent's Home, as well as the Hebrew Ladies' Benevolent Society, participated in COSD fundraising campaigns.[173]

Finally, Denver, and to a lesser extent Boulder, shared with most other urban centers the blurring of private and public aid during the Progressive

Era. Historian Michael Katz has identified this blurring as one of the major features of America's welfare state.[174] In Costilla and Teller Counties, the interdependence between private and public assistance, while important, always remained informal. In Denver, and to some degree in Boulder, however, the relationship between private and public aid became more formalized. In Denver, public funds regularly supported several private relief associations. The Jewish Relief Society, for instance, received fuel and groceries from the county to distribute to consumptive Jewish families. Public funds also partially supported the Woman's Club free baths.[175]

The city poured large sums of money into the Charity Organization Society of Denver. When Jacobs, Reed, Hart, O'Ryan, and Carr had formed the COSD, they wanted the association to investigate all relief cases, dispense some outdoor aid, and jointly raise money for the various private charities and institutions that belonged to the COSD. The founding members hoped to weed out "undeserving" relief applicants through investigation, provide appropriate relief for those truly in need, and streamline fundraising appeals to a single annual campaign. While Denver's citizens initially greeted the formation of the COSD with great enthusiasm, filling the Tabor Opera House to capacity for its annual meetings, the nation's economic decline in 1893 severely dampened that enthusiasm. As silver prices plunged, mines and smelters closed, causing thousands of unemployed workers to descend on Denver seeking relief. Overwhelmed by the rapid and growing influx of impoverished men, the COSD turned to the city for assistance. In 1893, Denver appropriated ten thousand dollars for the COSD and thereafter made annual appropriations of between just under eight to twelve thousand dollars. By 1910, a particularly good fundraising year, the city's annual appropriation still accounted for just over 30 percent of the COSD budget.[176] This notion of using public funds to maintain a private relief society was not limited to Denver. In nearby Boulder County, both the city of Boulder and the county commissioners likewise appropriated funds for the Associated Charities of Boulder.[177]

But the blurring of boundaries between private and public aid often went beyond the use of public resources to support private charities. Private and public relief organizations often maintained a fluid mixing of responsibilities, duties, services, and personnel. Prior to becoming Gertrude Vaile's hand-picked successor for Denver's Bureau of Charities, Florence Hutsinpillar, for example, had worked for the Denver Federation for Charity and Philanthropy, the successor of the COSD.[178] The Associated Charities of Boulder would make "investigations at [the] request of county commissioners" and agreed to report all "permanent" cases to officials.[179] Likewise, in Denver the COSD, as well as other volunteers, would often help investigate county relief applicants. Denver even took over the running of several privately operated social welfare programs. The city assumed control of the Woman's Club free baths at the League House and later took over the library started by the Neighborhood House settlement.[180] When the city and county of Denver appropriated annual funds for the COSD, public officials clearly spelled out, if not dictated, what they expected of the privately operated relief society. "This Association shall take care of all emergency work arising from transients in the city and county of Denver."[181] Public officials even went so far as to make COSD funding contingent on having two city council members sit on the COSD's Board of Trustees.[182]

During floods, the blurring of private and public relief structures became especially evident. Neighborhoods along the South Platte River and Cherry Creek occasionally suffered from rising water. Even though these floods varied in severity, the city did not tap into its outdoor relief funds to assist flooded neighborhoods. Instead, authorities mainly relied on a combination of public emergency funds and private money collected from special events, concerts, or dances to aid flood victims. The mayor usually appointed a temporary commission, consisting of a mixture of private citizens, often active in charity work, and public officials, to handle all flood-related assistance. These commissions then assumed authority to investigate all claims and distribute funds to worthy applicants. For smaller floods, these temporary commissions doled out approximately eight hundred dollars. Larger floods, like the 1912 Cherry Creek flood that displaced over five hundred families, required up to seven thousand dollars. These funds paid for moving expenses, rent, bedding, clothing, coal, groceries, meals, and lodging.[183]

This blurring of relief organizations brings into question the characterization of the Progressive Era as a period when the welfare state expanded. Political theorist Alan Wolfe has described this blurring between private and public agencies as a "franchise state." According to Wolfe, the state delegates its power to a private agency that can then exercise authority in the name of the state.[184] And indeed the examples from Boulder, and to a greater extent from Denver, clearly reveal this "franchise state" behavior. When Denver, under the leadership of Gertrude Vaile, decided to revamp its public charity system in 1912 and end its annual subsidy to the COSD, this did not represent a dramatic policy shift from private to public relief. For the city had been actively involved, through funding and decision-making, in the administration of COSD for years prior to 1912. Thus, the COSD was never a completely private organization, but rather it often acted as an extension of the city and county government. The changes in Denver's funding policies represented more of a partial consolidation of welfare responsibility rather than an outright expansion of state accountability for its needy. In a sense, the city and county of Denver simply reduced the number of franchises serving its poor residents. Yet, at the same time, the city did not completely end all of its dependency on philanthropic organizations. When two local private charities tried to bill Denver for cases referred to them by the city's welfare department, Vaile made it clear that Denver neither could nor would assume responsibility for all "city cases."[185] While the ending of annual subsidies did cause the COSD to teeter on the brink of dissolving, philanthropic institutions still continued to operate and provide services. And with the blurring of public and private relief prior to 1912, poor folk probably noticed little change with the ending of public subsidies to the COSD.

For the five smaller counties—Boulder, Costilla, Lincoln, Montezuma, Teller, and the Ute Mountain Reservation—even a partial consolidation of welfare services never materialized during the Progressive Era. But the absence of consolidation in the smaller communities did not represent a dominance of private relief, but rather, the continued dominance of public welfare. In four of the five smaller counties, public relief did not assume new responsibilities or new importance during the early twentieth century, but rather, public aid remained the most important form of assistance throughout the entire period. In Teller County a switch did occur from a reliance on private relief to a reliance on public aid. Yet Teller's switch occurred not for ideological reasons linked to the expansion of the welfare state, but rather, due to social, economic, and political events that destroyed the county's informal, privately operated welfare safety net. In the end, practical concerns motivated Teller County to assume a larger responsibility for its needy citizens. The depiction of the Progressive Era as simply an expansion of the welfare state misses both the complexity of previous relief practices and the day-to-day implementation of assistance programs.

Local conditions molded each community's use of private relief organizations and charitable institutions. In some counties, like Lincoln and Montezuma, this meant an absence of any privately operated or funded organization specifically focused on aiding needy citizens. In Costilla, though, residents were able to sustain one such society directed at helping poor people, while in Teller County residents could tap into a rather extensive privately operated welfare safety net. Denver's impoverished citizens had a multitude of religious-, ethnic-, and class-based institutions and organizations, as well as publicly funded facilities, to choose from. County poor farms and county hospitals all took on various characteristics depending on local population levels, funding amounts, existing problems, and management decisions. Cultural attitudes toward institutions likewise influenced how needy people utilized them. But in the end, poor people noticed few changes during the Progressive Era in the roles that private relief associations and charitable institutions played in their lives.

One attempt to minimize, if not override, the strong influence of local conditions in shaping Progressive Era relief policies was the mothers' pension movement. Middle-class female reformers, in particular, wanted both to improve the levels of aid that poor mothers received and to standardize welfare policies across the state. By passing a statewide mothers' pension law, reformers appeared to be on the verge of creating a uniform welfare policy. Yet, the enforcement, or often the lack of enforcement, of mothers' pensions clearly reveals the difficulty in overcoming the strong influences of local practices.

CHAPTER FOUR

So Little Change—
Mothers' Pensions

On April 9, 1910, Emily Freeburg's husband, John, died after a long battle with kidney problems. During his last year, John could not work, and Boulder County commissioners paid his last two months of medical bills. The Miners' Union assumed all his funeral expenses as John's long illness and death had left his family destitute. After her husband's burial, Emily, a Swede who had left school at the age of twelve, faced the difficult challenge of supporting herself and her family. At the time, society offered few employment opportunities for women, especially unskilled immigrant women, and the chances of finding a well-paying job that could accommodate the demands of single parenthood were essentially nonexistent. In addition, eight months after her husband's death, Emily gave birth to Anna, her third daughter. With three children to support, all under the age of seven, Emily turned to one of the few jobs open to women, washing laundry. For the next ten years, she performed the backbreaking task of washing to provide for her family. Yet, by 1920, Emily's health began to fail, and she could no longer solely sustain her family, now just two daughters. In June 1920, a Boulder County judge granted Emily Freeburg a mothers' pension of fifteen dollars per month.[1]

Mothers' pensions, also called mothers' compensation, widows' pensions, or mothers' aid, was a Progressive Era social welfare reform that aimed to halt the common practice of removing children from their homes and placing them in institutions simply due to their families' poverty. This new type of welfare allowed local governments, usually counties, to make cash payments, often long term (that is for several years), to impoverished single mothers so that they could devote their full attention to child rearing by removing the need to earn a wage. These pensions were ultimately intended to both lift single mothers, mainly widows, out of poverty and remove the stigma usually associated with poor relief.

Mothers' pensions have inspired a great deal of attention from scholars. In fact, no other aspect of Progressive Era welfare has generated so much literature. For the most part, authors have characterized these pensions as a major turning point in this nation's welfare practices. Historian Molly Ladd-Taylor claims that the "mothers' pensions movement was one of the most successful reforms of the early twentieth-century United States."[2] John Drew views these pensions as a "remarkable change in American relief policy," and Gwendolyn Mink goes so far as to rest the entire modern welfare state on mothers' pensions.[3] Many scholars view mothers' pensions as helping to usher in a two-tiered, gendered welfare system that applies means- and morality-tested standards for female recipients while it applies fixed-qualification criteria for male recipients.[4] Thus, for many writers, mothers' pensions act as a clean break from previous welfare practices.

Yet, despite the large volume of material on mothers' compensation, most of this literature offers little help when we try to assess the impact of these pensions on the actual lives of impoverished women. The question, "Did mothers' pensions radically alter the delivery of aid for poor mothers?" remains largely unanswered. Christopher Howard noticed this trend, lamenting that we know very little about the "difference mothers' pensions made in the lives of single mothers and their children."[5] This chapter aims to address this analytical gap. We need to ask if the lives of Emily Freeburg and her two daughters changed much once they received a pension. And we need to assess how and if mothers' pensions differed from previous poor relief practices.

The few historical studies that do assess the implementation of mothers' pensions are more tempered in their claims about the effects of the pensions. Howard, for example, reasons that "mothers' pensions never lived up to the promise held out by Progressive reformers."[6] Historian Joanne Goodwin examines the implementation of mothers' pensions in Chicago, and she likewise concludes that the city's pension program failed to live up to its potential.

Thwarted by limited funds and staffs, political infighting, and racial and eth-nic divisions, the mothers' pension program, writes Goodwin, stumbled from the very beginning. Focusing on implementation, Goodwin does not view mothers' pensions as a major breakthrough in welfare practices.[7]

An examination of the implementation of mothers' pensions in Colorado also reveals little change from previous relief practices. Many Colorado coun-ty commissioners simply ignored the new law, choosing not to enforce it. Other communities delayed enacting the welfare act for months and some-times for years. For mothers in these counties, pensions obviously made little or no difference in their impoverished situations. In fact, in many counties key components of pensions were already established prior to or independent of the state's mothers' compensation law. The existence of these similar practices or goals made mothers' pensions seem redundant and unnecessary, further discouraging implementation. Often those counties that did enact mothers' aid did so in a manner that simply continued existing relief practices. In these cases, mothers' pensions became only another form of outdoor aid and not a major transformation in assistance. And even when enacted, mothers' com-pensation faced persistent problems of underfunding and small staffs. Colorado's mothers' pensions, like Chicago's, fell well short of accomplishing all that its backers had promised.

But unlike Goodwin's examination, this study argues that the key reason for the failure of mothers' pensions to alter the welfare system rests with the continued influence of local circumstances on the delivery of aid. One of the many aims of the mothers' pension movement was to create uniform welfare practices within a state. Yet, pensions failed to achieve this goal since they were unable to override the strength of local conditions and customs. Many of the same factors that molded a community's public poor relief system and private charities also shaped how, or even if, mothers' pensions were enacted. A coun-ty's current public relief measures, the contributions of private charities, the policy decisions of local officials, and the local economic opportunities for women, all influenced how a county chose to implement mothers' pensions. And since pensions were generally dependent on local taxes for support and left local officials in charge of determining eligibility requirements, the influence of local conditions remained a vital component of mothers' com-pensation. In the end, mothers' pensions, considered by many scholars as one of the key accomplishments of Progressive Era reformers, actually made few changes in poor relief practices.

Campaigning for Mothers' Pensions

The campaign for mothers' pensions swept the nation during the twentieth century's second decade as forty states enacted some form of pension legislation. Colorado led efforts to establish such laws by becoming the second state, after Illinois, to approve statewide mothers' compensation in 1912 and the first state to do so by popular vote. The mothers' pension movement brought together a coalition of women's groups, juvenile court judges, and social workers. These supporters promised that pensions would help alleviate some of society's injustices as well as remove the shame often associated with receiving assistance. But not all favored mothers' pensions. Many charity workers, including some very prominent individuals, along with representatives from children's institutions, vigorously fought these new forms of welfare. Opponents argued, in brief, that if public officials administered mothers' pensions, it would be a step backward, a return to unregulated and corrupt relief methods.

The 1909 White House Conference on the Care of Dependent Children provided the spark that ignited the mothers' pension movement. President Theodore Roosevelt invited over two hundred child welfare advocates from charity societies, settlement houses, juvenile courts, children's institutions, and public relief programs to Washington to grapple with the issue of the nation's growing number of dependent children. According to census figures, about ninety-three thousand dependent children resided in orphanages and children's homes, and thousands more, probably at least fifty thousand more, lived in private homes with foster parents. "The interests of the nation," stated President Roosevelt, "are involved in the welfare of this army of children no less than in our great material affairs." After two days, these child welfare advocates presented President Roosevelt with a list of fourteen unanimously agreed-to resolutions aimed at improving conditions for dependent children.[8]

Most important to this study, the 1909 White House Conference endorsed a proposal that advocated that dependent children should not be removed from their homes and placed in institutions because of poverty. "Home life is the highest and finest product of civilization," stated the conference's summary report. "It is a great molding force of mind and character. Children should not be deprived of it except for urgent and compelling reasons." Only due to "inefficiency" or "immorality," according to conference participants, should children be taken from their homes. Children suffering from "temporary misfortune" or the absence of a "normal bread-winner, should as a rule, be kept with their parents." Communities, the report suggested, should provide aid or a pension for impoverished parents who require assistance in maintaining "suitable homes for the rearing of children." The resolution strongly encouraged that this assistance come from private charities rather than public sources; nevertheless, the conference did hedge a bit on this preference, stating that "aid should be given by such methods and from such sources as may be determined by the general relief policy of each community."[9]

While the 1909 White House Conference proposed aid for needy parents, especially widows, it did not offer any type of concrete legislation to address the situation. At the time, the legal authority to assist impoverished parents clearly rested with local and, to a lesser degree, with state jurisdictions. But, the conference was successful in publicizing the need for pensions, especially with President Roosevelt's strong endorsement. Still, mothers' aid became one of the most hotly contested social reforms of the Progressive Era despite the conference's unanimous endorsement.

Advocates for mothers' pensions rested their support on several different rationales. First, and probably most important, widows, and to a much lesser degree, deserted or unwed mothers, elicited sympathy from society. As previously discussed, social workers and the public almost unanimously considered widows to be a group deserving aid, even long-term assistance. Thus, politicians and proponents could exploit this sentiment in appealing for pensions.[10] Supporters also championed the benefits of home life over institutions. "The place for the child is in its own home, with its own parents," asserted Judge Ben Lindsey, Denver's pioneering juvenile court judge, during the closing dinner for the 1909 White House Conference.[11] Pensions, in theory, would allow mothers to remain at home, devoting their full attention to their children while maintaining a "morally sound" home environment. This would reinforce a woman's maternal role by keeping her out of the paid workforce and in the home. "The prime duty of the man is to work, to be the breadwinner; the prime duty of the woman is to be the mother, the housewife," asserted President Roosevelt.[12] In addition to protecting motherhood, pensions were also cost-effective when compared to institutionalization, argued supporters. Why pay institutions to raise children when their own mothers could raise them for less? Plus, mothers could provide that special nurturing and bonding, that maternal love, that only mothers could offer their children. "There is no love like a mother's love," observed Chicago's juvenile Judge Merritt Pinckney.[13]

Many favored mothers' pensions for their potential to transform the welfare state and expand women's claims to citizenship. Some reformers viewed mothers' pensions as a first step toward the ultimate goal of creating some form of comprehensive social insurance for all impoverished mothers, not just single ones, and of expanding the state's responsibility for other groups as well. Mothers' pensions "will prove at least a good entering wedge for those social and industrial insurance laws," stated Lindsey, "that must come in time as the public is educated to their necessity."[14] These reformers viewed the unpaid work performed by mothers as essential toward producing good citizens and a strong nation. Pensions were simply a small and first acknowledgment by the government of this work. "The child is the state and the state is the child," argued Lindsey.[15] Mothers' pensions implied, much like soldiers' pensions, that women were serving the state. Thus, these pensions could be viewed, not as charity, but as a right. By giving pensions, instead of poor relief, to impoverished mothers some of the stigma associated with receiving assistance would be removed. And as Joanne Goodwin points out, some reformers initially linked mothers' pensions with the "expansion of married women's rights" and claims of women's full citizenship.[16] For these supporters, pensions represented a form of social justice to rectify, at least partially, the situation of poor women, and they hoped, in the near future, the condition of all women.

Finally, reformers called for mothers' pensions because other forms of assistance had been terribly inadequate. Private charity organizations had failed to provide properly for an overwhelming number of needy widows and their children. In New York City, for example, "the great relief societies of the city were too poor in money to take care of families of widows properly."[17] Farther north in Massachusetts, private charity had left "the children of the self-respecting widow hungry."[18] Proponents of mothers' pensions argued that since private charities had been unable to care for widows and their children, communities should use public funds to support them. What really mattered, in the end, was not where the money came from, argued supporters, but rather that widows and their children received assistance to maintain their homes. Regarding the fears about corruption and waste, advocates like Pinckney believed that public relief should indeed follow proper and thorough casework methods. Both "private and public relief, when administered without proper inquiry and investigation," warned Pinckney, "are harmful and demoralizing. The success of either method is chiefly a matter of administration."[19]

Opponents of mothers' pensions put up a vocal and persistent fight to halt these new measures. Many officials from children's institutions as well as charity workers, especially those associated with the Charity Organization Society (COS) movement, including New York's Edward Devine, Frederic Almy, and Mary Richmond, and Massachusetts's C. C. Carstens, opposed mothers' pensions. As a whole, this group argued that indeed widows and their dependent children were worthy of aid, and that children should remain in their own homes. "We are all agreed," wrote Mary Richmond, "that families are being broken up which should be kept together; that mothers are being overworked with disastrous results to themselves and to their children."[20] The dispute arose over not whom to help but rather how best to deliver assistance to these needy mothers and their children.

The use of public funds and public officials to administer mothers' pensions horrified opponents. The COS movement had aimed to eliminate or at least reduce the public sector's role in providing relief. Mothers' compensation would dramatically challenge this goal. Richmond feared that mothers' aid had the potential to expand at a far greater and faster rate than the politically charged Civil War soldiers' pensions had. Furthermore, Richmond reasoned that "veterans are a diminishing class unless we have another big war; not so with mothers."[21] Some also raised concerns that mothers' pensions would become corrupt as they would be administered by political appointees rather than by trained social workers. Almy believed that the public would be unwilling to pay the salaries required to hire and retain skilled social workers. This failure would be disastrous, according to Almy, as "untrained relief is poisonous to the poor."[22] Early inspections of Chicago's mothers' pension program seemed to confirm these fears. Chicago's probation officers, wrote Carstens, performed a "meager investigation," and as a consequence "presented certain facts which were wholly inadequate for determining whether or not a pension was advisable."[23] The use of the public sector to administer mothers' pensions could also threaten the very existence of the COS movement. In places where public funds dominated a community's relief strategies, private charities often struggled to survive, finding it difficult to raise enough money. Almy, Richmond, and Denver's Gertrude Vaile had all noticed this inverse relationship.[24]

Finally, some objected to mothers' pensions because the proposed aid measures failed to address the root of the problem, and, in fact, had the potential to worsen the situation. Mothers' compensation did nothing to prevent the circumstances that caused male breadwinners to die, leaving women in the difficult situation of trying to support a family. Instead of using public resources to support widows, argued opponents, communities should use public funds to combat diseases and unsafe working environments that killed off male workers. These preventive measures would reduce both the number of widows and the need for pensions. In addition, by using public funds for compulsory insurance programs—workmen's compensation and sickness and old age benefits—there would, once again, be little need for mothers' aid.[25] Edward Devine objected to mothers' pensions, in part, because they did not function as a true pension nor as a sound social insurance policy with beneficiaries making regular contributions.[26] Mothers' compensation also did not address the issue of low wages for working women. In fact, Richmond theorized that pensions might actually "subsidize the sweated industries in the large cities" thus reinforcing women's already low wages, and making it even more difficult for impoverished women to support themselves.[27]

Amidst all these debates, various places began experimenting with different forms of pension-like measures to assist needy mothers and their children. As early as 1906, some California juvenile judges began liberally interpreting sections of the state constitution so as to use county funds to maintain children in their parents' impoverished homes following San Francisco's earthquake and fire. In Michigan, officials could use school funds to help needy parents, and in Oklahoma widowed mothers could receive a type of school scholarship equivalent to the earnings of a child. Milwaukee County, Wisconsin, set up a special fund that the juvenile court could use to aid families. The Missouri legislature approved the first specific mothers' pension act in 1911, which applied only to Kansas City. That same year, the legislature in Illinois ratified the nation's first statewide mothers' pension law.[28]

Cooperation between Judge Ben Lindsey of Denver's juvenile court and middle-class women from the Colorado Federation of Women's Clubs led efforts to enact Colorado's mothers' compensation law. Lindsey had received worldwide attention for his pioneering work with children, and on a regular basis he witnessed how hardworking widows struggled to maintain their families. When Missouri and Illinois approved mothers' pensions, he visited both Kansas City and Chicago to investigate how these new laws operated. Using Illinois's law as a rough model, he crafted Colorado's Mothers' Compensation Act with greater safeguards against possible corruption than found in the Illinois act.[29] Throughout the campaign for Colorado's mothers' pensions, Lindsey served as a prominent spokesman for the measure, repeatedly defending the initiative, in the press and in pamphlets, when attacked by opponents. Not only could he use his celebrity status to generate publicity for the act, but he also used his relations with other nationally known social reformers like Chicago's Jane Addams and Judge Pinckney to obtain endorsements for Colorado's proposal.[30]

While Lindsey occupied much of the spotlight throughout the campaign, middle-class women from the Colorado Federation of Women's Clubs (CFWC) created the backbone of the mothers' compensation effort. Since 1893, when Colorado women received the right to vote, they had played an important role in proposing and pushing for a range of reforms with the Women's Clubs of Colorado often leading these legislative efforts. By 1911, the Legislative Committee of the CFWC had become a major political power-broker in the state. That year, for example, the committee endorsed twenty-one measures that encompassed a comprehensive reform agenda including a child labor law, an eight-hour law for women, a miner's eight-hour law, minimum wages for teachers, workmen's compensation, teachers for the adult blind, an anti-cigarette law, regulation of dance halls, and funding for a state forester. Out of their office in the state capitol, the legislative committee held weekly meetings, sent out over three thousand letters on various measures, asked for hearings on certain acts, and protested against other bills. In all, the CFWC flexed its political muscle as eleven of the twenty-one proposed measures became law.[31] The women of the CFWC Legislative Committee believed that "if our nation is to survive and maintain its high standard of morality we must not build up its commerce on the souls and bodies of our women and children." Indeed, the very purpose of the committee was to deal "solely with legislation that affects humanity, educational matters, and the home. We must, therefore, combat the lobbyists of corporate interests."[32] Thus, when the 1911 state legislature failed to approve a mothers' pension bill and an eight-hour workday for women, two measures proposed by the CFWC and both key elements of their reform agenda, the women used the initiative to place both bills on the 1912 ballot.[33]

Colorado's proposed statewide Mothers' Compensation Act had four main components. The law allowed parents to reclaim their children from the State Home for Dependent and Neglected Children. In the past, once a judge committed a child to the state home, parents had no legal method to recover their child even if circumstances at home improved. Second, when a child was adopted or placed in a temporary foster home, then the state, according to the intended measure, should, "as far as practicable," place that child in a home that conformed to the religious beliefs of the parents. While this provision was not mandatory, it at least gave parents some comfort knowing that authorities had to consider religious beliefs when placing a child. The act also established methods for providing and dispensing of pensions for dependent or neglected children. "If the parent or parents of such dependent or neglected child are poor and unable to properly care for such child, but otherwise are proper guardians, and it is for the welfare of such child to remain at home," then the courts may determine the amount of money needed "to enable the parent or parents to properly care for such child." In counties with populations over one hundred thousand (only Denver had such a large population) the juvenile court would handle these pension cases, while in all other counties the county court would be in charge. But the courts would not have complete control over the pensions. Rather, the courts and county commissioners held different responsibilities, with power essentially divided between the two. While the courts could determine who received aid and at what levels, county commissioners made appropriations for the pensions. The purpose behind this division of power was to prevent potential misuse of county funds. Finally, to combat wife and child desertion, the Mothers' Compensation Act required commissioners in counties with over twenty thousand residents to "establish and maintain workhouses or proper facilities for the detention and employment of men convicted of non support of women and children." Commissioners would use any money earned by these men to help carry out the mothers' pension law.[34]

Opponents of Colorado's proposed mothers' pensions launched a series of "bitter attacks" in an attempt to sway voters.[35] A small group of philanthropists, including those associated with the State Home for Dependent and Neglected Children, spoke out against the initiative. While opponents had numerous objections, their main concerns revolved around fears that the proposed law would dramatically increase expenditures. They argued that "the cost to counties and the state would be prohibitive in carrying out the altruistic provisions" because they believed, in part, that the compensation law would create a costly new bureaucracy to investigate and report on mothers.[36] Opponents also anticipated a large number of needy mothers applying for the pensions, which would surely overwhelm county treasuries, and they also feared a huge influx of impoverished mothers to Colorado seeking support. The maintenance of county workhouses would likewise be expensive. In addition, opponents argued that the new law would cause great harm to the self-respect and personal pride of mothers. "It will mean the permanent pauperization of every woman and child that comes under its baneful influence." Finally, some worried that the State Home for Dependent and Neglected Children would be completely emptied if the act won approval. Supporters of the initiative responded to each one of these concerns, pointing out that in some instances opponents had simply misread the law, while in other cases they had exaggerated the potential consequences of the measure. Lindsey repeatedly cited Illinois' experiences with mothers' pensions to show how Colorado's initiative would most likely change relief practices.[37]

Despite opponents' vigorous attacks, Colorado voters overwhelmingly approved the statewide Mothers' Compensation Act. Only one of the sixty-two counties voted against the measure, and throughout the state it carried more than a two-to-one margin of victory. Boulder, Costilla, Denver, Lincoln, Montezuma, and Teller Counties all approved the act.[38] The *Denver Post* credited the voting power of women with the measure's strong showing at the ballot boxes. "Women Come Out Almost Solidly For Mothers' Compensation Act" read a *Denver Post* headline.[39] Indeed, the women of the CFWC Legislative Committee claimed "a large share of the victory" since they had initiated the measure.[40]

But the Mothers' Compensation Act's huge victory did not halt attacks on the measure. In fact, the initiative's success seemed only to increase the onslaught as opponents continued to lash out. Four days after the election, an article appeared in the *Denver Times* accusing voters of being "susceptible to sudden attacks of hysteria" for approving the law. The article claimed that most voters had not read nor understood the measure, and that the title had misled many citizens.[41] Almost a month after the election, the State Board of Charities and Corrections held a debate on the compensation act. Supporters and opponents thoroughly debated the measure, often repeating issues and concerns that were already addressed prior to the election.[42]

An attempt by a state legislator to modify the Mothers' Compensation Act proved most threatening. Charles Dailey proposed a bill that would remove the courts, both county and juvenile, from the compensation act and allow county commissioners "to pay indigent parents for the care of their children" without the court's input. In the end, Dailey's bill failed to win approval.[43]

Soon after Colorado approved mothers' compensations, other states passed similar laws. In twenty-seven of the forty-two state assemblies that met in 1913, mothers' pensions were part of the agenda. Legislatures in Washington, Oregon, California, Michigan, Ohio, Pennsylvania, Indiana, Minnesota, Nebraska, New Jersey, and New York all grappled with either studying, debating, or approving aid to needy mothers.[44] By the end of 1913, nineteen states had approved statewide mothers' pensions. Two years later, nine more states did so, and by 1920 a total of forty states had passed mothers' compensation laws.[45] The rapid spread of these laws across the nation seemed like a "wildfire," and according to historian Mark Leff, almost no other social justice issue "mustered a better legislative record."[46]

Lack of Implementation

Did mothers' pensions make a difference in the lives of impoverished women? For many needy women in Colorado, mothers' compensation made essentially no difference during the early twentieth century. Women on the Ute Mountain Reservation could not even apply for pensions because the new state law did not cover them, and most county commissioners and county judges simply never enacted the Mothers' Compensation Act despite its overwhelming support. Six months after the new law went into effect (January 22, 1913), only four counties had made appropriations to begin its operation.[47] By June 1915, seventeen counties had partially enacted mothers' compensations, and three years later, still only one-third of Colorado's counties had carried out, at least in part, the act.[48] The State Board of Charities and Corrections lamented this poor implementation, noting that if "the Mothers' Compensation Act is to mean anything, it should be in force in every county in the State."[49] This lack of enforcement was not limited to Colorado. In Illinois, for instance, two years after its mothers' pension law went into effect, only 16 out of the 102 counties carried out the measure.[50] Enforcement seemed to have improved dramatically by 1916 as 73 Illinois counties implemented, at least partially, mothers' aid.[51] Still the problem of getting communities to enact pension laws remained a persistent issue for almost all states. Mothers' pensions, observed Emma Lundberg of the U.S. Children's Bureau, "offers perhaps the most obvious arguments as to the futility... of placing laws on the statute books but failing to make them practically effective."[52]

In this study of six Colorado counties, Costilla and Montezuma did not implement mothers' pensions, and Lincoln only used the new law once before abandoning it. These three rural counties did not disregard the Mothers' Compensation Act out of ignorance. The campaign for pensions, as noted above, was hotly debated throughout the state, and since voters approved the act through an initiative, all sections of Colorado knew of the law. In addition, the lack of implementation cannot be conveniently dismissed, as Edith Abbott and Sophonisba Breckinridge did in their study of the mothers' pension law in Illinois, as taking place in the "poorer and more backward counties" of the state.[53] In Colorado, no such pattern emerged with regard to which rural counties did or did not enforce pensions. Costilla, Lincoln, and Montezuma Counties chose not to utilize the Mothers' Compensation Act because the new measure would not have substantially altered existing relief practices. In fact, all three counties, to varying degrees, were already delivering aid in such a way as to conform to many of the main goals of mothers' pensions.

In many respects, Costilla County's outdoor poor relief practices succeeded best in fulfilling most of the aims of Colorado's mothers' compensation. Costilla already offered long-term assistance, provided cash relief (after April 1917), attached little stigma or shame to receiving help, and encouraged aid recipients to remain in their own communities. These four characteristics of Costilla's poor relief system paralleled many of the key objectives of the mothers' pension movement. Yet, Costilla fulfilled these goals through indirect channels and methods that did not conform to the ideals of Progressive Era reform. While historians have associated the aims of mothers' pensions with efforts by largely urban, Protestant, Anglo-Saxon Americans trying to impose "American" cultural values on impoverished immigrants and African Americans, evidence from Costilla County suggests a slightly different interpretation. Although Costilla never formally implemented mothers' pensions, it fulfilled many of the law's intentions through rural, Hispanic, Catholic traditions.

Costilla County already offered long-term assistance to its residents prior to the approval of mothers' pensions. As mentioned in chapter 1, Costilla's aid recipients averaged the longest duration on poor relief, averaging close to three years (34.64 months). The few widows (twenty-four) who did receive aid in Costilla ranged from twenty-three to seventy-two years of age and remained on county poor rolls for various lengths of time. Genobeva Lopez, thirty years old and with three little children, received county assistance for only four months before she remarried. But Anastasia Gallegos, age forty-two with several small children, remained on the county poor books for four years.[54] Maternalism, however, did not motivate Costilla's long-term relief practices because most everyone, both males and females, remained on county relief for extremely long periods. Women averaged 33.67 months on aid, while males averaged slightly longer times, 36.40 months (see Table 17).

Indeed, the importance of family and community motivated the county's policies long before Progressive Era reformers realized the significance of home life. Costilla's aid system already operated on an assumption that poor people would stay in their homes and communities. The county provided only small amounts of monthly aid, with women averaging just $4.83 per month, hardly enough to support an individual, much less a family.[55] Thus, poor residents had to tap into other forms of assistance, such as support from nearby relatives, use of the barter and subsistence economy, and help from the Penitentes in order to survive. While all these forms of assistance supplemented the meager levels of county poor relief, more important, these informal relief strategies required that the poor person remain in, and be a part of, the community. As a consequence, Costilla's citizens would not remove children from their homes due to poverty. In fact, the county placed no children in the State Home for Dependent and Neglected Children during the first two decades of the twentieth century.[56] Costilla's poor relief, both from the county treasury and from other informal sources, was acutely centered around community and place. Absent either one, Costilla's relief failed to function adequately. The strong sense of community and place were key goals of the mothers' pension movement, and yet Costilla already incorporated, albeit informally, these concepts into its relief practices.

Costilla County also provided its needy mothers with cash assistance instead of in-kind aid, another major component of Colorado's Mothers' Compensation Act. In April 1917, Costilla's commissioners abandoned their practice of dispensing aid through individual accounts at local merchants by unanimously voting to "pay for the support of the county poor in cash (or by check)."[57] Convenience seemed to be the motivating factor behind this change in policy. Under the previous system, the commissioners had to transfer accounts from one store to another whenever a recipient moved or used a different store.[58] Some aid recipients even shopped across the border in Costilla, New Mexico, the nearest town to their place of residence.[59] By giving cash directly to the poor, the commissioners no longer had to transfer accounts or keep track of local merchants' poor records. Thus, almost five years after voters approved direct cash payments to indigent parents through mothers' pensions, Costilla County officials fulfilled this same objective by delivering all assistance in the form of monthly cash payments.

Finally, receiving aid in Costilla County carried little stigma, just as supporters of mothers' compensation had desired. Mothers' pensions were "a recognition by the state that the aid is rendered, not as a charity," wrote Judge Lindsey, "but as a right—as justice due mothers whose work in rearing their children is a work for the state as much as that of the soldier who is paid by the state for his services on the battlefield."[60] According to Lindsey, this sense of recognition for services rendered for the well-being of the state would remove any blemish associated with pensions. Yet, in Costilla County the stigma of receiving poor relief had largely been eliminated, although not through the enactment of mothers' pensions or by acknowledging a mother's service to the state. Instead, a combination of overall economic circumstances and religious beliefs washed away much of poor relief's shame. The vast majority of Costilla's residents were poor, and at any moment almost anyone could find themselves in need of aid. In addition, the county's barter and subsistence economy required constant mutual cooperation among community members. With such widespread poverty and frequent dependence on one another, attaching shame to those receiving assistance would, in a sense, humiliate the entire community. More importantly, the strong influence of Catholicism, through the Penitentes, elevated charitable acts. For not only was it "Christ-like" to aid the needy, but the poor were also "blessed" and deserving of compassion and respect. With Costilla County fulfilling so many key components of mothers' pensions, the new law hardly seemed groundbreaking, or for that matter, even worthy of implementing. Clearly, mothers' compensation offered little new to the county's needy women.

Lincoln and Montezuma Counties did not succeed to the same degree as Costilla did in fulfilling so many of the goals of the mothers' pension movement. Neither Lincoln nor Montezuma generally offered long-term aid for its residents. Both provided the shortest average times on relief, just 6.38 months for Lincoln and 7.57 months for Montezuma. Women did fare slightly better, averaging 8.22 months of relief in Lincoln, and 8.71 months of aid in Montezuma (see Table 17). Despite these low numbers, both communities still embraced a few of the concepts present in Colorado's Mothers' Compensation Act. Lincoln and Montezuma Counties did, on occasion, support widows for extended periods. Lincoln's Mary Yoder received assistance for herself and her three children for thirty-two months. Montezuma officials granted Mrs. Augusta Kirk, age thirty-five, and her large family, just over $1,350 in assistance over a three and a half year period.[61] Even in places where commissioners tended to give public relief only in short durations, exceptions were often made for widowed mothers. Thus, the notion that mothers' pensions introduced the idea of long-term assistance for needy mothers disregards the policies of communities prior to the law's approval. Likewise, the actual practices of commissioners clearly indicate that it would be wrong to assume that a county that did not implement mothers' pensions also did not offer impoverished mothers long-term aid.

Both Lincoln and Montezuma Counties provided cash relief for recipients years prior to pensions. The practice of using cash was somewhat uncommon in both communities, more uncommon in Lincoln than in Montezuma, but women still occasionally did get aid in cash. In May 1909, Mrs. B. F. Cease of Lincoln County, for example, received $25 due to her husband's illness. Montezuma's Lizzie Stiles, age twenty-eight, received $135 in cash over an eleven-month period after her husband deserted the family.[62] Thus, at the same time that Judge Lindsey and other mothers' pension supporters were vigorously working to block an attempt to alter the state's recently passed mothers' compensation law, which would have allowed county commissioners the right to pay indigent parents without any judicial oversight, Lincoln and Montezuma Counties were already doing just that. And Costilla County would soon begin a similar policy. The fact that urban reformers like Lindsey were obviously so unaware of the daily realities of relief practices in other sections of the state suggests an extremely narrow knowledge base from which Progressive Era reformers acted, at least in terms of welfare issues.

Providing cash aid was not the only way that communities tried to assist needy mothers. Montezuma's Georgia Denby, the one who stayed briefly at the poor farm, essentially directed her own relief by informing officials of her needs. "I am very sorry," began Denby's letter to her commissioners, dated May 27, 1912, "but I will have to ask a little help of the county as I am not able to get enough work to support us all." Denby's husband had not sent any money since the end of March, and the family was beginning to need assistance. She went on to request only "eight or ten dollars" for flour, meat, and potatoes since she could "earn enough to keep up other things."[63] But Denby would not see her husband again. As a result, beginning in June 1912, Denby, deserted and with a "large family," began regularly receiving county aid in the form of supplies. That next summer, Denby wrote to the commissioners requesting to "please have the July warrant cashed but not the August. We can get along until winter when there will be less work, so I will not ask again for any money until November."[64] By 1914 or 1915, Denby entered the poor farm for a short time for reasons that are unknown. But in March 1917, Denby once again wrote, this time requesting that her son be given five dollars "in cash this month instead of in trade" since she would only use ten dollars in trade that month.[65] Finally, in February 1921, almost nine years after first receiving public relief, Denby wrote her county commissioners to request that they "please discontinue signing any more warrants for me from the Poor Fund. It was a great help to us for a long time and I thank you."[66] Denby, to a degree, regulated her own relief. She not only largely determined the starting and ending dates, but she also stopped and started aid as needed and tried to alter the type of relief delivered. While Denby's case may have been unusual, her story does show the extent to which communities sometimes tried to accommodate single mothers, obviously within certain acceptable limits and with prodding from relief recipients, even though mothers' pensions were not implemented.

Lincoln County's sole attempt to implement mothers' compensation reveals the shortcomings of the law, at least in the eyes of local officials. In February 1914, Eva Pease, a forty-one-year-old widow with seven children, ranging in ages from two to fifteen years old, began receiving county aid. At first, this assistance took the form of ten to twenty dollars worth of monthly supplies. Then in March 1915, Pease appeared in county court asking for "an allowance sufficient to enable her to properly care for and educate" her children. Whether Pease or county officials initiated this action is not clear;

however, authorities did cooperate with the proceedings. After ensuring that Pease was in good health, of "good moral character," and that the children should "remain at home," Lincoln County Judge J. W. Veal granted Pease a mothers' compensation worth twenty dollars per month.[67]

At first glance, it appears as if Pease's circumstances improved. Indeed, mothers' compensation guaranteed Pease twenty dollars per month, a doubling of some of her previous assistance levels. Plus, she now received cash, not in-kind relief. But the changes brought on by mothers' compensation were superficial and lasted for only a few months. While the court claimed to have investigated Pease's situation, the thoroughness of that inquiry seems no different than previous poor relief investigations. The court, for instance, seemed unable to list how much Pease earned each month and could only offer the broadest characterizations of her circumstances. The fact that Pease lived forty miles from Hugo, Lincoln's county seat, may have discouraged any investigation, especially one that may have simply duplicated work already performed by the county commissioners. More important, Judge Veal ordered Pease to receive mothers' compensation only until September 1915. After that point, the court had to reorder the payments.[68] Why the judge restricted mothers' compensation to only six months remains unknown, but Pease obviously did not expect such a short duration. In December she wrote to Veal stating that she had "not received the widows check since in September. I hope you have not forgotten us. Hoping to hear from you soon."[69] But instead of approving more mothers' compensation, county officials simply resumed Pease's poor relief, twenty dollars in monthly supplies.[70]

Lincoln County's experiment with mothers' compensation proved brief, as Pease held the distinction of being the county's first and last resident to get a pension. In the end, mothers' pensions seemed, at least to county authorities, only to duplicate the county's existing poor relief efforts while adding an additional layer of bureaucracy, the role of the judicial branch, to an already functioning welfare system. So when Martha Stetson, deserted by her husband and already receiving county aid, asked Judge Veal for mothers' compensation, the county simply continued providing her with in-kind aid instead of granting a pension. Stetson had hoped that the pension would have provided her with more than what she was currently receiving, and quite possibly she preferred, as did other poor relief recipients, cash assistance instead of in-kind aid. "I am alone on a homestead," wrote Stetson in

December 1915. "Have no fuel. And must certainly suffer unless I get help."[71] But since Lincoln County officials saw little difference between mothers' pensions and poor relief, there seemed no reason to hassle with the cumbersome procedures of the compensation law to help Stetson. For Lincoln and Montezuma Counties, mothers' pensions offered little substantial change to existing policies. As a result, county officials ignored Colorado's Mothers' Compensation Act.

Enacting Mothers' Pensions

While commissioners in Costilla, Lincoln, and Montezuma Counties basically disregarded mothers' pensions, other locales did eventually enact the new law. Boulder and Teller both enforced Colorado's Mothers' Compensation Act, although each began implementation at drastically different times. Boulder County officials initiated the pension law in May 1914, almost a year and a half after its effective date. Despite Boulder's delay, the county was still one of the first in the state to enact the measure. Meanwhile, in Teller County, Gladys Pryor received that county's first mothers' pension in November 1920, almost eight years after the effective date.[72] Why such a difference in starting dates? Just as local circumstances and relief practices determined why Costilla, Lincoln, and Montezuma did not enforce mothers' pensions, local conditions likewise influenced when Boulder and Teller began issuing pensions.

Teller County's long delay in enforcing mothers' pensions comes as a bit of a surprise because its citizens seemed well informed and supportive of the measure. A few weeks prior to the election, the *Cripple Creek Times* ran an article explaining and quoting much of the proposed initiative.[73] On election day, although just under 69 percent of Colorado's voters approved the Mothers' Compensation Act, in Teller County the measure fared much better with just over 85 percent voting in favor.[74] Teller's voters provided the measure with one of its highest margins of victory, and the highest margin among the six counties in this study.

Yet despite the initiative's overwhelming political victory, Teller County officials did not enact the measure when it passed. In a sense, the local economic conditions seemed to have nullified the victory at the ballot box. Even though the county's mining economy started to take a downturn at this time, for women, especially unmarried women, Teller continued, as previously mentioned, to offer more job opportunities than many other locations. In 1910, just over 64 percent of Teller's unmarried women—widowed, single, or divorced—worked, while only a little more than 46 percent of the nation's unmarried women were employed.[75] With Teller's relatively good job prospects for women, county officials rarely gave outside aid to women simply due to an absence of a male breadwinner. Instead, commissioners expected healthy single, divorced, and widowed women to seek out employment. As a result of these expectations and the relatively decent job prospects, mothers' pensions remained unenforced in Teller County despite its huge electoral victory.

The economic situation in Teller, however, continued to deteriorate over the next few years. The completion of several drainage tunnels only temporarily solved the problems of underground flooding and only delayed, for a few years, the depletion of gold veins.[76] By 1915, the area was overrun "with men out of employment." The local newspaper reported that "there are at least 500 miners in the neighborhood of Victor seeking work," and the same held true for the town of Goldfield.[77] Several smaller communities in Teller County—Altman, Elkton, Gillett, Goldfield, and Independence—all experienced dramatic population reductions as workers and their families moved away when mining and milling companies reduced or ceased operations.[78] In Victor's and Cripple Creek's business districts, vacancies increased, and buildings began collapsing due to natural decay, lack of maintenance, and because people appropriated building materials. In some instances, property owners razed their own buildings to reduce property taxes and to sell off materials for construction projects in other locations.[79] Despite all of these visible signs of deterioration, the local newspaper, in 1917, tried to reassure residents that there was "nothing wrong with the Cripple Creek [mining] district." The editor reasoned that rumors about "the district . . . facing disaster" should be disregarded as the "district will still be producing its millions in gold after the present generation has gone to the far away shore."[80] With just over ten million dollars in gold production that year, the newspaper was not completely misguided in its optimism.[81]

But by 1920 any hopeful signs of returning to a booming, or even a stable, economy had clearly disappeared. After 1917, gold production dramatically declined. In 1920, the Cripple Creek Mining District produced only a little over $4.3 million in gold, a huge reduction from 1900 when the area pulled $18 million in gold from the ground.[82] Like its gold output, Teller County's population also sharply declined over the years. In 1900, the county housed 29,002 residents, but ten years later less than half that number, 14,351, still resided there. By 1920, Teller's population had once again shrunk by over half to only 6,696 residents (see Table 1). The Cripple Creek Mining District's golden era had definitely come to an end.

As Teller County's economy continued to decay, so too did women's employment prospects. When mining and milling operations closed, jobs for women also began disappearing, as the male workers that they had served moved to new locations. Thus, Teller's job situation for women had become anything but exceptional. Unlike ten years earlier, when figures for women's employment radically differed between Teller and the rest of the nation, by 1920 the two sets of data essentially mirrored one another. In 1920, only 49.8 percent of Teller's unmarried women worked, a drop of almost 15 percent from 1910. Meanwhile, nationally 46.4 percent of unmarried women were employed (see Table 18).[83] Teller County had become rather typical in what it could offer women for paid work.

The downturn in women's job opportunities meant that the issue of enforcing mothers' compensation warranted reconsideration. With the decrease in women's employment, Teller County officials could no longer expect unmarried women to support themselves and their children. As a result, commissioners slowly moved forward with enacting the state's Mothers' Compensation Act. In November 1919, commissioners approved collecting taxes for mothers' pensions.[84] A year later, County Judge Karl W. Farr awarded Teller's first mothers' pension to Gladys Pryor at fifteen dollars per month. The following month, December 1920, Judge Farr approved twenty dollars per month for Ida Olson, and by March 1921 Mrs. Ernest Adams became the third Teller County woman to receive mothers' compensation.[85]

Although Teller's economic health played the largest role in determining when officials enacted mothers' pensions, political factors were not completely irrelevant, at least not by 1919. As early as 1917, political pressure began mounting to improve implementation of the Mothers' Compensation Act. At the time, only one-third of Colorado's counties enacted some portion of the state's pension law. Governor Julius C. Gunter called on legislators to extend the "scope and operation" of mothers' pensions. "The present law," stated Governor Gunter, "is impracticable in its operation in that the County Commissioners do not appropriate any specific funds for this purpose. We recommend to your consideration legislation needed to make this law effective."[86] The governor's efforts proved unsuccessful, but two years later members of the legislature proposed a bill that required every county "to provide sufficient money to carry out the provisions of the Mothers' Compensation Act."[87] Under the proposed law, each county would establish a "Mothers' Compensation Fund" maintained by a special levy.[88] The goal behind the measure was to force counties to implement mothers' aid by collecting money specifically set aside for pensions. The proposed bill passed both houses of the state legislature without a single vote in opposition.[89] The approval of the new law may have played a small role in Teller County's decision to begin offering mothers' compensations. But the degree of influence that this new law had on county commissioners should not be overstated. For despite the bill's broad support, by 1924 only a little over half of Colorado's counties enacted, at least in part, mothers' compensations.[90] Costilla County, for instance, authorized the new tax without ever implementing pensions.[91] In the end, the new law may have nudged Teller's commissioners toward enacting the state's Mothers' Compensation Act.

Unlike Teller County, Boulder already provided long-term aid for many of its single mothers prior to the 1912 initiative. As explained in chapter 1, women in Boulder had few job opportunities, making them largely dependent on male breadwinners for support. As a result of these poor employment options, Boulder County officials were more likely to grant women public outdoor aid, often for long durations, due to unemployment and due to a husband's death, injury, desertion, or nonsupport than in Teller County (see Table 8). Mrs. M. S. Wheatley, for example, a thirty-five-year-old widow with five children, ranging in ages from five months to ten years, received almost four years of county aid.[92] As a whole, Boulder County women averaged the second longest time on relief, just over nineteen months (see Table 17).

Even though Boulder already provided long-term aid to many single mothers, the county still decided to enact pensions. Unlike Costilla, Lincoln, Montezuma, and Teller Counties, which all had only a handful of widows with children receiving aid, Boulder County had a large number of widows on its poor books. From 1912 to 1920, thirty-two widows made up just over 21 percent of all of Boulder's female relief recipients with a listed cause of distress.[93] Boulder County had a large enough number of widows to make the implementation of mothers' compensation seem like a worthwhile endeavor. As a result, county commissioners began enforcement of mothers' pensions in May 1914. Nonetheless, although mothers' pensions did result in some minor changes, for all essential purposes, the implementation of the act so closely followed existing aid patterns that it did not signify a new beginning in welfare.

Because one of the basic concepts behind mothers' pensions, long-term aid, was already well established in Boulder prior to voter approval of mothers' compensation, the actual implementation of the law did not disturb the county's relief practices. In fact, officials basically transferred women from one account, poor relief, to another account, mothers' pensions. The experiences of Lulu Seaman illustrate this transition. In February 1910, Seaman's husband contracted pneumonia. For the next three weeks he battled the illness, finally dying from it on March 16, 1910. Nine months later, Seaman, thirty-five years old, and her five children, three boys and two girls all under the age of thirteen, began receiving outdoor assistance. At first the county provided ten dollars of monthly aid in the form of coal, provisions, and rental payments. By May 1914, however, Seaman began receiving her monthly ten dollars of aid in cash as Boulder County had granted her a mothers' pension.[94] Seaman's relief had simply changed from in-kind aid to cash assistance as a result of pensions. Eight other women who had also previously received outdoor aid switched to pensions.[95] After May 1914, many Boulder County women who in the past would have received in-kind outdoor assistance now qualified for cash payments from mothers' compensation. Thus implementation of pensions were not so much an expansion of Boulder's welfare practices, in the sense that they did not attract new clientele that previously would not have received aid, but rather pensions simply changed the type of aid received.

Boulder's mothers' pensions followed other patterns already begun by the poor relief program. Under the county's outdoor assistance, female recipients received only small amounts of help, averaging $9.32 in monthly aid.[96] This level of assistance could only partially support a needy person, and county officials never expected such low monthly payments to maintain wholly an individual, much less an entire family. Mothers' pensions essentially continued this same trend of only providing partial support for needy women. Most Boulder County women accepting mothers' compensation received between ten and twelve dollars per month during the first years of enactment. By 1919, monthly pension payments generally increased to fifteen or twenty dollars. Such low payments prevented pensions from fulfilling their stated aims of

keeping mothers out of the workforce, allowing them to devote their full attention to raising their children and improving the family's standard of living. Due
to the meager levels of support, women receiving pensions needed to seek out
wage work. And although the Boulder County judge repeatedly acknowledged
that a mother's "earnings are not sufficient to properly care for herself and [her]
children," the court did not raise the level of monthly pension payments, nor
did the court demand that mothers stop working once pensions started.[97]
Clearly, the court viewed mothers' aid as only a supplement, and not a substitute, for earned wages.

This is not to say that impoverished women in Boulder noticed
absolutely no difference between mothers' pensions and poor relief. One of
the few differences, and probably the most important, was the use of cash
in the pension program. Unlike Costilla, Lincoln, and Montezuma Counties,
Boulder very rarely gave cash to the poor. Boulder's commissioners only
twice gave cash to needy people prior to mothers' compensation. Recipients
of pensions also seemed to have received a consistently higher, although
only slightly higher, monthly payment than from relief funds. And while outdoor assistance fluctuated with seasonal demands, especially with an
increase in coal use during the winter, mothers' pensions, for better or worse,
provided a constant dollar amount for each month regardless of the season
or the weather conditions.

The investigation of pension applicants also changed, to a degree.
According to Colorado's compensation law, the court would "appoint proper persons for the purpose of investigation, visitation, the keeping of records,
and the making of reports."[98] In Boulder County, the probation officer investigated each applicant using a one-page standardized form that contained
factual, means, and morality questions. The officer wrote down the applicant's address, the names, ages, and grade level of each child, the names and
locations of pastors and school teachers, and a brief general description of
the reasons for the family's destitution. Mothers were asked if they belonged
"to any society, benefit, or otherwise," and if they owned any property.
Officers noted the character of the neighborhood with regard to "saloons,
pool halls, etc.," the applicant's use of tobacco and "any intoxicating liquors,"
and the children's attendance at church services.[99] The one-page completed form constituted the basis for the judge's decision on whether or not to
grant a pension. In the past, no doubt, the probation officer did not investigate relief applicants. The new inquiry, with a set form and most likely only

one or two investigators, standardized, to a point, Boulder's mothers' pensions, but it may have also initiated greater intrusion into and restrictions upon the lives of poor women. Mary Billings lost her mothers' pension when a county commissioner advised the court not to provide her with cash relief because "she uses very poor judgment in expending the funds."[100]

Many of these changes, however, do not seem as dramatic as initial impressions indicate. The legislation for mothers' pensions did not begin the practice of investigating poor relief applicants. At some level, all counties, except for Costilla, regularly questioned those applying for aid. In most cases, the inquiry consisted of only a brief visit from a county commissioner or from some other selected person. Usually the county pauper book listed the applicant's address, name, age, number of family members, and cause of distress. In many ways, county officials had already been gathering much of the information being collected for mothers' pensions years prior to the new law. While the county had not specifically compiled data on means- or morality-tested questions, these concerns were already present, if only implicit, when dispensing outdoor assistance. Communities with small populations tended to know already the habits and behaviors of aid recipients. The notion that mothers' pensions dramatically increased the level of intrusion into the lives of poor folk simply disregards the practices and customs of counties prior to the law.

While the involvement of the judicial branch in mothers' pensions definitely added an additional layer of bureaucracy to the county's relief practices, the role of the court should not be exaggerated nor assumed to be strictly negative. Although the court could and did halt pensions, the county commissioners had also halted poor relief in the past. And even though a few women lost their pensions due to unacceptable behavior, the vast majority of women who lost their pensions did so simply because of changes in their economic circumstances, marital status, or residency. In Mary Krauss's case, the court halted pensions when her son turned sixteen under the assumption that he "is capable of earning her [a] living."[101] Ethel B. Reid stopped receiving a pension once she started teaching school, and Jean Martin's remarriage halted her pension.[102] The involvement of the court could be a means for women to increase their pensions. Lulu Seaman, for example, asked Judge Ingram for an increase in her monthly compensation due to an illness. He responded to the request by permanently increasing her monthly compensation to fourteen dollars, a four dollar increase.[103]

Finally, Boulder County officials seemed to follow a relaxed attitude, as they did with poor relief, toward monitoring the behavior of most pension recipients. The experiences of Minnie Cope and Seaman testify to this loose management. Once the court approved mothers' compensation for Cope, commissioners mailed her a booklet of monthly vouchers. During the latter part of each month, Cope was to sign a voucher and mail it to the commissioners, who would then issue "a warrant for the amount as shown by the enclosed order." Cope could then cash the warrant at a bank in Longmont, her place of residence.[104] The idea of using the mail to implement a program that aimed to monitor the home situation would seem absurd to most supporters of mothers' pensions. But in a large rural county, covering 764 square miles, the policy made complete sense. Only when the post office returned Cope's vouchers did county officials learn that she had left the county. And only when Seaman wrote to Judge Ingram informing him that she had remarried and that he could now discontinue her compensation did the county learn of her change in marital status.[105] Clearly, officials had little contact with most pension recipients once they were granted aid. Boulder's mothers' compensation program followed the same relaxed monitoring begun by its outdoor aid. The changes initiated by mothers' pensions tended to be only slight variations on Boulder County's existing poor relief practices.

Mothers' Pensions in the City and County of Denver

Denver, like Boulder, became one of the first communities to implement mothers' pensions. The Queen City began its pension program in March 1913, only a few weeks after the new law's effective date, and over a year before Boulder began its efforts. But unlike Boulder, several Denver officials invested their reputations on the successful implementation of the welfare measure. Judge Lindsey, Gertrude Vaile, and Florence Hutsinpillar, Vaile's successor, all devoted a great deal of energy to the aid program. Mothers' pensions in Denver represented the climax of Progressive Era welfare reform, embodying all the promises and hopes that reformers had for transforming poor relief practices. As a result, the city's pension program received a fair amount of publicity. Yet, the implementation of mothers' pensions in Denver remained closely linked with the city's poor relief practices and any changes made were more incremental than profound. As with Boulder County,

Denver's mothers' pensions failed to alter significantly the delivery of aid or achieve the goals set out by advocates.

Largely absent from the initial debate over mothers' pensions, Gertrude Vaile hesitated before becoming more involved. In October 1912, almost one month prior to the election, Vaile had accepted an invitation from the Russell Sage Foundation "to investigate the workings and results" of the year-old pension law in Illinois. Vaile viewed the measure as imprudent because it provided pensions for all poor mothers. Since Colorado's proposed compensation act largely patterned itself on the law in Illinois, she likewise frowned upon it as well. "Any mother," stated Vaile, "could get a pension just by showing to the satisfaction of the court that she and her husband were unable to keep their children at home because of poverty."[106] At the time, her opposition to Colorado's proposed mothers' pension law was not a complete surprise. Vaile had worked for two years with the United Charities of Chicago as a district visitor and later as a district superintendent. Charity workers like Vaile often feared political meddling in any publicly funded and administered relief. While she clearly disapproved of Colorado's proposed law, she still realized that the measure enjoyed widespread support; to campaign against the bill would bring her "into direct opposition to the people with whom I must heartily and tactfully work if I am to be of any further use in the charities situation here [in Denver]."[107] Hoping not to upset important members of the city's charity establishment, and being out of state during the time leading up to the election, Vaile essentially chose not to voice her opinions too strongly.

Immediately following the election, Vaile won appointment to Denver's Board of Charities and Corrections, as already mentioned, and her views toward mothers' pensions quickly changed. In less than a year, she went from opposing pensions to supporting "public pensions for destitute widowed mothers."[108] Vaile reasoned that mothers' pensions were logical, and thus justified, because the "state has long declared in many ways its responsibility for the training and rearing of children."[109] Mothers who tried to "perform the unnatural and impossible task of being both father and mother," argued Vaile, placed too great a burden on themselves and their children, a burden that the state could not "safely permit."[110] Her support for pensions also rested on notions of democracy. "Why," questioned Vaile, "should a good mother have to depend upon the alms of her more fortunate neighbor for the opportunity to perform her natural and civic duty of bringing up her children?"[111] Indeed, all members of society should help support, through taxes, such a mother because it is society that benefits from her maternal qualities. Finally, Vaile favored the mothers' compensation act for its preventive aspects. After a few months of operating Denver's mothers' aid program, she happily noticed that pensions seemed to assist families before conditions deteriorated to the point of disaster.[112]

While Vaile's change in attitude appeared drastic, she nevertheless carefully qualified her support for pensions. She did not agree, for example, that deserted mothers should be "pensioned even as widows," as Colorado's law stipulated.[113] More important, her support for mothers' compensation rested on the notion that pensions would be administered through a "constructive, individual, case-by-case treatment."[114] Public agencies, argued Vaile, could only safely administer pensions through the use of individual casework techniques. These methods were especially crucial for those "newly developing forms of relief like mothers' pensions, which deliberately aim to remove the stigma of dependency from the recipients."[115] She called upon all public officials to properly investigate and to thoroughly supervise mothers' pension recipients so that tax dollars would not be wasted or misused.

Vaile maneuvered so that she and the Board of Charities and Corrections would maintain control of mothers' compensations. Given her initial doubts about pensions, she wanted to monitor closely the new program. According to the law, Judge Lindsey's juvenile court would be in charge of mothers' pensions. Yet realizing that the juvenile court lacked experience in relief work and lacked the number of probation officers necessary to properly assume that responsibility, Vaile suggested to Lindsey that he appoint the board to investigate applicants and to supervise recipients. The appointment of the board would not only allow Vaile to regulate pensions, but it would also avoid the wasteful practice of investigating applicants twice, once by the juvenile court and once by the county, as Chicago did. Lindsey followed Vaile's advice, working out an agreement to have the board operate mothers' pensions, with the court basically approving the board's recommendations.[116] This setup simply placed a bureaucratic veneer of change over the city's relief practices. Since Lindsey accepted "the [board's] recommendation[s], almost without question," Vaile and the Board of Charities and Corrections remained firmly in control of mothers' pensions, despite appearances of change and promises of sharing responsibility with the juvenile court.[117]

With this arrangement, Denver's mothers' pensions became, in many ways, simply another form of poor relief, a subset of the city's outdoor aid measures. The same city employees who investigated all relief applicants now investigated all pension applicants. In either case, the inquiry seemed almost identical. Like poor relief, pension applicants completed a form listing a range of personal information that the bureau's staff then used to research "the circumstances of the family."[118] While Vaile reported that "more than one mother" withdrew her pension application upon learning that relatives and other references must be contacted, this same procedure was common for all outdoor relief applicants.[119] At the time that the board assumed responsibility for mothers' pensions, the staff was already too small to carry out proper individual casework methods for outdoor relief recipients. This same problem now plagued the mothers' pension program. Since the staff was "too small to give the quality of supervision" that Vaile desired, the Bureau of Charities tried instead to "see that the house is reasonably well-managed, that the children's school reports are satisfactory, [and] that their health is looked after."[120] Like relief recipients, only pensioned mothers in a crisis situation received more than occasional attention from the staff. By the late teens or early twenties, an additional caseworker supervised all mothers' pension recipients after their initial investigation. Yet even with this new hire, the amount of contact remained infrequent at best. The caseworker had a "short interview" twice a month with each mother when pension warrants were given out, and she only "aimed . . . to visit each family in the home at least once in two months." But even these home visits were often discontinued for "well-known families." In 1920 and 1921, for instance, slightly over 75 percent of Denver's pensioned mothers had only one home visit, or less, each month.[121] The degree to which the Bureau of Charities monitored pension recipients mirrored, in most cases, the amount of contact that outdoor relief recipients received.

Mothers' compensation became, in many ways, dependent upon outdoor aid. During the city's first year of offering pensions, 1913, most of the recipients were simply transferred from poor relief to pensions, just as in Boulder County. Of the twenty-eight families that first received pensions that year, twenty-six were already receiving public aid.[122] Because the city refused to provide sufficient funds to care for all qualified women under the pension program, the bureau had to rely on poor relief to support many qualified women. In 1920 and 1921, half of Denver's applicants for mothers' pensions had to wait at least eight months before receiving a pension, and 36 percent had to wait a year or longer. In June 1920, seventy-three families received pensions and another eighty-two were on the wait list.[123] While a family waited for one of the few available pensions, the city gave "relief to many mothers for long periods of time, often for a year or over, out of funds allotted to poor relief, before it became possible to get them mothers' pensions."[124] In addition to supporting partially those waiting for pensions, outdoor relief also, on occasion, supplemented mothers' pensions. In 1917 and 1918, for example, four mothers received outdoor relief as a supplement to their pensions. While three of these mothers received only small amounts of in-kind aid, $3.00 to $8.60, one Russian mother suffering from tuberculosis with four children obtained slightly over $43.00 of assistance in addition to her regular pension.[125] Outdoor aid clearly played a crucial role in helping to maintain Denver's mothers' compensations.

The small size of the city's mothers' pension program, both in terms of fiscal budget and number of recipients, meant that it remained secondary, but linked, to outdoor relief. At the same time that the city began allocating funds for pensions in 1913, it also reduced the budget for outdoor relief. In 1912, Denver spent $60,850.78 for outdoor relief, a new high in the city's welfare spending. The following year that amount dropped to $51,327.46 while mothers' pensions received its first funds, $4,784.16. In 1914, the budget for mothers' pensions more than doubled to $9,998.46, the city's outdoor relief funds decreased to only $43,516.53. Funding levels for both programs stabilized over the next few years before increasing again in 1918 (see Table 20).[126] Denver officials, like those in Boulder, obviously viewed mothers' pensions not as a program that would expand the city's welfare responsibilities but rather as a program that would care for those who would have received outdoor relief in the past.

In response to the city's meager funding of mothers' pensions, reformers pressured the city for more money. A year after Denver started its pension program, Judge Lindsey began petitioning for higher levels of support. In March 1914, Lindsey requested "additional appropriation[s] for the Juvenile Court and for the Mothers' Compensation act."[127] The next month, he again asked for "an additional appropriation," this time requesting a specific amount, two thousand dollars, "for the Mothers' Compensation Law."[128] In both instances, his efforts failed to secure any increases in funding.[129] The following year, a group from the Woman's Club of Denver led by Mabel Costigan and Marie Miller appeared before the city council "to secure an enlarged appropriation for Mothers' Compensation."[130] Like Lindsey's previous attempts, the women's efforts failed to persuade city officials to increase funding levels. Only with the passage of the 1919 law that required a mothers' pension tax did Denver's pensions receive a substantial increase in money. From 1919 to 1920, the budget in Denver for mothers' pensions jumped from $17,260.85 to $29,756.00 due to the new tax law (see Table 20).

With a relatively small budget, Vaile, and later her successor Florence Hutsinpillar, kept the number of pension recipients low. Rather than thinly distribute the small budget among many qualified mothers, Vaile decided that it was best to try to properly support a few women. "We feel strongly that if a pension is to be granted at all," wrote Vaile, "it should be sufficient to exempt the family from the need of any other charitable relief and maintain a wholesome and dignified standard of living. Only on that basis can a family be expected to live as they should."[131] Hutsinpillar continued this basic policy at least into the early 1920s as Denver "had the highest proportion of families [receiving mothers' pensions] with adequate incomes," according to a Children's Bureau study of how nine communities implemented pensions.[132] By following such a policy, however, Denver mothers' aid program remained small, extremely small. In March 1916 only twenty-nine women received pensions, while in June 1921 seventy-three did.[133]

Despite efforts to provide sufficient levels of support for the few families that did receive mothers' aid, the women receiving pensions, much like poor relief recipients, still had to supplement their pensions in order to cover expenses. Pensions were supposed to allow single mothers the opportunity to devote their full attention to child rearing by removing their need to earn a wage. However, Vaile and the Bureau of Charities expected mothers, from the very beginning, to contribute to their own support. The question for Vaile was not if a mother should supplement a pension but rather "how much the mother can supplement the pension without sacrifice of her health or neglect of the children." When determining how much cash each mother should receive, the bureau subtracted "what the family can provide from their own resources."[134] Even though Denver supported its pension recipients at relatively high levels, 67 percent of these mothers were nevertheless still earning a regular wage. While the bureau recommended that mothers spend no more than three days a week away from home, some needed to work well beyond the recommended limit. In June 1921, six of the seventy-three mothers receiving pensions worked six days a week away from home. The practice of women working while receiving pensions was not isolated to Denver or Boulder. In Chicago, according to historian Joanne Goodwin, 60 percent of mothers' pension recipients earned a wage, while in Minneapolis 59 percent worked, and in Cincinnati all pensioned women worked.[135] Families supplemented their pensions through other means as well. In some cases, children worked or relatives offered help, while in others private charities, public outdoor aid, or other sources of income assisted pension recipients. In Denver, every family supplemented their mothers' pension through some form or combination of outside income.[136] Denver's compensations were never intended nor implemented in such a manner as to completely support their recipients. Instead, the Bureau of Charities disbursed mothers' pensions in a way that closely resembled the city's outdoor relief program, which also only provided partial assistance.

Denver's implementation of mothers' compensation did not dramatically alter the city's relief system; nevertheless, it did, as in Boulder County, produce some changes. Most importantly, mothers' pensions provided cash for its recipients instead of in-kind aid. Like Boulder, Denver had in the past only distributed in-kind assistance to its outdoor relief recipients until it began using small amounts of cash in emergency situations. The use of cash for mothers' pensions provided one of the few tangible differences between the city's outdoor relief and pension program. In addition, mothers' pensions may have actually increased both the levels of support and the total time receiving aid. Due to missing records, a direct comparison between poor relief and pensions is unfortunately impossible. However, given that Vaile made a concentrated effort to increase pensions, although still not to adequate levels, one can reasonably assume that mothers' compensation offered higher levels of support than outdoor relief. We do know that in 1916, pensioned families averaged $27.62 in aid per month, which would appear to be substantially higher than what relief applicants received.[137] Likewise, even though it appears that Denver used its outdoor aid to maintain some people for long periods, pensions may have more frequently provided long-term assistance. Of the seventy-three women on mothers' compensation in June 1921, for example, at least seventeen had been receiving pensions for two years or longer.[138] Still, overall, Denver's pension program looked more like the city's existing poor relief practices than a bold new type of aid.

Mothers' pensions, at several levels, mirrored outdoor relief more than they established new practices for the nation's welfare state. Evidence from Colorado challenges claims that mothers' pensions were a form of "new social spending."[139] Instead, pensions, at best, became a subset of poor relief programs, or were closely linked to them. At worst, officials simply refused to enact them. Likewise, because mothers' pensions followed patterns already firmly established by local outdoor aid practices, they failed to break from the past. After examining previous welfare practices, which had already accomplished much of what compensation advocates wanted, and considering the inadequate implementation of pensions, one must conclude that mothers' pensions were a disappointment, if not a failure, in improving the lives of impoverished women during the Progressive Era.

These basic trends in implementing mothers' pensions were not completely unique to Colorado, as other regions of the nation followed similar patterns. Observations about mothers' pensions from the period repeatedly mention the lack of implementation, variances among communities, and similarities with poor relief. By 1921, Emma Lundberg had concluded that mothers' pensions "have been largely ineffective because of failure to make necessary funds available."[140] Communities either did not fund mothers' compensations at all or funded them at such inadequate amounts as to make the pensions available to only a few women at extremely low levels. In Pennsylvania, only half of all eligible mothers received pensions, due to low appropriations, resulting in "giving a little to all the families."[141] Variations in the implementation of mothers' pensions among different communities also continued to be a problem. At the broadest level, mothers' pension laws varied considerably among states as they differed over who qualified for aid, how much property a recipient could own, how much aid could be given, and who administered and funded pensions.[142] As in Colorado, dramatic differences appeared among counties. Edith Abbott observed that outside of Cook County (Chicago) there were "precisely 101 Illinois counties, with nearly 101 different pension policies."[143] In Pennsylvania, Mary Bogue noted that because of the local control of mothers' pension programs there was "great divergence in standards" among the state's counties.[144] Finally, observers consistently commented on the similarity between pensions and poor relief. Early on, Frederic Almy remarked that Chicago's mothers' pensions looked "like mere relief," and in neighboring Lake County, just north of Chicago, the local judge there "saw no difference between the purpose of widow's pensions and the old outdoor relief system."[145] In Ohio, although the state legislature, like other state legislatures, did not intend for mothers' pensions to be another form of poor relief, it nevertheless was observed that the measure in practice "actually becomes something of a relief measure."[146]

The failure of mothers' pensions to substantially change relief practices rests with the fact that the new pension laws largely left local communities in control of implementation. In Colorado, as in most states, county property taxes funded mothers' pensions, just as they did outdoor poor aid. Even in states which stipulated that the state and the counties would share the cost of funding pensions, the state still often failed to provide its share of money. In both Minnesota and Virginia state governments did not reimburse counties for pension expenses despite laws that required the state to do so.[147] In addition, mothers' pensions continued the practice of allowing local officials, either county commissioners or judges, or some combination of the two, to determine a person's eligibility for assistance. As a result, officials still used local standards to determine both if a person qualified for aid and how that assistance should be delivered. Even in states where some form of state supervision accompanied mothers' pensions, locals still maintained a large degree of control either by controlling the funding of pensions or by controlling their administration. By leaving in place local control, mothers' pension programs failed to radically alter poor relief practices.

Just as advocates for pensions were disappointed with the inadequate assistance levels provided to needy mothers, so too were Colorado's adult blind residents disappointed with their own situation. During the early twentieth century, blind adults became frustrated with society's refusal to either gainfully employ them or to offer sufficient poor relief. As a consequence, a group of blind activists joined together to improve their employment options and, eventually, the relief they received. But unlike mothers' pensions advocates, blind activists created a new form of welfare, blind benefits, which actually transformed the delivery of aid, removing the aid from local control and placing blind activists in charge of it.

CHAPTER FIVE

Transforming the Welfare State— Blind Benefits

KATACAN KROELL BEGAN RECEIVING POOR RELIEF FROM THE BOULDER COUNTY commissioners in December 1907. Kroell was a blind fifty-seven-year-old, and like other recipients of Boulder County aid, he took in a small amount of provisions each month. Farther south in Costilla County, Albinia de Madrid started county assistance in January 1916. Seventy-two-year-old de Madrid, like Kroell, was blind, and she received the same basic relief as other Costilla residents. De Madrid welcomed four dollars each month in store credit (cash payment after April 1917) from county commissioners who increased her relief to five dollars per month in 1918. The same year that de Madrid's name first appeared on Costilla's poor rolls, William Henderson began receiving public assistance in Teller County. Henderson, forty-three years old, was blind like Kroell and de Madrid. In 1916, Henderson accepted just over sixty-seven dollars in aid; the next year the county granted him just over sixty-two dollars in assistance.[1]

In 1919 and 1920, Kroell, de Madrid, and Henderson all experienced a marked improvement in their levels of public aid. With the passage of the 1918 statewide initiative, the Act for the Relief of the Adult Blind, commonly referred to as blind benefits, blind pensions, or blind aid, the amount of assistance for all three dependent blind citizens increased. The new law provided up to $300 annually in cash relief for each impoverished blind resident. As a result, beginning in 1919, Boulder's Kroell no longer accepted small amounts of monthly provisions. Instead, he received $300 in cash each year. Likewise, Costilla's de Madrid went from receiving only $60 to $300 per year. And Teller's William Henderson jumped to $275 in 1920, a huge increase from the $56.25 he received in 1918 or the $69.05 he shared with his blind brother the following year.[2] The experiences of Kroell, de Madrid, and Henderson reveal how blind benefits dramatically changed poor relief practices. For not only did assistance levels substantially rise but all counties implemented the new law within a few months of its effective date. Blind benefits, no doubt, quickly improved the lives of poor blind residents.

Despite the effectiveness of blind benefits, authors have written surprisingly little about them. The recent outpouring of literature on the development of the welfare state in the first part of the twentieth century has completely ignored blind benefits.[3] This void seems especially surprising considering the many similarities between blind benefits and mothers' pensions. Both movements happened during the same period, spread quickly from state to state, lacked any national organizational or individual leadership, encountered resistance from established charity and social workers, and tried to separate their form of assistance from general poor relief. General overviews of America's twentieth-century welfare policies likewise miss the opportunity to discuss blind benefits.[4] And even when authors specifically address the history of blind people, benefits still only receive brief attention.[5]

Regardless of the almost complete absence of a discussion of blind benefits in the historical literature, this new form of assistance significantly changed the welfare state. Blind benefits, for the first time during the Progressive Era, represented a welfare reform effort that succeeded in radically altering how communities dispensed poor relief. Unlike mothers' pensions, which either duplicated existing practices or, at best, slightly altered how counties helped impoverished women, blind benefits clearly broke with previous policies, completely changing how and who decided assistance levels. The new blind aid law essentially removed local officials from almost all decisions about supporting needy blind residents by creating a statewide Blind Benefit Commission to administer the measure. Also, the blind aid application clearly defined the criteria for qualifying for assistance. With blind benefits, no longer would local circumstances dictate the delivery of aid; instead, a new, uniform relief policy would be established.

Blind aid also transformed poor relief by helping to usher in the beginnings of the modern welfare state. Blind benefits assisted with introducing the trend of interest groups determining how welfare policies and money would be implemented and divided.[6] Earlier efforts by interest groups to create and control welfare practices proved either temporary or ineffective. Civil War pensions, for instance, did indeed become a type of turn-of-the-century disability and old age benefit largely administered by veterans themselves, but, as veterans died, the pension program became less and less significant, especially after 1910, with fewer and fewer surviving veterans.[7] Middle-class women were able to get mothers' pensions approved, but they were unable to get them fully implemented and funded. Blind citizens represented one of the best organized, most determined, and politically sophisticated interest groups trying to alter the welfare state during the Progressive Era. Advocates for the blind played critical roles in designing, promoting, and most importantly enforcing benefits. The blind community successfully formed and independently controlled their own portion of the state's welfare pie, a piece consisting of several coordinated programs. Blind people in Colorado created, staffed, and managed the publicly funded state teacher for the adult blind, the workshop for the blind, the blind benefits program, as well as the privately operated Adult Blind Home. Clients and potential clients of welfare had become the authorities and administrators of aid. Blind benefits helped to initiate the permanent fragmentation of the welfare state, which resulted in targeting specific relief programs and policies for specific groups. One of the goals of mothers' pension advocates was the separation of pensions from public aid. These efforts proved unsuccessful. Activists for the blind, however, succeeded in creating a clear division between blind aid and poor relief. In the 1930s, the New Deal would further balkanize public assistance by allowing interest groups to claim a portion of the welfare state as their own. The efforts of Progressive Era advocates for the blind helped to begin this permanent division of the welfare state.

Blind People in America

Early-twentieth-century attitudes toward blind people tended to characterize them as automatically needy and helpless. "The sentiment instantly excited at the sight of the blind," according to Harry Best, a prominent early-twentieth-century researcher on blindness and the blind, "is one of overwhelming pity for their condition." Much like widows, blind women and men (and most physically and mentally disabled people) occupied a permanent, and to a certain degree "honored," place among what society considered the worthy or deserving poor. This tendency to lump all blind people into a single category as needy resulted in a blurring of differences among them. Instead of viewing the blind as individuals with variations among them, society generally assumed that all blind people shared similar characteristics of dependency.[8] This stereotyping, as we will see, had contradictory results. On the one hand, it constantly created barriers to social advancement and economic security. Yet, as with widows, this societal belief in dependency allowed social reformers to justify special relief measures for blind people.

Given society's view of blind adults as needy and as part of the deserving poor, numerous states passed laws that tried to remove some obstacles for blind citizens by allowing them special privileges or fewer financial burdens. In Alabama, Indiana, Minnesota, Nebraska, Ohio, and Rhode Island, among others, legislatures exempted blind residents from prohibitions against begging or asking for alms. In some states, blind people could peddle goods without a license, and in New York City blind residents could obtain a free license to sell goods and newspapers or play music in public areas. Numerous states throughout the South, Midwest, and Northeast exempted blind adults from poll taxes and some property taxes. New Mexico allowed those supervising community irrigation ditches to provide, free of charge, enough water for a three-acre farm for any blind man or widow.[9] These statutes lessened some financial obligations and opened some employment options for blind people; however, these laws mainly offered only minimal job opportunities and failed to produce any long-term improvements in the lives of most indigent blind women and men.

As a consequence, the overall employment situation for blind adults remained dismal. Sight plays a key role in carrying out so many occupations that, without it, common tasks suddenly become more difficult, more time consuming, and occasionally impossible. Discrimination against blind people compounded this already burdensome situation. For although society considered blind women and men as part of the deserving poor, nevertheless, the public rarely offered them jobs. Like women, blind people had limited employment options and were usually relegated to low-paying jobs.

Given the discrimination against them and the physical disadvantages of not having eyesight, blind adults found it difficult to find and maintain employment. In 1910, for example, only about 17 percent of the nation's blind residents were gainfully employed, compared to just over 53 percent for the general population.[10] As a result of this bleak employment picture, the vast majority of blind adults faced a possibility of lifetime unemployment. Helen Keller, deaf and blind since the age of nineteen months, once remarked that the "heaviest burden on the blind is not blindness, but idleness." Keller attributed this idleness to the difficulty of moving around without assistance and the lack of employment.[11]

Even for those blind people fortunate and skillful enough to find and maintain employment, their jobs often did not lead them to become self-supporting. While blind adults worked in numerous fields, for the most part, however, they congregated in only a handful of occupations. Blind women and men tended to work in broom making, chair caning, carpet and rug making, weaving, basket making, piano tuning, peddling, and performing and teaching music. In addition, many blind females took up plain and fancy sewing to earn money. Yet by no means did this employment generally produce enough income to sustain someone. Many of these jobs—broom making, chair caning, carpet and rug making, weaving, and basket making—were often carried out in workshops for the blind, where employment was often erratic, and pay was well below a living wage. Likewise, peddling goods often amounted to little more than begging by selling token items—pencils, matches, and shoestrings—door to door, and sewing also failed to provide steady, well-paying work. As a result of these circumstances, only 6.6 percent of the entire blind population claimed to be self-supporting in 1910.[12]

Because they were unable to earn an adequate income, blind people had to rely on other means of support. A small number maintained themselves with their family's wealth, but the vast majority of the adult blind, 80 to 90 percent, had to piece together an existence with help from family members, friends, public assistance, or private aid. Families or friends supported from 25 to 45 percent of the blind population. Yet, many relatives were themselves poor and could offer little assistance, and many blind adults had no surviving families. As a result, many blind people depended on some form of charity or a combination of different forms of help. Approximately 7 to 12 percent of blind residents permanently lived in homes or institutions operated by philanthropic societies. Public assistance or public institutions maintained the remaining blind population. From about 12 to 25 percent received some type of outdoor public aid, while county poor farms and almshouses housed close to 6 percent of all the nation's blind residents in 1910.[13]

Although the blind largely depended on others for support, they still organized to change their circumstances. Blind people, as well as their friends and professionals, created numerous associations to address the educational, social, and economic issues affecting their lives. At the time, two national societies existed. The first of these organizations, the American Association of Instructors of the Blind (AAIB), formally organized in 1871. During the late nineteenth and early twentieth centuries, almost "all public expenditures for the blind," writes historian Frances A. Koestler, "were devoted to education and thus funnelled through" schools for blind children. As a result of this focus, society considered school superintendents and their staffs (members of AAIB) "undisputed experts on all aspects of blindness."[14] In 1895, a new group limited to blind members only, the American Blind People's Higher Education and General Improvement Association, formed in St. Louis, Missouri, to address ways of providing blind adults with post-secondary education and to grapple with other general issues. In 1905, the group abandoned its unwieldy name, becoming the American Association of Workers for the Blind (AAWB), reduced its emphasis on higher education, and opened its membership to the sighted.[15] In many respects, the AAWB challenged the exclusive authority and power of the AAIB by adding a more democratic voice, through its large and open membership, to policy debates. The AAWB, according to Robert Irwin, an influential activist for the blind during the first half of the twentieth century, "represented the rank and file of blind people as well as of workers for the blind."[16] The AAWB signified an important development toward self-advocacy and interest group politics by allowing blind people a say, for the first time and with a very powerful voice, in issues that concerned them.

The AAWB's willingness to tackle the need for a uniform system of embossed type in 1905, probably the most divisive issue facing the blind community, showed the organization's boldness and the desire of blind people to improve their quality of life. At the time, four systems of raised print were used in the United States: Line type, Moon type, New York Point, and American Braille.[17] The use of so many different forms of embossed type caused problems. The printing of books or magazines in any form of raised print was an expensive undertaking, and the competing forms of tactile print limited the market for these goods. The use of different embossed types also divided blind citizens. Not only were blind people often unable to communicate with one another, but the use of various forms of raised print had created extremely hostile divisions within the nation's blind community. Supporters of each embossed type passionately fought to protect their own dot system and vigorously attacked the dot system of their opponents. This disagreement reached such intensity that it eventually became known as the "war of the dots." In 1917, after years of study and debate, the AAWB endorsed the adoption of Revised Braille, a new modification of British Braille, as the sole form of embossed print.[18]

In addition to the AAWB, blind people organized numerous local and state groups during the early twentieth century. In 1903, a group of blind citizens formed the Maine Association for the Blind, and farther south the Massachusetts Association for Promoting the Interests of the Blind came into existence. Out west, the Scotoic Aid Society of Missouri incorporated in 1907, and a year later the Western Association for the Blind formed in Utah.[19] Many of these associations, especially the local ones, served mainly as social clubs or alumni associations for graduates from various private or public institutions, but some groups did engage in forms of self-help by seeking out employment, offering loans to start businesses, and providing benefits for illness, disability, and death.[20] The Scotoic Aid Society of Missouri, for instance, hoped "to lend a helping hand to adult blind" by establishing an industrial workshop where adults could learn trade skills and produce goods.[21] Several of the state-level groups were formed with the clear aim of actively lobbying governments to expand or improve public support for blind citizens. Maine's Association for the Blind organized to pressure the state legislature to fund and construct "an industrial school for the blind," while in Massachusetts blind people had come together to ask the state to establish a "temporary commission to investigate the condition and needs of the adult blind."[22] Often a dedicated individual, such as Maine's William J. Ryan, a blind man, became the main force behind some of these state organizations. In other areas blind residents teamed up with women's groups, religious leaders, or a wealthy benefactor like New York's Moses Charles Migel to promote their causes.[23] Blind people also maintained periodicals that allowed local communities to stay informed of events and debates in other parts of the nation. The *Matilda Ziegler Magazine for the Blind* and the *Outlook for the Blind*, the two most important publications in terms of advocacy, both began publishing in 1907.[24] In the course of the Progressive Era, blind citizens had become a well organized and an informed interest group.

Expanding the Welfare State

Events in Colorado mirrored many of these national trends, with small groups of activists forming coalitions, lobbying public officials, and enlarging the role of the state. Instrumental in the Centennial State's expansion of public services for blind residents was the work of Jennie Caward. Born in Buffalo, Illinois, in 1862, Caward lost the use of one eye at the age of nine after an accident. By the age of seventeen, she was teaching school when her other eye began to fail. At the age of twenty-two, Caward entered the Kansas School for the Blind, and after graduation she taught privately in Kansas and in the Indian Territory (Oklahoma) before moving to Colorado in 1905 at the age of forty-three. Realizing, after her arrival, that there were no state provisions to serve the adult blind, Caward began to work to improve their situation.[25]

At the time, almost all public funding for services for blind people, regardless of location, went to large state educational institutions, and Colorado proved no exception to this pattern. In Colorado Springs, the Colorado School for the Deaf and Blind opened in 1877 to educate deaf and blind residents under the age of twenty-one. The problem was that the vast majority of the adult blind population lost their eyesight as adults, making them largely ineligible for state schools. In 1900, nearly three-quarters of the adult blind in the United States "became blind after reaching twenty years of age."[26] And the situation may have been even worse in Colorado because of mining accidents. The state's Board of Charities and Corrections observed that a high percentage of the adult blind had been "injured by accidents in mines, which, perhaps accounts for the large number of such unfortunates in this state as compared with some others."[27] While census figures for the blind population fluctuated wildly, still, in 1920, Colorado had the sixth highest rate of blindness in the nation.[28] This realization that most blind people lost their eyesight as adults led to a vigorous "movement to render efficient assistance to adults" in various parts of the nation.[29]

Advocates pushed for an increase in employment options for the adult blind. "The blind are suffering from many ills," wrote Newel Perry, a turn-of-the-century activist, "but most of their troubles would cease if they could only secure employment which would yield them a livelihood."[30] Creating special workshops for blind adults seemed to be the solution for their lack of wages. The workshop movement began in the mid-nineteenth century when school superintendents realized that their students often had few chances for employment after graduation. Schools for the blind had initially hoped that their graduates could use their education and training to become self-supporting. Yet, society offered few meaningful employment opportunities for blind graduates despite their skills. Maryland's school for the blind reported that students had "been taught habits of industry at school, but because they cannot earn enough by their labor to supply both board and clothing, they must either beg or go to the almshouse."[31] In response to this bleak situation, schools began opening sheltered workshops for their graduates and eventually for other blind adults. In 1850, the Perkins Institution in Massachusetts started one of the first workshops, employing only males. By the late nineteenth and early twentieth centuries "a wave of . . . employment institutions for the blind spread over the country" as schools, states, and private associations opened sheltered workshops.[32] California's legislature began funding a workshop in 1885, and two years later Illinois started one in Chicago. Soon other states followed, and private organizations also founded workshops in Pittsburgh, Trenton, Cincinnati, and San Francisco, to name just a few locations.[33]

Jennie Caward led efforts in Colorado to establish a state-funded workshop. Almost immediately after her arrival in the state, Caward began meeting with many of Denver's blind adults and other interested parties, and soon they petitioned the legislature for support of a sheltered workshop. In 1907, their efforts quickly paid off when the state agreed to open the Colorado Industrial Workshop for the Blind in Denver. Like other sheltered workshops, Colorado's specialized in broom making, chair caning, basket making, beadwork, and brush making. Mr. T. F. Myers, a blind man who had worked for obtaining state funding, became the manager of the workshop and began a trend of placing advocates for the blind into new state positions created largely through their own lobbying efforts. Once within these new jobs, activists, as we will see, often used their positions as springboards to push for improved services, to organize further the blind community, and to expand state aid for blind adults.[34]

Jennie Caward's lobbying efforts did not stop with the opening of the workshop. In 1911, Caward sought out financial support from the Colorado

Industrial Workshop for the Blind, 1079 Jason Street, Denver, Colorado,
1909. Broom manufacturing soon became the sole focus of the workshop.
Denver Municipal Facts, *20 November 1909, 11. Courtesy of Denver*
Public Library, Western History Collection.

Federation of Women's Clubs for small classes to teach blind adults. The
Women's Clubs' Social Science Department responded to Caward's request by
providing her with twenty dollars per month for the classes. At the same time
that the Women's Clubs funded Caward's classes, they also drafted a bill asking for public money to support permanently a state teacher for the adult
blind. Members of the Women's Clubs assisted in writing the act and "successfully mothered it" along. The bill became law in 1911, and, as before, an advocate for the blind, this time Mrs. Jennie Jackson, formerly Jennie Caward,
assumed the newly created position as Colorado's teacher for the adult blind.[35]

Jackson used her new job to reach out to Colorado's adult blind population scattered across mountains and plains. She crisscrossed the state,
visiting and teaching blind people. "To reach my students," wrote Jackson,
"I have walked many miles, made a number of short trips in automobiles,

ridden hundreds of miles in street cars, and at least, 2,787 miles upon the railway" over a two-year period. She made just over one thousand calls teaching not only reading and writing but also crocheting, knitting, beadwork, and hammock making.[36] Jackson even arranged to sell her students' goods as she traveled the state. In Cripple Creek, she displayed "crochet work, tatting, hammocks and similar articles" made by Teller County's blind residents in the window of the Lewis and Eagle drug store.[37] Similar sales were held, often with "valuable assistance from members of the Woman's Clubs," at the state fair in Pueblo and in Durango, Leadville, and Denver.[38] All money received from the sale of goods went to the makers of the various articles.

Jackson's travels across the state revealed the isolating conditions that blind people faced during the early twentieth century, especially in rural communities. Adult blind pupils repeatedly remarked how thankful they were for her lessons and visits. "Do you know, I think your coming was a miracle," commented one student, and another exclaimed, "You have opened a new world to me."[39] Even in circumstances where it appeared that Jackson could offer little help, she still managed to find a way to teach some skill that provided greater independence. In Las Animas County, for example, most blind residents were elderly Hispanics who spoke only Spanish and were largely illiterate in both Spanish and English. Yet, when Jackson provided self-threading needles, one "elderly woman cried aloud for joy when she had threaded a needle," commenting to the interpreter, "'Now I can sew all I want to, for I won't have to wait for some one to thread my needle.'"[40]

Equally important as Jackson's formal duties of visiting and teaching was her informal role as the main contact person for blind people. Jackson's position placed her as the one common link for the state's scattered blind community. Traveling from county to county, Jackson connected blind adults with not only herself and the services she provided but also to one another and to the state's largest blind community located in Denver. Through Jackson's efforts as a teacher, messenger, and organizer, the blind could now count on people from beyond the Denver area to lobby for changes and increases in public support. The visibility of the state's blind community expanded as it represented almost every section of the state. Jackson had single-handedly created a lobbying and support network for Colorado's blind citizens.

While the creation and funding of both the state teacher position and the sheltered workshop provided dramatic increases in state services for blind residents, nevertheless, neither Jackson nor others were satisfied with these gains. Advocates turned their attention to the many shortcomings found at the Colorado Industrial Workshop for the Blind. The workshop struggled with erratic and low state funding levels that forced it to simplify operations and to eliminate manufacturing of all but the most profitable goods. In April 1909, the workshop discontinued chair caning and brush manufacturing and soon thereafter basket making and all beadwork halted as the production of brooms became the shop's sole focus.[41] The lack of funds also meant that workspace remained tight and, during the winter months, unsafe owing to poor ventilation.[42] The minimal levels of state funding as well as the limited space restricted the workshop's ability to employ many blind adults. In 1909, for instance, the workshop employed, on average, only fourteen blind people each day; three years later that average had fallen to less than twelve blind employees per day.[43] The low number of blind laborers did not go unnoticed as the State Board of Charities and Corrections lamented the workshop's ability to train only "a very scanty number of the blind of the state."[44] Uncertainty over the shop's continued operation due to erratic funding discouraged the recruitment of new employees as the superintendent constantly feared closure each time supplies ran low.[45]

For those men and women employed at the workshop, self-maintenance often remained an elusive goal. During the workshop's first few years, all blind employees were paid "33 1/3 per cent above the union scale for hand work." The higher wages increased per capita production costs, but it also enabled some blind workers to support themselves and their families. Of the fourteen men and six women employed in 1910, seven of the men were completely self-supporting but none of the women could claim such success.[46] Yet even this limited attempt to pay a living wage lasted for only a brief period due to financial pressures. As early as 1912, the workshop adopted a new policy that required beginning blind employees "to spend approximately six months in learning the work before receiving any considerable remuneration." During this training period, private or public charity assisted in supporting these new employees. This revised policy also discouraged the recruitment of laborers.[47]

Advocates for the blind began pressing state officials to address the workshop's many shortcomings. Providing better living conditions for new employees became one of their early demands. Workshop superintendent Joseph A. Claudon used his position to lobby for the state to provide room and board, or even a home, to support many of these needy workers. Because it often took "approximately, one year for a blind person, who has not been engaged in any mechanical pursuit for years to learn the work," wrote Claudon, the workers are "not self-supporting, and many never become so." If the state provided room and board, or a home, many more of the state's blind adults could take advantage of the industrial training offered at the workshop. Claudon repeatedly mentioned this idea in his reports to officials, but the state never acted on his requests.[48] "The policy of our State towards her blind," wrote Claudon, "is one which does not make for their most desirable advancement and independence, and does not compare favorably with that of other great States."[49]

Unable to convince the state to provide funding for room and board, or to maintain a home, activists turned to their own resources to solve the financial problems faced by new workshop employees. Advocates formed their own association and in 1913 opened the Adult Blind Home in Denver by "renting a double house" with "eleven rooms on each side" to separate the sexes. Supported by fees, donations, and solicitations, the Blind Home housed three men and one woman on opening day and worked closely with the workshop to set room and board rates based on an individual's earnings.[50] The Blind Home made it more feasible to live on a low income by providing affordable and comfortable housing to employees unable to support themselves.

The Blind Home did not, however, get at the root of the problem for the blind community. Superintendent Claudon and the Board of Control for the workshop continued to decry, for example, inefficient practices due to erratic state funding. The board strongly recommended that the workshop receive its "entire appropriation," and the board also asked for additional state money for purchasing land and constructing a new building in order to improve working conditions, expand operations, and properly store materials.[51] In 1913, the board succeeded in realizing a large portion of its goals by pooling together various funds to construct a new one-story workshop.[52] Yet the opening of the new building failed to solve many of the shortcomings that had plagued the workshop. The one-story building could not accommodate many more workers than the old site. In 1914, for instance, sixteen to twenty-two blind employees labored at the workshop, but the facility was "insufficient to afford work for many more."[53] When Mrs. Coates from the State Board of Charities and Corrections visited the new shop, she noticed several workers coughing and reported that "all of the workmen complain of the dust, and they should, for it is unpleasant and insanitary." Ventilation remained a concern as "the dust arising from the broom corn and the fumes from sulphur used in bleaching the corn are very unpleasant," wrote Coates, "and must be unhealthy."[54] In addition, employees working in the new facility were still unable to fully support themselves with their earnings.[55] The new building failed to solve any of the major problems—lack of space, poor ventilation, an unstable financial future, and achieving self-maintenance—that had previously limited the workshop's ability to serve the state's blind community.

Just as the new building fell short in helping blind workers, the Adult Blind Home also failed to fulfill its stated mission. By March 1915, occupancy at the home had increased to fourteen, thirteen men and one woman, with eight of the men employed at the workshop. The Blind Home and the workshop continued cooperating to assist those who were new to broom making, and residents enjoyed hearty meals and a clean living environment. But the Blind Home never really achieved its goal of offering affordable housing to lots of laborers so that they could take advantage of the workshop. The home faced instability and always remained a small operation. When the first matron for the home left, she took all her furniture "leaving the lower floor quite bare." And almost two years after its opening, bedrooms in the Blind Home still contained "little furniture." This barebones operation depended heavily on donations to refurnish the downstairs and remain open.[56] As a result of the Blind Home's continued shortcomings, the State Board of Charities and Corrections once again renewed calls for the use of public funds to support new workshop employees. "It is necessary to enlarge the scope of the institution," argued the board, "by providing either a dormitory and kitchen or a fund from which the indigent blind may be assisted during the obviously long period the training entails."[57] Despite efforts by the blind community to address the housing needs of impoverished blind workers, the results fell far short of what was needed to make employees of the workshop self-sufficient.

Fighting for Blind Benefits

Efforts both to expand and upgrade Colorado's Industrial Workshop for the Blind as well as efforts to establish and maintain the Blind Home failed to alter circumstances in any significant way for the blind community. Yet, the experiences gained from these attempts would prove invaluable in transforming the welfare state and in dramatically improving living standards for blind adults. By the early to mid-1910s, Colorado's blind community had become extremely knowledgeable about dealing with the state. Jackson had developed working relations with public officials and had successfully initiated and maintained connections with Colorado's Women's Clubs, one of the state's most powerful interest groups. Through her many travels, Jackson had also linked together Colorado's adult blind community, and thus they could now express their wants and desires in a collective voice. Finally, advocates had realized the importance of targeting goals that would realistically assist most of the state's blind adults. Gainful employment through sheltered workshops or through jobs in the public or private sector remained an important aim; still, the events of the early twentieth century showed that obtaining this goal would require long-term advocacy. Societal views were so entrenched concerning the helplessness of blind residents that activists had made little headway in opening doors of employment. Because Colorado's financial commitment to the workshop remained minimal, advocates turned their attention to securing blind benefits as a way to help eliminate poverty among the state's blind community.

The idea of providing blind adults with a special pension or benefit was not a new notion or unique to Colorado. In fact, for some time New York City's blind population had received a special form of aid from the municipal government. Beginning in 1866, New York City's Department of Charities started the nation's first public pension for the adult blind by giving monetary assistance to impoverished blind men and women. By 1897, New York City set aside seventy-five thousand dollars per year for the blind pension program, which limited each person to no more than one hundred dollars in annual aid.[58] During the Progressive Era, states began passing legislation creating statewide assistance programs for the blind. Ohio became the first to pass such a law in 1898, with other states soon following.[59] Illinois passed a blind relief act in 1903 that made compliance optional for each county, and Wisconsin approved a similar law four years later. Kansas ratified a pension law in 1911 that covered blind residents as well as people "who had lost one or both hands, or one or both feet, or who were otherwise disabled, and who were otherwise unprovided for."[60] By 1919, thirteen states had approved specific blind benefit laws. "Special 'blind pensions' and 'blind relief laws' seem to be the order of the day throughout the country," observed Robert Irwin.[61]

As the movement for blind benefits gained momentum, debates over the merits of these new laws received greater attention and publicity. For the most part, social workers and charity workers came out strongly against these new measures while the general blind community enthusiastically endorsed them. Social and charity workers expressed horror at the notion of giving relief to a group of citizens without first thoroughly investigating their circumstances. The delivery of New York City's blind pension, for example, especially upset James Forbes, mendicancy officer for the New York Charity Organization Society, who described the distribution of funds as a form of "barbarism." To Forbes, the mixing and equal treatment of recipients of questionable moral character with those of supposedly higher standards all under the common rubric of blindness seemed a "senseless criminal method of distribution."[62] Others cited the potentially demoralizing influence on a recipient's character due to receiving blind aid. Social workers feared that pensions would discourage blind adults from seeking out employment or trying to improve their lot, perhaps even resulting in "inertness and indolence."[63] Professionals in social work raised questions about corruption, fraud, trickery, and the importance of treating each individual in a flexible case-by-case manner as opposed to treating someone as a member of a fixed class or group.[64] "There does not seem to be any absolutely sound reason," wrote Eugene T. Lies, general superintendent of Chicago's United Charities, "for picking out a special class of disabled person for special relief."[65] Finally, opponents believed that communities already had an adequate system to support the needy blind—public poor relief.[66]

Those in favor of blind benefits rested their support for special assistance on a number of basic arguments. Activists Robert and Mary Irwin, who generally opposed blind pensions, ironically best summarized the overarching justification for benefits: "Blindness itself is a sufficiently well-defined cause of poverty to require special treatment at the hands of the state."[67] As mentioned before, those who were blind found it nearly impossible to secure and maintain a job that paid a living wage. "It cannot be denied," observed Robert Irwin, "that the handicap of blindness forces the most efficient sightless person down far nearer the poverty border line than he would otherwise be."[68] Because of limited opportunities and the difficulty of learning new skills, blindness and poverty often went hand in hand, thus requiring a special pension. In addition, given the rather permanent nature of their poverty, reasoned proponents of benefits, blind adults should not have to deal with the stigma of applying for poor relief. "Many a self-respecting blind person," wrote the Irwins, "has been submitted to a humiliating investigation whenever relief has been applied for."[69] Not only did blind people perceive the application process for relief as degrading but the levels of support proved terribly inadequate. Ohio's Dr. Louis Stricker could hardly believe the depth of poverty that he witnessed among the state's blind residents. "The scenes of poverty and degradation disclosed were a revelation," wrote Stricker. "One could scarcely understand how, amid all the existing agencies for relief, such poverty and distress could remain hidden and continue without adequate relief."[70] Although blind benefits were often not enough to completely maintain an indigent person, the levels of support were usually much higher than what poor relief provided. And even though supporters acknowledged the possibility of fraud, benefits still appeared to be "the simplest, the most direct, and probably the most economical of all the measures available for giving necessary assistance to the blind."[71]

As the two sides of the blind benefits debate squared off, the issue and language of pensions became a recurring theme. During the Progressive Era, social reformers proposed a number of pension-like schemes in an attempt to involve the state in protecting the well-being and security of its citizens. Blind benefits, like mothers' pensions, contributed to this mix of proposals. Opponents to blind aid insisted that these new laws did not qualify as real pensions because pensions were paid in "recognition of a past service" or "something given for services previously rendered."[72] Using these definitions, the newly enacted laws that aimed to help the blind surely did not qualify as pensions. These laws clearly made a person's financial needs a key criterion for receiving assistance. Blind aid laws in Illinois and Wisconsin allowed public assistance only if a person's annual income did not exceed $250, while Ohio's blind relief law required that counties give aid only to those individuals deemed needy.[73] Given the need-based qualifications that states had written into their statutes, opponents branded these laws not as pensions but rather as "a specialized kind of poor relief" or simply as a "public outdoor relief" measure directed toward the indigent blind.[74]

Yet, despite this obvious evidence of requiring financial need for assistance, advocates for blind benefits persisted in viewing these same laws not as a type of poor relief but rather as a form of pension. This difference in interpretation rested not upon ignorance of these laws, as blind people themselves wrote most of the nation's blind relief laws. Instead, proponents took into account similarities with other pension schemes, their own motivations for enacting these laws, and, most notably, the implementation of these new acts. Like supporters of mothers' pension measures, advocates for blind benefits pulled ideas from other pension plans. In Michigan, activists drew "helpful suggestions from the fields of kindred philanthropic movements, such as those of old age pensions, teachers' retirement funds, mothers' pensions, and the like."[75] Even Robert Irwin argued that if existing poor relief measures failed to provide properly for blind people, then activists should use mothers' pension laws as a model for creating blind benefits.[76]

But more important than borrowing ideas from similar proposals was the sense of a "right" to public support based on traditional male roles. In many ways, much as supporters of mothers' pensions spoke about widows, activists for the blind likewise argued that society's obligation toward the blind stemmed from the contributions that blind people had made to society's development. But unlike mothers' pensions advocates, who rested their arguments for state support on ideas that the nation benefited from maternal child-care practices, supporters of blind benefits based their arguments on contributions that male wage earners had made to society. The Board of Control for Colorado's Industrial Workshop for the Blind, for instance, drew a parallel between veterans and the blind. Elderly and disabled veterans in Colorado could reside at the state's Soldiers' and Sailors' Home because of their past service, sacrifice, and "loyalty to the government." Yet, argued the board, blind people had also dedicated themselves to building the nation and, much like veterans, had sacrificed themselves for the common good. Many blind adults, stated the board, "were injured as the result of accidents occurring while they were engaged as miners and in developing the resources which have made it possible for this state to reach the proud position which it now occupies."[77] Because of this sacrifice, blind benefits were not a type of welfare but rather a pension that blind people had earned through hard, physical, honorable work while employed in some of the most masculine of all occupations.

A slightly different, but more radical, view of this same male wage earner right to a pension surfaced during a discussion on Colorado's need for blind benefits. In 1916, Mr. Stone, a Denver advocate for blind aid, believed that "the blind were just as independent as any body else and if given a chance to do so would make their own living." But society, claimed Stone, had wrongly grouped all blind adults into one class as "'the Blind.'" This single classification assumed that all blind people were unable to work or support themselves. Because of this stereotyping and discrimination, Stone argued, the "blind have as much right to a pension as any other person who becomes unable to work whether or not a city fireman or city policeman or in the army or navy."[78] Thus for Stone, blind benefits would at least partially rectify the impoverished position in which society, and not individual blind people, had placed most blind men by denying them their roles as male breadwinners.

The linking of blind aid with the traditional male role as a family's main wage earner reflected the male dominance within the blind community as well as a desire to associate benefits with new successful pension programs. In 1920, males numerically dominated the blind population, accounting for just over 57 percent of the nation's blind community and almost 63 percent of Colorado's.[79] Evidence that mining caused a significant number of cases of blindness does not materialize in census data; however, male employment clearly did cause high rates of blindness. Male rates of blindness significantly increase, and diverge from females, between the ages of twenty and forty-five, when "males are most actively engaged in industry" and susceptible to injury from accidents.[80] This association of blindness with male wage earning provides some basis for viewing blind benefits as a pension for jobs previously performed. But just as important must have been the desire to distance benefits from the dismal record of mothers' pension programs. By comparing blind benefits to more successfully implemented job-related pensions—military, police, and fire—activists lessened any possible association with the underfunded and partially enforced mothers' pensions and strengthened notions that blind benefits were a wage earner's "right."

At the same time that activists spoke passionately about a "right" for benefits, the implementation of these new blind aid laws cemented their views of these measures as true pensions. The public's generally favorable view of blind aid resulted in a tendency to downplay financial need in determining eligibility. In "far too many counties," reported Robert and Mary Irwin, "need is but a secondary consideration after the facts of residence and blindness have been established. The result has been," continued the Irwins, "to convert the laws creating a special relief for the needy blind into a pension for the blind, regardless of need." While sloppy investigations partially accounted for these practices, the Irwins also acknowledged that "an underlying conviction on the part of a large mass of the public that there should be a pension for the blind" played an important role in fostering these habits.[81] In terms of implementation, blind relief laws were indeed evolving into pensions, regardless of the legal restrictions that supposedly limited aid to the indigent.

Given the high level of public support for blind benefits, the success in transforming these aid laws into pensionlike programs, the increase in assistance these measures provided, and the failure of sheltered workshops in solving the problems of limited employment options, Colorado's blind community turned its attention to securing benefits. At first, Jennie Jackson seemed, once again, to assume complete responsibility for convincing the legislature to expand state services, this time to fund blind aid. Beginning in 1913, Jackson began pursuing blind benefits by approaching state officials about her proposal.[82] Yet, unlike her previous efforts, this initial attempt made little headway.

Only with assistance from the Society of United Workers for the Blind of Colorado, a local group consisting of both blind and sighted members but clearly dominated by blind people, did benefits move forward in any substantial manner. Formed in 1915, Colorado's United Workers for the Blind aimed to help and encourage blind residents by providing a number of services for the community—holding social events, collecting clothes for the indigent, and serving as a lobbying group. While Jackson played a prominent role in founding and running the United Workers, Lucius (Lute) M. Wilcox led the newly formed organization. Wilcox came to Denver in 1876 from Pennsylvania and Ohio where he began his newspaper career. Once in Colorado, he worked as a reporter before publishing and owning *Field and Farm*, an influential weekly agricultural paper based in Denver. Wilcox accomplished all this with limited and deteriorating vision. Born blind in one eye, Wilcox began losing sight in his other eye at the age of fifteen, and by the time he reached the age of forty-four he was totally blind. Yet, despite losing his vision, Wilcox continued editing and publishing his weekly paper.[83] Under Wilcox's leadership, the United Workers quickly formed a committee in 1915 to introduce a blind pension bill in the state legislature. Although the group actively worked for the act's passage, the blind relief bill once again failed to win approval.[84]

The following year, the United Workers again began the process of preparing a blind benefit bill for the legislature, but this time, they were better organized and got an earlier start. In September 1916, Wilcox addressed the United Workers concerning plans for the upcoming legislative session, while another member reviewed the previous year's failed efforts. By November, a three-person Legal Committee had formed, and members openly debated employment and pension plans to assist the needy.[85] By January 1917, however, the United Workers halted their own efforts and threw their support behind another pension bill introduced by Pitkin County Representative James M. Downing. Promising an annual pension of $180 for "helpless, adult blind," the proposed bill seemed to have the best chance of winning approval. Downing, himself blind, used an emotional appeal to propel the bill forward. Standing before his colleagues, "his sightless orbs mutely re-echoing his story as half-suppressed sobs arose here and there," Downing, "told of the plight these unfortunates were in and of the failure of the state to properly provide for them." Downing's eloquent appeal had left scarcely "a dry eye in the assembly chamber," reported the *Rocky Mountain News*. When the applause from the assembly chamber died down, the House voted unanimously to support the pension plan.[86] The blind community happily welcomed the good news and enthusiastically thanked Downing for his "touching and eloquent" speech and for "introducing and fathering" the bill along.[87] When the bill reached the Senate, however, its good fortune quickly ended. Once the Finance Committee received the pension bill, its chairman, Senator George E. West, "an avowed opponent of all pension legislation," pigeonholed the proposal, killing any hope of passing blind benefits through the state legislature.[88] The United Workers petitioned the legislature one last time during the Extraordinary Session called in response to America's entry into World War I. Yet, this time they even failed to place their pension act on the assembly's agenda.[89]

After four unsuccessful attempts to win legislative approval of a blind aid bill, the United Workers decided to use a different approach, the initiative, to accomplish their goal. By September 1917, the Legal Committee had prepared a report comparing blind benefit laws in various states and drafted its own proposed bill. After reading the act and holding a brief discussion, the United Workers voted to accept the proposal and place it on next year's ballot.[90] With the beginning of the new year, the United Workers, along with their supporters, began collecting signatures for their initiative, entitled an Act for the Relief of the Adult Blind. The public wholeheartedly supported the proposal. "So enthusiastic were our friends," reported Jennie Jackson, "that they sent in about seven thousand more signatures than were required by law."[91]

The Colorado Federation of Women's Clubs endorsed the blind benefit measure, and citizens continued to show their enthusiasm for the proposal in November 1918, when the measure won by an almost fourteen-to-one margin, receiving the largest majority ever by an initiated bill in Colorado.[92] Several days after the election victory, the United Workers for the Blind and their supporters gathered to celebrate. Over one hundred people came together to hear piano, violin, and vocal solos and duets as well as readings of poetry and literature. While people listened, they enjoyed an assortment of sandwiches, pies, and doughnuts. "The adoption of this bill," joyously proclaimed Jackson, "will be a great benefit to many of the blind of this state."[93]

Transforming the Welfare State

The implementation of the new blind benefit law not only helped many of Colorado's blind adults but it also transformed the state's public assistance practices. Blind benefits, unlike mothers' pensions and other Progressive Era reform efforts, overrode, for the first time, the influence of local circumstances in determining the delivery of aid. The ability of blind benefits to change the welfare state rested partially with the wording of the new measure. Advocates, through their research of other states' laws, had carefully crafted Colorado's blind benefit act so as to guarantee, almost completely, the successful implementation of the new measure by minimizing or eliminating the authority of local county officials and social workers while at the same time maximizing the power of the newly created statewide Blind Benefit Commission, which oversaw the new measure. Likewise, the continued role that activists played in monitoring the law, in gaining control of the Blind Benefit Commission, and in calling for a further expansion of public support for blind adults remained a key reason for the measure's success. In the end, despite attempts by Denver's social workers to gain control over benefits, advocates succeeded, as they had done earlier with the state teacher and the workshop, in expanding and controlling the new state service for the blind. But this time, they had created a much larger program that dramatically improved the lives of indigent blind people and revolutionized the state's welfare system.

Colorado's blind residents greeted the new aid law with a true feeling of appreciation. "I wish I could express in fitting words," wrote one unidentified blind resident, "the joy and deep sense of gratitude which I felt when I heard that the relief law had passed. I wish that all the blind in Colorado could, in some befitting manner, express their thanks to the kind voters, and particularly to those who, by their labor and efforts, started the movement. Let me, as one, thank you [Jennie Jackson] and the 'Workers for the Blind' for all that you have done for us," concluded the blind citizen. Another unidentified blind resident expressed a degree of comfort and security about the new law. "I hope that I shall never need it [blind benefits], but it is a great satisfaction to know that it is there if I do." During her travels throughout the state, Jackson received many words of gratitude and praise from her students and other members of the blind community concerning the state's new blind aid law.[94]

Within only a few months, changes began to materialize. By the beginning of July 1919, for example, Costilla County commissioners received notice to transfer three relief applicants from their poor rolls to blind benefits. At the same time, three additional county residents, who had previously not received any type of public support, also started receiving blind aid.[95] Thus, as with mothers' pensions, many of the first recipients of blind benefits came from county poor relief programs. But unlike mothers' pensions, the new blind aid act quickly assumed responsibility for those who would have previously not qualified for public aid. Other counties besides Costilla quickly implemented the new blind benefit law, including Boulder, Denver, Lincoln, Montezuma, and Teller Counties. In fact, by the end of 1919, blind benefits' first year of operation, all Colorado counties had enacted the new law, although only 73 percent of the state's counties (forty-six out of sixty-three counties) actually used the measure.[96] The county commissioners who did not distribute blind benefits did so not as a result of noncompliance but rather because no qualified blind residents had applied for aid within their jurisdiction. This rapid and universal implementation (the blind benefit law did not apply to residents of the Ute Mountain Ute Indian Reservation) differs dramatically from the sparse enforcement of the state's mothers' pension act. Three years after mothers' pensions' effective date (January 22, 1913), only about twenty-one counties had enacted the law, and most of these counties only partially carried out the measure.[97]

One reason for the widespread enactment of blind benefits was that the act created a new state levy to help fund the measure. According to the blind benefit law, the state had to collect "a sufficient sum" to pay for half of the measure's costs, with counties responsible for paying the other half. Mothers' pensions never had access to state funds. Even in 1919, when reformers managed to get a special tax approved to support mothers' pensions, this new levy still required counties, and not the state, to raise the necessary money. By involving the state, activists for the blind had assured themselves that at least half of the funds would be raised and had avoided total dependence on county commissioners, who were generally extremely reluctant to use taxes for welfare programs. In a sense, the state levy for benefits partially liberated the indigent blind from the power of local officials. Indeed, by removing county commissioners' control in raising relief funds, the state levy limited the authority of local officials in regulating the implementation of the new measure.[98]

The creation of the Blind Benefit Commission and the application procedure also played an important role in achieving universal implementation and reducing the power of local officials. In order to administer the new blind aid measure, the voter-approved law created a three-member Blind Benefit Commission consisting of the auditor of the state, the superintendent of public instruction, and a secretary appointed by the governor. When indigent blind people applied for benefits, they applied not to their county commissioners or local social workers, as had been the case with poor relief and mothers' pensions, but rather to their county clerk and recorder, county physician, and ultimately the Blind Benefit Commission. In fact, the benefit law seemed to go out of its way to avoid county commissioners. Each potential recipient filed an application and an affidavit with the county clerk and recorder stating his or her residency status, age, financial need, and lack of eyesight. In addition, two citizens also provided affidavits supporting the applicant's claims. The county clerk and recorder then immediately referred the applicant to the county physician for an eye examination. From this information the Blind Benefit Commission determined whether a person qualified for assistance and how much aid should be given. Once the commission reached a decision, they informed the county clerk and recorder who then instructed the county commissioners to issue quarterly warrants for the applicant.[99]

The blind benefit application eliminated any formal investigation by county officials. In an attempt to avoid the stigma associated with county aid and to differentiate blind aid from poor relief, the benefit law prevented the use of a person's character or moral behavior as criteria for assistance. Instead, the blind benefit law focused completely on a person's financial status, eyesight, age, and his or her length of residency in the state and county as conditions for aid. And the act clearly defined each one of these qualifications. An applicant, for example, must have an annual "income through earnings or otherwise" of less than $360 and, of course, must be declared blind by the county physician.[100] The tight focus of the three-page application along with the well-defined guidelines prevented county officials from meddling in the operation of blind benefits. County commissioners could not establish their own local criteria for assistance, nor could they impose additional standards for aid. The use of the county physician to certify a person's blindness introduced a degree of professional authority that clearly overrode any possible objections that commissioners may have had and reinforced the notion that blindness, and not character flaws, caused a blind person's poverty. The blind benefit law cleverly avoided traditional poor relief practices that allowed local officials to determine who qualified for assistance.

As a consequence of the law's guidelines, blind benefits largely succeeded in eliminating county commissioners from the decision-making process. And most county commissioners seemed to quickly relinquish their authority and roles as investigators with little or no complaint. In fact, some county commissioners became completely unaware of just who applied for blind benefits and how far along in the application process they were. Montezuma County commissioners seemed surprised, almost taken aback, when they learned that the Blind Benefit Commission had approved a resident's application for assistance in October 1919: "It appearing to the Board that Evelyn F. Tozer, a blind person, has made application to the Colorado Blind Benefit Commission . . . and it further appearing to the Board that said application has been approved." Despite being caught off guard, the commissioners did not challenge the application or the commission's order to provide aid.[101]

Almost all county commissioners not only accepted those whom the Blind Benefit Commission selected as deserving of aid, but they also raised no objections to the levels of support that the commission approved. The new law stated that the Blind Benefit Commission "shall fix the amount in such sum as it finds necessary, considering the circumstances of the applicant." Yet, the act did set a maximum amount of $300 per year that the commission could award each applicant.[102] Advocates had designed the act so that the indigent blind would no longer have to tolerate the low levels of assistance often found in county poor relief programs. The Blind Benefit Commission, for instance, granted Evelyn Tozer from Montezuma County

$300 each year, well above the county's average annual level of just under $170 for female aid recipients.[103] In Lincoln County, the commission allotted Charles E. Millisack $300 per year, an amount almost three times higher than the county's average annual amount of just over $105 for males on poor relief.[104] Indigent blind residents in Boulder, Denver, and Teller, as well as from other Colorado counties, likewise received assistance from the Blind Benefit Commission at levels well above what their local counties had previously allowed. Yet, despite this trend of granting much higher levels of aid, most county commissioners accepted the commission's levels of assistance with no objections. The fact that the state reimbursed each county for half of all blind benefit expenses may partly explain this acceptance. In the case of Lincoln's Charles Millisack, for example, the state's reimbursement of $150 meant that it only cost Lincoln about $45 more for Millisack's higher blind aid than the county's average poor relief. The state's $150 reimbursement for Montezuma's Evelyn Tozer's blind aid actually lowered the county's portion to less than the average paid to female poor relief recipients.

Denver, however, became the one exception to this trend of counties relinquishing authority to the Blind Benefit Commission. Within a few weeks of its effective date, the United Workers began noticing problems with Denver's willingness to fully enact the new measure. In April 1919, members of the United Workers spoke of the "handicap" or burden that Denver's Bureau of Charities placed on the city's benefit applicants and asked for help with the problem.[105] In September, Lute Wilcox accused Denver's Bureau of Charities of blocking "two applicants for relief," even though both were "worthy cases." Wilcox went on to advise "all who are receiving the relief to keep a careful record of their receipts."[106] The situation only deteriorated further over the next several months, and by June 1920 the United Workers filed a formal protest "against the Bureau of Charities and the way in which they mishandled the Blind Benefit work."[107]

The lack of any formal investigation became the sticking point between Denver's Bureau of Charities and the United Workers. The bureau wanted a formal investigation of applicants and wanted to transform the blind benefit law into a modified form of county poor relief by insisting on a large degree of local control in investigating applicants, by deciding who should get aid, and by setting relief levels. This request to alter a relief measure was not the first time that the Bureau of Charities had tried to extend its legal authority beyond what a law stipulated. A few years earlier, the board had successfully assumed control of the city's mothers' pension program through an agreement with Judge Lindsey that largely circumvented a key element of the pension law— distinguishing mothers' pensions from poor relief. Indeed, Denver's mothers' pensions had become simply another form of poor relief with the same personnel administering both programs and treating recipients in a similar manner. At the time, Gertrude Vaile argued that the mothers' pension program needed the professional expertise and individual casework techniques that trained social workers could provide in order to guard public funds from waste, fraud, and deception. Vaile's successor, Florence Hutsinpillar, and the Bureau of Charities likewise argued that blind benefits needed professional oversight. The bureau also disliked that the county clerk and recorder, a person obviously not trained in social work practices, exclusively handled and processed blind benefits.[108]

As with mothers' pensions, Denver used a legal technicality both to expand the authority of the Bureau of Charities and to try and temper those aspects of the benefit law that had transferred decision-making power from local officials to the Blind Benefit Commission. After consulting with the city attorney and studying the new act, city officials decided to make Hutsinpillar a "deputy" county clerk without any additional pay so that she could now "legally" administer the blind benefit measure. In addition, the board used a phrase in the new law that allowed county clerks and recorders to send "any further information or evidence in [their] possession" to the Blind Benefit Commission as justification for formally investigating each blind aid applicant. As a result, Denver's Bureau of Charities sent written recommendations to the Blind Benefit Commission, and Hutsinpillar personally attended each commission meeting to keep a watchful eye on proceedings.[109]

While similar tactics had worked for the Bureau of Charities in maintaining control of the city's mothers' pension program, this time it failed. The United Workers could not block the city's investigation of relief applicants or halt Hutsinpillar's attendance at meetings; still, Denver's social workers seemed to have little influence over the implementation of benefits. Regardless of Hutsinpillar's attempts to control assistance, the Blind Benefit Commission had taken a firm stand in favor of generously dispensing aid. During the first two years of implementation, 1919 and 1920, the commission considered 554 applicants statewide, granting aid in 519 cases. Thus, slightly over 93 percent of all blind aid applicants received assistance.[110] In addition, after four years of operation, the Commission granted over 97 percent of all blind aid recipients the maximum amount of three hundred dollars per year.[111] The commission's implementation of blind benefits made the new relief measure almost a guaranteed three hundred dollar annual pension for the state's indigent blind adults. Denver's attempts to control the new act, including Hutsinpillar's attendance at commission meetings, failed to derail either one of these trends or lessen the authority of the Blind Benefit Commission. In fact, by 1920, almost 56 percent of the state's blind community received some form of public aid, by far the highest percentage in the nation.[112]

The key reason for the failure of Denver's social workers to gain control over blind benefits was that activists successfully ruled over the benefits, just as they had done with the state teacher and workshop. The United Workers kept a close watch not only on how Denver implemented the new law but also on how other counties, regardless of their location, enforced the new measure. When the county clerk and recorder from Conejos County, located along the New Mexico border, failed to fully carry out the new act, for instance, Lute Wilcox and the United Workers quickly expressed concern. Wilcox told "of the Devil's own time down in Conejos [C]ounty to get the county clerk to do his duty."[113] In 1921, the United Workers succeeded in having Henrietta Wilcox, the sighted wife of Lute Wilcox and a strong advocate for the blind, appointed secretary of the Blind Benefit Commission, the most powerful position on the commission. Henrietta Wilcox provided "sympathetic and tireless labor" toward her new responsibilities and used her new position to call for higher levels of support.[114] The "amount of $300 per annum is wholly inadequate for the maintenance of most of the blind beneficiaries," she wrote to Governor Oliver H. Shoup. According to Henrietta Wilcox, this was especially true for those too old and weak to work and for heads of dependent families.[115] By the early 1920s, the Blind Benefit Commission acted as a firm advocate for blind residents. In a sense, the commission had become an extension of the blind community and worked so closely with the United Workers that for all practical purposes the two groups spoke with a single voice. Colorado's blind citizens had clearly claimed a portion of the state's welfare system as their own.

■

The blind benefit movement radically transformed the delivery of Colorado's Progressive Era poor relief by establishing a number of firsts. Blind benefits centralized, for the first time, relief authority in a statewide commission that assumed most of the responsibilities previously held by county commissioners. The Blind Benefit Commission decided not only who received assistance but also how much aid the county should grant. The blind aid application completely bypassed, for the first time, county commissioners and even Denver's social workers. By establishing the criteria for qualifying for aid, the blind aid act kept local officials from determining who received aid, the duration of aid, and the amount of aid. More generally, the benefit law overrode, for the first time, the effects of a county's local circumstances in deciding the delivery of assistance. Finally, blind benefits carved up, for the first time, a portion of county-level public outdoor relief as the exclusive domain of a single group.[116]

The blind community's hold over their piece of the welfare pie—blind benefits, the workshop, and the state teacher position—would prove only temporary. During the mid-1920s, these welfare policies would come under attack from an odd coalition of opponents. Despite local activists' attempts to defend their control of these agencies and the structure of these various programs, the activists would be dislodged from their positions of authority and the programs profoundly modified. Yet, the concept of a separate aid program for blind adults would continue, albeit at reduced levels. Other forms of county-level assistance would escape political scrutiny until the Great Depression, operating much as they had during the late nineteenth and early twentieth centuries.

CHAPTER SIX

Change, Continuity, and Conclusion

AFTER TELLER COUNTY'S WILLIAM HENDERSON SWITCHED FROM POOR RELIEF to blind benefits in 1920, he continued to accept benefits, with his assistance levels increasing from $275 per year to the maximum annual amount of $300. In 1926, Henderson's relative good fortune came to a halt as his annual assistance dropped to only $180.[1] What had changed to alter Henderson's situation so quickly? In the early 1920s, activists firmly controlled and generously disbursed blind benefits, allowing the indigent blind an almost guaranteed pension. In addition, blind aid enjoyed strong political support from the outgoing Governor Oliver H. Shoup who, in 1923, called for "additional financial assistance" for blind benefits.[2] Yet by 1925, departing Governor William E. Sweet now characterized blind aid as too costly and called for a complete restructuring of blind benefits and of other state services for blind adults.[3] Soon, advocates would lose their command over benefits, the workshop, and the state teacher, while the distribution and amount of blind aid would be greatly reduced. Why this sudden reversal in attitude and policy?

With both the placement of Henrietta Wilcox on the Blind Benefit Commission and the successful blocking of social workers' attempts to gain control over blind aid, the blind community could rightfully claim blind benefits as "theirs." Activists had written the law, placed the measure on the ballot, campaigned for its approval, closely monitored its implementation, defended it from attacks, and actively administered the act. Blind men and women clearly controlled a portion of the welfare pie. But that control would prove to be only temporary. In just a few years, the United Workers, blind benefits, and other services for blind adults came under attack from an odd assortment of groups. Denver's Community Chest, the eventual successor of the Charity Organization Society and the forerunner to United Way; Gertrude Vaile, the former head of Denver's Bureau of Charities; Helen Keller; the American Foundation for the Blind; and the Ku Klux Klan all attacked either the United Workers, blind benefits, or other programs for blind residents for various, often unrelated, reasons. The combination of these attacks ultimately succeeded in dislodging advocates' control over state services for blind adults. Yet, the idea of a separate relief fund for indigent blind citizens would remain, although funded at much lower levels and intended for fewer recipients.

Meanwhile, other welfare programs operated much as they had during the previous decades. In the 1920s, local circumstances continued to shape the delivery of relief as county officials still administered and funded assistance programs. County poor farms and hospitals remained open and, in some cases, were even expanded. The implementation of mothers' pensions continued to be thwarted by the familiar concerns of a lack of compliance and a lack of funds. Efforts by interest groups to solve these two problems proved unsuccessful. Thus, pensions remained a subset of public aid, and the counties that did enact mothers' aid usually only enforced a portion of it. As a result of these trends, Colorado's poor relief practices on the eve of the New Deal looked much like late-nineteenth- and early-twentieth-century welfare policies. Indeed, except for the scaled-back blind benefits, the Progressive Era had left surprisingly little to show for many years of reform.

Reorganizing State Services for Blind Adults

The activists' control of blind benefits, the workshop, and the state teacher challenged the authority and power of the newly emerging class of professional social workers like Florence Hutsinpillar and Gertrude Vaile. Of course, this was not the first time that these new professionals were challenged. Clients and their families often created their own methods for maintaining control over their own lives independent of social workers' desires and aims. Peggy Pascoe charts, for example, how Chinese women in a San Francisco mission home dedicated to instilling Anglo-Victorian values and habits managed, ironically, to retain the serving of Chinese food in the home.[4] In Los Angeles, working-class parents, according to Mary Odem, used new juvenile courts "for their own purposes, namely to restrain children whose behavior conflicted with family needs and expectations."[5] Yet, activists' successful efforts to create, expand, and manage state services for blind adults offered a significantly more serious challenge to the authority and control that social workers had over assistance. Instead of challenging reformers directly within existing programs or institutions, the blind community chose to carve out their own practices and establishments that were not only independent of both social workers and local politicians but were also under the control of the blind themselves. According to social workers, this situation of having an interest group manage their own assistance was simply unacceptable, unprofessional, and in need of change.

The first blow came in October 1923, when Guy T. Justis, director of Denver's Community Chest, requested that the United Workers halt their efforts in assisting the indigent blind and allow other organizations to assume this task. By having other groups take responsibility for the needy blind, Justis would have increased the power of trained charity workers and social workers and decreased the United Workers' self-advocacy role. Lute Wilcox and the United Workers quickly expressed outrage at the notion of abandoning the indigent. Wilcox argued that the United Workers knew the city's blind population and already helped a large percentage of them. Many of Denver's blind residents were "fighting the great battle of bread and butter for daily subsistence. Many of these people are homeless and friendless," wrote Wilcox, "and under the proposed arrangement they would get practically nothing." Wilcox concluded his letter of protest by stating that "we cannot agree to the proposition that we are to be divorced from helping the needy blind of Denver."[6] Wilcox and other United Workers' members clearly realized the importance of maintaining contact with the indigent blind not only to make sure that the needs of the poor were being met but also to continue advocating for them. In the end, Wilcox and the United Workers strongly believed that the blind themselves, and not trained social workers, could best monitor and represent the interests of the state's impoverished blind population.

Calls for the increased involvement of professionally trained social workers also shaped Gertrude Vaile's attempt to remake Colorado's services for blind adults. Vaile had been the executive secretary of Denver's Bureau of Charities until 1917, when she resigned to become director of civilian relief for the American Red Cross's Rocky Mountain Division. Two years later, she left for the Family Service Association of America to take a position as associate field director for the area west of the Mississippi River. In March 1924, Governor William Sweet appointed Vaile secretary of the newly formed Department of Charities and Corrections, the successor to the State Board of Charities and Corrections.[7] During her short term as the department's secretary, Vaile characterized blind benefits as "expensive but unsatisfactory and chaotic." Vaile lamented the limited amount of vocational training available for the state's blind adults. She argued that blind benefits diminished "efforts of the blind toward self-support" and even went so far as to claim that blind citizens were unhappy with the aid. In her view, the efforts of the state teacher, the Colorado Industrial Workshop for the Blind, and the Blind Benefit Commission needed to be coordinated and focused on promoting independence instead of dependency. Vaile recommended the creation of a State Blind Commission that would oversee the state teacher, the workshop, and blind benefits and "whose efforts should be, first, to give the blind every help and opportunity to be independent and, second, to give them such relief as they may need where independence is not fully possible."[8] Vaile clearly hoped to wrest control of the state's blind services away from activists and place it in the hands of trained social workers while reducing state expenditures. All of Vaile's goals clearly reflected Denver's previous failed attempt to alter blind aid.

Advocates for the blind were furious with Vaile. She had completely distorted the blind community's concerns and exaggerated the lack of coordination among the state's various blind programs. (Vaile had used similar tactics of exaggeration and distortion years earlier when she had called for the restructuring of Denver's outdoor relief.) Colorado's blind community had always strongly preferred independence and employment instead of dependency and relief, establishing the state teacher, the workshop, and the Blind Home as tools to help people become self-supporting. Yet, despite these diligent efforts, most of the state's blind population remained unemployed and poor. The workshop trained only a small number of blind workers despite persistent attempts by activists to expand the facility. Blind benefits became a necessity not because people did not want to work, as Vaile suggested, but because of a lack of employment. "I have quite a list of those who are willing and anxious to work," lamented Jennie Jackson. "They would be glad to earn their own way if they could, instead of accepting the [blind] benefit."[9] And Colorado's blind services were hardly "chaotic." Instead, the state's blind programs were closely linked; the state teacher, the workshop, and the Blind Benefit Commission all worked together to coordinate their services. A few workshop employees, for example, received a small amount of blind benefits to supplement their low wages, and Jackson obviously informed her students about blind aid.[10] The state's different blind services were certainly organized, but activists for the blind, and not trained social workers, controlled and coordinated these programs, and this bothered Vaile. When the United Workers heard of the reorganization proposal, Henrietta Wilcox concisely summed up the plan as an attempt by Vaile "to take over the Blind [Benefit] Commission." As in the past, the United Workers quickly formed a committee, headed by Lute Wilcox, to meet with politicians to explain why the blind community opposed Vaile's ideas.[11]

Although the United Workers used a well-proven strategy to try to protect their interests, the political landscape had changed dramatically in only a few years. Two new powerful players had entered the political arena and had altered the playing field by creating competing ideologies that drowned out the United Workers' message. First, in June 1921, members of the American Association of Workers for the Blind (AAWB), including Colorado's Jennie Jackson, gathered in Vinton, Iowa, for their ninth biennial convention. During the convention, AAWB members approved forming a new national organization, the American Foundation for the Blind (AFB), "for supplementing and co-operating with all activities in behalf of the blind."[12] The AFB would tackle issues that were "too technical and too comprehensive to be handled by local organizations" while also promising not to encroach "in a manner detrimental to local interests."[13] By May 1923, the new national organization took over publishing the *Outlook for the Blind*, a magazine begun in 1907 by the Massachusetts Association for Promoting the Interests of the Blind, and the AFB's strong antipension stance and almost absolute belief that employment would soon lift the indigent blind out of poverty reverberated throughout a string of editorials and articles.[14]

Shortly thereafter, the AFB's antipension views were both directly and indirectly running roughshod over the interests of Colorado's United Workers for the Blind. Governor Sweet asked the AFB in 1924 to participate on a committee to survey the state's work for the blind and make recommendations to the legislature. The AFB could have deferred to the local United Workers, who were extremely knowledgeable about Colorado's habit of providing low levels of financial support for vocational programs and knew in great detail the state's history of aid to the indigent blind through both blind benefits and county poor relief programs. Instead, the AFB not only accepted the governor's invitation but also endorsed a recommendation, much like Vaile's plan, to reorganize the state's three agencies working with the adult blind—the workshop, the state teacher, and blind benefit commission—under a single commission.[15] At about the same time that the committee released its recommendations for reorganizing the state's blind programs, Helen Keller arrived in Denver in early 1925 on a fund-raising tour for the AFB. Keller spoke to packed and overflowing meeting halls on numerous occasions over a period of several days, emphasizing the AFB's ideology. In front of the Colorado Assembly, Keller called on the need to teach the blind skills so that they could become self-supporting and "happy members of society." She went on to tell state legislatures that "the great need of the blind is not charity, but opportunity."[16] At another gathering with Keller, blind assembly member Frank M. Mobley rose to endorse the AFB's work and "declared that the pension for the blind in Colorado has resulted in an unhealthy psychology among them and toward them in the state."[17] The local United Workers for the Blind simply could not counter the wave of antibenefit publicity generated by Keller's visit.

At the same time that the American Foundation for the Blind captured the attention of both public and political officials, a second social movement, the Ku Klux Klan, entered the political center ring. Resurrected by William Joseph Simmons in 1915 on top of Stone Mountain in Georgia, the rise of the second Klan initially failed to attract much of a following. Yet after Simmons hired two experienced promoters, the fledging Klan bloomed into a nationwide organization with one million members.[18] Combining racism, nativism, anti-Semitism, anti-Catholicism, law and order, and its own version of Protestant morality, the Klan spread west to Colorado, becoming a powerful political force.[19] In 1921, the Klan surfaced in Denver under the direction of local physician John Galen Locke, preaching "one hundred per cent Americanism."[20] While Colorado's Klan targeted African Americans and Jews, "Catholics," according to historian Robert Goldberg, "bore the brunt of the Klan hatred."[21] By 1924, Colorado's Klan operated a well-disciplined political machine that captured control of the city of Denver, the state's

Republican Party, the lower house of the assembly, numerous judgeships, and the governorship. During his inaugural address, Klan-backed Governor Clarence Morley called for banning the use of sacramental wine, imposing rigid immigration restrictions, ending the public defender act, abolishing several government boards and agencies, reducing government expenses, and caring for the state's unfortunates in an "intensely humane, but not profligate" manner.[22]

Morley's desire for a more efficient government meshed well with calls by the American Foundation for the Blind and Gertrude Vaile for reorganizing the state's services for the adult blind, although the motivations differed for each person or group. Vaile's preference for change rested on Progressive Era notions that only professional experts, in this case trained social workers, could efficiently and properly manage social welfare programs. The AFB, on the other hand, wanted to increase the state's funding for vocational training while decreasing blind benefits. And Morley used the issue of efficiency as a means to achieve his goal of removing Catholics and Jews from governmental boards and replacing them with Klan supporters or placing the boards under agencies already controlled by the Klan. Morley hoped to make his slogan, "Every Man under the Capitol Dome a Klansman" a reality by entrenching Klansmen in the state's administrative bodies so that Klan control would continue long after he left office.[23]

Like prey surrounded by a pack of wolves, blind social services quickly fell to their many attackers. A group of Democratic and Republican senators not linked to the Klan successfully blocked almost all of Morley's Klan-inspired agenda; nevertheless, in 1925 the legislature voted almost unanimously to overhaul completely services for blind adults.[24] In a bill partially sponsored by blind representative Mobley, the assembly created a single State Commission for the Blind, just as Vaile and the AFB had wanted, to oversee the workshop, the state teacher, and blind benefits. The act clearly articulated the state's new approach toward helping blind residents: "The Commission shall never undertake the permanent support or maintenance of any blind person; the main object of this act is to aid the blind to become self-supporting rather than to afford them permanent support at public expense." The measure rolled back all the changes that had distinguished blind benefits from other forms of public assistance. Now, no one under the age of forty could qualify for blind benefits as the state offered only vocational training to those under forty. Also, potential blind benefit recipients now had to apply first to their county commissioners, who could investigate all applicants and who submitted a report or recommendation to the State Commission for the Blind. The act eliminated the $360 annual income level that previously determined who qualified for blind benefits and in its place required one to be "a public charge or liable to become so through want of financial means or of ability to earn a livelihood."[25] Under the new law, blind benefits had become just another form of poor relief. In the words of Lute Wilcox, the "unfriendly legislature . . . killed our good old Benefit law."[26]

Activists for the blind had few ways to protest the new act. The board of directors for the United Workers met to discuss "ways and means of handling the new Blind law," and Wilcox viewed the act as "unfair" and suggested that funds be raised to hire an attorney to take the case "to the Supreme Court."[27] Yet, several months later, Wilcox realized that the United Workers could do little to change the law, admitting that "all we can do is watch and wait."[28] Lacking a large number of voters willing to punish politicians for altering the law, the blind community remained essentially powerless to mount an effective defense or counterattack. While the United Workers waited, the new State Commission for the Blind and county commissioners went to work. In May 1925, before the state implemented the new law, 1,078 residents received blind benefits, with over 91 percent (984) getting the maximum annual amount of three hundred dollars. Eighteen months later, only 527 people received assistance, with just over 64 percent (340) welcoming the maximum three hundred dollars.[29] Because the new law allowed county commissioners to involve themselves in the investigation of blind benefit applicants, different levels of support for the indigent blind re-emerged among the various counties.[30] Thus, blind benefits now simply mirrored local poor relief practices.

Although the new commission succeeded in reducing blind benefits, it failed to expand vocational training and never taught an employable skill to most blind residents. While the number of state teachers did increase from one to four, Jennie Jackson lost her job.[31] The commission found the state unwilling to increase vocational services. Commission members quickly realized that "the facilities for . . . [vocational] training in Colorado are meagre" and voiced all too familiar complaints that the single workshop needed to expand, served too few residents, and trained employees in only one job skill, broom making.[32] Activists had already known of these shortcomings and had been petitioning officials for years to expand the workshop and increase vocational opportunities. The new commission fared no better than the activists had in achieving these goals, as the commission was still asking for more funds to expand the workshop in 1930.[33]

Even though Colorado's blind community lost control over the various state programs serving blind residents, the notion that blind people should receive a separate piece of the welfare pie still persisted. In Colorado, blind benefits continued at reduced levels into the 1930s, and by 1931 twenty-four states had passed some form of blind pension legislation. While not all these laws were mandatory, blind citizens usually still managed to obtain higher levels of support than other needy groups.[34] Because of the blind community's success in getting these laws approved and enforced, the original proposal for the 1935 Social Security Bill did not include a specific provision for blind adults. Still, the Senate Finance Committee created a new section in the Social Security legislation, Title X, that provided $3 million in federal matching funds "for aid to the needy blind." Despite strong lobbying from Helen Keller and the American Foundation for the Blind to amend the bill to fund vocational training instead of relief, Title X, Aid to the Blind as it became known, remained only a relief measure in its final version.[35]

Other Welfare Programs in the 1920s

Blind benefits were not the only social welfare program affected by Governor Morley's Klan-inspired agenda. During the same legislative session that gutted the blind aid law, the Department of Charities and Corrections also fell victim to Morley's desire to shut agencies not controlled by Klan members. When the Senate refused to abolish the already underfunded Department of Charities and Corrections in 1925, Morley simply fired Gertrude Vaile, since civil service rules did not protect her, and transferred the two remaining employees to other agencies.[36] While the department still officially existed on paper, nevertheless, lacking any personnel, Morley's actions essentially destroyed the agency.[37] Denver's social workers protested Vaile's firing, and telegrams and letters from around the nation poured into the governor's office.[38] "No better evidence of Klan incompetency and Klan bigotry could be mentioned," wrote Judge Ben Lindsey, himself a subject of Klan attacks, "than this arbitrary removal by the Klan governor of Miss Vaile."[39] When members of the National Conference of Social Work gathered in Denver that summer, they gave Governor Morley a "slap in the face" by electing Vaile as their next president and by holding a session addressing "The Menace of Racial and Religious Intolerance."[40]

Surprisingly silent in the uproar over Vaile's dismissal and the closing of the department was Vaile herself. According to her younger sister, Lucretia Vaile, Gertrude decided not to protest her discharge since at the time the governor and his supporters did not know that the Department of Charities and Corrections had supervisory authority "over all charitable organizations in the state including some Catholic ones." Gertrude feared, according to her sister, that if she fought for her job the governor would become informed of this power, and he would then most likely "appoint a Klan successor in Gertrude's place," putting the Catholic institutions in "serious risk."[41]

Although the Klan quickly rose to power, the organization just as quickly lost its dominance. Colorado's Klan experienced a series of missteps and encountered increasingly well-organized opposition that quickly weakened its tight grip on political authority. Links to corruption and graft rings, violations of prohibition laws, accusations of mail fraud and kidnapping, charges of federal income tax evasion, internal power struggles, and eventually a splitting of the organization into various factions all contributed to the Klan's demise. As the Klan stumbled, opposition groups publicly challenged the Klan in political contests, ridiculed the organization in newspapers for poor judgment, and chided the group for disregarding the law. By 1926, the Klan's political machine broke down as Morley lost his re-election bid, and other politicians distanced themselves from the secret organization.[42]

After the Klan's demise, few changes were rolled back. The Department of Charities and Corrections remained on the books, but without any personnel, until 1933, when the general assembly officially abolished the department and formed the Division of Public Welfare. After her dismissal, Gertrude Vaile moved to Story County, Iowa, where she simultaneously headed the Social Service Bureau and served as the executive secretary of the Ames Social Service League. In the autumn of 1928, ill health forced Vaile's return to Denver. However, in 1930 she began teaching at the University of Minnesota, where she remained until her retirement in 1946.[43] Another blind benefit bill passed the legislature in 1927, which softened the 1925 act. The newest law now allowed applicants less than forty years old to receive benefits when the commission determined the situation to be "extreme."[44] Despite this legal maneuver, the state's spending for blind benefits remained largely unchanged.[45]

While blind benefits experienced a roller-coaster ride during the 1920s, mothers' pensions, on the other hand, remained far more stable, though still hindered by limited funds and lax enforcement. After the passage of the 1919 law requiring counties to collect a specific tax, not exceeding one-eighth of one mill (a mill equals one-thousandth of a dollar), for mothers' pensions, supporters almost immediately began calling for an increase in that levy. Governor Shoup appointed eight juvenile and county court judges to his Committee on Child Welfare Legislation in 1920 to make recommendations to next year's general assembly. The committee put forth fourteen bills, including one to increase the tax for mothers' pensions from one-eighth to one-half of one mill. According to the committee, the one-eighth levy "has proven to be absolutely inadequate" and the one-half-mill levy recommendation represented a compromise. Indeed, Florence Hutsinpillar and her fellow social workers had called for not "less than three-fourths of one mill" to properly operate mothers' pensions. The judges, however, believed that a smaller request would be more likely to win approval and would still be sufficient to care for needy mothers and their children. Despite this cautious strategy, the judges' suggested levy increase, as well as all the other proposals, failed to win acceptance.[46]

Completely defeated, Governor Shoup reorganized the committee the following year, requesting that members from six prominent women's organizations participate in the committee's work. The new group decided to continue pushing for an increase in the mothers' pensions levy along with seven other proposals. With the women's active help, four bills won approval; however, the increase in the mothers' pension tax failed to pass. Once again, the committee recommended the four remaining bills to the 1925 general assembly, but made little headway competing with the Klan.[47] Not only had supporters failed to gain more money for mothers' pensions, but the state legislature's approval of the 1923 Maternity Benefit Act, which provided financial assistance for mothers six months before and six months after birth, used the same pool of money set aside for mothers' pensions.[48] Thus, the Maternity Act increased the potential number of women asking for aid while keeping the overall amount of money constant.

Because of the failure to increase the levy for mothers' compensation, counties that collected the tax and used it for pensions still needed to find ways to increase funding or alter implementation. Teller County, for instance, began collecting the one-eighth-mill levy for mothers' pensions in late 1919, yet, by early 1923, the tax appeared insufficient to meet the county's pension needs. As a result, Teller's commissioners began supplementing most pensions with additional support from the county's general poor relief fund.[49] This tactic not only circumvented the legal tax limit placed on mothers' compensations, but it also blurred what little division existed between pensions and poor relief. In Denver, meanwhile, Florence Hutsinpillar and the Bureau of Charities succeeded in partially distinguishing mothers' compensation from poor relief by using new social work techniques with pension recipients. Beginning in 1920, the bureau formed an advisory council of seven pensioned mothers who met monthly with staff members to decide how family budgets should be determined, to plan recreation for the children, and to advise on household management. A year later, the bureau had organized all seventy-odd mothers into small groups that met monthly to hear guest speakers on a variety of child welfare topics.[50]

Supporters of mothers' pensions still continued to push for universal compliance. In 1924, only thirty-six out of sixty-three Colorado counties administered mothers' pensions, and for most of these communities commissioners enacted only portions of the law.[51] This low level of enforcement shocked some residents. In 1925, after the Kiwanis Club had surveyed the state's child welfare practices, the club demanded that the twenty-seven counties not implementing mothers' pensions "obey the law" by granting assistance.[52] The following year, the Colorado Federation of Women's Clubs adopted a resolution urging its members "to ascertain the condition of their county with regard to compliance with the provisions of this law [mothers' compensation] and to make an earnest effort to secure observance of this law."[53] Yet despite these calls for enforcement, the state's mothers' aid act remained underfunded and only sporadically enacted. By the mid-1920s, mothers' pensions looked like a stalled and failed reform effort that had achieved legislative victories but had been unable to attain implementation.

At the same time that mothers' pensions stalled, the various county institutions around the state continued operating and serving the needy. Montezuma's dilapidated poor farm still housed a small number of the county's indigent, including four men and one woman, in June 1924.[54] Boulder's combined county hospital and poorhouse and Teller's county hospital, likewise, still assisted the needy. In Denver, the poor farm remained at its fertile location and continued producing large quantities of dairy products, vegetables, poultry, and meat. By mid-decade, overcrowding at the poor farm once again became a concern for officials. In 1925, prisoners transported bricks to the poor farm for a new twenty-five-bed dormitory. The following year, the city planned another dormitory, this time for forty-five beds, in order to bring the farm's capacity up to two hundred residents.[55] Over at the Denver County Hospital, the city council approved construction of a new one-hundred-bed tuberculosis ward in 1920, representing the first publicly funded facility for consumptive patients in a city overwhelmed by indigent tubercular sufferers. Yet, in just a few years, the county hospital would once again struggle with overcrowding as a shortage of space forced the placement of beds in hallways and aisles, prodding doctors to call for a new five-hundred-bed facility.[56] Tuberculosis, however, was not the cause of overcrowding. The flow of migrant consumptives had begun to decline rapidly by mid-decade as "lungers" no longer sought out climate for a cure.[57] On the Ute Mountain Ute Indian Reservation, medical doctors and nurses still battled with medicine men over the right to care for the ill and injured, and hospital use remained infrequent and highly conditional.[58]

By the late 1920s, Colorado, and the nation, began sliding into an economic decline. The severity of the Great Depression transformed the county-level poor relief system. In 1933, the Colorado legislature finally approved and enacted an old age pension law that relied on a combination of state and county funds, mainly taxes on alcohol. The new statewide law provided a maximum monthly grant of thirty dollars and required county courts to investigate each applicant and set assistance levels.[59] In Costilla County, the Depression caused such desperate conditions that the traditional reliance on the Penitentes for a large share of the community's relief became impractical; the organization was simply unable to handle the demands for aid. As a result, almost 58 percent of Costilla's families received government assistance, the state's second highest percentage.[60] Meanwhile, the Depression forced Lincoln County commissioners both to abandon their reliance on outdoor relief and to concentrate their indigent in a newly opened poor farm. The poor farm remained in operation for only two years, 1932 and 1933, before closing amid complaints of being too costly to operate, in addition to charges of occupants being physically abused.[61] In Montezuma County, the Red Cross rationed flour and feed grain to needy residents in the summer of 1932.[62] At the same time, Denver began cutting back on performing casework because "there was neither the time nor the staff to continue individualized case treatment." To save money the city started regularly refusing mothers' pensions to women with only one child.[63] Out-of-work professional men formed the Unemployed Citizens' League of Denver (UCLD) in 1932 to organize self-help relief among the indigent. Relying on a barter system, these men used donated goods and facilities to run a bakery, cut firewood, mine coal, harvest crops, mend shoes, collect clothes, print a weekly paper, distribute food, cut hair, repair houses, and even teach English classes. At its peak, the UCLD claimed over thirty thousand members.[64]

As counties experienced changes in their relief practices, new federal programs initiated by President Franklin D. Roosevelt also affected local communities. In early 1934, for example, Congress passed the Gold Reserve Act, which set the price of gold at $35.00 an ounce, a substantial increase from its previous value of $20.67. With the price increase and lower labor costs, mining activity in the Cripple Creek District once again expanded, reversing years of economic decline. Buildings that had been closed and vacated reopened as people filled up hotels, rooming establishments, and empty houses in Teller County.[65] Practices on the Ute Mountain Reservation also suddenly changed. Until 1933, all residents had received rations, as had been the custom for decades, and the Office of Indian Affairs continued to place annuity payments into Individual Indian Accounts, although these checks had dropped to fifty dollars per year by 1932.[66] The following year, the Office of Indian Affairs halted the use of Individual Indian Accounts and issued rations to only "the old and very needy."[67] Almost three years later, Jack Miller, leader of the Mountain Utes, still "bitterly resent[ed] the stoppage of the rationing system" as he continued to cite the 1868 treaty, the first agreement signed between Utes and the federal government, as proof that "the Utes were to receive food, clothing and cash from the United States forever."[68] Despite Miller's persistent protests, the Office of Indian Affairs refused to resume rations or cash payments and succeeded in transforming practices that had been legal obligations into a type of poor relief. But even those who still received rations faced hardships during the Depression. In 1938, members of the Ute Mountain Council affixed their thumb prints to a petition asking the federal government to use $750 in tribal funds to purchase beef "for the support of the old, sick, blind and indigent people of this reservation" because "the rations issued . . . have been inadequate."[69]

A flood of New Deal programs—the Civilian Conservation Corps, the Agricultural Adjustment Administration, the Federal Emergency Relief

Administration, the Indian Reorganization Act, Aid to Dependent Children, Old Age Insurance, Old Age Assistance, and Aid to the Blind—to name just a few, all changed how states and counties assisted poor residents. These various New Deal measures subdivided indigent people into separate relief programs with specific eligibility criteria and different types and levels of aid. This trend of subdividing the welfare state, partially initiated by blind people during the Progressive Era, became a permanent feature of America's modern welfare state during the 1930s. No longer would the elderly, the disabled, the unemployed, the widowed, or the orphaned be grouped together under one common heading as the "poor," receiving the same common form of county-level assistance.

Conclusion

In order to gain a clear understanding of how needy residents encountered poor relief, this study has purposely focused on the daily implementation of Progressive Era welfare policies in various western settings. The welfare state during the late nineteenth and early twentieth centuries was a diverse, complex, and largely localized effort that was molded by a wide range of forces. Any attempt to change relief practices had to grapple with overcoming these many strong local influences.

A variety of state- and society-centered practices contributed to how communities structured their aid programs. Many local conditions—settlement patterns, religious beliefs, local economies, employment opportunities, philanthropic traditions, existing relief policies, decisions by local officials, and state laws—all affected how counties gave out assistance. In the end, these local influences distinguished each community's publicly funded aid program from one another. In Costilla County, relief recipients received small amounts of assistance for extremely long durations because the community had established an elaborate safety net for needy residents and because maintaining the community's social fabric was highly valued. But in Lincoln and Montezuma Counties, commissioners gave the needy substantially larger amounts of aid for much shorter periods because these residents were in more desperate circumstances and lacked any other relief alternatives. These two communities quickly cut off aid recipients if they could not succeed in the market economy. Meanwhile, in Boulder and Teller

Counties, the employment options for single, impoverished women largely determined if they received aid.

Even in Denver, local circumstances still influenced how public aid was distributed. Reformers like Gertrude Vaile found it difficult to dislodge previous relief practices. Despite wanting to implement individualized casework methods, Vaile instead found herself continuing the practice of using a standard dole of food and coal orders to assist the needy. And of course, the influx of poor migrant tubercular sufferers both overwhelmed the city's aid programs and shaped Vaile's attitudes concerning the role of federal assistance. For Vaile, impoverished "lungers" came to represent not just a medical concern but rather a social problem needing the skills of trained social workers. Indeed, Vaile's beliefs and decisions as well as local political battles affected how Denver chose to aid the poor.

Local circumstances likewise shaped the role that private charities and institutions played in a community's relief strategies. Low populations, for instance, discouraged commissioners and private organizations in both Costilla and Lincoln Counties from establishing a hospital or a poor farm during the Progressive Era. Yet, Lincoln's officials and residents still sought out institutional care outside of their county boundaries, while Costilla's impoverished Hispanic residents did not send county members to institutions. The existence of a strong kinship network in Costilla, as well as a belief in Lincoln that these establishments could help solve problems, seems to best explain these very different preferences for institutional use. Meanwhile the practices and policies of unions, lodges, fraternal associations, and millionaire Winfield Stratton created an informal welfare system in Teller that substantially lessened any need for county aid. On the Ute Mountain Ute Indian Reservation, use of the hospital became a cultural battle between medicine men and medical doctors. In Boulder, the use of the hospital on the University of Colorado campus served as a substitute for a county hospital. And in Denver, the existence of so many privately operated charities provided a vast number of alternatives to the city's poor residents. Private charities and institutions, like public assistance, did not escape from the overwhelming influence of local conditions.

The distribution of relief presented a fluid, ever-changing picture. On the Ute Mountain Reservation, for instance, widespread poverty, previous practices, and protests largely thwarted any attempts by the Office of Indian Affairs to change rations and annuity payments into a type of poor relief during the Progressive Era. Yet, in 1933, officials halted annuity payments and used rations as relief despite the continuation of these same circumstances and behaviors on the reservation. In Montezuma, the commissioners' decision to maintain a poor farm superseded the fact that the county lacked a large enough population to make the establishment cost-effective. And of course, Vaile's beliefs, as well as existing poor relief practices in Denver, essentially nullified mothers' pensions in the city. Only the blind benefit law overrode, for a time, the many powerful local influences.

The use of a community-wide perspective allows for an inclusive investigation of assistance practices. Most important, with this perspective we can see how poor people themselves actually experienced the many relief options offered to them. Since impoverished residents could often choose to use either public or private sources of aid, the type of aid selected varied depending on a person's needs and their location. In addition, some needy individuals moved among the various options. Relief for the poor often amounted to a mix of private and public aid, with the two types of assistance complementing one another. In Costilla County, the Penitentes' good deeds supplemented the county's low levels of aid, while in Denver, and to a lesser extent in Boulder, the division between public and private assistance was blurred as public money and county officials often played essential roles in private relief efforts.

Supporters of mothers' pensions had hoped to transform the Progressive Era welfare state. Advocates for mothers' pensions believed that their plan would create a separate assistance category for single impoverished mothers that would provide long-term, cash assistance without the stigma of poor relief. Some reformers even expected mothers' pensions to be the first step in expanding the state's responsibility toward all mothers. After a heated debate, Colorado became the second state to approve mothers' pensions, and the first to do so by popular vote. Yet, despite all the bold rhetoric and the overwhelming electoral victory, mothers' pensions failed to alter the welfare state in any substantial manner. Many counties simply refused to implement the new measure. But this refusal rested not with an ignorance of or disagreement with the new law, but rather with the fact that mothers' pensions differed little from existing practices. Some counties already offered long-term assistance and cash payments for widows with children. Other counties provided single mothers with a large degree of flexibility with their aid. Counties that did use mothers' pensions, even those that only partially enacted the law, administered it much as they did their poor relief programs. Local officials generally used the same personnel and procedures to operate both programs, and often counties mixed poor relief funds with mothers' pensions, thus blurring any difference that reformers had hoped to establish between the two. In the end, mothers' pensions resembled existing relief efforts and reflected local practices instead of breaking new ground largely because the Mothers' Compensation Act left in place local control and funding.

Blind benefits, however, did indeed transform the Progressive Era welfare state. Beginning near the turn of the century, blind people began organizing themselves into associations to voice their opinions on issues that affected their lives. These local and state organizations started addressing a number of concerns including the dismal employment prospects that many blind adults encountered. Local activists quickly succeeded in gaining state funding for a state teacher and a workshop for blind adults to help address the lack of jobs. But the small size of Colorado's workshop severely limited employment to only a handful of laborers. An attempt to improve the situation by creating a home that would offer low-cost housing for workshop employees failed to better the workers' circumstances in any meaningful way. Frustrated by the few job prospects, activists pushed for blind benefits as a way to help the indigent. Blocked by politicians in the general assembly, Colorado's blind community successfully used the initiative system to win approval for benefits. These new blind benefits overrode local conditions, for the first time, and established a uniform statewide welfare policy. No longer could local officials determine who received blind benefits or set aid levels. In addition, advocates monitored enforcement and successfully defeated Denver's attempt to remake benefits into a form of poor relief. Activists gained control of the Blind Benefit Commission, the state teacher, and the workshop, and they used their new positions of power to press for a further expansion of state support for poor blind adults.

While the blind community succeeded in altering and in controlling a portion of the welfare state, this would prove only temporary. During the 1920s, blind benefits and the role of local advocates came under attack from several different fronts. Gertrude Vaile and the Community Chest disliked the fact that trained professionals were not directing the state's services for blind adults. The American Foundation for the Blind wanted to increase vocational training while decreasing benefits. At the same time, politicians

loyal to the Ku Klux Klan wanted to cut costs and place their own supporters in control of state agencies. The convergence of these very different
forces overwhelmed the local blind community and their efforts to defend
benefits and maintain control of state programs. As a consequence, the state
legislature rolled back the portions of the blind benefit law that had taken
power away from local officials. With these changes, blind benefits simply
resembled county poor relief practices.

Despite this defeat, the notion of separate aid for blind adults remained
a permanent feature of the state's welfare efforts. While the number of people receiving blind aid decreased and the amount of yearly assistance
declined, still the basic concept that one group of needy citizens should
receive a different type of help than other poor residents remained intact.
The efforts of activists for the blind helped to initiate the trend of interest
groups influencing welfare policy and spending. This trend has continued
to be a key characteristic of America's modern welfare state.

On the eve of the Great Depression, Colorado's poor relief system,
except for the reduced blind benefits, looked much as it had during the late
nineteenth and early twentieth centuries, with local circumstances continuing to dictate how communities distributed assistance. Thus, a poor person's location determined the type and amount of relief that one received.
This trend of continuity seems, at first, a bit surprising given how dedicated
reformers were trying to instill new relief practices, and how much success
western Progressives had in altering other areas of government policy. But
while Progressive Era welfare theories and advocates offered bold claims of
transformation, the actual implementation of those ideas at the local level
failed to produce the changes promised. In the end, most poor people at the
close of the Progressive Era encountered a poor relief system that had
remained remarkably unchanged.

Appendix

TABLE 1

Populations of Counties and County Seats, 1890–1920

COUNTY / COUNTY SEAT	1890	1900	1910	1920
Costilla /	3,491	4,632	5,498	5,032
San Luis	—	731	956	550
Montezuma /	1,529	3,058	5,029	6,260
Cortez	332	125	565	541
Lincoln /	689	926	5,917	8,273
Hugo	—	—	343	838
Teller /	—	29,002	14,351	6,696
Cripple Creek	—	10,147	6,206	2,325
Boulder /	14,082	21,544	30,330	31,861
City of Boulder	3,330	6,150	9,539	10,006
Denver	106,713	133,859	213,381	256,491

SOURCES: U.S. Bureau of the Census, *Thirteenth Census of the United States, Abstract of Census with Supplement for Colorado* (Washington, D.C.: Government Printing Office, 1913), 33 and 585–86; Colorado Board of Immigration, *Year Book of the State of Colorado, 1922* (Denver: Eames Brothers, 1922), 114–18. Please note that beginning in 1902 the city and county of Denver had the same boundaries. The figures for Denver for 1890 and 1900 represent the population totals for the city while the figures for 1910 and 1920 represent totals for the city and county of Denver.

TABLE 2

Average Amount of Outdoor Aid Received per Month

County	AVERAGE AMOUNT OF OUTDOOR AID PER MONTH	TOTAL NUMBER OF AID RECIPIENTS
Boulder (1907–25)	$9.19	1043
Costilla (1891–1906 & 1913–19)[a]	$4.97	181
Lincoln (1909–22)	$18.51	231
Montezuma (1901–19)	$30.90	131
Teller (1912–20)[b]	$19.74	695

Sources: *Boulder County Pauper Book*, vols. 1–4, County Clerk and Recorder Office, Boulder County Courthouse, Boulder, Colorado; *Costilla County Poor Book*, vols. 1–3, County Clerk and Recorder Office, Costilla County Courthouse, San Luis, Colorado; *Lincoln County Poor Record*, County Clerk and Recorder Office, Lincoln County Courthouse, Hugo, Colorado; *Montezuma County Poor Records*, 1901–1919, County Clerk and Recorder Office, Montezuma County Courthouse, Cortez, Colorado; *Montezuma County Poor Reports*, 1901–1910 and 1912–1919, Boxes 4967A and 4968A, Colorado State Archives, Denver, Colorado; *Teller County Poor Reports*, 1912–1920, Boxes 4967A and 4968A, Colorado State Archives, Denver, Colorado.

Note: Please note that because of inconsistent data, totals may change slightly among the various tables depending on the subject matter.

[a]These figures exclude C. L. Cowgill who received $1,765.00 in assistance over sixty months for what appears to be a stay at a hospital. Cowgill averaged $29.42 per month. If Cowgill is included the average received per month increases to $5.11.

[b]Teller's data include both outdoor aid and assistance given at the county hospital.

TABLE 3

Average Total Number of Months Receiving Outdoor Aid

County	Average Number of Months Receiving Aid	Total Number of Aid Recipients
Boulder (1907–25)	16.39	1043
Costilla (1891–1906 & 1913–19)[a]	34.64	181
Lincoln (1909–22)	6.38	231
Montezuma (1901–19)	7.57	131
Teller (1912–20)[b]	7.90	695

Sources: Same as Table 2. (See note from Table 2).

[a]These figures exclude C. L. Cowgill who appears to have stayed at a hospital.

[b]Teller's data include both outdoor aid and assistance given at the county hospital.

TABLE 4

Number and Percentage of "Elderly" as a Cause of Distress

COUNTY	NUMBER OF ELDERLY	PERCENTAGE OF TOTAL
Boulder (1907–25)	52	12.62%
Costilla (1891–1906 & 1913–19)	83	30.07%
Lincoln (1909–22)	11	6.43%
Montezuma (1901–19)	21	14.46%
Teller (1912–20)[a]	39	4.17%

Sources: Same as Table 2. (See note from Table 2).

[a]Teller's data include both outdoor aid and assistance given at the county hospital.

TABLE 5

Average Age of Women and Men Receiving Outdoor Aid

County	Avg. Female Age / N	Avg. Male Age / N
Boulder (1907–25)	43.56 / 217	50.03 / 138
Costilla (1891–1906 & 1913–19)	57.76 / 124	64.91 / 67
Lincoln (1909–22)	40.62 / 37	47.01 / 71
Montezuma (1901–19)	39.40 / 20	58.87 / 38
Teller (1912–20)[a]	48.21 / 257	53.83 / 334

Sources: Same as Table 2. (See note from Table 2).

[a]Teller's data include both outdoor aid and assistance given at the county hospital.

TABLE 6

Number and Percentage of Relief Cases Sent Away

County	Number	Percentage of Total
Boulder (1907–25)	28	2.67%
Costilla (1891–1906 & 1913–19)	0	0%
Lincoln (1909–22)	77	32.91%
Montezuma (1901–19)	8	6.02%
Teller (1912–20)[a]	13	1.19%

Sources: Same as Table 2. (See note from Table 2).

[a]Teller's data includes both outdoor aid and assistance given at the county hospital.

TABLE 7

Number and Percentage of Employed Unmarried
Women by Marital Status, 1910[a]

COUNTY	DIVORCED WOMEN EMPLOYED N / %	SINGLE WOMEN EMPLOYED N / %	WIDOWED WOMEN EMPLOYED N / %	TOTAL UNMARRIED WOMEN EMPLOYED N / %
Boulder	7 / 38.89%	337 / 45.79%	125 / 45.96%	469 / 45.71%
Teller	20 / 80%	134 / 65.37%	79 / 58.96%	233 / 64.01%

Sources: U.S. Bureau of the Census, *Population Schedules of the Thirteenth Census of the United States, 1910*, Microfilm Publication, Reels 113 and 125, National Archives and Records Administration.

[a]These figures are based on a random sampling of one of every three females seventeen years and older in both Boulder and Teller Counties.

TABLE 8
Female Causes of Distress, 1912–1920

County	"Beyond Control"[a] N / %	"Personal Distress"[b] N / %
Boulder	79 / 53.4%	69 / 46.6%
Teller[c]	21 / 4.8%	417 / 95.2%

Sources: *Boulder County Pauper Book*, vols. 1–4, Boulder Courthouse; *Teller County Poor Reports*, 1912–1920, State Archives.

[a]"Beyond Control" includes: husband's death, husband's illness, husband's injury or disability, husband's nonsupport, husband's desertion, and no work for women.

[b]"Personal Distress" refers to causes of distress that strike individual women: sickness, old age, insanity, operations, and blindness.

[c]Teller's data include both outdoor aid and assistance given at the county hospital.

TABLE 9

Average Amount of Aid per Month on a Yearly Basis

County	Avg. Amount of Aid per Month	Number of Recipients
Costilla (1891–1906 & 1913–19)	$5.03	771
Denver (1906–10)[a]	$5.52	1,594
Lincoln (1909–22)	$19.14	294
Montezuma (1901–19)	$26.84	217
Teller (1912–20)[b]	$21.06	1,159

Sources: *Costilla County Poor Book*, vols. 1–3, Costilla Courthouse; *Denver County Poor Reports*, 1906–1910, Box 4967A, State Archives; *Lincoln County Poor Record*, Lincoln Courthouse; *Montezuma County Poor Records*, 1901–1919, Montezuma Courthouse; *Montezuma County Poor Reports*, 1901–1910 and 1912–1919, State Archives; *Teller County Poor Reports*, 1912–1920, State Archives.

Note: The figures used in this table differ from those in Table 2. Because of how Denver's records were organized, it is only possible to calculate the amount of monthly aid for each year when using Denver's records. Table 2 shows the amount of monthly aid per recipient over their entire time on relief. Also note that because of the way Boulder County records were kept, it is not possible to break down Boulder's data into yearly figures.

[a]Denver's figures are based on a random sampling of one of every three relief recipients.

[b]Teller's data include both outdoor aid and assistance given at the county hospital.

TABLE 10

Average Number of Months Receiving Aid per Year

County	Avg. Number of Months	Number of Recipients
Costilla (1891–1906 & 1917–19)[a]	10.26	620
Denver (1906–10)[b]	3.57	1,594
Lincoln (1909–22)	3.52	294
Montezuma (1901–19)	4.48	217
Teller (1912–20)[c]	6.15	1,077

Sources: Same as in Table 9.

Note: The figures used in this table differ from those in Table 3. Because of how Denver's records were organized, it is only possible to calculate the number of months that a person received aid for each year when using Denver's records. Table 3 shows the average number of months a person received aid over their entire time on relief. Also note that because of the way Boulder County records were kept, it is not possible to break down Boulder's data into yearly figures.

[a]Dates for Costilla County are slightly different for this table because of the manner in which data was originally recorded.

[b]Denver's figures are based on a random sampling of one of every three relief recipients.

[c]Teller's data include both outdoor aid and assistance given at the county hospital.

TABLE 11

Average Amount of Monthly Aid per Year by Nativity,
Denver County, 1906–1910[a]

NATIVITY	AVERAGE AMOUNT OF MONTHLY AID	NUMBER OF RECIPIENTS
U.S.	$5.72	968
All Foreign-born	$5.20	626
Italy	$4.39	39
Ireland	$4.91	120
Russia	$4.33	127
England	$4.92	48
Germany	$5.84	96
Sweden	$4.24	44
Southern & Eastern Europe[b]	$4.37	187

Sources: *Denver County Poor Reports,* 1906–1910, State Archives.

Please note that because of inconsistent data, totals may change slightly among the various tables using the *Denver County Poor Reports*. In addition, since only a select number of nativities are listed above, their total does not equal the total for all foreign-born.

[a]Denver's figures are based on a random sampling of one of every three relief recipients.

[b]This group includes immigrants identified as being from Hungary, Italy, Poland, Romania, and Russia.

TABLE 12

Average Household Size of Aid Recipients by Nativity,
Denver County, 1906–1910[a]

NATIVITY	AVERAGE HOUSEHOLD SIZE	NUMBER OF AID RECIPIENTS
U.S.	2.77	974
All Foreign-born	3.20	634
Italy	4.49	39
Ireland	2.77	121
Russia	3.89	130
England	2.54	48
Germany	3.29	98
Sweden	3.04	45
Southern & Eastern Europe[b]	3.97	190

Sources: *Denver County Poor Reports,* 1906–1910, State Archives.
(See note from Table 11).

[a]Denver's figures are based on a random sampling of one of every three
relief recipients.

[b]This group includes immigrants identified as being from Hungary,
Italy, Poland, Romania, and Russia.

TABLE 13

Average Number of Months Receiving Aid per Year by
Nativity, Denver County, 1906–1910[a]

NATIVITY	AVERAGE NUMBER OF MONTHS	NUMBER OF AID RECIPIENTS
U.S.	3.23	968
All Foreign-born	4.10	626
Italy	6.36	39
Ireland	4.83	120
Russia	4.03	127
England	3.38	48
Germany	3.90	96
Sweden	4.66	44
Southern & Eastern Europe[b]	4.39	187

Sources: *Denver County Poor Reports*, 1906–1910, State Archives.
(See note from Table 11).

[a]Denver's figures are based on a random sampling of one of every
three relief recipients.

[b]This group includes immigrants identified as being from Hungary,
Italy, Poland, Romania, and Russia.

TABLE 14

Average Amount of Yearly Aid, Denver County, 1906–1910 and 1915–1919 (1906 = 100)[a]

YEAR	WHOLESALE PRICE INDEX	AVERAGE YEARLY AID	AID INDEX	NUMBER OF AID RECIPIENTS
1906	100	$15.61	100	203
1907	105	$12.80	82	242
1908	101.3	$15.43	98.8	386
1909	109.1	$15.05	96.4	401
1910	113.8	$17.87	114.5	388
1915	111.9	$21.49	137.7	317
1916	137.8	$26.43	169.3	274
1917	189.4	$35.53	227.6	284
1918	211.3	$31.79	203.6	215
1919	223.1	$36.49	233.8	202

Sources: *Denver County Poor Reports*, 1906–1910 and 1915–1919, Box 4967A, State Archives; U.S. Bureau of the Census, *Historical Statistics of the United States Colonial Times to 1970*, Part 1 (Washington, D.C.: Government Printing Office, 1975), 199.

[a]Denver's figures are based on a random sampling of one of every three relief recipients.

TABLE 15

Leading Causes of Distress, Denver County, 1906–1910 and 1915–1919[a]

CAUSE OF DISTRESS	NUMBER OF AID RECIPIENTS	PERCENTAGE
Sickness	660	22.12%
Old Age	514	17.23%
Unemployed	419	14.04%
Tuberculosis	331	11.09%
Widow	263	8.81%
Total[b]	**2,984**	**100%**

Sources: *Denver County Poor Reports*, 1906–1910 and 1915–1919, State Archives.

[a]Denver's figures are based on a random sampling of one of every three relief recipients.

[b]The total figures represent all causes of distress, many of which are not listed above.

TABLE 16

Nativity of Aid Recipients for the Charity Organization Society of Denver and for Denver County, 1906 and 1909

NATIVITY	COSD N / %	DENVER COUNTY N / %
U.S.	3,746 / 58.07%	2,894 / 54.87%
Germany	588 / 9.11%	354 / 6.71%
Ireland	598 / 9.27%	372 / 7.05%
England	234 / 3.63%	118 / 2.24%
Sweden	197 / 3.05%	133 / 2.52%
Norway	65 / 1.01%	16 / 0.30%
Italy	218 / 3.38%	186 / 3.53%
France	91 / 1.41%	10 / 0.19%
Wales	45 / 0.70%	2 / 0.04%
Russia	133 / 2.06%	618 / 11.72%
Scotland	120 / 1.86%	41 / 0.78%
Denmark	47 / 0.73%	30 / 0.57%
Others	369 / 5.72%	500 / 9.48%
Total	**6,451 / 100%**	**5,274 / 100%**

Sources: *Denver County Poor Reports*, 1906 and 1909, State Archives; *Nineteenth Annual Report of the Charity Organization Society of Denver* (Denver, 1906), 17, Western History Collection, Denver Public Library; *Twenty-Second Annual Report of the Charity Organization Society of Denver* (Denver, 1909), 19, Western History Collection, Denver Public Library.

Note: The figures for both the COSD and Denver County include all family members and are not a random sampling.

TABLE 17

Average Total Number of Months Receiving
Outdoor Aid per Person

COUNTY	AVG. MONTHS FOR FEMALES / N	AVG. MONTHS FOR MALES / N	AVG. MONTHS FOR ALL / N
Boulder (1907–25)	19.15 / 624	14.52 / 309	16.39 / 1045
Costilla (1891–1906 & 1913–19)	33.67 / 118	36.40 / 65	34.64 / 183
Lincoln (1909–22)	8.22 / 72	6.57 / 128	6.38 / 231
Montezuma (1901–19)	8.71 / 35	8.70 / 76	7.57 / 131
Teller (1912–20)[a]	8.64 / 276	7.40 / 410	7.90 / 695

Sources: Same as Table 2.

Note: Please note that because some cases do not list a sex, the total may not equal the sum of the females and males and the percentage average of months may be less than either percentage of both males or females as in Lincoln and Montezuma Counties.

[a]Teller's data include both outdoor aid and assistance given at the county hospital.

TABLE 18

Number and Percentage of Employed Unmarried Women by
Marital Status, Teller County, 1910 and 1920[a]

YEAR	DIVORCED WOMEN EMPLOYED	SINGLE WOMEN EMPLOYED	WIDOWED WOMEN EMPLOYED	TOTAL UNMARRIED WOMEN EMPLOYED	PERCENTAGE UNMARRIED WOMEN EMPLOYED
1910	20	134	79	233	64.01%
1920	8	56	43	107	49.77%

Sources: U.S. Bureau of the Census, *Population Schedules of the Thirteenth Census of the United States, 1910*, Microfilm Publications, Reel 125, National Archives and Records Administration; U.S. Bureau of the Census, *Population Schedules for the Fourteenth Census of the United States, 1920*, Microfilm Publications, Reel 172, National Archives and Records Administration.

[a]These figures are based on a random sampling of one of every three females seventeen years and older in Teller County.

TABLE 19

Number and Percentage of Employed Unmarried Women by Marital Status, Boulder County, 1910 and 1920[a]

YEAR	DIVORCED WOMEN EMPLOYED	SINGLE WOMEN EMPLOYED	WIDOWED WOMEN EMPLOYED	TOTAL UNMARRIED WOMEN EMPLOYED	PERCENTAGE UNMARRIED WOMEN EMPLOYED
1910	7	337	125	469	45.71%
1920	12	376	121	509	49.51%

Sources: U.S. Bureau of the Census, *Population Schedules of the Thirteenth Census of the United States, 1910*, Microfilm Publications, Reel 113, National Archives and Records Administration; U.S. Bureau of the Census, *Population Schedules for the Fourteenth Census of the United States, 1920*, Microfilm Publications, Reels 155 and 156, National Archives and Records Administration.

[a]These figures are based on a random sampling of one of every three females seventeen years and older in Boulder County.

TABLE 20

Denver County Expenditures on Outdoor Relief and Mothers' Pensions, 1910–1921

YEAR	OUTDOOR RELIEF ($)	MOTHERS' PENSIONS ($)	TOTAL ($)
1910	12,000.00		12,000.00
1911	58,194.05		58,194.05
1912	60,850.78		60,850.78
1913	51,327.46	4,784.16	56,111.62
1914	43,516.53	9,998.46	53,514.99
1915	44,211.00	10,039.53	54,250.53
1916	43,516.53	9,989.00	53,505.53
1917	42,789.59	11,999.80	54,789.39
1918	56,399.82	16,801.80	73,201.62
1919	57,607.46	17,260.85	74,868.31
1920	61,783.97	29,756.00	91,539.97
1921	64,024.72	34,855.00	98,879.72

Sources: Grace Eleanor Wilson, "The History and Development of the Denver Bureau of Public Welfare," 57, see related footnote in Chapter 2, note 16; *Biennial Report of Health and Charity, City and County of Denver, Colorado, 1924–1925,* 7,Western History Collection, Denver Public Library.

Abbreviations

The following titles and abbreviations are used to identify frequently cited archives, collections, and terms.

Boulder Courthouse	Clerk and Recorder Office, Boulder County Courthouse, Boulder, Colorado
CHS	Colorado Historical Society, Denver, Colorado
CL Boulder	Carnegie Library, Boulder, Colorado
Columbia Library	Columbia University Rare Book and Manuscript Library, New York City
Comm. of Lincoln Commissioners	Communications of Lincoln County Commissions, Box 1-546
Con. Ute	Consolidated Ute Agency 1879–1952
Costilla Courthouse	Clerk and Recorder Office, Costilla County Courthouse, San Luis, Colorado
CSU Archives	Colorado State University Archives, Fort Collins, Colorado
Denver City Building	City Clerk and Recorder Office, Denver City and County Building, Denver Colorado
GP/DPL	Government Publications, Denver Public Library, Denver, Colorado
Limon Library	Limon Memorial Library, Limon, Colorado
Lincoln Courthouse	Clerk and Recorder Office, Lincoln County Courthouse, Hugo, Colorado
MD/LC	Manuscript Division, Library of Congress, Washington D.C.

Mont. Box 9	Montezuma County Commissioners Records, File Box 9
Montezuma Courthouse	Clerk and Recorder Office, Montezuma County Courthouse, Cortez, Colorado
NARA	National Archives and Records Administration
NARM	National Archives, Rocky Mountain Region, Denver, Colorado
NFB Colorado	National Federation of the Blind of Colorado, Littleton, Colorado
RG 75	Record Group 75
State Archives	Colorado State Archives, Denver, Colorado
Teller Courthouse	Clerk and Recorder Office, Teller County Courthouse, Cripple Creek, Colorado
UC Archives	University of Colorado Archives, Boulder, Colorado
WHC/DPL	Western History Collection, Denver Public Library, Denver, Colorado

Notes

Introduction

1. *Lincoln County Poor Record*, 25, 28, 33, and 36, Lincoln Courthouse.
2. For an overview of the development of welfare history see Clarke A. Chambers, "Toward a Redefinition of Welfare History," *Journal of American History* 73 (September 1986): 407–33. Many of my observations about the field of welfare history parallel Chambers' article. Also see Robert H. Bremner, "The State of Social Welfare History," in *The State of American History*, ed. Herbert J. Bass (Chicago: Quadrangle Books, 1970), 89–98.
3. Robert H. Bremner, *From the Depths: The Discovery of Poverty in the United States* (New York: New York University Press, 1956).
4. Nathan Irvin Huggins, *Protestants Against Poverty: Boston's Charities, 1870–1900* (Westport, Conn.: Greenwood Publishing, 1971); Allen F. Davis, *Spearheads for Reform: The Social Settlements and the Progressive Movement, 1890–1914* (New York: Oxford University Press, 1967); Clarke A. Chambers, *Seedtime of Reform: American Social Service and Social Action, 1918–1933* (Minneapolis: University of Minnesota Press, 1963); Roy Lubove, *The Professional Altruist: The Emergence of Social Work as a Career, 1880–1930* (Cambridge, Mass.: Harvard University Press, 1965).
5. Joan Waugh, *Unsentimental Reformer: The Life of Josephine Shaw Lowell* (Cambridge, Mass.: Harvard University Press, 1997); Kathryn Kish Sklar, *Florence Kelley and the Nation's Work: The Rise of Women's Political Culture, 1830–1900* (New Haven, Conn.: Yale University Press, 1995); Ellen Fitzpatrick, *Endless Crusade: Women Social Scientists and Progressive Reform* (New York: Oxford University Press, 1990); Mina Carson, *Settlement Folk: Social Thought and the American Settlement Movement, 1885–1930* (Chicago: University of Chicago Press, 1990); Linda Gordon, *Pitied But Not Entitled: Single Mothers and the History of Welfare* (New York: Free Press, 1994); Gwendolyn Mink, *The Wages*

of Motherhood: Inequality in the Welfare State, 1917–1942 (Ithaca, N.Y.: Cornell University Press, 1995); Molly Ladd-Taylor, *Mother-Work: Women, Child Welfare, and the State, 1890–1930* (Urbana: University of Illinois Press, 1994); Linda Gordon, "Black and White Visions of Welfare: Women's Welfare Activism, 1890–1945," *Journal of American History* 78 (September 1991): 559–90; Robyn Muncy, *Creating a Female Dominion in American Reform 1890–1935* (New York: Oxford University Press, 1991); Theda Skocpol, *Protecting Soldiers and Mothers: The Political Origins of Social Policy in the United States* (Cambridge, Mass.: Harvard University Press, 1992); Elizabeth N. Agnew, *From Charity to Social Work: Mary E. Richmond and the Creation of an American Profession* (Urbana: University of Illinois Press, 2004).

6. Walter I. Trattner, *From Poor Law to Welfare State: A History of Social Welfare in America* (New York: Free Press, 1974).

7. Allen J. Matusow, *The Unraveling of America: A History of Liberalism in the 1960s* (New York: Harper and Row, 1984), 217–42; James W. Trent, Jr., *Inventing the Feeble Mind: A History of Mental Retardation in the United States* (Berkeley: University of California Press, 1994); Linda Gordon, *Heroes of Their Own Lives: The Politics and History of Family Violence* (New York: Penguin Books, 1988); Alice O'Connor, *Poverty Knowledge: Social Science, Social Policy, and the Poor in Twentieth-Century U. S. History* (Princeton, N.J.: Princeton University Press, 2001); Patrick J. Kelly, *Creating a National Home: Building the Veterans' Welfare State* (Cambridge, Mass.: Harvard University Press, 1997); Timothy A. Hacsi, *Second Home: Orphan Asylums and Poor Families in America* (Cambridge, Mass.: Harvard University Press, 1997); Michael Katz, *The Undeserving Poor: From the War on Poverty to the War on Welfare* (New York: Pantheon Books, 1989).

8. Skocpol, *Protecting Soldiers and Mothers.*

9. Edwin Amenta, *Bold Relief: Institutional Politics and the Origins of Modern American Social Policy* (Princeton, N.J.: Princeton University Press, 1998).

10. An example of this division is the debate between Linda Gordon and Theda Skocpol over their books *Pitied But Not Entitled* and *Protecting Soldiers and Mothers.* See Gordon, "Gender, State and Society: A Debate with Theda Skocpol;" Skocpol, "Soldiers, Workers, and Mothers: Gendered Identities in Early U.S. Social Policy;" and Gordon, "Response to Theda Skocpol;" all in *Contention* 2 (Spring 1993): 139–89; Stephen Skowronek, *Building a New American State: The Expansion of National Administrative Capacities, 1877–1920* (New York: Cambridge University Press, 1982); Theda Skocpol, "Bringing the State Back In: Strategies of Analysis in Current Research," in *Bringing the State Back In*, ed. Peter B. Evans, Dietrich Ruechemeyer, and Theda Skocpol (New York: Cambridge University Press, 1985), 3–37.

11. Waugh, *Unsentimental Reformer;* Agnew, *From Charity to Social Work*; Jean Bethke Elshtain, *Jane Addams and the Dream of American Democracy* (New

York: Basic Books, 2002). For another excellent example of the influence of Protestantism on charity practices see James A. Denton, *Rocky Mountain Radical: Myron W. Reed, Christian Socialist* (Albuquerque: University of New Mexico Press, 1997).

12. David Rothman, *The Discovery of the Asylum: Social Order and Disorder in the New Republic* (Boston: Little, Brown and Company, 1971).

13. Frances Fox Piven and Richard A. Cloward, *Regulating the Poor: The Functions of Public Welfare* (New York: Vintage Books, 1971).

14. Ladd-Taylor, *Mother-Work*. Also see Seth Koven and Sonya Michel, "Womanly Duties: Maternalist Politics and the Origins of Welfare States in France, Germany, Great Britain, and the United States, 1880–1920," *American Historical Review* 95 (1990): 1076–1108.

15. Paula Baker, "The Domestication of Politics: Women and American Political Society, 1780–1920," in *Women, the State, and Welfare*, ed. Linda Gordon (Madison: University of Wisconsin Press, 1990), 55–91, quotes, 72.

16. Gordon, *Pitied But Not Entitled*; Mink, *Wages of Motherhood*, 3–52; Skocpol, *Protecting Soldiers and Mothers*. Of course, the issue of race also played an important role in determining welfare benefits.

17. Joanne L. Goodwin, *Gender and the Politics of Welfare Reform: Mothers' Pensions in Chicago, 1911–1929* (Chicago: University of Chicago Press, 1997); Suzanne Mettler, *Dividing Citizens: Gender and Federalism in New Deal Public Policy* (Ithaca, N.Y.: Cornell University Press, 1998); Sonya Michel, *Children's Interests/Mothers/ Rights: The Shaping of America's Child Care Policy* (New Haven, Conn.: Yale University Press, 1999); K. Walter Hickel, "War, Region, and Social Welfare: Federal Aid to Servicemen's Dependents in the South, 1917–1921," *Journal of American History* 97 (March 2001): 1362–91; Alice Kessler-Harris, *In Pursuit of Equity: Women, Men, and the Quest for Economic Citizenship in 20th-Century America* (New York: Oxford University Press, 2001); Michael B. Katz, *The Price of Citizenship: Redefining the American Welfare State* (New York: Henry Holt and Company, 2001).

18. Bremner, *From the Depths*, 201; Trattner, *From Poor Law*, 136–211; James T. Patterson, *America's Struggle Against Poverty, 1900–1985* (Cambridge, Mass.: Harvard University Press, 1986), 23.

19. Gordon, *Pitied But Not Entitled*, 37.

20. Mink, *Wages of Motherhood*, 3.

21. Michael B. Katz, *Improving Poor People: the Welfare State, the "Underclass," and Urban Schools as History* (Princeton, N.J.: Princeton University Press, 1995), 23–24; Gordon, *Pitied But Not Entitled*; Mink, *Wages of Motherhood*; Barbara J. Nelson, "Origins of the Two-Channel Welfare State: Workmen's Compensation and Mothers' Aid," in *Women, the State, and Welfare*, ed. Linda Gordon (Madison: University of Wisconsin Press, 1990), 123–51.

22. Bremner, *From the Depths*, 223; Patterson, *America's Struggle*, 27; Clarke A. Chambers, "'Uphill All the Way': Reflections on the Course and Study of Welfare History," *Social Service Review* 66 (December 1992): 501.

23. Roy Lubove, *The Struggle for Social Security, 1900–1935* (1968; reprint, Pittsburgh, Pa.: University of Pittsburgh Press, 1986), 111.

24. Gordon, *Pitied But Not Entitled*; Muncy, *Female Dominion*; Mink, *Wages of Motherhood*.

25. Michael B. Katz, *Poverty and Policy in American History* (New York: Academic Press, 1983), ix. Katz partially tries to remedy the situation by examining a detailed case history of a needy family and by presenting a statistical analysis of New York's poorhouses, see pages 17–54. Other vivid descriptions of the daily realities of the poor can be found in Beverly Stadum, *Poor Women and Their Families: Hard Working Charity Cases, 1900–1930* (Albany: State University of New York Press, 1992); Ruth Wallis Herndon, *Unwelcome Americans: Living on the Margin in Early New England* (Philadelphia: University of Pennsylvania, 2001); Sherri Broder, *Tramps, Unfit Mothers, and Neglected Children: Negotiating the Family in Late Nineteenth-Century Philadelphia* (Philadelphia: University of Pennsylvania Press, 2002); Kenneth L. Kusmer, *Down and Out, on the Road: The Homeless in American History* (New York: Oxford University Press, 2002); and Simon P. Newman, *Embodied History: The Lives of the Poor in Early Philadelphia* (Philadelphia: University of Pennsylvania Press, 2003).

26. Chambers, "Toward a Redefinition," 411. Others have also cited the need to abandon the top-down focus on reformers and social workers. See Allen F. Davis, "Social Welfare History," *Reviews in American History* 2 (September 1974): 343–47; Raymond A. Mohl, "Mainstream Social Welfare History and Its Problems," *Reviews in American History* 7 (December 1979): 469–76.

27. Ladd-Taylor, *Mother-Work*, 148. Also see Mettler, *Dividing Citizens*. Judith Sealander questions whether members of women's clubs really embraced their rhetoric about mothers' pensions. See Judith Sealander, *Private Wealth and Public Life: Foundation Philanthropy and the Reshaping of American Social Policy from the Progressive Era to the New Deal* (Baltimore, Md.: Johns Hopkins University Press, 1997), 107–9.

28. Goodwin, *Gender and Welfare Reform*, 185.

29. Katz, *Poverty and Policy*, 5. For the importance of local and regional factors see Elna C. Green, ed., *The New Deal and Beyond: Social Welfare in the South since 1930* (Athens: University of Georgia Press, 2003). Lynn Hollen Lees also argues for the importance of focusing on the local implementation of relief. See Lynn Hollen Lees, *The Solidarities of Strangers: The English Poor Laws and the People, 1700–1948* (New York: Cambridge University Press, 1998).

30. Skocpol, *Protecting Soldiers and Mothers*, 465–66.

31. Listed below is a sampling of this concentrated focus. For Boston see Robert W. Kelso, *The History of Public Poor Relief in Massachusetts, 1620–1920* (1922; reprint, Montclair, N.J.: Patterson Smith, 1969); Nathan Irvin Huggins, *Protestants Against Poverty: Boston's Charities, 1870–1900* (Westport, Conn.: Greenwood Publishing, 1971); Gordon, *Heroes of Their Own Lives*; Peter C. Holloran, *Boston's Wayward Children: Social Services for Homeless Children, 1830–1930* (1989; reprint, Boston: Northeastern University Press, 1994); Susan Traverso, *Welfare Politics in Boston, 1910–1940* (Amherst: University of Massachusetts Press, 2001); For Chicago see Goodwin, *Gender and Welfare Reform*; Anne Meis Knupfer, *Reform and Resistance: Gender, Delinquency, and America's First Juvenile Court* (New York: Routledge, 2001). Michael Willrich, *City of Courts: Socializing Justice in Progressive Era Chicago* (New York: Cambridge University Press, 2003). For New York City see Robert E. Cary, Jr., *Paupers and Poor Relief in New York City and its Rural Environs, 1700–1830* (Philadelphia: Temple University Press, 1988); Gordon, *Pitied But Not Entitled*. For Philadelphia see John K. Alexander, *Render Them Submissive: Responses to Poverty in Philadelphia, 1760–1800* (Amherst: University of Massachusetts Press, 1980); Priscilla Ferguson Clement, *Welfare and the Poor in the Nineteenth-Century City: Philadelphia, 1800–1854* (Cranbury, N.J.: Associated University Press, 1985); Broder, *Tramps, Unfit Mothers*; Newman, *Embodied History*. Also see Kusmer, *Down and Out*, for a focus on the homeless in Boston, Philadelphia, New York City, and Chicago. Examples from south of the Mason-Dixon line are also largely missing from the historiography. Recently, a pair of edited works has partially addressed this oversight. See Elna C. Green, ed., *Before the New Deal: Social Welfare in the South, 1830–1930* (Athens: University of Georgia Press, 1999) and Green, ed., *The New Deal and Beyond*. Also see Elna C. Green, *This Business of Relief: Confronting Poverty in a Southern City, 1740–1940* (Athens: University of Georgia Press, 2003).

32. J. W. Magruder, "Pensions to Widows—Discussion," in *Proceedings of the National Conference of Charities and Corrections, 1912* (Fort Wayne, Ind.: Fort Wayne Printing, 1912), 496.

33. Paul Kleppner, "Voters and Parties in the Western States, 1876–1900," *Western Historical Quarterly* 14 (January 1983): 49–68; Martin Shefter, "Regional Receptivity to Reform: The Legacy of the Progressive Era," *Political Science Quarterly* 98 (Fall 1983): 459–83.

34. For an excellent example of these trends see John Paul Enyeart, "'By Laws of Their Own Making': Political Culture and the Everyday Politics of the Mountain West Working Class, 1870–1917" (PhD dissertation, University of Colorado, Boulder, 2002).

35. For some examples of a similar approach, see Julie Greene, *Pure and Simple Politics: The American Federation of Labor and Political Activism, 1881–1917* (New York: Cambridge University Press, 1998); Colin J. Davis, *Power at Odds: The 1922 National Railroad Shopmen's Strike* (Urbana: University of Illinois Press, 1997), 1–7; Charles Bright and Susan Harding, "Processes of Statemaking and Popular Protest: An Introduction," in their edited collection *Statemaking and Social Movements: Essays in History and Theory* (Ann Arbor: University of Michigan Press, 1984), 1–15.

36. *Cripple Creek Times and Victor Daily Record*, 12 May 1914, 3; *Teller County Poor Reports*, 1913–1919, Boxes 4967A and 4968A, State Archives.

37. Katz, *Improving Poor People*, 21.

38. *First Biennial Report of the State Board of Charities and Corrections of Colorado* (Denver: Smith-Brooks, 1893), 7.

39. From the very beginning, the board battled with local officials over the collection of this data. "It has been more difficult," concludes the first biennial report of the board, "to get the co-operation of the County Clerks and Sheriffs, especially in the giving of statistics." By no means was this a one-time problem as a version of this same refrain appears repeatedly throughout the board's biennial reports. See, the *First Report Board of Charities and Corrections*, 43.

40. I used the Q&A database software for all my data entry and calculations. Q&A, originally designed for business use, proved both flexible and powerful enough to address all my needs without the rigidity of the Statistical Package for the Social Sciences (SPSS). Flexibility was a key requirement for this project because the format of the pauper records varied from county to county and sometimes a county's format would change over the years.

41. *Thirteenth Census of the United States, 1910*, vol. 2 (Washington, D.C.: Government Printing Office, 1913), 191; *Fourteenth Census of the United States, 1920*, vol. 3 (Washington, D.C.: Government Printing Office, 1922), 147.

42. *Fourteenth Census of the United States, 1920*, vol. 2 (Washington, D.C.: Government Printing Office, 1922), 36. For Colorado, the actual percentages of foreign-born were 16.9 percent in 1900, 16.2 percent in 1910, and 12.7 percent in 1920. In 1910, Rhode Island with 33 percent, Massachusetts with 31.5 percent, and New York with 30.2 percent foreign-born led the nation.

43. Marianne L. Stoller, "La Tierra y la Merced," in *La Cultura Constante de San Luis*, ed. Randall Teeuwen (n.p.: San Luis Museum Cultural and Commercial Center, 1985), 12.

44. Randall Teeuwen, "La Gente de la Tierra," in *La Cultura Constante de San Luis*, ed. Randall Teeuwen (n.p.: San Luis Museum Cultural and Commercial Center, 1985), 9.

45. Stoller, "La Tierra," 14.

46. David William Lantis, "The San Luis Valley, Colorado: Sequent Rural Occupance in an Intermontane Basin" (PhD dissertation, Ohio State University, 1950), 126–29; Stoller, "La Tierra," 14–15.

47. Lantis, "San Luis Valley," 385.

48. Marta Weigle, *Brothers of Light, Brothers of Blood: The Penitentes of the Southwest* (Albuquerque: University of New Mexico Press, 1976); Maclovio C. Martinez, "The Penitente," in *La Cultura Constante de San Luis*, ed. Randall Teeuwen (n.p.: San Luis Museum Cultural and Commercial Center, 1985), 26–33.

49. Ira S. Freeman, *A History of Montezuma County Colorado: Land of Promise and Fulfillment* (Boulder, Colo.: Johnson Publishing, 1958), 119.

50. Ibid., 27–28, 49, 55–56, and 111–13.

51. Ibid., 96–103.

52. Richard K. Young, *The Ute Indians of Colorado in the Twentieth Century* (Norman: University of Oklahoma Press, 1997), 15–38 and map on 60; Freeman, *History of Montezuma County*, 119. The Ute Mountain Ute Indian Reservation actually encompasses a small part of neighboring La Plata County and a portion of New Mexico. During the late nineteenth and early twentieth centuries these sections were sparsely populated. The vast majority of Utes lived in the western section of the reservation near Towaoc in Montezuma County.

53. To give the reader a sense of the size of these counties, Rhode Island is 1,054 square miles and Delaware is 1,933 square miles. Costilla County is larger than Rhode Island, while Montezuma County and Lincoln County are larger than either Rhode Island or Delaware.

54. Laura Solze Claggett, ed., *History of Lincoln County, Colorado* (Dallas, Tex.: Curtis Media Corporation, 1987), 2; Lincoln County Historical Society, *Lincoln County: From the Beginning to 1940* (Marceline, Mo.: Walsworth Publishing, n.d.), 3.

55. Elliott West, *The Contested Plains: Indians, Goldseekers, and the Rush to Colorado* (Lawrence: University Press of Kansas, 1998), 1–93; Carl Ubbelohde, Maxine Benson, and Duane A. Smith, *A Colorado History*, 7th ed. (Boulder, Colo.: Pruett, 1995), 166.

56. West, *Contested Plains*, 310; Ubbelohde, Benson, and Smith, *Colorado History*, 101–9; Richard White, *"It's Your Misfortune and None of My Own": A History of the American West* (Norman: University of Oklahoma Press, 1991), 94–97.

57. Claggett, *History of Lincoln County*, 3.

58. Lincoln County Historical Society, *From the Beginning*, 3, 28, 46, and 54; Claggett, *History of Lincoln County*, 4 and 8.

59. Dale Cooley and Mary Liz Owen, eds., *Where the Wagons Rolled: The History of Lincoln County and the People Who Came Before 1925* (Limon: Eastern Colorado Printery, 1985), 9.

60. Donald Ray Storey, "An Investigation of the Early Dry Farming Movement in Colorado and Its Effect Upon the Development of Elbert and Lincoln Counties Between 1905 and 1915" (MA thesis, Kansas State Teachers College, 1971), 128.

61. Storey, "An Investigation," 141; U.S. Department of Agriculture, "Dry Farming in Eastern Colorado: A Study of 151 Farms in Lincoln and Washington Counties, Farm Year 1922," (Washington, D.C.: 1924), 4, CSU Archives.

62. U.S. Department of Agriculture, "Dry Farming in Eastern Colorado," 10; Cooley and Owen, *Wagons Rolled*, 18.

63. Marshall Sprague, *Money Mountain: The Story of Cripple Creek Gold* (Lincoln: University of Nebraska Press, 1953), 3–75; Carl Abbott, Stephen J. Leonard, and David McComb, *Colorado: A History of the Centennial State*, 3rd ed. (Niwot: University Press of Colorado, 1994), 113–14.

64. Robert Guilford Taylor, *Cripple Creek* (Bloomington: Indiana University Press, 1966), 45.

65. The Colorado Bureau of Mines reported gold and silver production in terms of dollar value instead of tonnage. It does not appear that the state took into account inflation and deflation. *Fifteenth Biennial Report of the State of Colorado Bureau of Mines, 1917–1918* (Denver: Eames Brothers, 1919), 197; *Thirteenth Census of the United States—Abstract of Census with Supplement for Colorado, 1910* (Washington, D.C.: Government Printing Office, 1913), 604.

66. Taylor, *Cripple Creek*, 32.

67. Elizabeth Jameson, *All That Glitters: Class, Conflict, and Community in Cripple Creek* (Urbana: University of Illinois Press, 1998), 25.

68. Walter A. Wyckoff, "The Rampart Range: Ten Years After," *Scribner's Magazine*, October 1908, 498.

69. Elizabeth Ann Jameson, "High-Grade and Fissures: A Working-Class History of the Cripple Creek, Colorado, Gold Mining District, 1890–1905" (PhD dissertation, University of Michigan, 1987), 49.

70. Jameson, *All That Glitters*, 140–60.

71. Jameson, "High-Grade and Fissures," 132.

72. Phyllis Smith, *A Look at Boulder: From Settlement to City* (Boulder, Colo.: Pruett, 1981), 11–13.

73. Mabel Guise Montgomery, *A Story of Gold Hill Colorado: Seventy-odd Years in the Heart of the Rockies* (Boulder, Colo.: The Book Lode, 1987), 10.

74. Smith, *Look at Boulder*, 49.

75. Smith, *Look at Boulder*, 49; Duane A. Smith, *Silver Saga: The Story of Caribou, Colorado* (Boulder, Colo.: Pruett, 1974), 191 and 98.

76. Tungsten, a recently discovered mineral, created a small, short boom in the early twentieth century. See, Isabel M. Becker, *Nederland: A Trip to Cloudland* (Denver: South Becker Press, 1989), 57 and 61; Smith, *Look at Boulder*, 133 and 134; R. D. George, *The Main Tungsten Area of Boulder County, Colorado* (Boulder, Colorado, 1916), 76, CL Boulder; *Boulder County Miner*, 6 August 1914; *State of Colorado Bureau of Mines Annual Report for the Year 1920* (Denver: Smith-Brooks Printing, 1921), 11.

77. *Thirteenth Census of the United States, Abstract, 1910*, 585.

78. *Agricultural Possibilities of Boulder County* (Boulder, Colo.: Boulder Commercial Association, 1907), 1, 3, and 4, CL Boulder.

79. Carolyn Conarroe, *The Louisville Story* (Boulder, Colo.: Johnson Publishing, 1979), 3–4.

80. *Drumm's Pocket Map of Boulder County, Colorado*, (1908), CL Boulder.

81. *Thirteenth Census of the United States, Abstract, 1910*, 33.

82. *Fourteenth Census of the United States, 1920*, vol. 3, 141–42.

83. West, *Contested Plains*, 97–113; Stephen J. Leonard and Thomas J. Noel, *Denver: Mining Camp to Metropolis* (Niwot: University Press of Colorado, 1990), 3–8; Ubbelohde, Benson, and Smith, *Colorado History*, 56–67. For an excellent overview of Denver's early development see David Brundage, *The Making of Western Labor Radicalism: Denver's Organized Workers, 1878–1905* (Urbana: University of Illinois Press, 1994), 7–24; Denton, *Rocky Mountain Radical*, 8–21.

84. Leonard and Noel, *Denver*, 116–27. For an overview of how Denver shaped the regional economy see Kathleen A. Brosnan, *Uniting Mountain and Plain: Cities, Law, and Environmental Change along the Front Range* (Albuquerque: University of New Mexico Press, 2002).

85. *Thirteenth Census of the United States, 1910*, vol. 2, 44.

Chapter One

1. *Montezuma County Commissioners Records*, vol. 3, 258, Montezuma Courthouse.

2. *Costilla County Commissioners Records*, vol. 6, 427, Costilla Courthouse.

3. Some scholars have already observed some variances among counties in the delivery of assistance. See Michael B. Katz, *In the Shadow of the Poorhouse: A Social History of Welfare in America* (New York: Basic Books, 1986), 38–39; George A. Warfield, "Public Poor Relief in Missouri: An Investigation of the Ethics and Efficiency" (MA thesis, University of Denver, 1915); George A. Warfield, *Outdoor Relief in Missouri: A Study of its Administration by County Officials* (New York: Survey Associates, 1915). These authors, however, have not accounted for the differences among county poor relief practices.

4. Katz, *Shadow of the Poorhouse*, 36–57; James T. Patterson, *America's Struggle Against Poverty, 1900–1985* (Cambridge, Mass.: Harvard University Press, 1986), 20–25; Walter I. Trattner, *From Poor Law to Welfare State: A History of Social Welfare in America* (New York: Free Press, 1974), 75–95.

5. Linda Gordon, *Pitied But Not Entitled: Single Mothers and the History of Welfare* (New York: Free Press, 1994); Gwendolyn Mink, *The Wages of Motherhood: Inequality in the Welfare State, 1917–1942* (Ithaca, N.Y.: Cornell University Press, 1995); Molly Ladd-Taylor, *Mother-Work: Women, Child Welfare, and the State, 1890–1930* (Urbana: University of Illinois Press, 1994); Robyn Muncy, *Creating a Female Dominion in American Reform 1890–1935* (New York: Oxford University Press, 1991); Theda Skocpol, *Protecting Soldiers and Mothers: The Political Origins of Social Policy in the United States* (Cambridge, Mass.: Harvard University Press, 1992); Joanne L. Goodwin, *Gender and the Politics of Welfare Reform: Mothers' Pensions in Chicago, 1911–1929* (Chicago: University of Chicago Press, 1997).

6. George Warfield falls into the trap of labeling the administrators of rural poor relief in Missouri as unwilling to follow the practices of cities. George A. Warfield, "The County as a Unit in Charity Administration: Outdoor Relief," in *Proceedings of the National Conference of Social Work, 1918* (Chicago: Rogers and Hall Printers, 1918), 250–52.

7. *Morning Times-Citizen*, 18 Feb. 1902, 1; also see *Morning Times-Citizen*, 19 Feb. 1902, 1 and 5; *Morning Times-Citizen*, 25 Feb. 1902, 5; C. L. Stonaker, "Colorado," in *Proceedings of the National Conference of Charities and Corrections, 1902* (Boston: George H. Ellis, 1902), 29.

8. "Sociological Conference," *University of Colorado Bulletin* 14 (July 1914): 11 and 8.

9. "Baccalaureate Address and Commencement Oration," *University of Colorado Bulletin* 7 (June 1907): 21; Woman's Club of Boulder, 28 February 1918, Folder 17, Box 1, BHS 268, CL Boulder.

10. *Costilla County Poor Book*, vol. 1, Costilla Courthouse. Costilla County's poor records stop in 1906 and resume again in 1913. Madrid may have actually continued on county aid beyond 1906.

11. Colorado Board of Immigration, *Year Book of the State of Colorado, 1920* (Denver: Welch-Haffner Printing, 1920), 208.

12. Carol J. Carter, "History of Sacred Heart Parish," (MA thesis, Adams State College, 1961), 10.

13. *San Luis Valley News*, 9 Nov. 1912, 1.

14. Erl H. Ellis, *Colorado Mapology* (Fredrick, Colo.: Jende-Hagan Book Corporation, 1983), 188; *San Luis Valley News*, 1 March 1913, 1; Thomas J. Noel, Paul F. Mahoney, and Richard E. Stevens, *Historical Atlas of Colorado* (Norman: University of Oklahoma Press, 1994), 16.

15. *San Luis Valley News,* 2 Nov. 1918, 1.

16. *State Board of Charities and Corrections Minutes, 1916,* 210, Box 18626, State Archives.

17. David William Lantis, "The San Luis Valley, Colorado: Sequent Rural Occupance in an Intermontane Basin" (PhD dissertation, Ohio State University, 1950), 130.

18. Lantis, "San Luis Valley," 131; Ron Sandoval, "The San Luis Vega," in *La Cultura Constante de San Luis,* ed. Randall Teeuwen (n.p.: San Luis Museum Cultural and Commercial Center, 1985), 18.

19. Sandoval, "San Luis Vega," 18–24.

20. Lantis, "San Luis Valley," 133.

21. Sandoval, "San Luis Vega," 18.

22. Lantis, "San Luis Valley," 385; Olibama Lopez Tushar, *The People of "El Valle": A History of the Spanish Colonials in the San Luis Valley* (Denver, 1975), 51; Arnold A. Valdez and Maria A. Valdez, "The Culebra River Villages of Costilla County: Village Architecture and Its Historical Context, 1851–1940," the National Park Service, Colorado Historical Society, and the State Historic Preservation Office (n.p.: 1991), 34.

23. Sandoval, "San Luis Vega," 18–20. For an overview of attempts to enforce the Treaty of Guadalupe Hidalgo see Richard Griswold del Castillo, *The Treaty of Guadalupe Hidalgo: A Legacy of Conflict* (Norman: University of Oklahoma Press, 1990). Articles VIII and IX of the Treaty of Guadalupe Hidalgo guaranteed existing property rights.

24. Frances Leon Swadesh, *Los Primeros Pobladores: Hispanic Americans of the Ute Frontier* (Notre Dame, Ind.: University of Notre Dame Press, 1974), 147.

25. *Fifth Biennial Report of the State Board of Charities and Corrections, 1900* (Denver: Smith-Brooks, 1901), 76.

26. *Costilla County Commissioners Records,* vol. 3, 117, other examples include pages 7, 18, 44, and 92, Costilla Courthouse.

27. Ibid., 7.

28. Marta Weigle, *Brothers of Light, Brothers of Blood: The Penitentes of the Southwest* (Albuquerque: University of New Mexico Press, 1976), 96. For examples of lay activism in the Midwest and Northeast see Deirdre M. Moloney, *American Catholic Lay Groups and Transatlantic Social Reform in the Progressive Era* (Chapel Hill: University of North Carolina Press, 2002).

29. Weigle, *Brothers of Light,* xi.

30. Alex M. Darley, *The Passionists of the Southwest or the Holy Brotherhood* (Pueblo, Colo., 1893).

31. Weigle, *Brothers of Light,* quote 24, also see 53–54.

32. Alice Corbin Henderson, *Brothers of Light: The Penitentes of the Southwest* (New York: Harcourt, Brace, and Company, 1937), 10.

33. Henderson, *Brothers of Light*, 58; Weigle, *Brothers of Light*, xvii, 75, and 139; Darley, *Passionists of the Southwest*, 15; Dorothy Woodward, "The Penitentes of New Mexico" (PhD dissertation, Yale University, 1935), 288–89.

34. Weigle, *Brothers of Light*, 151; Virginia McConnell Simmons, "The Penitentes: Remnant of a Vanishing Lifestyle," *San Luis Valley Historian* 24 (1992): 21.

35. William Wallrich, "Auxiliadoras de la Morado," *Southwestern Lore* 16 (June 1950): 6–7, quote 7.

36. Weigle, *Brothers of Light*, 151. The trend of Catholic women supplementing and following men's charity efforts also surfaces with middle-class Catholics. See Moloney, *Catholic Lay Groups*, 167–204. Yet, since so few sources exist documenting the activities of the Auxiliadoras, it is not possible to determine if women actually acted on their own instead of following the Enfermero.

37. Woodward, "Penitentes of New Mexico," 288; Simmons, "Penitentes," 20; Tushar, *People*, 65.

38. Simmons, "Penitentes," 24.

39. S. Omar Barker, "Los Penitentes," *Overland Monthly and Out West Magazine* 82 (April 1924): 180.

40. Ibid.

41. Henderson, *Brothers of Light*, 58.

42. The exact figure is 47.83 percent. *Costilla County Poor Book*, vols. 1–3, Costilla Courthouse.

43. John Opie, *The Law of the Land: Two Hundred Years of American Farmland Policy* (Lincoln: University of Nebraska Press, 1987), 101.

44. Donald Ray Storey, "An Investigation of the Early Dry Farming Movement in Colorado and Its Effect Upon the Development of Elbert and Lincoln Counties Between 1905 and 1915" (MA thesis, Kansas State Teachers College, 1971), 141–42; U.S. Department of Agriculture, "Land Use in Lincoln County, Colorado," (n.p.: 1938), 5, CSU Archives; U.S. Department of Agriculture, "Dry Farming in Eastern Colorado: A Study of 151 Farms in Lincoln and Washington Counties, Farm Year 1922," (Washington, D.C.: 1924), 4, CSU Archives.

45. Colorado Board of Immigration, *Year Book of the State of Colorado, 1918* (Denver: Brock-Haffner, 1918), 152.

46. Opie, *Law of the Land*, 102. Also see Pamela Riney-Kehrberg, *Rooted in Dust: Surviving Drought and Depression in Southwestern Kansas* (Lawrence: University Press of Kansas, 1994), 7–8.

47. *Rocky Mountain News*, 9 Jan. 1891, 3.

48. Robert G. Dunbar, "Agricultural Adjustments in Eastern Colorado in the Eighteen-Nineties," *Agricultural History* 18 (January 1944): 41–52.

49. Mary Wilma M. Hargreaves, *Dry Farming in the Northern Great Plains, 1900–1925* (Cambridge, Mass.: Harvard University Press, 1957), 83–125; Paul W. Gates, *History of Public Land Law Development* (Washington, D.C.: Government Printing Office, 1968), 503.

50. Hargreaves, *Dry Farming*, 92–98, quote 92.

51. *Range Ledger*, 23 Sept. 1905, 2.

52. Storey, "An Investigation," 128; *Range Ledger*, 4 July 1908, 6.

53. *Empire Magazine, Denver Post*, 28 September 1975, 38.

54. Ira S. Freeman, *A History of Montezuma County Colorado: Land of Promise and Fulfillment* (Boulder, Colo.: Johnson Publishing, 1958), 266; Linda Dishman, "Ranching and Farming in the Lower Dolores River Valley," in *The River of Sorrows: The History of the Lower Dolores River Valley*, ed. Gregory D. Kendrick (Denver: National Park Service, 1981), 29.

55. *Montezuma Journal*, 19 Aug. 1904, 2.

56. Richard White, *"It's Your Misfortune and None of My Own": A History of the American West* (Norman: University of Oklahoma Press, 1991), 230. In Lincoln County, above average precipitation was reported for every year between 1911 and 1920, with the exceptions of 1911 and 1913. See Storey, "An Investigation," 145.

57. *Range Ledger*, 3 July 1915, 4.

58. Martha Kollath, oral history interview, 28 March 1979, Limon Library.

59. Ruth Cunningham, ed., *Homesteaders and Other Early Settlers, 1900–1930: Western Cheyenne County, Colorado* (Cassville, Mo.: Litho Printers, 1985), 243–44.

60. Carrie Wheeler, affidavit, 13 May 1911, Comm. of Lincoln Commissioners, Lincoln Courthouse.

61. *Range Ledger*, 14 April 1904, 2. Also see *Range Ledger*, 18 March 1911, 3.

62. Gates, *Public Land Law*, 504; Freeman, *History of Montezuma County*, 144.

63. Freeman, *History of Montezuma County*, 145.

64. Ibid. Only a small difference in the amount of precipitation could mean the difference between success or failure. See Rodman W. Paul, *The Far West and the Great Plains in Transition, 1859–1900* (New York: Harper and Row, 1988), 232.

65. Nora Marie Dreier, oral history interview, no date, Limon Library.

66. Henry McCabe, *Cowboys, Indians, and Homesteaders* (n.p.: Desert Press, 1975), 279.

67. Esther Johnson, "Karval, Colorado," *Colorado Magazine* 6 (March 1929): 64; Veronica Cirbo, "My Grandparents," 2, Historical Essay Contest—Student Papers, Special Collections, Penrose Library, Colorado Springs, Colorado; Kollath, oral history interview.

68. McCabe, *Cowboys*, 281.

69. Cirbo, "My Grandparents," 3.

70. McCabe, *Cowboys*, 282.

71. *Range Ledger*, 6 April 1918, 3.

72. Clara Robbins, Statement of Paupers, 29 July 1916, Comm. of Lincoln Commissioners, Lincoln Courthouse; O. B. Schenk, affidavit, 27 October 1911, Comm. of Lincoln Commissioners, Lincoln Courthouse.

73. Maud Armack to Lincoln County commissioners, 12 October 1925, Comm. of Lincoln Commissioners, Lincoln Courthouse.

74. *Range Ledger*, 6 April 1918, 3.

75. V. Jenkins to Lincoln County commissioners, 15 April 1912, Comm. of Lincoln Commissioners, Lincoln Courthouse.

76. M. S. Balsiger to Mr. Robert Durham, 28 August 1916, Mont. Box 9, Montezuma Courthouse.

77. Mrs. Gust Velander to Lincoln County commissioners, no date, Comm. of Lincoln Commissioners, Lincoln Courthouse.

78. Charley Miller, J. H. Billingsley, Daisey Morris, R. H. Bailey, E. J. Murray, Melina Murray, B. E. Hampton, A. C. Short to Montezuma County commissioners, 26 February 1917, Mont. Box 9, Montezuma Courthouse.

79. Ibid.

80. *Lincoln County Commissioners Record*, book 2, 76–77, Lincoln Courthouse.

81. Dunbar, "Agricultural Adjustments," 47 and 50. Farmers in Baca County, Colorado failed in their efforts to secure seed from their county commissioners in 1890, *Baca County Commissioners Record*, vol. 1, 103, County Clerk and Recorder Office, Baca County Courthouse, Springfield, Colorado; Susan Sterett found similar cases in Kansas, see "Serving the State: Constitutionalism and Social Spending, 1860s–1920s," *Law & Social Inquiry* 22 (Spring 1997): 321.

82. Henry Wolf to Montezuma County commissioners, 24 February, no year, Mont. Box 9, Montezuma Courthouse.

83. James Gariss to Mr. A. S. Johnson, 6 June 1912, Comm. of Lincoln Commissioners, Lincoln Courthouse.

84. Martha Stetson, Statement of Paupers, 6 March 1915, Comm. of Lincoln Commissioners, Lincoln Courthouse.

85. James Gariss to County Clerk, 1 April 1912, Comm. of Lincoln Commissioners, Lincoln Courthouse.

86. Carrie Wheeler, affidavit, 13 May 1911, Comm. of Lincoln Commissioners, Lincoln Courthouse.

87. Esther Johnson, "Karval, Colorado," *Colorado Magazine* 6 (March 1929): 64; Glen R. Durrell, "Homesteading in Colorado," *Colorado Magazine* 51 (Spring 1974): 95.

88. Donald Worster, *Dust Bowl: The Southern Plains in the 1930s* (New York: Oxford University Press, 1979), 6.

89. Ibid., 97. The importance of the market economy can also be seen in the 1930s, see Michael Johnston Grant, *Down and Out on the Family Farm: Rural Rehabilitation in the Great Plains, 1929–1945* (Lincoln: University of Nebraska Press, 2002), 5–6 and 33–34.

90. *Lincoln County Poor Record*, 27, Lincoln Courthouse.

91. Ruth Wallis Herndon, *Unwelcome Americans: Living on the Margin in Early New England* (Philadelphia: University of Pennsylvania Press, 2001); Kenneth L. Kusmer, *Down and Out, on the Road: The Homeless in American History* (New York: Oxford University Press, 2002), 20; Hendrik Hartog, "The Public Law of a County Court: Judicial Government in Eighteenth Century Massachusetts," *American Journal of Legal History* 20 (October 1976): 292–99.

92. For examples of high mobility rates see Worster, *Dust Bowl*, 83–84, 88, and 145–46.

93. *Lincoln County Commissioners Record*, book 3, 31, Lincoln Courthouse; Letters from V. Jenkins to Lincoln County commissioners, Comm. of Lincoln Commissioners, Lincoln Courthouse.

94. *Montezuma County Commissioners Records*, vol. 2, 437; also see vol. 3, 309, 398, and 446, both in Montezuma Courthouse.

95. U.S. Bureau of the Census, *Religious Bodies, 1906, Part 1, Summary and General Tables* (Washington, D.C.: Government Printing Office, 1910), 300 and 301.

96. While this attitude was formed in the second half of the nineteenth century, it continued into the early 1930s. See Trattner, *From Poor Law*, 80–82 and 86–93; Joan Waugh, *Unsentimental Reformer: The Life of Josephine Shaw Lowell* (Cambridge, Mass.: Harvard University Press, 1997), 121–83; Robert S. McElvaine, ed., *Down and Out in the Great Depression: Letters from the Forgotten Man* (Chapel Hill: University of North Carolina Press, 1983), 22 and 37–48.

97. Georgia Denby to Mr. Myler, 27 May 1912, Mont. Box 9, Montezuma Courthouse.

98. H. W. Edwards to Lincoln County commissioners, 6 December 1912, Comm. of Lincoln Commissioners, Lincoln Courthouse.

99. Charles J. Kappler, comp. and ed., *Indian Affairs: Laws and Treaties*, vol. 1 (Washington, D.C.: Government Printing Office, 1904), 556.

100. The Ute Mountain Ute Indian Reservation actually encompasses a small part of neighboring La Plata County and a portion of New Mexico. During the late nineteenth and early twentieth centuries these sections were sparsely populated. The vast majority of Utes lived in the western section of the reservation near Towaoc in Montezuma County. See Richard K. Young, *The Ute Indians of Colorado in the Twentieth Century* (Norman: University of Oklahoma Press, 1997), 17–38 and 60.

101. Francis E. Leupp, "The Southern Utes," in *Twenty-Seventh Annual Report of the Board of Indian Commissioners, 1895* (Washington, D.C.: Government Printing Office, 1896), 21; Harold Hoffmeister, "The Consolidated Ute Indian Reservation," *The Geographical Review* 35 (October 1945): 609.

102. Kappler, *Indian Affairs*, vol. 1, 620. The issue of adequate water supplies on the Ute Mountain Reservation has been an ongoing battle. Until 1990, water trucks brought water to the reservation. By the mid-1990s, the reservation finally received both a steady supply of safe drinking water and some water for business use. Still, tribal officials claimed that the federal government has not guaranteed all the tribe's water rights. See Young, *Ute Indians of Colorado*, 201-5.

103. Louis A. Knackstedt, "Southern Ute Agency," in *Thirty-First Annual Report of the Board of Indian Commissioners, 1899* (Washington, D.C.: Government Printing Office, 1900), 67; Frances Leon Swadesh, "The Southern Utes and Their Neighbors 1877-1926: An Ethnohistorical Study of Multiple Interaction in Contact-Induced Culture Change" (MA thesis, University of Colorado, Boulder, 1962), 66 and 129.

104. *Annual Report of the Commissioner of Indian Affairs, 1920* (Washington, D.C.: Government Printing Office, 1920), 131.

105. Marvin Kaufmann Opler, "The Southern Ute of Colorado," in *Acculturation in Seven American Tribes*, ed. Ralph Linton (New York: D. Appleton-Century, 1940), 187; Young, *Ute Indians of Colorado*, 65.

106. Frederick E. Hoxie, *A Final Promise: The Campaign to Assimilate the Indians, 1880-1920* (Lincoln: University of Nebraska Press, 1984).

107. Leupp, "Southern Utes," 20.

108. Knackstedt, "Southern Ute Agency," 67.

109. S. F. Stacher, "The Indians of the Ute Mountain Reservation, 1906-9," *Colorado Magazine* 26 (January 1949): 55.

110. Trachoma is a "chlamydial infection of the conjunctiva, the moist tissue that lines the eyelids and the white portion of the eyeball." Charles B. Clayman, ed., *The American Medical Association Family Medical Guide*, 3rd ed. (New York: Random House, 1994), 607.

111. "Prevalence of tuberculosis and trachoma among Indians, fiscal year ended June 30, 1912," in *Annual Report of the Commissioner of Indian Affairs, 1912* (Washington, D.C.: Government Printing Office, 1912), 171; *Fortieth Annual Report of the Board of Indian Commissioners, 1908* (Washington, D.C.: Government Printing Office, 1909), 7.

112. Paula Maria Allen, oral history interview by Sue Armitage, 14 July 1978, Cortez Public Library, Cortez, Colorado; Young, *Ute Indians of Colorado*, 66.

113. "Indian populations of the United States, exclusive of Alaska, June 30, 1913," in *Annual Report of the Commissioner of Indian Affairs, 1913* (Washington, D.C.: Government Printing Office, 1914), 50; *Census of the Ute Indians of Ute Mountain Agency, 1915–1922*, Microfilm Publication M595, RG 75, NARA.

114. Allen, oral history interview.

115. Stacher, "Indians of Ute Mountain Reservation," 56.

116. Charles J. Kappler, comp. and ed., *Indian Affairs: Laws and Treaties*, vol. 2 (Washington, D.C.: Government Printing Office, 1904), 992.

117. Kappler, *Indian Affairs*, vol. 1, 152.

118. *Montezuma Journal*, 6 April 1900, 4.

119. *Thirty-first Report of Indian Commissioners, 1899*, 17.

120. *Annual Report of the Commissioner of Indian Affairs, 1900* (Washington, D.C.: Government Printing Office, 1900), 9.

121. *Forty-first Annual Report of the Board of Indian Commissioners, 1909* (Washington, D.C.: Government Printing Office, 1910), 14.

122. *Thirty-first Report of Indian Commissioners, 1899*, 17; *Thirty-fifth Annual Report of the Board of Indian Commissioners, 1903* (Washington, D.C.: Government Printing Office, 1904), 11.

123. President Theodore Roosevelt quoted in *Thirty-Sixth Annual Report of the Board of Indian Commissioners, 1904* (Washington, D.C.: Government Printing Office, 1905), 6.

124. *Forty-first Report of Indian Commissioners, 1909*, 20.

125. *Thirty-first Report of Indian Commissioners, 1899*, 17. Also see *Annual Report of the Commissioner of Indian Affairs, 1911* (Washington, D.C.: Government Printing Office, 1911), 21.

126. Letter to Alfred H. Symons, Superintendent of Ute Mountain Agency, 1 December 1916, Folder 005/105, Box 2, Inspectors Reports, Con. Ute, RG 75, NARM. Frances Leon Swadesh argues that the Indian Office only permitted "competent Indians" to use their I.I.A. But it seems clear from correspondence between Alfred H. Symons and officials in Washington that the issue is not one of "competence" but rather one of being unable to work. Swadesh, "Southern Utes and Their Neighbors," 97–98.

127. Lurene Whyte, folder 006 status file, Box 6, Con. Ute, RG 75, NARM.

128. Jesse Bancroft and Enterpa Bancroft, folder 006 status file, Box 4, Con. Ute, RG 75, NARM.

129. Ida Fields, folder 006 status file, Box 4, Con. Ute, RG 75, NARM.

130. E. B. Merritt to Alfred H. Symons, 1 December 1916, Folder 005/105, Box 2, Inspectors Reports, Con. Ute, RG 75, NARM.

131. E. B. Merritt to Alfred H. Symons, 21 September 1916, Folder 005/105, Box 2, Inspectors Reports, Con. Ute, RG 75, NARM.

132. *Annual Report of the Commissioner of Indian Affairs, 1900,* 214.

133. Alfred H. Symons to the Commissioner of Indian Affairs, 7 December 1916, Folder 005/105, Box 2, Inspectors Reports, Con. Ute, RG 75, NARM.

134. Alfred H. Symons to the Commissioner of Indian Affairs, 30 September 1916, Folder 005/105, Box 2, Inspectors Reports, Con. Ute, RG 75, NARM.

135. Alfred H. Symons to the Commissioner of Indian Affairs, 7 Dec. 1916, Folder 005/105, Box 2, Inspectors Reports, Con. Ute, RG 75, NARM.

136. John Merry, Henry Goodman, John Benao, Tah-we-up, Calabas, Bill Coyote, Big Tom, Toree, Blue Nose, Jim Bancroft, Jake House, Ha-gar, and James Bush to Franklin K. Lane, 6 February 1915, Box 2, Ute Mountain Central Classified Files 1907–1939, RG 75, National Archives I, Washington, D.C.

137. Alfred H. Symons to the Commissioner of Indian Affairs, 7 Dec. 1916, Folder 005/105, Box 2, Inspectors Reports, Con. Ute, RG 75, NARM; Alfred H. Symons to the Commissioner of Indian Affairs, 30 Sept. 1916, Folder 005/105, Box 2, Inspectors Reports, Con. Ute, RG 75, NARM.

138. Alfred H. Symons to the Commissioner of Indian Affairs, 30 Sept. 1916, Folder 005/105, Box 2, Inspectors Reports, Con. Ute, RG 75, NARM.

139. Alfred H. Symons to the Commissioner of Indian Affairs, 7 Dec. 1916, Folder 005/105, Box 2, Inspectors Reports, Con. Ute, RG 75, NARM. This habit of protesting was not isolated to the Weeminuches. See Frederick E. Hoxie, *Talking Back to Civilization: Indian Voices from the Progressive Era* (Boston: Bedford/St. Martin's, 2001).

140. Teller County officials did not differentiate between indoor and outdoor aid. As a result, the Teller figures contain both types of assistance and thus do not solely represent outdoor aid. Because institutional aid tended to be more expensive than outdoor aid and because a sizable number of people died shortly after arriving at the county hospital, the inclusion of indoor aid distorts Teller's data by increasing the average amount of aid received per month while decreasing the average duration. Thus, much of Teller's data cannot be used in direct comparison with the other counties.

141. Merritt W. Pinckney, "Public Pensions to Widows: Experiences and Observations Which Lead Me to Favor Such a Law," reprinted in *Selected Articles on Mothers' Pensions,* comp. Edna D. Bullock (New York: H. W. Wilson Company, 1915), 142.

142. Mary E. Richmond and Fred S. Hall, *A Study of Nine Hundred and Eighty-Five Widows Known to Certain Charity Organization Societies in 1910* (1913; reprint, New York: Arno Press, 1974), 13.

143. Frederic Almy, "Public Pensions to Widows: Experiences and Observations Which Lead Me to Oppose Such a Law," reprinted in *Selected Articles on Mothers' Pensions,* comp. Edna D. Bullock (New York: H. W. Wilson Company, 1915), 153.

144. Richmond and Hall, *Nine Hundred Widows*, 14–16.

145. Almy, "Public Pensions to Widows," first quote, 155, second quote, 153.

146. Marshall Sprague, *Money Mountain: The Story of Cripple Creek Gold* (Lincoln: University of Nebraska Press, 1953), 298.

147. Frederick L. Hoffman, *Industrial Accident Statistics*, U. S. Department of Labor, Bureau of Labor Statistics, Bulletin 157, March 1915 (Washington, D.C.: Government Printing Office, 1915), 6.

148. "Boulder County Studies 1919–1921," *University of Colorado Bulletin* 21 (September 1921): 15 and 21.

149. "Accidents 1894–1919," A. A. Paddock Collection, CL Boulder; *Denver Catholic Register*, 21 Jan. 1908.

150. Hoffman, *Industrial Accident Statistics*, 6.

151. *Cripple Creek Times*, 6 Sept. 1912, 1.

152. *Cripple Creek Times*, 13 Aug. 1912, 1. Also see 30 July 1913, 2; 13 March 1914, 4; 6 Jan. 1918, 1; and 9 Sept. 1915, 5, all in the *Cripple Creek Times and Victor Daily Record*. Also see 24 Aug. 1912, 1; 10 Sept. 1912, 1; 5 Jan. 1913, 1; and 1 Jan. 1915, 5, all in the *Cripple Creek Times*.

153. Alan Derickson, *Workers' Health Workers' Democracy: The Western Miners' Struggle, 1891–1925* (Ithaca, N.Y.: Cornell University Press, 1988), 39–56. For an overview of silicosis see David Rosner and Gerald Markowitz, *Deadly Dust: Silicosis and the Politics of Occupational Disease in Twentieth-Century America* (Princeton, N.J.: Princeton University Press, 1991).

154. *Twelfth Biennial Report of the Bureau of Mines of the State of Colorado for Years 1911 and 1912* (Denver: Smith-Brooks, 1913), 126.

155. The Boulder and Teller figures come from a random sampling of every third female seventeen years and older from the 1910 census manuscripts. The exact figures for each county are 9.16 percent for Boulder and 9.57 percent for Teller.

156. *Thirteenth Census of the United States—Abstract of Census with Supplement for Colorado, 1910* (Washington, D.C.: Government Printing Office, 1913), 162 and 165.

157. Leanne Sander argues that widows from the Upper Clear Creek migrated to Denver to earn a living. Leanne Louise Sander, "'The Men All Died of Miners' Disease': Women and Families in the Industrial Mining Environment of Upper Clear Creek, Colorado, 1870–1900" (PhD dissertation, University of Colorado, Boulder, 1990).

158. *Denver Times*, 17 June 1900, 3.

159. Anne Ellis, *The Life of an Ordinary Woman* (1929; reprint, Boston: Houghton Mifflin Company, 1990), 204–10.

160. Julian Street, "Colorado Springs and Cripple Creek," *Collier's Weekly* 21 (November 1914): 30.

161. Elizabeth Jameson argues that "most adult women were economically dependent on male breadwinners" in the Cripple Creek Mining District in 1900. What I am arguing is that women, especially unmarried women, were less dependent in Teller than in Boulder. Jameson never provides a comparison to test if women in Teller were more or less dependent on male breadwinners than in other communities. Elizabeth Jameson, *All That Glitters: Class, Conflict, and Community in Cripple Creek* (Urbana: University of Illinois Press, 1998), 117.

162. *Abstract of the Fourteenth Census of the United States, 1920* (Washington, D.C.: Government Printing Office, 1923), 560.

Chapter Two

1. Frank J. Bruno, "Expert's Opinion on Denver Charity Work," *City of Denver*, 25 July 1914, 11, WHC/DPL; *Second Annual Report of the Social Welfare Department of the City and County of Denver for the Year Ending December 31, 1914*, 98, GP/DPL.

2. Frank J. Bruno, *Trends in Social Work as Reflected in the Proceedings of the National Conference of Social Work 1874–1946* (New York: Columbia University Press, 1948), 211.

3. Boris D. Bogen, "The 'Cincinnati Method' of Treating Consumption," *Charities and the Commons* 18 (13 July 1907): 418.

4. *Thirteenth Census of the United States, 1910*, vol. 2 (Washington, D.C.: Government Printing Office, 1913), 191.

5. *Minutes of the State Board of Charities and Corrections, 1914*, 355–56, Box 18626, State Archives.

6. Ibid., 9, 13, 152, 153, and 358.

7. Ibid., 9, 13, and 153. Also see David Brundage, *The Making of Western Labor Radicalism: Denver's Organized Workers, 1878–1905* (Urbana: University of Illinois Press, 1994), 20–21.

8. *Thirteenth Census, 1910*, vol. 2, 218.

9. Brundage, *Western Labor Radicalism*, 23.

10. Clyde Lyndon King, *The History of the Government of Denver with Special Reference to its Relations with Public Service Corporations* (Denver: Fisher Book Company, 1911), 199.

11. Robert L. Perkin, *The First Hundred Years: An Informal History of Denver and the Rocky Mountain News* (Garden City, N.Y.: Doubleday and Company, 1959), 407–8.

12. *Proceedings and Ordinances of the Denver City Council,* vol. R, 554, Denver City Building; *Proceedings and Ordinances for the City and County of Denver,* vol. T, 258, Denver City Building.

13. *Denver County Poor Reports,* 1906–1910, Box 4967A, State Archives.

14. "City Board of Charities and Corrections: Report for the Year 1912 of Outdoor Relief for the Poor," *City of Denver,* 31 May 1913, 1, WHC/DPL.

15. *Denver Post,* 1 Jan. 1912, 12.

16. Grace Eleanor Wilson, "The History and Development of the Denver Bureau of Public Welfare," 2, unpublished paper found at the Denver Department of Social Services' informal archives; author has a copy in his possession. Final version of the paper can also be found at Grace Eleanor Wilson, "The History and Development of the Denver Bureau of Public Welfare" (MA thesis, University of Denver, 1938).

17. *Denver Post,* 1 Jan. 1912, 12. For information about coal orders see Wilson, "History of the Denver Bureau of Public Welfare," 2.

18. "Report for the Year 1912 of Outdoor Relief," 4, WHC/DPL.

19. Ibid.

20. Ibid., 3; also see, *Denver Post,* 1 June 1913, sec. 1, 5.

21. Wilson, "History of the Denver Bureau of Public Welfare," 2.

22. *Denver Post,* 1 Jan. 1912, 12.

23. J. Paul Mitchell, "Municipal Reform in Denver: The Defeat of Mayor Speer," *Colorado Magazine* 45 (Winter 1968): 42–60; George Creel, *Rebel at Large: Recollections of Fifty Crowded Years* (New York: G. P. Putnam's Sons, 1947), 94–119; Ben B. Lindsey and Harvey J. O'Higgins, *The Beast* (New York: Doubleday, Page and Company, 1911).

24. William Bennett Munro, *The Government of American Cities,* 4th ed. (New York: Macmillian Company, 1930), 302–20.

25. Clinton Rogers Woodruff, "Fundamental Principles Involved in Commission Government," in *City Government by Commission,* ed. Clinton Rogers Woodruff (New York: D. Appleton and Company, 1911), 21–43.

26. Lyle W. Dorsett, *The Queen City: A History of Denver* (Boulder, Colo.: Pruett, 1977), 157–58.

27. Wilson, "History of the Denver Bureau of Public Welfare," 1. Wilson indicates that with the 1905 court decision blocking the merging of the city and county offices two separate sets of relief officials existed from 1905–1912. I have found no other evidence that corroborates the maintenance of separate city and county relief officials during this time.

28. Wilson, "History of the Denver Bureau of Public Welfare," 3; Harold A. Morse, "A Social History of the Department of Social Services" (1994): 28–29, in author's possession; *Bulletin*, September 1947, 2, Box 1, Gertrude Vaile Collection, Columbia Library; Bureau of Municipal Research, *Report on a Survey of the Department of Social Welfare of the City and County of Denver* (New York, 1914), 23, 75, and 76; Gertrude Vaile, "Principles and Methods of Outdoor Relief," in *Proceedings of the National Conference of Charities and Corrections, 1915* (Chicago: Hildmann Printing, 1915), 481.

29. *Denver Republican*, 8 Oct. 1912, 10.

30. William H. Byers, *Encyclopedia of Biography of Colorado: History of Colorado*, vol. 1 (Chicago: Century Publishing and Engraving Company, 1901), 237–39, quote 239; *Rocky Mountain News*, 23 Jan. 1924, 11.

31. *Rocky Mountain News*, 23 Jan. 1924, 11; Woman's Club of Denver, *Minutes of the Social Science Department, 1902–1903*, 7 and 18, CHS.

32. Woman's Club of Denver, *Minutes of the Meetings of the Executive Board of the Social Science Department, 1904–1906*, 1 and 7, CHS.

33. *Rocky Mountain News*, 23 Jan. 1924, 11 and 16 June 1925, 1; *Denver Republican*, 8 Oct. 1912, 10; Margaret E. Rice, "Gertrude Vaile, 1878–1954," *Social Casework* 35 (December 1954): 449; "Vaile, Gertrude (1878–1954)," in *Encyclopedia of Social Work*, vol. 15, ed. Harry L. Lurine (Albany, N.Y.: Boyd Printing, 1965), 807–8.

34. *Denver Republican*, 8 Oct. 1912, 10.

35. *Denver Republican*, 8 Nov. 1912, 10. Also see class bulletins (1901–1906, 1908–1909, and 1911–1912) from Vassar College, Box 1, the Gertrude Vaile Collection, Columbia Library.

36. Vaile first presented her ideas at a sociological conference at the University of Colorado in the summer of 1914. Several months later, the *Survey* presented Vaile's same ideas to a national audience by reprinting her original paper. Gertrude Vaile, "Some Social Problems of Public Outdoor Relief," *University of Colorado Bulletin* 14 (July 1914): 8–16; also reprinted with the same title in *Survey* 34 (3 March 1915): 15–17.

37. Vaile, "Principles of Outdoor Relief," 479–84.

38. Arthur P. Kellogg, "The Trend of the Times in Charity," *Survey* 34 (29 May 1915): 205.

39. "Report for the Year 1912 of Outdoor Relief," 4, WHC/DPL.

40. Quote, "Board of Charities and Corrections," *City of Denver*, 27 Dec. 1913, 8, WHC/DPL; Vaile, "Principles of Outdoor Relief," 480; *Minutes Board of Charities and Corrections, 1914*, 214, State Archives; "Report for the Year 1912 of Outdoor Relief," 4, WHC/DPL.

41. Bureau of Municipal Research, *Survey of the Department of Social Welfare*, 83; "Report for the Year 1912 of Outdoor Relief," 1, WHC/DPL.

42. Quote, Bureau of Municipal Research, *Survey of the Department of Social Welfare*, 83; *Minutes Board of Charities and Corrections, 1914*, 214, State Archives; "Report for the Year 1912 of Outdoor Relief," 5, WHC/DPL; "Board of Charities and Corrections," 8, WHC/DPL.

43. *First Annual Report of the Social Welfare Department of the City and County of Denver, Colorado, for the Year Ending December 31, 1913*, 70, GP/DPL.

44. Vaile, "Principles of Outdoor Relief," 480.

45. "Report for the Year 1912 of Outdoor Relief," 1 and 4, WHC/DPL.

46. Wilson, "History of the Denver Bureau of Public Welfare," 4–5 and 11–12; *Rocky Mountain News*, 6 June 1915, sec. 3, 6.

47. "Board of Charities and Corrections," 8–9, WHC/DPL; *Minutes Board of Charities and Corrections, 1914*, 214, State Archives; Vaile, "Principles of Outdoor Relief," 481.

48. Vaile, "Principles of Outdoor Relief," 481.

49. Wilson, "History of the Denver Bureau of Public Welfare," 4.

50. Robyn Muncy, *Creating a Female Dominion in American Reform 1890–1935* (New York: Oxford University Press, 1991).

51. Wilson, "History of the Denver Bureau of Public Welfare," 13 and 50.

52. Bruno, "Expert's Opinion," 11, WHC/DPL.

53. *Second Annual Report of the Social Welfare Department, 1914*, 97, GP/DPL.

54. Wilson, "History of the Denver Bureau of Public Welfare," 13.

55. "Report for the Year 1912 of Outdoor Relief," 1, WHC/DPL; *Denver Post*, 1 June 1913, sec. 1, 5.

56. *Denver Post*, 1 June 1913, sec. 1, 5.

57. "Report for the Year 1912 of Outdoor Relief," 1, WHC/DPL.

58. "Report for the Year 1912 of Outdoor Relief," 4, WHC/DPL; Bureau of Municipal Research, *Survey of the Department of Social Welfare*, 84; "Board of Charities and Corrections," 4, WHC/DPL; *Denver Post*, 24 Nov. 1912, sec. 3, 4.

59. *Denver Post*, 18 June 1913, 8.

60. *Denver Post*, 1 June 1913, sec. 1, 5.

61. "Board of Charities and Corrections," 6, WHC/DPL; "Report for the Year 1912 of Outdoor Relief," 4, WHC/DPL; *Denver Post*, 28 Jan. 1914, 6.

62. Teller County was the only community, besides Denver, that listed alcoholism and drug addiction as reasons for receiving public assistance. For the five years from 1899 to 1903, Teller spent over $6,600 on morphine and whiskey cures to end individual addictions. Teller's notorious red-light district fostered substance abuse and perpetuated addictions. As mining activity slowed and many red-light establishments closed, the problems of addiction declined but did not completely disappear.

63. Bureau of Municipal Research, *Survey of the Department of Social Welfare*, 86; *Second Annual Report of the Social Welfare Department, 1914*, 102, GP/DPL; "Report for the Year 1912 of Outdoor Relief," 4, WHC/DPL.

64. *First Annual Report of the Social Welfare Department ,1913*, 70, GP/DPL.

65. Wilson, "History of the Denver Bureau of Public Welfare," 13.

66. Bureau of Municipal Research, *Survey of the Department of Social Welfare*, 84–86.

67. Kellogg, "Trend of the Times in Charity," 206; Vaile, "Principles of Outdoor Relief," 482–84; Wilson, "History of the Denver Bureau of Public Welfare," 6.

68. *Minutes of the State Board of Charities and Corrections, 1915*, 59 and 135, Box 18626, State Archives. For a description of conditions that homeless men encountered before 1912 in Denver see Edwin A. Brown, *"Broke" The Man Without the Dime* (Boston: Four Seas Company, 1920), 3–27. For an examination of homelessness in the Midwest see Frank Tobias Higbie, *Indispensable Outcasts: Hobo Workers and Community in the American Midwest, 1880–1930* (Urbana: University of Illinois Press, 2003).

69. *Denver Times*, 3 Dec. 1914, [editorial page] and 4 Dec. 1914, [editorial page]; "Recommendations of Taxpayer Committee for 1915 Budget," 4 and 5, Box 1, Gertrude Vaile Collection, Columbia Library; Letter to *Rocky Mountain News*, 4 Aug. 1914, Box 1, Gertrude Vaile Collection, Columbia Library.

70. Wilson, "History of the Denver Bureau of Public Welfare," 8–9.

71. *Second Annual Report of the Social Welfare Department, 1914*, 96, GP/DPL.

72. The effect of wartime inflation on relief was not limited to Denver. See, John B. Dawson, "The Significance of the Rise in Relief-Giving During the Past Five Years," in *Proceedings of the National Conference of Social Work, 1922* (Chicago: University of Chicago Press, 1922), 228–36.

73. "Tuberculosis Subsidies Challenged in Colorado," *Survey* 35 (18 March 1916): 711.

74. Sheila M. Rothman, *Living in the Shadow of Death: Tuberculosis and the Social Experience of Illness in American History* (New York: Basic Books, 1994), 13 and 179–80; Richard Harrison Shryock, *National Tuberculosis Association, 1904–1954* (New York: National Tuberculosis Association, 1957), 25 and 62–63.

75. Rothman, *Living in the Shadow*, 184.

76. Elizabeth Dobell, "Some Impressions of a Seeker After Health," *Survey* 32 (8 August 1914): 480.

77. Ibid.

78. Ibid., 482.

79. Katherine Ott, *Fevered Lives: Tuberculosis in American Culture since 1870* (Cambridge, Mass.: Harvard University Press, 1996), 40.

80. Charles Denison, *Rocky Mountain Health Resorts: An Analytical Study of High Altitudes in Relation to the Arrest of Chronic Pulmonary Disease* (Boston: Houghton, Mifflin and Company, 1881); Charles Fox Gardiner, *The Care of the Consumptive* (New York: G. P. Putman's Sons, 1900); Thomas Crawford Galbreath, *Chasing the Cure in Colorado* (Denver: Thomas Crawford Galbreath, 1907).

81. Rothman, *Living in the Shadow*, 18–22 and 131–60.

82. Dobell, "Some Impressions," 479.

83. Jeanne Abrams, *Blazing the Tuberculosis Trail: The Religio-Ethnic Role of Four Sanatoria in Early Denver* (Denver: Colorado Historical Society, 1990); Alice Elizabeth Boggs, "The History and Development of the Tuberculosis Assistance Program in Colorado" (MA thesis, University of Denver, 1943), 9–16; Jeanne Abrams, "Chasing the Cure: A History of the Jewish Consumptives' Relief Society of Denver" (PhD dissertation, University of Colorado, Boulder, 1983), 1–56; James Giese, "Tuberculosis and the Growth of Denver's Eastern European Jewish Community: The Accommodation of an Immigrant Group to a Medium-Sized Western City, 1900–1920" (PhD dissertation, University of Colorado, Boulder, 1979), 101–52.

84. Abrams, *Blazing the Tuberculosis Trail*, 23, 59, and 67–71; *Minutes of the State Board of Charities and Corrections, 1915*, 174 and 179, State Archives; Boggs, "Tuberculosis Assistance Program in Colorado," 14; *First Annual Report of the Social Welfare Department, 1913*, 59 and 75, GP/DPL; "Annual Report of the Denver Anti-Tuberculosis Society for 1919," 2, WHC/DPL.

85. Dobell, "Some Impressions," 482.

86. Edward T. Devine, "Denver's Tuberculosis Problem," *Survey* 42 (24 May 1919): 320.

87. *First Annual Report of the Social Welfare Department, 1913*, 71, GP/DPL.

88. Jessamine S. Whitney, *A Report on the Indigent Migratory Consumptive in Certain Cities of the Southwest*, Treasury Department, Public Health Reports, vol. 38, no. 12, 23 March 1923, 588–89.

89. Gertrude Vaile, "Federal Aid for Consumptives: Would the Kent Bill Help?" *Survey* 37 (30 December 1916): 354.

90. Wilson, "History of the Denver Bureau of Public Welfare," 13.

91. *Twelfth Annual Report of the Charity Organization Society of Denver, Colorado, November 1, 1899*, 6, WHC/DPL.

92. *Denver Times*, 18 Sept. 1902, 12.

93. *Second Annual Report of the Social Welfare Department, 1914*, 100, GP/DPL.

94. Denver's Jewish leaders quickly understood that the movement of indigent tubercular sufferers required special attention. The National Jewish Hospital required that each of its patients obtain a sponsor, an individual or a charity society, which guaranteed to pay for the return of the patient or to support the patient if he or she decided to remain in Colorado after being discharged. In addition, the National Conference of Jewish Charities adopted a series of "Transportation Rules" to define residency, transiency, and local responsibility for charity care. Even with these safeguards in place, the influx of indigent tubercular sufferers still strained Denver's Jewish community, and differences still arose over which communities were responsible for discharged patients. See Garfield A. Berlinsky, "The Story of the Opposition of the National Jewish Hospital for Consumptives to the Local Jewish Charities of Denver" (1915): 4, WHC/DPL; Giese, "Tuberculosis and the Growth of Denver's Eastern European Jewish Community," 355–408; Moses Collins, "How the Jewish People Care for Their Consumptive Poor," *Jewish Outlook*, 21 July 1905, 3.

95. First quote, Letter from the State Board of Charities and Corrections, 2 January 1912, Box 10154, State Archives; second quote, Rev. Dr. W. S. Friedman, "The Wrong of Sending Advanced Consumptives Away From Home," in *Proceedings of the National Conference of Charities and Correction, 1909* (Fort Wayne, Ind.: Fort Wayne Printing, 1909), 208.

96. "Annual Report of the Denver Anti-Tuberculosis Society for 1919," 2–3, WHC/DPL.

97. Senate Committee on Public Health and National Quarantine, *To Provide Federal Aid in Caring for Indigent Tuberculous Persons and for other Purposes*, 64th Cong., 1st sess., Rept. 746, Serial Set 6899, 8.

98. "Not Consumptives' Utopia," *Survey* 28 (20 July 1912): 569.

99. "Discussion on Tuberculosis," in *Proceedings of the National Conference of Charities and Corrections, 1899* (Boston: George H. Ellis, 1900), 345–46.

100. Frank M. Bruno, "A National Sanatorium for the Tuberculous," in *Proceedings of the National Conference of Charities and Corrections, 1908* (Fort Wayne, Ind.: Fort Wayne Printing, 1908), 140–44.

101. "The Problem of Poor Lungers Who Go West," *Survey* 32 (18 April 1914): 67.

102. Theda Skocpol, *Protecting Soldiers and Mothers: The Political Origins of Social Policy in the United States* (Cambridge, Mass.: Harvard University Press, 1992).

103. Philip King Brown, "Interstate Traffic in Tuberculosis: The Argument for the Kent Bill," *Survey* 36 (29 July 1916): 459.

104. Robert J. Newton, "On the Other Hand An Affirmative Answer to the Question: 'Will the Kent Bill Help?'" *Survey* 37 (10 February 1917): 547.

105. First quote, Vaile, "Federal Aid for Consumptives," 354; "Tuberculosis Subsidies," *Survey* 35 (18 March 1916): 711; second quote, Gertrude Vaile, Letter to the Editor, *Survey* 37 (17 March 1917): 702.

106. *Rocky Mountain News*, 26 March 1916; Gertrude Vaile memo, 2 March 1916, Box 1, Gertrude Vaile Collection, Columbia Library.

107. Quote, "Tuberculosis Subsidies," *Survey* 35 (18 March 1916): 711; Vaile, "Federal Aid for Consumptives," 355.

108. Newton, "On the Other Hand," 548.

109. Quote, Gertrude Vaile, "Interstate Control of Tuberculosis: Will the Kent Bill Help?" Twelfth Annual Meeting of the National Association for the Study and Prevention of Tuberculosis, 9; also see "Settlement Law as an Element in the Solution of the Problem of Migratory Tuberculosis;" "The Need of Uniform Laws of Settlement;" and Gertrude Vaile to the Transportation Committee, 20 February 1915; all in Box 1, Gertrude Vaile Collection, Columbia Library.

110. Quote, Vaile, "Federal Aid for Consumptives," 356; Newton, "On the Other Hand," 548.

111. Senate Committee on Public Health, *Federal Aid in Caring for Indigent Tuberculous Persons*, 6.

112. Brown, "Interstate Traffic in Tuberculosis," 459–60.

113. Ibid., 459.

114. Newton, "On the Other Hand," 546.

115. "Annual Report of the Denver Anti-Tuberculosis Society for 1919," 1–2, WHC/DPL.

Chapter Three

1. *Minutes of the State Board of Charities and Corrections, 1913*, 259, Box 18626, State Archives.

2. *Minutes of the State Board of Charities and Corrections, December 12, 1916 to November 12, 1918*, 223–24, Box 18626, State Archives.

3. *Articles of Incorporation and Constitution and By-Laws of the Associated Charities of Boulder* (Boulder, Colo., 1913), 21, CL Boulder.

4. For some examples of the division of social welfare history, see Beverly Stadum, *Poor Women and Their Families: Hard Working Charity Cases, 1900–1930* (Albany: State University of New York Press, 1992); Robyn Muncy, *Creating a Female Dominion in American Reform 1890–1935* (New York: Oxford University Press, 1991); Theda Skocpol, *Protecting Soldiers and Mothers: The Political Origins of Social Policy in the United States* (Cambridge, Mass.: Harvard University Press, 1992); Peggy Pascoe, *Relations of Rescue: The Search for Female Moral Authority in the American West, 1874–1939* (New York: Oxford University Press, 1990); Molly Ladd-Taylor, *Mother-Work: Women, Child*

Welfare, and the State, 1890–1930 (Urbana: University of Illinois Press, 1994); Joanne L. Goodwin, *Gender and the Politics of Welfare Reform: Mothers' Pensions in Chicago, 1911–1929* (Chicago: University of Chicago Press, 1997); Gwendolyn Mink, *The Wages of Motherhood: Inequality in the Welfare State, 1917–1942* (Ithaca, N.Y.: Cornell University Press, 1995); Linda Gordon, *Pitied But Not Entitled: Single Mothers and the History of Welfare* (New York: Free Press, 1994); Linda Gordon, ed., *Women, the State, and Welfare* (Madison: University of Wisconsin Press, 1990); Seth Koven and Sonya Michel, eds., *Mothers of a New World: Maternalist Politics and the Origins of Welfare States* (New York: Routledge, 1993); David J. Rothman, *Conscience and Convenience: The Asylum and Its Alternatives in Progressive America* (Boston: Little, Brown, 1980); Timothy A. Hacsi, *Second Home: Orphan Asylums and Poor Families in America* (Cambridge, Mass.: Harvard University Press, 1997); Matthew A. Crenson, *Building the Invisible Orphanage: A Prehistory of the American Welfare System* (Cambridge, Mass.: Harvard University Press, 1998).

5. Michael B. Katz, *Improving Poor People: the Welfare State, the "Underclass," and Urban Schools as History* (Princeton, N.J.: Princeton University Press, 1995), 5.

6. Glen R. Durrell, "Homesteading in Colorado," *Colorado Magazine* 51 (Spring 1974): 96; see also James E. Fell, Jr., *Limon, Colorado Hub City of the High Plains 1888–1952* (Boulder, Colo.: Limon Heritage Society, 1997), 12–13.

7. Dale Cooley and Mary Liz Owen, eds., *Where the Wagons Rolled: The History of Lincoln County and the People Who Came Before 1925* (Limon: Eastern Colorado Printery, 1985), 67, for information on other churches in Lincoln County see pages 26, 68, 94, 117, 132–33, and 177; also see Laura Solze Claggett, ed., *History of Lincoln County, Colorado* (Dallas, Tex.: Curtis Media Corporation, 1987), 16–23.

8. Ira S. Freeman, *A History of Montezuma County Colorado: Land of Promise and Fulfillment* (Boulder, Colo.: Johnson Publishing, 1958), 40, 68, and 69.

9. Esther Johnson, "Karval, Colorado," *Colorado Magazine* 6 (March 1929): 64.

10. For some examples of social gatherings in Lincoln County, see Durrell, "Homesteading," 101–10.

11. *Thirteenth Census of the United States—Abstract of Census with Supplement for Colorado, 1910* (Washington, D.C.: Government Printing Office, 1913), 586; Colorado Board of Immigration, *Year Book of the State of Colorado, 1922* (Denver: Eames Brothers, 1922), 116–21.

12. Cooley and Owen, *Wagons Rolled*, 68; Claggett, *History of Lincoln County*, 16–17.

13. David William Lantis, "The San Luis Valley, Colorado: Sequent Rural Occupance in an Intermontane Basin" (PhD dissertation, Ohio State University, 1950), 147.

14. Frances Leon Swadesh, *Los Primeros Pobladores: Hispanic Americans of the Ute Frontier* (Notre Dame, Ind.: University of Notre Dame Press, 1974), 147.

15. Durrell, "Homesteading," 106.

16. *Fifth Biennial Report of the State Board of Charities and Corrections, 1900* (Denver: Smith-Brooks, 1901), 76.

17. U.S. Bureau of the Census, *Paupers in Almshouses, 1910* (Washington, D.C.: Government Printing Office, 1915), 13. This same pattern of an absence of poor farms is also evident in the heavily Hispanic regions of Texas along the Mexican border. See Debbie Mauldin Cottrell, "The County Poor Farm System in Texas," *Southwestern Historical Quarterly* 93 (October 1989): 173–74 and 178.

18. *Costilla County Poor Book*, vol. 1, 5–9 and vol. 2, 13, Costilla Courthouse.

19. *Costilla County Commissioners Records*, vol. 6, 422–23, Costilla Courthouse.

20. *Lincoln County Poor Record*, 1909–1922, Lincoln Courthouse; *Montezuma County Poor Records*, 1901–1919, Montezuma Courthouse.

21. *Lincoln County Poor Record*, 2, 4, 5, 9, and 17, Lincoln Courthouse.

22. *Montezuma County Poor Records*, 6, Montezuma Courthouse.

23. Atherton was sent to the National Home for Disabled Volunteer Soldiers, *Montezuma County Commissioners Records*, vol. 2, 87, Montezuma Courthouse; *Montezuma County Commissioners Records*, vol. 4, 28, Montezuma Courthouse.

24. Robert A. Trennert, *White Man's Medicine: Government Doctors and the Navajo, 1863–1955* (Albuquerque: University of New Mexico Press, 1998), 1.

25. *Superintendents' Annual Narrative and Statistical Reports, 1910*, 318, Navajo Springs, Microfilm Publication Reel 90, RG 75, NARA.

26. *Superintendents' Annual Narrative and Statistical Reports, 1911*, 336, Navajo Springs, Microfilm Publication Reel 90, RG 75, NARA.

27. *Superintendents' Annual Narrative and Statistical Reports, 1917*, 3, Ute Mountain, Microfilm Publication Reel 161, RG 75, NARA.

28. *Superintendents' Annual Narrative and Statistical Reports, 1922*, 73 and 74, Ute Mountain, Microfilm Publication Reel 161, RG 75, NARA.

29. Marvin Kaufmann Opler, "The Southern Ute of Colorado," in *Acculturation in Seven American Tribes*, ed. Ralph Linton (New York: D. Appleton-Century, 1940), 195.

30. Diane T. Putney, "Fighting the Scourge: American Indian Morbidity and Federal Policy, 1897–1928" (PhD dissertation, Marquette University, 1980), 55.

31. S. F. Stacher, "The Indians of the Ute Mountain Reservation, 1906–9," *Colorado Magazine* 26 (January 1949): 54.

32. *Superintendents' Reports, 1911*, 336, Reel 90, RG75, NARA.

33. Stacher, "Indians of Ute Mountain Reservation," 54; *Superintendents' Reports, 1911*, 336, Reel 90, RG 75, NARA.

34. *Superintendents' Reports, 1910*, 318, Reel 90, RG 75, NARA; *Report of Special Indian Agent W. W. McConihe on the Inspection of the Ute Mountain School and Agency and Reservation, August 1, 1916*, 27, Box 2, Central Classified Files 1907–1939, Ute Mountain, RG 75, National Archives I, Washington, D.C.; *Superintendents' Annual Narrative and Statistical Reports, 1920*, 897, Ute Mountain, Microfilm Publication Reel 161, RG 75, NARA.

35. *Superintendents' Annual Narrative and Statistical Reports, 1917*, 847, Ute Mountain, Microfilm Publication Reel 161, RG 75, NARA.

36. Frances Leon Swadesh, "The Southern Utes and Their Neighbors 1877–1926: An Ethnohistorical Study of Multiple Interaction in Contact-Induced Culture Change" (MA thesis, University of Colorado, Boulder, 1962), 166–70.

37. Stacher, "Indians of Ute Mountain Reservation," 54–55.

38. *Superintendents' Annual Narrative and Statistical Reports, 1916*, 824, Ute Mountain, Microfilm Publication Reel 161, RG 75, NARA; *Superintendents' Annual Narrative and Statistical Reports, 1918*, 873, Ute Mountain, Microfilm Publication Reel 161, RG 75, NARA.

39. *Superintendents' Annual Narrative and Statistical Reports, 1925*, 148, Consolidated Ute, Microfilm Publication Reel 29, RG 75, NARA; Robert A. Trennert does not raise this issue of competency in his study of government doctors and the Navajo people despite mentioning the work of Dr. Albert Wigglesworth who was hardworking, spoke the Navajo language, and "had created a special bond with his patients," see Trennert, *White Man's Medicine*, 128–29.

40. *Tenth Biennial Report of the State Board of Charities and Corrections of Colorado, 1910* (Denver: Smith-Brooks, 1910), 93.

41. *Minutes Board of Charities and Corrections, 1916 to 1918*, 223, State Archives.

42. Alan Derickson, *Workers' Health Workers' Democracy: The Western Miners' Struggle, 1891–1925* (Ithaca, N.Y.: Cornell University Press, 1988), 63. In Cleveland, Ohio, changes in policy resulted in the removal of women from the poorhouse during the late-nineteenth century. See Marian J. Morton, *And Sin No More: Social Policy and Unwed Mothers in Cleveland, 1855–1990* (Columbus: Ohio State University Press, 1993), 31–34. For more changes in poor farm policies see Bruce Smith, "Poor Relief at the St. Joseph County Poor Asylum, 1877–1891," *Indiana Magazine of History* 86 (June 1990): 178–96 and Elna C. Green, *This Business of Relief: Confronting Poverty in a Southern City, 1740–1940* (Athens: University of Georgia Press, 2003). David Wagner's *The Poorhouse: America's Forgotten Institution* (Lanham, MD: Rowman & Littlefield Publishers, 2005) does address the changing nature of poorhouses and poor farms.

43. Michael B. Katz, *In the Shadow of the Poorhouse: A Social History of Welfare in America* (New York: Basic Books, 1986), 3–35; David J. Rothman, *The Discovery of the Asylum: Social Order and Disorder in the New Republic* (Boston: Little, Brown and Company, 1971), 180–205; Simon P. Newman, *Embodied History: The Lives of the Poor in Early Philadelphia* (Philadelphia: University of Pennsylvania Press, 2003), 16–39.

44. *Minutes of the State Board of Charities and Corrections, 1911,* 116, Box 18626, State Archives; for other examples see *Minutes of the State Board of Charities and Corrections, 1912,* 82, Box 18626, State Archives; *Minutes of the State Board of Charities and Corrections, 1915,* 38, Box 18626, State Archives; *Minutes Board of Charities and Corrections, 1916 to 1918,* 223 and 139, State Archives.

45. Bureau of Municipal Research, *Report on a Survey of the Department of Social Welfare of the City and County of Denver* (New York, 1914), 81.

46. *Denver Municipal Facts,* 3 February 1912, 15, WHC/DPL.

47. *Thirteenth Biennial Report of the State Board of Charities and Corrections of Colorado* (Denver: Eames Brothers, 1916), 35.

48. *Montezuma County Commissioners Records,* vol. 3, 39, Montezuma Courthouse.

49. Freeman, *History of Montezuma County,* 267.

50. *Montezuma County Commissioners Records,* vol. 3, 67, Montezuma Courthouse.

51. *Montezuma County Commissioners Records,* vol. 3, 169, 178, 182, 212, 221, 227, 245, 266, and 459, Montezuma Courthouse.

52. *Montezuma Journal,* 13 August 1914, 2.

53. *Montezuma Journal,* 20 August 1914, 2. Also see 27 August 1914, 1–2; 14 January 1915, 2; 28 October 1915, 2; 27 January 1916, 1, all in the *Montezuma Journal.*

54. *Montezuma Journal,* 9 November 1916, 2.

55. *Minutes of the State Board of Charities and Corrections, 1914,* 295, Box 18626, State Archives.

56. *Minutes Board of Charities and Corrections, 1914,* 335, State Archives.

57. First quote, *Montezuma Journal,* 20 August 1914, 2; second quote, *Montezuma Journal,* 27 August 1914, 2.

58. *Minutes of the State Board of Charities and Corrections, 1916,* 241, Box 18626, State Archives.

59. *Minutes Board of Charities and Corrections, 1914,* 262, State Archives.

60. *Montezuma County Commissioners Records,* vol. 3, 123, Montezuma Courthouse.

61. *Minutes Board of Charities and Corrections, 1916,* 241, State Archives. This notion of poor farm residents not wanting interference from officials can also be seen in Philadelphia's almshouse. See Newman, *Embodied History,* 36–39.

62. *Twelfth Biennial Report of the State Board of Charities and Corrections of Colorado* (Denver: Smith-Brooks, 1914), 59; *Fourteenth Biennial Report of the State Board of Charities and Corrections of Colorado* (Denver: Eames Brothers, 1918), 58.

63. *Minutes Board of Charities and Corrections, 1915*, 191, State Archives.

64. *Minutes Board of Charities and Corrections, 1914*, 295, State Archives; *Minutes Board of Charities and Corrections, 1916*, 241, State Archives.

65. *Montezuma County Commissioners Records*, vol. 3, 150, Montezuma Courthouse.

66. Sanford Charles Gladden, *The Early Days of Boulder Colorado*, 1572–1580, vol. 2, CL Boulder; Anne Quinby Dyni, "History of Boulder County Poor Farm and Hospital," 1–11, CL Boulder; Anne Quinby Dyni, "Historic Time Line for Boulder County Poor Farm," 1–5, CL Boulder.

67. Quote, *Minutes of the State Board of Charities and Corrections, 1918*, 223, Box 18626, State Archives; *Minutes Board of Charities and Corrections, 1913*, 259, State Archives.

68. *Minutes Board of Charities and Corrections, 1915*, 257, State Archives.

69. *Sixth Biennial Report of the State Board of Charities and Corrections* (Denver: Smith-Brooks, 1903), 105–6.

70. Reports from the State Board of Charities and Corrections vary as to how many beds were available at Boulder's poor farm. The 1912 report lists 34 beds, the 1914 report lists 19 beds, and the 1916 report lists 18 beds. *Eleventh Biennial Report of the State Board of Charities and Corrections* (Denver: Smith-Brooks, 1912), 89; *Twelfth Report Board of Charities and Corrections*, 59; *Thirteenth Report Board of Charities and Corrections*, 54.

71. *Boulder County Pauper Book*, vols. 1–4, Boulder Courthouse. Data for 1917 is missing.

72. *Boulder County Pauper Book*, vols. 1–4, Boulder Courthouse.

73. *Minutes Board of Charities and Corrections, 1912*, 82, State Archives; *Minutes Board of Charities and Corrections, 1915*, 257, State Archives.

74. *Minutes Board of Charities and Corrections, 1915*, 257, State Archives.

75. *Minutes Board of Charities and Corrections, 1912*, 82, State Archives.

76. *Minutes Board of Charities and Corrections, 1913*, 259, State Archives.

77. *Minutes Board of Charities and Corrections, 1918*, 223, State Archives.

78. Michael B. Katz, *Poverty and Policy in American History* (New York: Academic Press, 1983), 89; see also Derickson, *Workers' Health*, 62–63.

79. Nell Jones, oral history interview by Stephanie Widener, 1976, tape 164, CL Boulder.

80. Ruth Kinney, oral history interview with author, 13 May 1999, Boulder, Colorado.

81. The original contract stated that the county would receive one free bed and University Hospital staff would also oversee the medical needs of county poor farm residents. In 1902, university regents and county commissioners agreed to change this clause, dropping the oversight of the poor farm in exchange for one additional free bed. *University of Colorado Regents Minutes*, 13 April 1898 to 18 January 1911, the contract is located inside the back cover, 19–22, 89–91, and 97, UC Archives; William E. Davis, *Glory Colorado! A History of the University of Colorado 1858–1963* (Boulder, Colo.: Pruett, 1965), 113.

82. *Minutes of the State Board of Charities and Corrections, 1908–1910,* 294, Box 66917, State Archives; *Tenth Report of State Board of Charities and Corrections*, 94.

83. *University Regents Minutes*, 13 April 1898 to 18 January 1911, contract located inside the back cover, UC Archives.

84. "Boulder County Studies 1919–1921," *University of Colorado Bulletin* 21 (9 September 1921): 27 and 33.

85. Davis, *Glory Colorado*, 155–161; Frederick S. Allen and others, *The University of Colorado 1876–1976* (New York: Harcourt Brace Jovanovich, 1976), 60–62. By 1920, university officials openly acknowledged that the hospital was of little use to them. See, President's Office, Folder 5, Box 21, UC Archives.

86. *Minutes Board of Charities and Corrections, 1916 to 1918,* 223, State Archives.

87. "Report of the Investigator for the State Board of Charities and Corrections," 12 July 1921, 32, Box 26959, State Archives.

88. Elizabeth Jameson, *All That Glitters: Class, Conflict, and Community in Cripple Creek* (Urbana: University of Illinois Press, 1998), 76 and 265.

89. Ibid., 87.

90. Ibid., 91.

91. Ibid. Labor unions also played an important role in helping needy miners in eastern portions of Boulder County, see *Minutes Board of Charities and Corrections, 1908–1910,* 294, State Archives.

92. Anne Ellis, *The Life of an Ordinary Woman* (1929; reprint, Boston: Houghton Mifflin Company, 1990), 205–6. For an overview of the importance of fraternal societies see David T. Beito, *From Mutual Aid to the Welfare State: Fraternal Societies and Social Services, 1890–1967* (Chapel Hill: University of North Carolina Press, 2000). Also see Beatrix Hoffman, *The Wages of Sickness: The Politics of Health Insurance in Progressive America* (Chapel Hill: University of North Carolina Press, 2001), 9–18.

93. Jameson, *All That Glitters*, 114–25.

94. *Evening Telegraph*, 17 February 1902, 1.

95. Marshall Sprague, *Money Mountain: The Story of Cripple Creek Gold* (Lincoln: University of Nebraska Press, 1953), 213–15.

96. Ibid., 194–95.

97. Frank Waters, *Midas of the Rockies: The Story of Stratton and Cripple Creek*, 3rd ed. (Chicago: Sage Books, 1949), 152–53; *Denver Times*, 15 September 1902, 4; *Cripple Creek Times*, 10 July 1912, 2.

98. *Minutes of the State Board of Charities and Corrections, 1898–1904*, 1 May 1901, page 2 of letter, Box 66917, State Archives.

99. C. L. Stonaker, "Colorado State Conference of Charities," *Charities* 8 (1 March 1902): 236; *Morning Times-Citizen*, 19 February 1902, 1 and 5 and 25 February 1902, 5.

100. The exact opening date of Teller County's hospital is a bit unclear. County commissioners accepted the completed building on April 16, 1902 and stated that it was "now ready for occupancy." But the only newspaper account of the opening puts the commencement date on May 13, 1902. See *Teller County Commissioner Records*, 316–17, vol. 2, Teller Courthouse; *Denver Times*, 13 May 1902, 7.

101. *Minutes Board of Charities and Corrections, 1911*, 172, State Archives; *Minutes Board of Charities and Corrections, 1913*, 264, State Archives.

102. Sprague, *Money Mountain*, 229. Stratton's will continued his generosity by using the bulk of his estate, worth six million dollars, to establish and maintain a home for aged poor and dependent children of El Paso County. He named the home for his father, Myron Stratton. Yet, because the state had carved Teller County largely out of El Paso County in 1899 and because Stratton had not rewritten his will to reflect this change, Teller's citizens could not take advantage of the Myron Stratton Home in Colorado Springs. See, Waters, *Midas of the Rockies*, 277–325; Sprague, *Money Mountain*, 229–31; Jameson, *All That Glitters*, 47.

103. Robert Guilford Taylor, *Cripple Creek* (Bloomington: Indiana University Press, 1966), 10.

104. Ibid., 125.

105. *Thirteenth Census of the United States, Abstract*, 604; *Fifteenth Biennial Report of the State of Colorado Bureau of Mines, 1917–1918* (Denver: Eames Brothers, 1919), 197.

106. Jameson, *All That Glitters*, 199–225 and 241–42.

107. *Minutes Board of Charities and Corrections, 1913*, 264, State Archives. State reports list various numbers of beds in the Teller County Hospital. See *Tenth Report of State Board of Charities and Corrections*, 93; *Eleventh Report Board of Charities and Corrections*, 89; *Twelfth Report Board of Charities and Corrections*, 58; *Thirteenth Report Board of Charities and Corrections*, 54.

108. *Teller County Poor Reports*, 1909, 1910, and 1912–1919, Boxes 4967A and 4968A, State Archives.

109. *Cripple Creek Times and Victor Daily Record*, 10 May 1914, 11–12, quotes on 12; *Cripple Creek Times*, 2 October 1914, 2.

110. *Cripple Creek Times and Victor Daily Record*, 18 December 1918, 2; also see 19 October 1918, 4; 21 October 1918, 8; and 1 November 1918, 2, all in the *Cripple Creek Times and Victor Daily Record*.

111. *Cripple Creek Times and Victor Daily Record*, 1 November 1918, 2; *Teller County Poor Reports*, 1912–1920, State Archives.

112. Quote from Bureau of Municipal Research, *Survey of the Department of Social Welfare*, 108; see also 101–7 for information about Steele Hospital.

113. "Municipal Lodging House," *City of Denver*, 21 December 1912, 14, WHC/DPL; John W. Ford, "Consecrated to the Uplift of Humanity," *City of Denver*, 21 December 1912, 1 and 4, WHC/DPL.

114. *Minutes Board of Charities and Corrections, 1913*, 28, State Archives.

115. *Second Annual Report of the Social Welfare Department, 1914*, 104, GP/DPL.

116. *Minutes Board of Charities and Corrections, 1913*, 28, State Archives; *Minutes Board of Charities and Corrections, 1914*, 232, State Archives; *Second Annual Report of the Social Welfare Department 1914*, 104, GP/DPL; *First Annual Report of the Social Welfare Department of the City and County of Denver, Colorado, for the Year Ending December 31, 1913*, 73, GP/DPL; "Board of Charities and Corrections," *City of Denver*, 27 December 1913, 6, WHC/DPL.

117. *Second Annual Report of the Social Welfare Department, 1914*, 104, GP/DPL.

118. "City Board of Charities and Corrections: Report for the Year 1912 of Outdoor Relief for the Poor," *City of Denver*, 31 May 1913, 4, WHC/DPL.

119. *Minutes Board of Charities and Corrections, 1913*, 28, State Archives.

120. Ibid.

121. Ibid.; *Second Annual Report of the Social Welfare Department, 1914*, 104, GP/DPL; *Minutes Board of Charities and Corrections, 1914*, 232, State Archives.

122. *Minutes Board of Charities and Corrections, 1914*, 232, State Archives.

123. The practice of providing breakfast as well as requiring work of lodgers was not unusual. Private charities that operated lodging houses or wayfarers' lodges in other parts of the nation followed similar policies. See Kenneth L. Kusmer, *Down and Out, on the Road: The Homeless in American History* (New York: Oxford University Press, 2002), 74. Others argue that municipal lodging houses had little influence on homeless men's lives since most homeless men avoided these municipal lodging houses. See John C. Schneider, "Homeless Men and Housing Policy in Urban America, 1850–1920," *Urban Studies* 26 (February 1989): 90–99 and Todd Depastino, *Citizen Hobo: How a Century of Homelessness Shaped America* (Chicago: University of Chicago Press, 2003), 132–35.

124. *Denver Directory, 1913* (Denver: Ballenger and Richards, 1913), 1356; *Denver Directory, 1914* (Denver: Ballenger and Richards, 1914), 19 and 1361; *Denver Directory, 1915* (Denver: Will H. Richards, 1915), 19 and 1354; *Denver Directory, 1916* (Denver: Will H. Richards, 1916), 17 and 1367; *Denver Directory, 1917* (Denver: Will H. Richards, 1917), 15 and 1384; *Denver Directory, 1918* (Denver: Will H. Richards, 1918), 15 and 1436; *Denver Directory, 1919* (Denver: Gazetteer Publishing, 1919), 15 and 1499; *Denver Directory, 1920* (Denver: Gazetteer Publishing, 1920), 7 and 1627; *Denver Directory, 1921* (Denver: Gazetteer Publishing, 1921), 7.

125. *Second Annual Report of the Social Welfare Department, 1914,* 104, GP/DPL; Bureau of Municipal Research, *Survey of the Department of Social Welfare,* 93.

126. Bureau of Municipal Research, *Survey of the Department of Social Welfare,* 93.

127. *Denver Post,* 20 November 1912, 13; Bureau of Municipal Research, *Survey of the Department of Social Welfare,* 93.

128. *Second Annual Report of the Social Welfare Department, 1914,* 105, GP/DPL.

129. Izetta George, "Denver's Plan," in *Proceedings of the National Conference of Charities and Corrections, 1894* (Boston: George H. Ellis, 1894), 57. This practice of requiring those receiving assistance to work became increasingly more common and formalized during the 1870s and 1880s as wage labor and contract relations assumed supremacy according to Amy Dru Stanley in *From Bondage to Contract: Wage Labor, Marriage, and the Market in the Age of Slave Emancipation* (New York: Cambridge University Press, 1998), 98–137. Also see C. G. Truesdell, "Treatment of the Poor in Cities," *Chautauquan* 15 (1892): 183–87.

130. *Rocky Mountain News,* 21 July 1887, 8.

131. *Denver Post,* 20 November 1912, 13.

132. *Denver Directory, 1918,* 15 and 1436.

133. *Denver Times,* 16 April 1899, 4.

134. *Minutes Board of Charities and Corrections, 1916 to 1918,* 138, State Archives.

135. First quote, "County Farm Survey," *Municipal Facts,* December 1918, 15, WHC/DPL; other quotes, *First Annual Report of the Social Welfare Department,* 75, GP/DPL.

136. *First Annual Report of the Social Welfare Department,* 75, GP/DPL.

137. *Minutes Board of Charities and Corrections, 1916 to 1918,* 13, State Archives.

138. *Minutes Board of Charities and Corrections, 1916 to 1918,* 138–39, State Archives. Fulton and Walling may have overstated the quality of meals at the poor farm. By today's standards, a sample menu from 1925 shows a diet heavy in starches with few fruits or vegetables. See "The Denver Farm Prospers," *Municipal Facts,* November–December 1925, 17, WHC/DPL.

139. *Denver Times,* 16 April 1899, 4.

140. *Eighth Biennial Report of the State Board of Charities and Corrections* (Denver: Smith-Brooks, 1906), 154.

141. "How County Commissioners Conduct the County Institutions," *Denver Municipal Facts*, 4 December 1909, 5, WHC/DPL.

142. "Poor Farm," *Denver Municipal Facts*, 3 February 1912, 15, WHC/DPL.

143. Bureau of Municipal Research, *Survey of the Department of Social Welfare*, 78.

144. *Minutes Board of Charities and Corrections, 1915*, 39, State Archives.

145. Bureau of Municipal Research, *Survey of the Department of Social Welfare*, 78–79. Please note that because of fluctuating occupancy, the total number of poor farm residents is constantly changing.

146. Ford, "Consecrated to the Uplift of Humanity," 4.

147. *Second Annual Report of the Social Welfare Department, 1914*, 109, GP/DPL.

148. *Thirteenth Report Board of Charities and Corrections*, 35.

149. "Board of Charities and Corrections," 5; *Minutes Board of Charities and Corrections, 1914*, 215, State Archives. The city spent more money on the new barn ($25,000) than on the new dormitory and hospital ward ($5,000).

150. *Second Annual Report of the Social Welfare Department, 1914*, 109, GP/DPL.

151. *Rocky Mountain News*, 21 November 1925, 3; Bureau of Municipal Research, *Survey of the Department of Social Welfare*, 78–79; *Minutes Board of Charities and Corrections, 1916 to 1918*, 139, State Archives.

152. *Rocky Mountain News*, 21 November 1925, 3.

153. *Second Annual Report of the Social Welfare Department, 1914*, 77, GP/DPL.

154. T. M. Hunter, "The County Hospital," *Municipal Facts Monthly*, August 1920, 17, WHC/DPL.

155. Quote, *Second Annual Report of the Social Welfare Department, 1914*, 77, also see 78–79, GP/DPL; Bureau of Municipal Research, *Survey of the Department of Social Welfare*, 109–20; *Minutes Board of Charities and Corrections, 1914*, 108 and 118–20, State Archives; *Minutes Board of Charities and Corrections, 1913*, 25, State Archives.

156. "How County Commissioners Conduct the County Institutions," 5, WHC/DPL.

157. *Minutes Board of Charities and Corrections, 1914*, 119, State Archives.

158. *Second Annual Report of the Social Welfare Department, 1914*, 118, GP/DPL.

159. "The City and County Hospital," *City of Denver*, 9 November 1912, 5, WHC/DPL.

160. *Minutes Board of Charities and Corrections, 1913*, 25, State Archives.

161. Quotes, Bureau of Municipal Research, *Survey of the Department of Social Welfare*, 117; *Second Annual Report of the Social Welfare Department, 1914*, 78–79, GP/DPL; *First Annual Report of the Social Welfare Department*, 54, GP/DPL.

162. *Tenth Report Board of Charities and Corrections*, 83–84.

163. *Twelfth Report Board of Charities and Corrections,* 37. Denver's burden became so great that the city and county sued the state. See the *Eighteenth Biennial Report of the Board of Lunacy Commissioners of the Colorado Insane Asylum, 1913–1914* (Denver: Smith-Brooks, 1914), 11–14 and the *Nineteenth Biennial Report of the Superintendent of the Colorado Insane Asylum, 1915–1916* (Denver: Eames Brothers, 1916), 9–13. The issue of overcrowding was not isolated to Denver or Colorado. See David J. Rothman, *Conscience and Convenience,* 293–378.

164. *Thirteenth Report Board of Charities and Corrections,* 37.

165. *Minutes Board of Charities and Corrections, 1916 to 1918,* 96, State Archives; *Minutes Board of Charities and Corrections, 1914,* 118, State Archives.

166. For examples of Protestant proselytizing in public schools see Edward J. Larson, *Summer for the Gods: The Scopes Trial and America's Continuing Debate over Science and Religion* (Cambridge, Mass.: Harvard University Press, 1997), 75.

167. Mary J. Oates, *The Catholic Philanthropic Tradition in America* (Bloomington: Indiana University Press, 1995), 29. Also see Deirdre M. Moloney, *American Catholic Lay Groups and Transatlantic Social Reform in the Progressive Era* (Chapel Hill: University of North Carolina Press, 2002), 117–66.

168. Oates, *Catholic Philanthropic Tradition,* 7, 28–30, and 39; Dorothy M. Brown and Elizabeth McKeown, *The Poor Belong to Us: Catholic Charities and American Welfare* (Cambridge, Mass.: Harvard University Press, 1997), 3–4.

169. James A. Denton, *Rocky Mountain Radical: Myron W. Reed, Christian Socialist* (Albuquerque: University of New Mexico Press, 1997), 77–89; Thomas J. Noel, *Colorado Catholicism and the Archdiocese of Denver, 1857–1989* (Niwot: University Press of Colorado, 1989), 104–5; Guy T. Justis, "Twenty-Five Years of Social Welfare," issued by the Denver Community Chest, 15–16, WHC/DPL; Paul Jones, "Where it All Began! . . . The History of Mile High United Way," 2–3, WHC/DPL; "Golden Anniversary: 50 Years of Federated Human Service, 1887–1937," 2–4, WHC/DPL; Flora Helen Ringle Hurlbut, "History of the Federation of Charities in Denver" (MA thesis, University of Denver, 1933), 53–82.

170. *Sixteenth Annual Report of the Denver Charity Organization Society, 1903,* 9, WHC/DPL.

171. Olivier Zunz, *The Changing Face of Inequality: Urbanization, Industrial Development, and Immigrants in Detroit, 1880–1920* (Chicago: University of Chicago Press, 1982), 270–79. Also see Susan Traverso, *Welfare Politics in Boston, 1910–1940* (Amherst: University of Massachusetts Press, 2003), 13–26.

172. Isabel C. Barrows, ed., *Proceedings of the National Conference of Charities and Corrections, 1896* (Boston: George H. Ellis, 1896), 23; Oates, *Catholic Philanthropic Tradition,* 48–62.

173. Oates, *Catholic Philanthropic Tradition*, 48–62; Brown and McKeown, *Poor Belong to Us*, 60–61. It should be noted that, according to Brown and McKeown, Catholics in Duluth, Akron, Rochester, Detroit, Omaha, Kansas City, and St. Paul did indeed join in joint fund-raising with Protestants.

174. Katz, *Improving Poor People*, 25–26; Katz, *In the Shadow*, 42–46. For examples of this mixing of private and public aid see Mary Ann Irwin, "'Going About and Doing Good': The Politics of Benevolence, Welfare, and Gender in San Francisco, 1850–1880," *Pacific Historical Review* 68 (August 1999): 365–96; David Spinoza Tanenhaus, "Policing the Child: Juvenile Justice in Chicago, 1870–1925" (PhD dissertation, University of Chicago, 1997); Jacob S. Hacker, *The Divided Welfare State: The Battle over Public and Private Social Benefits in the United States* (New York: Cambridge University Press, 2002); Jennifer Klein, *For All These Rights: Business, Labor, and the Shaping of America's Public-Private Welfare State* (Princeton, N.J.: Princeton University Press, 2003).

175. *Minutes Board of Charities and Corrections, 1908–1910*, 265, State Archives; *The Woman's Club of Denver, 1907–1908* (Denver: Merchants Publishing, 1907), 13, CHS.

176. *Twenty-Third Annual Report of the Charity Organization Society of Denver* (Denver, 1910), 7, WHC/DPL; Hurlbut, "History Federation of Charities in Denver," 72.

177. *Boulder County Journal*, vol. 10, 28, Boulder Courthouse. The county appropriated $200. *City of Boulder Daily Journal*, Ledger M22, 306, CL Boulder. The city appropriated $500. *Minutes Board of Charities and Corrections, 1916 to 1918*, 228–29, State Archives.

178. Grace Eleanor Wilson, "The History and Development of the Denver Bureau of Public Welfare," 10, see related footnote, Chapter 2, note 16.

179. *Sixth Report Board of Charities and Corrections*, 127; *Seventh Biennial Report of the State Board of Charities and Corrections* (Denver: Smith-Brooks, 1905), 125.

180. For baths see, *The Woman's Club, Fifteenth Annual Announcement, 1908–1909* (Denver: Smith-Brooks, 1908), 15, CHS; "Neighborhood House," 2, WHC/DPL.

181. *City and County of Denver*, vol. T, 258, Denver City Building.

182. *City and County of Denver*, vol. R, 220 and 484, Denver City Building.

183. "The Work of Relief," 14 August 1909, 9; "Flood Fund Apportioned," 17 September 1910, 7; "Prompt Relief Given Flood Sufferers," 27 July 1912, 8; all in *Denver Municipal Facts*, WHC/DPL; "Cherry Creek Flood Fund," *City of Denver*, 26 October 1912, 11, WHC/DPL; *Twenty-fifth Annual Report of the United Charities of Denver* (Denver, 1912), 14, WHC/DPL.

184. Alan Wolfe, *The Limits of Legitimacy: Political Constrictions of Contemporary Capitalism* (New York: Free Press, 1977), 108–75.

185. Gertrude Vaile, "Principles and Methods of Outdoor Relief," in *Proceedings of the National Conference of Charities and Corrections, 1915* (Chicago: Hildmann Printing, 1915), 482; Arthur P. Kellogg, "The Trend of the Times in Charity," *Survey* 34 (29 May 1915): 206.

Chapter Four

1. Emily Freeburg, Mothers' Compensation Cases, Boulder County, Box 18318, State Archives; *Boulder County Pauper Book*, vol. 2, 96 and vol. 4, 139, Boulder Courthouse.

2. Molly Ladd-Taylor, *Mother-Work: Women, Child Welfare, and the State, 1890–1930* (Urbana: University of Illinois Press, 1994), 135.

3. John Drew, "Child Labor and the Mothers' Pension Movement," in *The American Welfare System: Origins, Structure, and Effects*, ed. Howard Gensler (Westport, Conn.: Praeger, 1996), 88; Gwendolyn Mink, *The Wages of Motherhood: Inequality in the Welfare State, 1917–1942* (Ithaca, N.Y.: Cornell University Press, 1995), 3.

4. Theda Skocpol, *Protecting Soldiers and Mothers: The Political Origins of Social Policy in the United States* (Cambridge, Mass.: Harvard University Press, 1992); Linda Gordon, *Pitied But Not Entitled: Single Mothers and the History of Welfare* (New York: Free Press, 1994); Mink, *Wages of Motherhood*, 3–52.

5. Christopher Howard, "Sowing the Seeds of 'Welfare': The Transformation of Mothers' Pensions, 1900–1940," *Journal of Policy History* 4 (1992): 195.

6. Howard, "Sowing the Seeds of 'Welfare,'"189; see also Ann Shola Orloff, "Gender in Early U.S. Social Policy," *Journal of Policy History* 3 (1991): 249–81; Mimi Abramovitz, *Regulating the Lives of Women: Social Welfare Policy From Colonial Times to the Present*, rev. ed. (Boston: South End Press, 1996), 200.

7. Joanne L. Goodwin, *Gender and the Politics of Welfare Reform: Mothers' Pensions in Chicago, 1911–1929* (Chicago: University of Chicago Press, 1997). Other writers have noted the failure of mothers' pensions. See Judith Sealander, *Private Wealth and Public Life: Foundation Philanthropy and the Reshaping of American Social Policy from the Progressive Era to the New Deal* (Baltimore, Md.: Johns Hopkins University Press, 1997), 100–127 and Sonya Michel, *Children's Interests/Mothers' Rights: The Shaping of America's Child Care Policy* (New Haven, Conn.: Yale University Press, 1999), 73–87. The courts often viewed mothers' pensions as a type of poor relief. See Susan M. Sterett, "Serving the State: Constitutionalism and Social Spending, 1860s–1920s," *Law and Social Inquiry* 22 (Spring 1997): 311–56. For a detailed study of several types of public pensions see Susan M. Sterett, *Public Pensions: Gender & Civic Service in the States, 1850–1937* (Ithaca, N.Y.: Cornell University Press, 2003).

8. *Proceedings of the Conference on the Care of Dependent Children*, 5–6, 60th Cong., 2nd sess., Senate Document 721, Serial 5400 (Washington, D.C.: Government Printing Office, 1909).

9. Ibid., 9–10.

10. Sealander, *Private Wealth and Public Life*, 107–13; Michel, *Children's Interests/Mothers' Rights*, 80–81.

11. *Conference on the Care of Dependent Children*, 217.

12. Ibid., 216.

13. Merritt W. Pinckney, "Public Pensions to Widows: Experiences and Observations Which Lead Me to Favor Such a Law," reprinted in *Selected Articles on Mothers' Pensions*, comp. Edna D. Bullock (New York: H. W. Wilson Company, 1915), 140. For an excellent study on why mothers' pensions became so popular see Matthew A. Crenson, *Building the Invisible Orphanage: A Prehistory of the American Welfare System* (Cambridge, Mass.: Harvard University Press, 1998).

14. Ben B. Lindsey, "The Mothers' Compensation Law of Colorado," *Survey* 29 (15 February 1913): 716.

15. *Conference on the Care of Dependent Children*, 216.

16. Goodwin, *Gender and Politics of Welfare Reform*, 4 and 21–55.

17. Robert W. Hebberd, "Relief to Needy Mothers in New York," in *Proceedings of the National Conference of Charities and Corrections, 1914* (Fort Wayne, Ind.: Fort Wayne Printing, 1914), 450. Also see Frank Tucker, "Pensions to Widows— Discussion," in *Proceedings of the National Conference of Charities and Corrections, 1912* (Fort Wayne, Ind.: Fort Wayne Printing, 1912), 494.

18. Clara Cahill Park, "Widows' Pensions," *Survey* 32 (20 June 1914): 331. Another related argument for the use of mothers' pensions was that there were too few Charity Organization Societies in the nation to care properly for all the needy widows. See Arthur P. Kellogg, "The Trend of the Times in Charity," *Survey* 34 (29 May 1915): 206.

19. Merritt W. Pinckney, "Public Pensions to Widows: Experiences and Observations Which Lead Me to Favor Such a Law," condensed version, in *Proceedings of the National Conference of Charities and Corrections, 1912* (Fort Wayne, Ind.: Fort Wayne Printing, 1912), 479.

20. Mary E. Richmond, "Motherhood and Pensions," *Survey*, 29 (1 March 1913): 774.

21. Richmond, "Motherhood and Pensions," 778.

22. Frederic Almy, "Public Pensions to Widows: Experiences and Observations Which Lead Me to Oppose Such a Law," in *Proceedings of the National Conference of Charities and Corrections, 1912* (Fort Wayne, Ind.: Fort Wayne Printing, 1912), 482.

23. C. C. Carstens, "Public Pensions to Widows with Children," *Survey* 29 (4 January 1913): 461.

24. Almy, "Public Pensions to Widows," 484; Kellogg, "Trend of the Times," 206; Mary Richmond, "Pensions to Widows—Discussion," in *Proceedings of the National Conference of Charities and Corrections, 1912* (Fort Wayne, Ind.: Fort Wayne Printing, 1912), 492; Roy Lubove, *The Struggle for Social Security, 1900–1935* (1968; reprint, Pittsburgh, Pa.: University of Pittsburgh Press, 1986), 101–4.

25. "New York Charities in Conference," *Survey* 28 (25 May 1912): 325–26; Max Senior, "Pensions to Widows-Discussion," in *Proceedings of the National Conference of Charities and Corrections, 1912* (Fort Wayne, Ind.: Fort Wayne Printing, 1912), 491–92; Sealander, *Private Wealth and Public Life*, 116–17.

26. Edward T. Devine, "Pensions for Mothers," reprinted in *Selected Articles on Mothers' Pensions*, comp. Edna D. Bullock (New York: H. W. Wilson Company, 1915), 176–88.

27. Richmond, "Motherhood and Pensions," 775. For a detailed discussion of Richmond's views about mothers' pensions see Elizabeth N. Agnew, *From Charity to Social Work: Mary E. Richmond and the Creation of an American Profession* (Urbana: University of Illinois Press, 2004), 122–25. Devine also speculates that employers would take advantage of mothers' pensions to avoid their responsibilities for a safe work environment, see Devine, "Pensions for Mothers," 182.

28. L. A. Halbert, "The Widows' Allowance Act in Kansas City," *Survey* 31 (28 February 1914): 675; Laura A. Thompson, comp., *Laws Relating to 'Mothers' Pensions' in the United States, Canada, Denmark, and New Zealand*, U.S. Department of Labor, Children's Bureau Publication 63 (Washington, D.C.: Government Printing Office, 1919), 7–8; Emma O. Lundberg, *Public Aid to Mothers with Dependent Children*, U.S. Department of Labor, Children's Bureau Publication 162 (Washington, D.C.: Government Printing Office, 1928), 3; Lubove, *Struggle for Social Security*, 99; Mary Ann Irwin, "'Going About and Doing Good': The Politics of Benevolence, Welfare, and Gender in San Francisco, 1850–1880," *Pacific Historical Review* 68 (August 1999): 384.

29. *Denver Times*, 4 November 1912, 12; *Denver Post*, 11 November 1912, 1; Ben B. Lindsey and George Eisleer, "A Pamphlet Containing Arguments in Favor of the Mothers' Compensation Act," Box 1, Ben Lindsey Papers, WHC/DPL; Ida L. Gregory, Clerk Juvenile Court, to the Honorable Mayor and Board of Supervisors, City and County of Denver, 18 November 1912, Box 134, Ben B. Lindsey Papers, MD/LC. For a refreshing approach to Lindsey's work see R. Todd Laugen, "Engendering Juvenile Courts and Political Machine Reform: The Masculine Politics of Denver's Ben B. Lindsey, 1900–1912," in author's possession.

30. *Denver Post*, 1 November 1912, 11; *Denver Post*, 3 November 1912, 10; Woman's Club of Denver to Lindsey inviting him to speak on mothers' compensation, August 1912, Box 133, Ben B. Lindsey Papers, MD/LC.

31. "Colorado," *Survey* 35 (23 October 1915): 86–87; *Colorado Federation of Women's Clubs Official Year Book, 1911–12*, 51–52, UC Archives; *The Woman's Club of Denver, Eighteenth Annual Announcement, 1911–1912* (Denver: Eastwood-Kirchner Printing, 1911), 14, Box 9, MSS 1662, CHS.

32. *Colorado Federation of Women's Clubs Official Year Book, 1913–14*, 56–57, UC Archives.

33. The 1912 election had thirty-two measures on the ballot. See Daniel P. Smith and Joseph Lubinski, "Direct Democracy During the Progressive Era: A Crack in the Populist Veneer?" *Journal of Policy History* 14 (2002): 349–83.

34. *Laws Passed at the Nineteenth Session of the General Assembly of the State of Colorado* (Denver: Western Newspaper Union, 1913), 694–96; Lindsey, "Mothers' Compensation Law," 714–16.

35. *Denver Post*, 11 November 1912, 1; also see *Denver Post*, 6 November 1912, 10.

36. *Denver Times*, 4 November 1912, 12.

37. Quote, *Denver Times*, 9 November 1912, 2. Also see *Denver Times*, 1 November 1912, 5 and 4 November 1912, 12; *Denver Post*, 11 November 1912, 1; Lindsey, "Mothers' Compensation Law," 716.

38. *Abstract of Votes Cast, 1912, State of Colorado* (Denver: Smith-Brooks, 1913), 190–91.

39. *Denver Post*, 8 November 1912, 1.

40. *Women's Clubs, Official Year Book, 1913–14*, 55, UC Archives.

41. *Denver Times*, 9 November 1912, 2.

42. *Minutes of the State Board of Charities and Corrections, 1912*, 103–4, Box 18626, State Archives; "The State Board of Charities and Corrections, Semi-Annual Conference Fall Session, 1912," Box 10154, State Archives; *Denver Post*, 3 December 1912, 1.

43. "A Pamphlet Containing a List and Explanation of Bills Concerning Women and Children Now Pending in the Nineteenth General Assembly," 18, Box 1, Ben Lindsey Papers, WHC/DPL; "Pension Legislation for Needy Mothers," *Survey* 29 (15 February 1913): 660–61; *House Journal of the General Assembly of the State of Colorado, Nineteenth Session* (Denver: Smith-Brooks, 1913), 55, 72, 1231, 1266, and 1382.

44. "Pension for Needy Mothers," 660–61; Drew, "Child Labor and Mothers' Pension," 84.

45. Skocpol, *Protecting Soldiers and Mothers*, 446–47; Mark H. Leff, "Consensus for Reform: The Mothers' Pension Movement in the Progressive Era," *Social Service Review* 47 (September 1973): 401.

46. Leff, "Consensus for Reform," 397; Ladd-Taylor, *Mother-Work*, 135.

47. *Twelfth Biennial Report of the State Board of Charities and Corrections of Colorado* (Denver: Smith-Brooks, 1914), 40.

48. *Thirteenth Biennial Report of the State Board of Charities and Corrections of Colorado* (Denver: Eames Brothers, 1916), 39; *Fourteenth Biennial Report of the State Board of Charities and Corrections of Colorado* (Denver: Eames Brothers, 1918), 57. The board lists Lincoln County as one of the communities enacting mothers' compensation, but according to Lincoln's *Poor Record*, the county was not enforcing the law. Thus I did not include Lincoln County in the total figure.

49. *Thirteenth Report Board of Charities and Corrections*, 39.

50. Sherman C. Kingsley, "The Working of the Funds to Parents Act in Illinois," in *Proceedings of the National Conference of Charities and Corrections, 1914* (Fort Wayne, Ind.: Fort Wayne Printing, 1914), 439.

51. Edith Abbott and Sophonisba P. Breckinridge, *The Administration of the Aid-to-Mothers Law in Illinois*, U. S. Department of Labor, Children's Bureau Publication 82 (Washington, D.C.: Government Printing Office, 1921), 131.

52. Emma O. Lundberg, "Aid to Mothers with Dependent Children," *Annals of the American Academy of Political and Social Science* 98 (November 1921): 101.

53. Abbott and Breckinridge, *Administration of the Aid-to-Mothers Law*, 131.

54. For Lopez see *Costilla County Poor Book*, vol. 3, 4, Costilla Courthouse; for Gallegos see *Costilla County Poor Book*, vol. 1, 10–13, Costilla Courthouse.

55. *Costilla County Poor Book*, 1891–1906 and 1913–1919, vols. 1–3, Costilla Courthouse.

56. *Third Biennial Report of the Board of Control of the Colorado State Home for Dependent and Neglected Children* (Denver: Smith-Brooks, 1900), 20; *Fourth Biennial Report of the Board of Control of the Colorado State Home for Dependent and Neglected Children* (Denver: Smith-Brooks, 1902), 17; *Fifth Biennial Report of the Board of Control of the Colorado State Home for Dependent and Neglected Children* (Denver: Smith-Brooks, 1904), 17; *Sixth Biennial Report of the Superintendent of the Colorado State Home for Dependent and Neglected Children to the Board of Control* (Denver: Smith-Brooks, 1906), 15; *Seventh Biennial Report of the Superintendent of the Colorado State Home for Dependent and Neglected Children to the Board of Control* (Denver: Smith-Brooks, 1908), 17; *Eighth Biennial Report of the Superintendent of the Colorado State Home for Dependent and Neglected Children to the Board of Control* (Denver: Smith-Brooks, 1910), 22; *Ninth Biennial Report of the Superintendent of the Colorado State Home for Dependent and Neglected Children to the Board of Control* (Denver: Smith-Brooks, 1912), 29; *Tenth Biennial Report of the Superintendent of the Colorado State Home for Children to the Board of Control* (Denver: Smith-Brooks, 1914), 58; *Eleventh Biennial Report of the Superintendent of the Colorado State Home for Children to the Board of Control* (Denver: Eames Brothers, 1916), 42; *Twelfth and Thirteenth Biennial Reports of the Superintendent of the Colorado State Home for Children to the Board of Control* (Denver: Eames Brothers, 1920), 9 and 18.

57. *Costilla County Commissioners Records*, vol. 6, 427, Costilla Courthouse.

58. Ibid., 183, 206, and 238.

59. Ibid., 175–76.

60. Lindsey, "Mothers' Compensation Law," 716.

61. For Yoder, see *Lincoln County Poor Record*, 25, 28, 33, and 36, Lincoln Courthouse; for Kirk see *Montezuma County Poor Reports*, 1901–1910 and 1912–1919, Box 4967A and 4968A, State Archives.

62. For Cease see *Lincoln County Poor Record*, 1, Lincoln Courthouse. For Stiles see *Montezuma County Poor Book*, vol. 1, 15–17, Montezuma Courthouse; *Montezuma County Poor Reports*, State Archives.

63. Georgia Denby to Montezuma County commissioners, 27 May 1912, Mont. Box 9, Montezuma Courthouse.

64. Georgia Denby to Montezuma County commissioners, 11 August 1913, Mont. Box 9, Montezuma Courthouse.

65. Georgia Denby to Montezuma County commissioners, 6 March 1917, Mont. Box 9, Montezuma Courthouse.

66. Georgia Denby to Montezuma County commissioners, 14 February 1921, Mont. Box 9, Montezuma Courthouse.

67. *Lincoln County Court Record and Judgement Book*, vol. 1, 510, Ledger 18460K, State Archives.

68. Ibid.

69. Eva Pease to Judge Veal, 8 December 1915, Comm. of Lincoln Commissioners, Lincoln Courthouse.

70. *Lincoln County Poor Record*, 42, Lincoln Courthouse.

71. Martha Stetson to County Judge, 11 December 1915, Comm. of Lincoln Commissioners, Lincoln Courthouse.

72. *Teller County Commissioners Records*, vol. 8, 214, Teller Courthouse.

73. *Cripple Creek Times*, 17 October 1912, 3. The newspaper's stance on the mothers' compensation act is a bit confusing. An editorial just two days before the election says, "As to the Mothers Compensation act, look for yourself as to the advisability of voting for it. We know that the Childrens Homes are opposed to it." Also see *Cripple Creek Times*, 3 November 1912, 4.

74. *Abstract of Votes Cast*, 1912, 190–91.

75. *Abstract of the Fourteenth Census of the United States, 1920* (Washington, D.C.: Government Printing Office, 1923), 560.

76. Robert Guilford Taylor, *Cripple Creek* (Bloomington: Indiana University Press, 1966), 120 and 132–33; Marshall Sprague, *Money Mountain: The Story of Cripple Creek Gold* (Lincoln: University of Nebraska Press, 1953), 267–71.

77. *Cripple Creek Times and Victor Daily Record*, 6 February 1915, 5.

78. Taylor, *Cripple Creek*, 134–39.

79. Ibid., 139–144.

80. *Cripple Creek Times and Victor Daily Record*, 23 December 1917, 12.

81. Sprague, *Money Mountain*, 297.

82. Ibid.

83. *Abstract of the Fourteenth Census, 1920,* 560.

84. *Teller County Commissioners Records,* vol. 8, 115, Teller Courthouse.

85. Ibid., 214 and 236.

86. *House Journal of the General Assembly of the State of Colorado, Twenty-First Session* (Denver: Brock-Haffner Press, 1917), 75.

87. *Laws Passed at the Twenty-Second Session of the General Assembly of the State of Colorado* (Denver: American Printing and Publishing, 1919), 531.

88. Ibid., 531–32. The levy was not to exceed one-eighth of one mill.

89. *House Journal of the General Assembly of the State of Colorado, Twenty-Second Session* (Denver: Smith-Brooks, 1919), 1268 and 1545–46; *Senate Journal of the General Assembly of the State of Colorado, Twenty-Second Session* (Denver: Smith-Brooks, 1919), 1116.

90. *First Biennial Report of the State Department of Charities and Corrections, 1923–24* (Denver: Bradford-Robinson, 1925), 35.

91. Works Progress Administration, *Inventory of County Archives of Colorado,* vol. 12, (Denver: Historical Records Survey, 1938), 16.

92. *Boulder County Pauper Book,* vol. 2, 60, Boulder Courthouse.

93. *Boulder County Pauper Book,* vols. 1–4, Boulder Courthouse.

94. *Boulder County Pauper Book,* vol. 2, 83, Boulder Courthouse; Lulu Seaman, Mothers' Compensation Cases, Boulder County, Box 18318, State Archives.

95. *Boulder County Commissioners Journal,* vol. 9, 458, 475, 476, and 503, Boulder Courthouse; *Boulder County Pauper Book,* vols. 1–4, Boulder Courthouse.

96. *Boulder County Pauper Book,* vols. 1–4, Boulder Courthouse.

97. Anna Scoville, Minnie Wiles, Belle Harris, and Katie Roberts, Mothers' Compensation Cases, Boulder County, Box 18318, State Archives.

98. *Laws Passed Nineteenth Session of the General Assembly,* 694–95.

99. Report of Investigator, Mothers' Compensation Cases, Box 18318, State Archives.

100. Mary Billings, Mothers' Compensation Cases, Boulder County, Box 18318, State Archives.

101. Mary Krauss, Mothers' Compensation Cases, Boulder County, Box 18318, State Archives.

102. *Boulder County Commissioners Journal,* vol. 10, 118 and 147, Boulder Courthouse.

103. Lulu Seaman, Mothers' Compensation Cases, State Archives.

104. Minnie Cope, Mothers' Compensation Cases, Boulder County, Box 18318, State Archives.

105. Lulu Seaman, Mothers' Compensation Cases, State Archives.

106. *Denver Republican*, 8 October 1912, 10; also see Gertrude Vaile to Mrs. Costigan, 11 November 1912, Box 134, Ben B. Lindsey Papers, MD/LC.

107. Quoted in Hace Sorel Tishler, *Self-Reliance and Social Security 1870–1917* (Port Washington, N.Y.: Kennikat Press, 1971), 153.

108. Gertrude Vaile, "Some Social Problems of Public Outdoor Relief," *Survey* 34 (3 March 1915): 16.

109. Gertrude Vaile, "Administering Mothers' Pensions in Denver," *Survey* 31 (28 February 1914): 673.

110. Vaile, "Some Social Problems," 16.

111. Vaile, "Mothers' Pensions in Denver," 673.

112. Ibid., 674.

113. Ibid.

114. Vaile, "Some Social Problems," 16.

115. Ibid.

116. Grace Eleanor Wilson, "The History and Development of the Denver Bureau of Public Welfare," 6–7, see related footnote Chapter 2, note 16; Vaile, "Mothers' Pensions in Denver," 673; "Board of Charities and Corrections," *City of Denver*, 27 December 1913, 9, WHC/DPL; Gertrude Vaile, "Public Administration of Charity in Denver," in *Proceedings of the National Conference of Charities and Corrections, 1916* (Chicago: The Hildmann Printing Company, 1916), 416.

117. *Proceeding of Conference on Mothers' Pensions*, U.S. Department of Labor, Children's Bureau Publication 109 (Washington, D.C.: Government Printing Office, 1922), 10.

118. Florence Nesbitt, *Standards of Public Aid to Children in Their Own Homes*, U.S. Department of Labor, Children's Bureau, Publication 118 (Washington, D.C.: Government Printing Office, 1923), 44–45.

119. Vaile, "Mothers' Pensions in Denver," 673.

120. Vaile, "Public Charity in Denver," 416.

121. Nesbitt, *Standards of Public Aid*, 48.

122. Vaile, "Mothers' Pensions in Denver," 673. Of the original twenty-eight women, two quickly remarried and stopped receiving pensions, sixteen were widows, eight were deserted, one's husband was a "hopeless invalid," and one's husband was in prison. See Vaile, "Mothers' Pensions in Denver," 673; "Board of Charities and Corrections," 9, WHC/DPL; *First Annual Report of the Social Welfare Department of the City and County of Denver, Colorado, for the Year Ending December 31, 1913*, 72, GP/DPL.

123. Nesbitt, *Standards of Public Aid*, 47.

124. Ibid., data 29, quote 47, also see 45.

125. *Denver County Poor Reports*, 1917 and 1918, Box 4968A, State Archives; for more examples of relief supplementing pensions see Gertrude Vaile to Ben Lindsey, 2 October 1915, Box 60, Ben B. Lindsey Papers, MD/LC.

126. In Boston, as spending for mothers' aid increased during the first several years of implementation, funding for other assistance programs decreased. By the early 1920s, this trend reversed itself due to political debates over welfare. See Susan Traverso, *Welfare Politics in Boston, 1910–1940* (Amherst: University of Massachusetts Press, 2003), 45 and 69–70. In Chicago, funding for mothers' pensions was inadequate during the first few years of implementation. See David Spinoza Tanenhaus, "Policing the Child: Juvenile Justice in Chicago, 1870–1925," (PhD dissertation, University of Chicago, 1997), 295.

127. *Proceedings and Ordinances of the City and County of Denver*, vol. 1, 165, Denver City Building.

128. Ibid., 181.

129. Ibid.

130. Quote, *The Woman's Club of Denver, Twenty-Third Annual Announcement, 1916–1917* (Denver: W. F. Robinson Printing, n.d.), 9, Box 9, MSS 1662, CHS; also see *Proceedings and Ordinances of Denver*, vol. 1, 483, Denver City Building.

131. Vaile, "Mothers' Pensions in Denver," 675.

132. Nesbitt, *Standards of Public Aid*, 21.

133. "City Social Service Mothers' Compensation Granted" memorandum, 25 March 1916, Box 1, Gertrude Vaile Collection, Columbia Library. Nesbitt, *Standards of Public Aid*, 47. In comparison, outdoor relief cared for 612 cases in 1919. See *Denver County Poor Reports*, 1919, Box 4968A, State Archives. In Boston, mothers' aid quickly became the city's largest aid program. See Traverso, *Welfare Politics in Boston*, 45.

134. Vaile, "Mothers' Pensions in Denver," 675.

135. Goodwin, *Gender and Politics of Welfare Reform*, 169; Nesbitt, *Standards of Public Aid*, 18; T. J. Edmonds and Maurice B. Hexter, "State Pensions to Mothers in Hamilton County, Ohio," *Survey* 33 (12 December 1914): 290.

136. Nesbitt, *Standards of Public Aid*, 17–20 and 23–24.

137. "City Social Service Mothers' Compensation Granted" memorandum, Gertrude Vaile Collection, Columbia Library. The trend of higher levels of support for mothers' pensions also surfaces in Boston. See Traverso, *Welfare Politics in Boston*, 45.

138. Nesbitt, *Standards of Public Aid*, 50.

139. Skocpol, *Protecting Soldiers and Mothers*, 424. Also see Gordon, *Pitied But Not Entitled*, 38.

140. Lundberg, "Aid to Mothers With Dependent Children," 98.

141. Mary F. Bogue, "The Greater Economy of Adequate Grants," in *Proceedings of the National Conference on Social Work, 1919* (Chicago: Rogers and Hall Company, 1919), 304; Mary F. Bogue, "Problems in the Administration of Mothers' Aid," in *Proceedings of the National Conference on Social Work, 1918* (Chicago: Rogers and Hall Printers, 1918), 351.

142. Thompson, *Laws Relating to 'Mothers' Pensions'*, 7–18.

143. Edith Abbott, "The Administration of the Illinois 'Funds to Parents' Laws," in *Proceedings of the Conference of Social Insurance*, U.S. Department of Labor, Bureau of Labor Statistics 212 (Washington, D.C.: Government Printing Office, 1917), 826.

144. Bogue, "Problems of Mothers' Aid," 350.

145. Frederic Almy, "Public Pensions to Widows: Experiences and Observations Which Lead Me to Oppose Such a Law," reprinted in *Selected Articles on Mothers' Pensions*, comp. Edna D. Bullock (New York: H. W. Wilson Company, 1915), 156; Abbott, "The Administration of the Illinois 'Funds to Parents' Laws," 827.

146. James F. Jackson, "Experience of Ohio in Relieving Needy Mothers," in *Proceedings of the National Conference of Charities and Corrections, 1914* (Fort Wayne, Ind.: Fort Wayne Printing, 1914), 446.

147. Mary F. Bogue, "Ten Years of Mothers' Pensions," *Survey* 49 (15 February 1923): 635.

Chapter Five

1. *Boulder County Pauper Book*, vol. 2, 20, vol. 3, 36, and vol. 4, 28, Boulder Courthouse; *Costilla County Poor Book*, vol. 2, 3 and vol. 3, 2, 17, 21, and 24, Costilla Courthouse; *Teller County Poor Reports*, 1916 and 1917, Boxes 4967A and 4968A, State Archives.

2. *Boulder County Poor Book*, vol. 4, 28, Boulder Courthouse; *Costilla County Poor Book*, vol. 3, 24, Costilla Courthouse; *Costilla County Commissioners Records*, vol. 7, 86–87, Costilla Courthouse; *Teller County Poor Reports*, 1918–1920, Boxes 4967A and 4968A, State Archives.

3. One reason for this absence in the literature is that blind benefits do not easily fit into the two-gendered welfare system that some scholars argue developed during the early twentieth century. In fact, blind benefits embodied characteristics from both dependent (female) and independent (male) forms of welfare. See Thomas A. Krainz, "Transforming the Progressive Era Welfare State: Activists for the Blind and Blind Benefits," *Journal of Policy History* 15 (2003): 224–25. For another example of welfare policies that do not fit into the two-gendered welfare track see Michael Willrich, "Home Slackers: Men, the State, and Welfare in Modern America," *Journal of American History* 87 (September 2000): 460–89.

4. Walter I. Trattner, *From Poor Law to Welfare State: A History of Social Welfare in America* (New York: Free Press, 1974); Michael B. Katz, *In the Shadow of the Poorhouse: A Social History of Welfare in America* (New York: Basic Books, 1986); James T. Patterson, *America's Struggle Against Poverty, 1900–1985* (Cambridge, Mass.: Harvard University Press, 1986).

5. Jacobus tenBroek and Floyd W. Matson, *Hope Deferred: Public Welfare and the Blind* (Berkeley: University of California Press, 1959); Frances A. Koestler, *The Unseen Minority: A Social History of Blindness in America* (New York: David McKay Company, 1976); C. Edwin Vaughan, *The Struggle of Blind People for Self-Determination: The Dependency-Rehabilitation Conflict: Empowerment in the Blindness Community* (Springfield, Ill.: Charles C. Thomas, 1993); Richard K. Scotch and Edward D. Berkowitz, "One Comprehensive System? A Historical Perspective on Federal Disability Policy," *Journal of Disability Policy Studies* 1 (Fall 1990): 2–19. One reason for this oversight is that the growing field of disability history has mainly focused on the post-World War II years. See Joseph P. Shapiro, *No Pity: People with Disabilities Forging a New Civil Rights Movement* (New York: Times Books, 1993). Scholars of disability history have recently begun focusing on pre-World War II events. See Paul K. Longmore and David Goldberger, "The League of the Physically Handicapped and the Great Depression: A Case Study in the New Disability History," *Journal of American History* 87 (December 2000): 888–922; Paul K. Longmore and Lauri Umansky, eds., *The New Disability History: American Perspectives* (New York: New York University Press, 2001). For an overview of disability history see Catherine J. Kudlick, "Disability History: Why We Need Another 'Other,'" *American Historical Review* 108 (2003): 763–93.

6. For an overview of the rise of interest group politics during the Progressive Era, see Elisabeth S. Clemens, *The People's Lobby: Organizational Innovation and the Rise of Interest Group Politics in the United States, 1890–1925* (Chicago: University of Chicago Press, 1997); Grant McConnel, *Private Power and American Democracy* (New York: Alfred A. Knopf, 1966).

7. In 1900, out of one million Civil War Union veterans 741,259 were receiving pensions. By 1915, pensions were given to 396,370 out of 424,000 surviving veterans. In 1920, the number of living Civil War veterans had drastically declined to only 244,000; five years later, only 127,000 would still be alive. See U.S. Bureau of the Census, *Historical Statistics of the United States, Colonial Times to 1970*, Bicentennial edition, pt. 2 (Washington, D.C.: Government Printing Office, 1975), 1145; Theda Skocpol, *Protecting Soldiers and Mothers: The Political Origins of Social Policy in the United States* (Cambridge, Mass.: Harvard University Press, 1992), 102–51, especially the table on 109; Jill Quadagno, *The Transformation of Old Age Security: Class and Politics in the American Welfare State* (Chicago: University of Chicago Press, 1988), 36–49.

8. Quote, Harry Best, *The Blind: Their Condition and the Work Being Done for Them in the United States* (New York: Macmillian Company, 1919), 83, see pages 86–88 on stereotyping.

9. Ibid., 26–29.

10. Ibid., 46.

11. Helen Keller, "The Heaviest Burden on the Blind," *Outlook for the Blind* 1 (April 1907): 10; Robert B. Irwin, *As I Saw It* (New York: American Foundation for the Blind, 1955), 169.

12. Best, *The Blind*, 43–63; Harry Best, *Blindness and the Blind in the United States* (New York: Macmillian Company, 1934), 217–58.

13. Best, *The Blind*, 74–77.

14. Koestler, *Unseen Minority*, 14.

15. Edward J. Nolan, "Historical Sketch," *Outlook for the Blind* 1 (April 1907): 17–18; Koestler, *Unseen Minority*, 14–15; Best, *The Blind*, 674–75; Richard Slayton French, *From Homer to Helen Keller: A Social and Educational Study of the Blind* (New York: American Foundation for the Blind, 1932), 248–50.

16. Irwin, *As I Saw It*, 29.

17. Irwin, *As I Saw It*, 3–8; Koestler, *Unseen Minority*, 37–38 and 91–96; Best, *The Blind*, 400–406; French, *From Homer to Helen Keller*, 166–67.

18. For an excellent description of failed reform attempts see Irwin, *As I Saw It*, 9–45; "New York Point or American Braille," *Outlook for the Blind* 3 (April 1909): 2; "1913 Report of the U.T.C." *Outlook for the Blind* 7 (July 1913): 23; "One Alphabet for All the Blind," *Survey* 38 (14 July 1917): 341–42; Best, *The Blind*, 406–10; Koestler, *Unseen Minority*, 37–38 and 91–96; French, *From Homer to Helen Keller*, 166–69. In 1918, the AAIB likewise endorsed the AAWB's decision.

19. "New Associations for the Blind," *Outlook for the Blind* 2 (July 1908): 59; "The Scotoic Aid Society of Missouri—a Foreword," *Outlook for the Blind* 1 (July 1907): 47; "Maine Association for the Blind," *Outlook for the Blind* 1 (April 1907): 3; Samuel F. Hubbard, "Association and Commission for the Blind," *Outlook for the Blind* 1 (April 1907): 4.

20. Best, *The Blind*, 676–78.

21. "The Scotoic Aid Society of Missouri," 47–48.

22. "Maine Association for the Blind," 3; Hubbard, "Association for the Blind," 4.

23. "Maine Association for the Blind," 3; Hubbard, "Association for the Blind," 4; Koestler, *Unseen Minority*, 37–44.

24. "Our New Year," *Outlook for the Blind* 7 (April 1913): 1; "Our Magazine's New Home," *Outlook for the Blind* 5 (October 1911): 53; Best, *The Blind*, 437–39.

25. *Denver Post*, 24 August 1933, 6; *Rocky Mountain News*, 24 August 1933, 6; "Mrs. Jennie Caward Jackson," *Outlook for the Blind* 27 (October 1933): 188–89; Jennie Caward Jackson, "My Record as a Worker for the Blind," FF7, Box 36, Gano and Laurena Senter Collection, WHC/DPL.

26. S. M. Green, "State Aid and Maintenance of the Adult Blind," in *Proceedings of the National Conference of Charities and Corrections, 1910* (Fort Wayne, Ind.: Archer Printing, 1910), 291. This statistical observation became widely known for the first time with the publication in 1906 of a special census report on the blind and deaf, U.S. Bureau of the Census, *Special Reports—The Blind and The Deaf, 1900* (Washington, D.C.: Government Printing Office, 1906).

27. *Seventh Biennial Report of the State Board of Charities and Corrections of Colorado, 1904* (Denver: Smith-Brooks, 1905), 129.

28. U.S. Bureau of the Census, *The Blind in the United States, 1920* (Washington, D.C.: Government Printing Office, 1923), 14.

29. Charles F. F. Campbell, "Problems of the Blind, Especially the Adult Blind" in *Proceedings of the National Conference of Charities and Corrections, 1912* (Fort Wayne, Ind.: Fort Wayne Printing, 1912), 79.

30. Newel Perry, "What do the Blind Want?" *Outlook for the Blind* 5 (October 1911): 69.

31. Quoted in Best, *The Blind*, 477, originally located in a Report of Maryland School, 1873, 11.

32. Irwin, *As I Saw It*, 151.

33. Best, *The Blind*, 509–12; for more information on the workshop movement, see pages 473–517; Irwin, *As I Saw It*, 151–58; tenBroek and Matson, *Hope Deferred*, 249–54. In 1893 Connecticut opened a workshop, followed by Michigan in 1903, New York in 1906, and Maryland in 1908.

34. "Colorado Workshop," *Outlook for the Blind* 1 (January 1908): 132; "Colorado Industrial Workshop for the Blind," *Outlook for the Blind* 1 (July 1907): 33–34; "Mrs. Jennie Caward Jackson," 188–89; *Rocky Mountain News*, 24 August 1933, 6; Efay Nelson Grigg, "The Colorado State Board of Charities and Corrections" (MA thesis, University of Denver, 1932), 97–98; *Denver Post*, 24 August 1933, 6.

35. Quote from *Colorado Federation of Women's Clubs Official Year Book, 1911–12*, 55, UC Archives; Mary Louise Sinton, "A History of the Woman's Club of Denver: 1894–1915" (MA thesis, University of Denver, 1980), 138; *Denver Post*, 24 August 1933, 6; *Rocky Mountain News*, 24 August 1933, 6; "Mrs. Jennie Caward Jackson," 188–89.

36. Quote, *Biennial Report of the State Teacher for the Adult Blind, 1916–1918* (Denver: Eames Brothers, 1919), 6, also see pages 8 and 10; for examples of travel see *Biennial Report of the State Teacher for the Adult Blind, 1914–1916* (Denver: Eames Brothers, 1916), 9–10.

37. *Cripple Creek Times and Victor Daily Record*, 27 August 1915, 2.

38. *State Teacher for the Adult Blind, 1916–1918*, 8.

39. *State Teacher for the Adult Blind, 1916–1918*, 1 and 6; for more examples of the condition of the blind see *State Teacher for the Adult Blind, 1914–1916*, 1, 6, and 9.

40. *Biennial Report of the State Teacher for the Adult Blind, 1918–1920* (Denver: Eames Brothers, 1920), 8.

41. *Report of the Board of Control of the Colorado Industrial Workshop for the Blind, 1910* (Denver: Smith-Brooks, 1910), 6; *Report of the Board of Control of the Colorado Industrial Workshop for the Blind, 1912* (Denver: Smith-Brooks, 1913), 3.

42. *Colorado Industrial Workshop for the Blind, 1912,* 11; *Colorado Industrial Workshop for the Blind, 1910,* 10.

43. *Colorado Industrial Workshop for the Blind, 1910,* 6; *Colorado Industrial Workshop for the Blind, 1912,* 9

44. *Eleventh Biennial Report of the State Board of Charities and Corrections of Colorado, 1912* (Denver: Smith-Brooks, 1912), 11.

45. *Colorado Industrial Workshop for the Blind, 1912,* 3.

46. *Tenth Biennial Report of the State Board of Charities and Corrections of Colorado, 1910* (Denver: Smith-Brooks, 1910), 20.

47. *Colorado Industrial Workshop for the Blind, 1912,* quote 3 and 11.

48. Quote, *Tenth Report Board of Charities and Corrections,* 21; *Colorado Industrial Workshop for the Blind, 1910,* 8; *Colorado Industrial Workshop for the Blind, 1912,* 11.

49. *Colorado Industrial Workshop for the Blind, 1910,* 9.

50. *Minutes of the State Board of Charities and Corrections, 1913,* 88, Box 18626, State Archives; *Minutes of the State Board of Charities and Corrections, 1914,* 121, Box 18626, State Archives; *Minutes of the State Board of Charities and Corrections, 1915,* 111, Box 18626, State Archives.

51. *Colorado Industrial Workshop for the Blind, 1912,* 4.

52. *Report of the Board of Control of the Colorado Industrial Workshop for the Blind, 1914* (Denver: Smith-Brooks, 1914), 4; *Minutes Board of Charities and Corrections, 1914,* 128, State Archives.

53. Quote, *Minutes Board of Charities and Corrections, 1914,* 128, State Archives; *Colorado Industrial Workshop for the Blind, 1914,* 7.

54. *Minutes Board of Charities and Corrections, 1914,* 128, State Archives.

55. Ibid.

56. Quotes, *Minutes Board of Charities and Corrections, 1915,* 111, State Archives; *Minutes of the State Board of Charities and Corrections, December 12, 1916 to November 12, 1918,* 103, Box 18626, State Archives.

57. *Thirteenth Biennial Report of the State Board of Charities and Corrections of Colorado* (Denver: Eames Brothers, 1916), 19.

58. Best, *The Blind,* 565; Robert B. Irwin and Evelyn C. McKay, *Blind Relief Laws: Their Theory and Practice* (New York: American Foundation for the Blind, 1929), 105.

59. J. P. Draper, "Abolition of Ohio's Pension Law," *Outlook for the Blind* 1 (April 1907): 12–13; Best, *The Blind*, 558 and 561. Ohio passed several revised acts which partially addressed constitutional concerns of the Ohio Supreme Court.

60. Best, *The Blind*, 568.

61. Robert B. Irwin, "Relation of Commission to Other Agencies," *Outlook for the Blind* 11 (April 1917): 39. The blind benefit movement first took hold in midwestern states—Ohio (1898), Illinois (1903), Wisconsin (1907)—before moving west and into the New England states—Kansas (1911), Iowa (1915), New Hampshire (1915), Maine (1915), Missouri (1916), Nebraska (1917), Idaho (1917), Colorado (1918), New Jersey (1918), Massachusetts (1919), and California (1919).

62. James Forbes, "A Feudal Survival—the Blind Pension," *Charities and the Commons* 15 (3 February 1906): 616 and 618.

63. Best, *The Blind*, 549; Robert B. Irwin and Mary B. Irwin, *Blind Relief Laws and Their Administration* (n.p.: Red Cross Institute for the Blind, 1919), 21.

64. Lucy Wright, "The Pension Question in Massachusetts," *Outlook for the Blind* 9 (January 1916): 75–76; Best, *The Blind*, 549; Irwin and Irwin, *Blind Relief Laws*, 4 and 21. Some opponents argued that an old age pension would be a better solution since effects of old age, which often included blindness along with other disabilities, caused much of the poverty among those asking for blind aid. See, Wright, "Pension Question in Massachusetts," 74; Best, *The Blind*, 550; Irwin and Irwin, *Blind Relief Laws*, 5.

65. Eugene T. Lies, "Public Outdoor Relief in Chicago," in *Proceedings of the National Conference of Charities and Corrections, 1916* (Chicago: The Hildmann Printing Company, 1916), 346.

66. Wright, "Pension Question in Massachusetts," 77–78; Irwin, "Relation of Commission," 41; Lies, "Public Outdoor Relief in Chicago," 347.

67. Irwin and Irwin, *Blind Relief Laws*, 5.

68. Irwin, "Relation of Commission," 39.

69. Irwin and Irwin, *Blind Relief Laws*, 5.

70. Louis Stricker, "Blindness in Hamilton County," *Studies from the Helen S. Trounstine Foundation* 1 (1 September 1918): 63.

71. Best, *The Blind*, 551.

72. First quote, Irwin and Irwin, *Blind Relief Laws*, 3; second quote, "Ohio Relief for the Blind," *Outlook for the Blind* 9 (October 1915): 45; see also Wright, "Pension Question in Massachusetts," 73.

73. Stricker, "Blindness in Hamilton County," 104; Irwin and Irwin, *Blind Relief Laws*, 20–24 and 27–28.

74. Irwin and Irwin, *Blind Relief Laws*, 3; "Ohio Relief for the Blind," 45.

75. Ambrose M. Shotwell, "Outdoor Relief for the Blind," *Outlook for the Blind* 11 (July 1917): 30.

76. Irwin, "Relation of Commission," 41.

77. *Colorado Industrial Workshop for the Blind, 1912*, 4–5. Labor leaders used a similar language when advocating for old age pensions. See Ann Shola Orloff, *The Politics of Pensions: A Comparative Analysis of Britain, Canada, and the United States, 1880–1940* (Madison: University of Wisconsin Press, 1993), 158.

78. *Society of the United Workers for the Blind of Colorado Minutes*, vol. 1, 46, NFB Colorado.

79. U.S. Bureau of the Census, *The Blind Population of the United States, 1920: A Statistical Analysis of the Data Obtained at the Fourteenth Decennial Census* (Washington, D.C.: Government Printing Office, 1928), 20–21.

80. U.S. Bureau of the Census, *The Blind Population, 1920*, 46.

81. Irwin and Irwin, *Blind Relief Laws*, 14.

82. *State Teacher for the Adult Blind, 1916–1918*, 8; Irwin and Irwin, *Blind Relief Laws*, 38.

83. *Denver Post*, 10 August 1941, sec. 1, 10; also see *Denver Post*, 18 January 1947, 2 and 23 January 1947, 4. According to James Wright, Wilcox was active in agrarian politics although he was never a Populist. He was, according to Wright, a silverite. See James Edward Wright, *The Politics of Populism: Dissent in Colorado* (New Haven, Conn.: Yale University Press, 1974), 181 and 242.

84. Irwin and Irwin, *Blind Relief Laws*, 38.

85. *United Workers Minutes*, vol. 1, 40 and 45–46, NFB Colorado.

86. Quotes, *Rocky Mountain News*, 31 January 1917, 2; *United Workers Minutes*, vol. 1, 52 and 56, NFB Colorado; Irwin and Irwin, *Blind Relief Laws*, 38.

87. *United Workers Minutes*, vol. 1, 56, NFB Colorado.

88. Quote, Irwin and Irwin, *Blind Relief Laws*, 38; *United Workers Minutes*, vol. 1, 58 and 60, NFB Colorado. Lute Wilcox and the United Workers discussed the possibility of recalling Senator West. See *United Workers Minutes*, vol. 1, 60–61, NFB Colorado.

89. *United Workers Minutes*, vol. 1, 66–67 and 72, NFB Colorado.

90. Ibid., 81.

91. Quote, *State Teacher for the Adult Blind, 1916–1918*, 8; *United Workers Minutes*, vol. 1, 94, NFB Colorado.

92. *Colorado Federation of Women's Clubs Official Year Book, 1918–1919*, 92–93, UC Archives. *Abstract of Votes Cast—1918 Election—State of Colorado* (Denver: Eames Brothers, 1919), 26–27; Irwin and Irwin, *Blind Relief Laws*, 38.

93. *United Workers Minutes*, vol. 1, 102–4, NFB Colorado.

94. *State Teacher for the Adult Blind, 1918–1920*, 7–8.

95. *Costilla County Commissioners Records*, vol. 7, 86–87, Costilla Courthouse.

96. *Biennial Report of Auditor of State of Colorado, 1919–1920* (Denver: Eames Brothers, 1920), see chart in back.

97. *Fourteenth Biennial Report of the State Board of Charities and Corrections of Colorado* (Denver: Eames Brothers, 1918), 57.

98. *Laws Passed at the Twenty-Second Session of the General Assembly of the State of Colorado* (Denver: American Printing and Publishing, 1919), 313 and 531–32; *Laws Passed at the Nineteenth Session of the General Assembly of the State of Colorado* (Denver: Western Newspaper Union, 1913), 694–96.

99. *Laws Passed at the Twenty-Second Session of the General Assembly*, 311–13; Blind Benefit Application, Box 26959, State Archives.

100. *Laws Passed at the Twenty-Second Session of the General Assembly*, 311–13, quote 311.

101. *Montezuma County Commissioners Records*, vol. 3, 579, Montezuma Courthouse.

102. *Laws Passed at the Twenty-Second Session of the General Assembly*, 312.

103. *Montezuma County Commissioners Records*, vol. 3, 579, Montezuma Courthouse; *Montezuma County Poor Reports*, 1901–10 and 1912–19, Boxes 4967A and 4968A, State Archives.

104. *Lincoln County Poor Record*, 1909–22, Lincoln Courthouse; Blind Benefits 1919–1920, Comm. of Lincoln Commissioners, Lincoln Courthouse.

105. *United Workers Minutes*, vol. 1, 117, NFB Colorado.

106. Ibid., 124.

107. Ibid., 140.

108. Rev. Charles F. Brooks, "The Activities and Administration of a State Central Authority for Work with the Adult Blind" (MA thesis, University of Denver, 1939), 85; Grace Eleanor Wilson, "The History and Development of the Denver Bureau of Public Welfare," 15–16, see related footnote Chapter 2, note 16.

109. Brooks, "Activities for Work with the Adult Blind," 85; Wilson, "History of the Denver Bureau of Public Welfare," 15–16.

110. *Report of Auditor of State of Colorado, 1919–1920*, 130.

111. Mrs. Lute Wilcox to Gov. Oliver H. Shoup, 1922, Box 26959, State Archives.

112. U.S. Bureau of the Census, *The Blind Population, 1920*, 110–111.

113. *United Workers Minutes*, vol. 1, 140, NFB Colorado.

114. *Biennial Report of Auditor of State of Colorado, 1921–1922* (Denver: Eames Brothers, 1923), 8.

115. Mrs. Lute Wilcox to Gov. Oliver H. Shoup, 1922, State Archives.

116. Colorado's blind benefit law also allowed recipients to cross county lines and still retain their rights to aid.

Chapter Six

1. "Report of the State Commission for the Blind From June 2, 1925 to November 30, 1926," File 10, Box 26962, State Archives.

2. *House Journal of the General Assembly of the State of Colorado, Twenty-Fourth Session* (Denver: Smith-Brooks, 1923), 39.

3. *House Journal of the General Assembly of the State of Colorado, Twenty-Fifth Session* (Denver: Welch-Haffner Printing, 1925), 20–21.

4. Peggy Pascoe, *Relations of Rescue: The Search for Female Moral Authority in the American West, 1874–1939* (New York: Oxford University Press, 1990), 102.

5. Mary E. Odem, *Delinquent Daughters: Protecting and Policing Adolescent Female Sexuality in the United States, 1885–1920* (Chapel Hill: University of North Carolina Press, 1995), 158. Also see Anne Meis Knupfer, *Reform and Resistance: Gender, Delinquency, and America's First Juvenile Court* (New York: Routledge, 2001); Sherri Broder, *Tramps, Unfit Mothers, and Neglected Children: Negotiating the Family in Late Nineteenth-Century Philadelphia* (Philadelphia: University of Pennsylvania Press, 2002); Frank J. Weed, "Bureaucratization as Reform: The Case of the Public Welfare Movement, 1900–1929," *Social Science Journal* 16 (October 1979): 79–89. For an overview of the professionalization of social work see Gary R. Lowe and P. Nelson Reid, eds., *The Professionalization of Poverty: Social Work and the Poor in the Twentieth Century* (New York: Aldine de Gruyter, 1999) and Roy Lubove, *The Professional Altruist: The Emergence of Social Work as a Career, 1880–1930* (Cambridge, Mass.: Harvard University Press, 1965).

6. Guy T. Justis to Mrs. Lute Wilcox, 12 October 1923 and Mr. Lute Wilcox to Guy T. Justis, 15 October 1923, *Society of the United Workers for the Blind of Colorado Minutes*, vol. 1, inside the back cover, NFB Colorado.

7. *Denver Times*, 23 August 1917, 1; *Rocky Mountain News*, 23 January 1924, 11; Grace Eleanor Wilson, "The History and Development of the Denver Bureau of Public Welfare," 17, see related footnote Chapter 2, note 16; Efay Nelson Grigg, "The Colorado State Board of Charities and Corrections," (MA thesis, University of Denver, 1932), 110; *First Biennial Report of the State Department of Charities and Corrections, 1923–24* (Denver: Bradford-Robinson, 1925), 7.

8. *First Report of Charities and Corrections, 1923–24*, 29–32.

9. *Biennial Report of the State Teacher for Adult Blind, 1918–1920* (Denver: Eames Brothers, 1920), 10.

10. *First Report of Charities and Corrections, 1923–24*, 33.

11. *United Workers Minutes*, vol. 1, 279, NFB Colorado.

12. Quote, "Vinton, 1921 A.A.W.B. Convention," *Outlook for the Blind* 15 (Summer 1921): 87; *Biennial Report of the State Teacher for Adult Blind, 1920–1922* (Denver: Eames Brothers, 1923), 6; Frances A. Koestler, *The Unseen Minority: A Social History of Blindness in America* (New York: David McKay Company, 1976), 13–24.

13. H. R. Latimer, "The Importance of Organization in Work for the Blind," *Outlook for the Blind* 16 (Summer 1922): 43.

14. For examples of this trend see, "Getting a Job for the Blind," *Outlook for the Blind* 16 (September 1923): 22–24; J. J. Childs, "Blindness as Affected by the Popular Attitude," *Outlook for the Blind* 17 (December 1923): 29–31; "Opportunity—Not Pity," *Outlook for the Blind* 17 (March 1924): 36; "The Right Man in the Right Place," *Outlook for the Blind* 18 (September 1924): 40; "Blindness Versus Employment," *Outlook for the Blind* 18 (December 1924): 49–50.

15. *First Report of Charities and Corrections, 1923–24*, 29; "American Foundation for the Blind, Nation-Wide Service," *Outlook for the Blind* 18 (March 1925): 6; "What the American Foundation for the Blind has Done During 1924 and 1925," *Outlook for the Blind* 19 (December 1925): 8.

16. *Rocky Mountain News*, 24 February 1925, 3.

17. *Rocky Mountain News*, 27 February 1925, 11.

18. Nancy MacLean, *Behind the Mask of Chivalry: The Making of the Second Ku Klux Klan* (New York: Oxford University Press, 1994), 3–7; Kathleen M. Blee, *Women of the Klan: Racism and Gender in the 1920s* (Berkeley: University of California Press, 1991), 17–23.

19. For an overview of the Klan's popularity in the West, see Shawn Lay, ed., *The Invisible Empire in the West: Toward a New Historical Appraisal of the Ku Klux Klan of the 1920s* (Urbana: University of Illinois Press, 1992).

20. Kenneth T. Jackson, *The Ku Klux Klan in the City, 1915–1930* (New York: Oxford University Press, 1967), 216.

21. Robert Alan Goldberg, *Hooded Empire: The Ku Klux Klan in Colorado* (Urbana: University of Illinois Press, 1981), 8.

22. *House Journal Twenty-Fifth Session*, 105–12, quote, 111.

23. Goldberg, *Hooded Empire*, 86.

24. Ibid., 87–95; *Senate Journal of the General Assembly of the State of Colorado, Twenty-Fifth Session* (Denver: Welch-Haffner, 1925), 1156; *House Journal Twenty-Fifth Session*, 1236–37. The notion that the Klan largely failed to carry out its agenda is a bit misleading with respect to welfare since this is the one area where the secret organization succeeded in obtaining many goals.

25. *Laws Passed at the Twenty-fifth Session of the General Assembly of the State of Colorado* (Denver: Eames Brothers, 1925), 168–76.

26. Lute Wilcox, "President's Report for 1925," *Society of the United Workers for the Blind of Colorado Minutes*, vol. 2, between pages 6 and 7, NFB Colorado.

27. *United Workers Minutes*, vol. 1, 299, NFB Colorado.

28. Wilcox, "President's Report for 1925," NFB Colorado.

29. "Report of the State Commission for the Blind From June 2, 1925 to December 1, 1926," 1, File 10, Box 26962, State Archives.

30. "The State-wide Social Welfare Survey of Colorado—The Administration of Colorado's Blind Benefit Act," 2–5, Folder 1, MSS 1224, CHS.

31. Myrtle Long to Laurena Senter, 13 July 1925, Gano and Laurena Senter Collection, FF7, Box 36, WHC/DPL. It appears that Jackson wrote to Myrtle Long requesting that Long contact Laurena Senter, leader of the women's KKK of Denver and Colorado, for assistance in regaining her job as a teacher for the adult blind.

32. "Report From June 2, 1925 to December 1, 1926," 2–4, State Archives.

33. "Biennial Report of the State Commission for the Blind, 1928–1930," 4, Box 13791, State Archives.

34. Harry Best, *Blindness and the Blind in the United States* (New York: Macmillian Company, 1934), 550–54.

35. Quote, Koestler, *The Unseen Minority*, 178, also see 176–79; Jacobus tenBroek and Floyd W. Matson, *Hope Deferred: Public Welfare and the Blind* (Berkeley: University of California Press, 1959), 59–63; Robert B. Irwin, *As I Saw It* (New York: American Foundation for the Blind, 1955), 178–81.

36. *Rocky Mountain News*, 1 March 1925, 11.

37. Grigg, "Colorado Board of Charities and Corrections," 57 and 109–13; *Rocky Mountain News*, 26 February 1925, 2; *Rocky Mountain News*, 28 February 1925, 2 and 1 March 1925, 11; *Denver Post*, 26 February 1925, 29.

38. *Rocky Mountain News*, 14 March 1925, 3; Newspaper Clipping, File 1, Box 27211, State Archives; also see "The Common Welfare," *Survey* 54 (15 April 1925): 75–76; Paul U. Kellogg, "The Social Workers in Denver," *Survey* 54 (15 July 1925): 425–30.

39. Ben B. Lindsey, "My Fight with the Ku Klux Klan," *Survey* 54 (1 June 1925): 274. The Klan played a major role in removing Judge Ben Lindsey from his seat. Colorado's Supreme Court disbarred Lindsey in 1929 on charges unrelated to the Klan. He eventually resettled in southern California.

40. Kellogg, "Social Workers in Denver," 429; *Rocky Mountain News*, 16 June 1925, 1 and 3; Charles A. Ellwood, "The Menace of Racial and Religious Intolerance," in *Proceedings of the National Conference of Social Work, 1925* (Chicago: University of Chicago Press, 1925), 18–26.

41. Undated note by L. V., Box 1, Gertrude Vaile Collection, Columbia Library.

42. Goldberg, *Hooded Empire*, 96–117; Jackson, *Klan in the City*, 230–31.

43. *Rocky Mountain News*, 1 September 1928, 5; Margaret E. Rice, "Gertrude Vaile, 1878–1954," *Social Casework* 35 (December 1954): 449.

44. *Laws Passed at the Twenty-Sixth Session of the General Assembly of the State of Colorado* (Denver: Eames Brothers, 1927), 210–14, quote 213.

45. "State-wide Social Welfare Survey of Blind Benefit Act," 1, CHS.

46. *Report of Governor Shoup's Committee on Child Welfare Legislation for Colorado* (Denver: Eastwood Printing, 1921), 10–12 and 63–71, quotes 66, Box 1, Ben Lindsey Collection, WHC/DPL; *1922 Report of Governor Shoup's Committee on Child Welfare Legislation for Colorado* (Denver: Eastwood Printing, 1922), 1, Box 1, Ben Lindsey Collection, WHC/DPL.

47. *1922 Report of Governor Shoup's Committee*, 1–2, WHC/DPL; *Report of Governor's Committee on Social and Child Welfare Legislation for Colorado, 1925*, 1–4, Box 1, Ben Lindsey Collection, WHC/DPL.

48. *Laws Passed at the Twenty-Fourth Session of the General Assembly of the State of Colorado* (Denver: Bradford-Robinson Printing, 1923), 204–7.

49. *Teller County Poor Record, 1923–1937*, vol. 23072L, State Archives.

50. Florence Nesbitt, *Standards of Public Aid to Children in Their Own Homes*, U.S. Department of Labor, Children's Bureau, Publication 118 (Washington, D.C: Government Printing Office, 1923), 49; Mary F. Bogue, "Ten Years of Mothers' Pensions," *Survey* 49 (15 February 1923): 636; Wilson, "History of the Denver Bureau of Public Welfare," 15, see related footnote Chapter 2, note 16. This practice of including welfare recipients with assisting in the operation of a welfare program predates these same practices found in the War on Poverty in the 1960s.

51. *First Report of Charities and Corrections, 1923–24*, 35. A 1921 survey of county judges conducted by Denver County found similar trends of nonenforcement. See "Remarks of County Judges Regarding Mothers' Compensation April, 1921," Box 4, Gertrude Vaile Collection, Columbia Library.

52. "Data From Child Welfare Report by Dr. Carstens, Colorado Report," 4, Box 82, Edmond C. Van Diest Manuscripts, Colorado College Special Collections, Colorado Springs, Colorado.

53. "Resolutions Adopted by the Colorado Federation of Women's Clubs at Greeley, September 17, 1926," *Colorado Club Woman* 6 (October 1926): 13 and 15.

54. "Montezuma County Poor Farm Report, 1924," Box 66945, State Archives.

55. *Denver Post*, 1 March 1925, 10; *Rocky Mountain News*, 21 November 1925, 3; "The Denver Farm Prospers," *Municipal Facts*, November-December 1925, 16–17, WHC/DPL; *Biennial Report Department of Health and Charity, City and County of Denver Colorado, 1924–1925*, 32–34, WHC/DPL.

56. "Tuberculosis Addition to City and County Hospital," *Municipal Facts*, January 1920, 14, WHC/DPL; "—'but the greatest of these is charity,'" *Municipal Facts*, November-December 1925, 3, WHC/DPL.

57. Alice Elizabeth Boggs, "The History and Development of the Tuberculosis Assistance Program in Colorado," (MA thesis, University of Denver, 1943), 23–28.

58. Marvin Kaufmann Opler, "The Southern Ute of Colorado," in *Acculturation in Seven American Tribes*, ed. Ralph Linton (New York: D. Appleton-Century, 1940), 195.

59. Efforts to create an old age pension in Colorado began as early as 1915. See Samuel R. Crawford, *The Old Age Pension Movement in Colorado* (Denver: Samuel R. Crawford, 1939), 6–14; Efay Nelson Grigg, "Social Legislation and the Welfare Program," in *Colorado and Its People: A Narrative and Topical History of the Centennial State*, ed. LeRoy R. Hafen, vol. 2 (New York: Lewis Historical Publishing, 1948), 345–46; James F. Wickens, *Colorado in the Great Depression* (New York: Garland Publishing, 1979), 338–39. For a comparative overview of the establishment of old age pensions see Ann Shola Orloff, *The Politics of Pensions: A Comparative Analysis of Britain, Canada, and the United States, 1880–1940* (Madison: University of Wisconsin Press, 1993).

60. Virginia McConnell Simmons, "The Penitentes: Remnant of a Vanishing Lifestyle," *San Luis Valley Historian* 24 (1992): 26; Marta Weigle, *Brothers of Light, Brothers of Blood: The Penitentes of the Southwest* (Albuquerque: University of New Mexico Press, 1976), 98; "State-wide Social Welfare Survey— Emergency Relief in Colorado," 6–7, File 12, MSS 1224, CHS. The actual percentage was 57.6 percent.

61. *Range Ledger*, 6 November 1931, 6; also see 27 November 1931, 2; 1 January 1931, 1; 22 December 1933, 2; 5 January 1934, 1, all in the *Range Ledger*. F. B. Fanger to P. E. Deatherage, 28 August 1933, County Home Report, File Draw, Lincoln Courthouse; Mrs. A. C. Hulse of Limon, Colorado to Governor William Adams, 20 November 1931, File 2, Box 26842, State Archives; also see James E. Fell, Jr., *Limon, Colorado: Hub City of the High Plains, 1888–1952* (Boulder, Colo.: Limon Heritage Society, 1997), 43.

62. Ira S. Freeman, *A History of Montezuma County Colorado: Land of Promise and Fulfillment* (Boulder, Colo.: Johnson Publishing, 1958), 285–86.

63. Wilson, "History of the Denver Bureau of Public Welfare," 19–23, quote 23, see related footnote Chapter 2, note 16.

64. Lyle W. Dorsett, *The Queen City: A History of Denver* (Boulder, Colo.: Pruett Publishing, 1977), 232–33; Robert G. Athearn, *The Coloradans* (Albuquerque: University of New Mexico Press, 1976), 276.

65. Robert Guilford Taylor, *Cripple Creek* (Bloomington: Indiana University Press, 1966), 147–50; Marshall Sprague, *Money Mountain: The Story of Cripple Creek Gold* (Lincoln: University of Nebraska Press, 1953), 298; David M. Kennedy, *Freedom From Fear: The American People in Depression and War, 1929–1945* (New York: Oxford University Press, 1999), 197.

66. G. E. E. Lindquist, "Consolidated Ute Indian Agency, Colo.," in *Annual Report of the Board of Indian Commissioners to the Secretary of the Interior, 1932* (Washington, D.C.: Government Printing Office, 1932), 24; Richard K. Young, *The Ute Indians of Colorado in the Twentieth Century* (Norman: University of Oklahoma Press, 1997), 82.

67. R. Trant, "Community Work on the Ute Mountain Reservation," 8, Box 1, Central Classified Files 1907–39, Consolidated Ute, RG 75, National Archives I, Washington, D.C.

68. Margaret Burge and Moris Burge, "Investigation of Southern Ute Reservation and Ute Mountain Reservation, October 1935," 22, Central Classified Files 1907–39, Consolidated Ute, RG 75, National Archives I, Washington, D.C.

69. "Petition of Ute Mountain Council Approved at Towaoc, Colorado on September 15th, 1938," Box 65, Central Classified Files 1907–39, Consolidated Ute, RG 75, National Archives I, Washington, D.C.

Index

The letters *n* or *t* following a page number denote a note or a table. The number of the note or table on that page follows the letter.